Linux®
Security Toolkit

Linux®
Security Toolkit

David A. Bandel

M&T Books
An imprint of IDG Books Worldwide, Inc.

Foster City, CA ◆ Chicago, IL ◆ Indianapolis, IN ◆ New York, NY

Linux® Security Toolkit

Published by
M&T Books
An imprint of IDG Books Worldwide, Inc.
919 E. Hillsdale Blvd., Suite 400
Foster City, CA 94404
www.idgbooks.com (IDG Books Worldwide Web site)

The image of the Linux penguin, Tux, was created by Larry Ewing (lewing@isc.tamu.edu) using the Gimp (http://www.gimp.org/) and was subsequently modified for use by IDG Books Worldwide on this book's cover by Tuomas Kuosmanen (tigert@gimp.org). Tuomas also used the Gimp for his work with Tux.

ISBN: 0-7645-4690-2

Printed in the United States of America

10 9 8 7 6 5 4 3 2 1

1B/RX/QU/QQ/FC

Distributed in the United States by IDG Books Worldwide, Inc.

Distributed by CDG Books Canada Inc. for Canada; by Transworld Publishers Limited in the United Kingdom; by IDG Norge Books for Norway; by IDG Sweden Books for Sweden; by IDG Books Australia Publishing Corporation Pty. Ltd. for Australia and New Zealand; by TransQuest Publishers Pte Ltd. for Singapore, Malaysia, Thailand, Indonesia, and Hong Kong; by Gotop Information Inc. for Taiwan; by ICG Muse, Inc. for Japan; by Intersoft for South Africa; by Eyrolles for France; by International Thomson Publishing for Germany, Austria and Switzerland; by Distribuidora Cuspide for Argentina; by LR International for Brazil; by Galileo Libros for Chile; by Ediciones ZETA S.C.R. Ltda. for Peru; by WS Computer Publishing Corporation, Inc., for the Philippines; by Contemporanea de Ediciones for Venezuela; by Express Computer Distributors for the Caribbean and West Indies; by Micronesia Media Distributor, Inc. for Micronesia; by Chips Computadoras

S.A. de C.V. for Mexico; by Editorial Norma de Panama S.A. for Panama; by American Bookshops for Finland.

For general information on IDG Books Worldwide's books in the United States, please call our Consumer Customer Service department at 800-762-2974. For reseller information, including discounts and premium sales, please call our Reseller Customer Service department at 800-434-3422.

For information on where to purchase IDG Books Worldwide's books outside the United States, please contact our International Sales department at 317-572-3337 or fax 317-572-4002.

For consumer information on foreign language translations, please contact our Customer Service department at 800-434-3422, fax 317-572-4002, or e-mail rights@idgbooks.com.

For information on licensing foreign or domestic rights, please phone +1-650-653-7098.

For sales inquiries and special prices for bulk quantities, please contact our Sales department at 800-434-3422 or write to the address above.

For information on using IDG Books Worldwide's books in the classroom or for ordering examination copies, please contact our Educational Sales department at 800-434-2086 or fax 317-572-4005.

For press review copies, author interviews, or other publicity information, please contact our Public Relations department at 650-653-7000 or fax 650-653-7500.

For authorization to photocopy items for corporate, personal, or educational use, please contact Copyright Clearance Center, 222 Rosewood Drive, Danvers, MA 01923, or fax 978-750-4470.

Library of Congress Cataloging-in-Publication Data
Bandel, David A. (David Allan), 1955-
   Linux Security Toolkit / David A. Bandel.
    p. cm.
   ISBN 0-7645-4690-2 (alk. paper)
    1. Linux. 2. Operating systems (Computers)
3. Computer security. I. Title.
QA76.76.063. B3624   2000
005.8--dc21   00-027004
                                 CIP

is a registered trademark or trademark under exclusive license to IDG Books Worldwide, Inc. from International Data Group, Inc. in the United States and/or other countries.

M&T BOOKS is a trademark of IDG Books Worldwide, Inc.

ABOUT IDG BOOKS WORLDWIDE

Welcome to the world of IDG Books Worldwide.

IDG Books Worldwide, Inc., is a subsidiary of International Data Group, the world's largest publisher of computer-related information and the leading global provider of information services on information technology. IDG was founded more than 30 years ago by Patrick J. McGovern and now employs more than 9,000 people worldwide. IDG publishes more than 290 computer publications in over 75 countries. More than 90 million people read one or more IDG publications each month.

Launched in 1990, IDG Books Worldwide is today the #1 publisher of best-selling computer books in the United States. We are proud to have received eight awards from the Computer Press Association in recognition of editorial excellence and three from Computer Currents' First Annual Readers' Choice Awards. Our best-selling *...For Dummies*® series has more than 50 million copies in print with translations in 31 languages. IDG Books Worldwide, through a joint venture with IDG's Hi-Tech Beijing, became the first U.S. publisher to publish a computer book in the People's Republic of China. In record time, IDG Books Worldwide has become the first choice for millions of readers around the world who want to learn how to better manage their businesses.

Our mission is simple: Every one of our books is designed to bring extra value and skill-building instructions to the reader. Our books are written by experts who understand and care about our readers. The knowledge base of our editorial staff comes from years of experience in publishing, education, and journalism — experience we use to produce books to carry us into the new millennium. In short, we care about books, so we attract the best people. We devote special attention to details such as audience, interior design, use of icons, and illustrations. And because we use an efficient process of authoring, editing, and desktop publishing our books electronically, we can spend more time ensuring superior content and less time on the technicalities of making books.

You can count on our commitment to deliver high-quality books at competitive prices on topics you want to read about. At IDG Books Worldwide, we continue in the IDG tradition of delivering quality for more than 30 years. You'll find no better book on a subject than one from IDG Books Worldwide.

John Kilcullen
Chairman and CEO
IDG Books Worldwide, Inc.

Eighth Annual Computer Press Awards ≥ 1992

Ninth Annual Computer Press Awards ≥ 1993

Tenth Annual Computer Press Awards ≥ 1994

Eleventh Annual Computer Press Awards ≥ 1995

Credits

ACQUISITIONS EDITOR
Laura Lewin

PROJECT EDITOR
Eric Newman

TECHNICAL EDITOR
Kurt Wall

COPY EDITOR
S.B. Kleinman

MEDIA DEVELOPMENT MANAGER
Stephen Noetzel

PERMISSIONS EDITOR
Lenora Chin Sell

MEDIA DEVELOPMENT SPECIALIST
Jason Luster

PROJECT COORDINATORS
Linda Marousek
Danette Nurse
Louigene A. Santos

GRAPHICS AND PRODUCTION SPECIALISTS
Robert Bihlmayer
Jude Levinson
Michael Lewis
Victor Pérez-Varela
Dina F Quan
Ramses Ramirez

PROOFREADING AND INDEXING
York Production Services

COVER DESIGN
W. Lawrence Huck

ILLUSTRATORS
Shelley Norris
Mary Jo Richards

BOOK DESIGNER
Jim Donohue

About the Author

David Bandel earned a Master of Aviation Management from Embry-Riddle Aeronautical University in 1989 at Ft. Campbell, Kentucky. He retired from 20 years in the Army in February 1996. While on active duty, he learned many of the basics of UNIX, working on DEC 5000s running Ultrix and Sun SparcStations running SunOS 4. His work in intelligence and security provided the background for continued security work, and taught him the kind of vigilance security requires. In 1993, he began dabbling in Linux, a hobby that quickly grew on him. Following retirement from active duty, he worked various contracts with the U.S. government at Ft. Lewis, Washington, performing system administration until landing a position with Custom Software Services (CSS) in Bellevue, Washington. At CSS, he worked on a wide variety of systems, maintaining, installing, and upgrading Sparc Solaris, HP-UX, AIX, SCO OpenServer, NT, and, of course, Linux systems. Most systems ran CSS software using either Informix IDS or MSSQL Server database backends. David is currently enjoying retirement in the Republic of Panama, consulting on network installations and writing about Linux. He and his wife and children live in David, Chiriqui Province, in the Republic of Panama.

To my loving wife, Silvia, and my children, Lisa and Vanessa

Preface

The principal reason for this book's existence is the ever-increasing number of home users connecting 24 hours a day, seven days a week to the Internet thanks to the emergence of services such as Road Runner and affordable adsl/xdsl services from the phone companies. This audience also includes all the small businesses out there that recognize that a Web presence is a necessity, and find in-house hosting the most economical solution although they do not have resources to spare to hire someone knowledgeable in security.

This book provides home users and small businesses (those without the resources for a well-equipped IT department) who have chosen Linux to learn about and put into practice good systems security. And while some of you may be skeptical that you can understand this information, most of it is actually quite basic. You may think that if the "big boys" like NASA and others can be cracked, and they have big budgets with folks who really know security, that you can be too. But they are working against much greater odds than you are. First, they are a high-visibility target, and oh, so very inviting. Second, they have so many systems and such a complex network that it is difficult to ensure every system is updated with the latest, most secure versions of software. Third, they are trying to bring a large number of services to an even larger number of people and stay on the cutting edge while doing so. And as anyone who's worked the cutting edge before will tell you, you're bound to bleed sometimes. Besides, the only truly secure system is one that is still in its box, not plugged in, locked in a back room, and if you still don't want anyone to tamper with it, that has you sitting on the box. But that system does you or anyone else absolutely no good.

What this book will do is help you build an understanding of your system from a security point of view, chapter by chapter, concept by concept. It will not make you a security expert by any means, but it will lay the groundwork necessary for more advanced material.

This book is intended as a guide for beginners and a review and reference for more experienced hands on the subject of Linux security. While this book was written with Caldera's OpenLinux in mind, and the tools built for a Caldera OpenLinux installation, the concepts apply to all distributions of Linux.

Many Linux neophytes make the mistake of believing that the different distributions are somehow different, as if they were back in 1988 looking at MS-DOS or DR-DOS. But in fact, nothing could be further from the truth. The Linux kernel that you'll rebuild comes from the same kernel source everyone else is using. The telnet daemon you'll almost certainly disable is the same regardless of the distribution. What the distributions bring to the table are varying installation procedures and even more varied administration tools. But beyond that, they use (essentially) the same libraries, the same server programs, the same basic file system layout, and they all share many of the same weaknesses.

So if you have a curiosity about basic system security – what it is, how it works, and how to improve it – you've come to the right place. The fact that you're reading this is testament enough to your curiosity.

How this book is organized

Linux Security Toolkit contains four parts.

Part 1: Your host

The chapters in Part I will help you understand the security of your host as it pertains to files, users, permissions, and how your host works. This section includes information on protecting your system from users authorized to log in to the system as well as how to protect your system from compromise during the boot process.

Part II: Your network

The chapters in Part II explain how your network works and what you need to understand about different categories of attacks on your system. This section will give you a good idea of what the bad guys are looking at so you can counter their efforts.

Part III: Firewalls and special-purpose software

The chapters in Part III explain how to use firewall software and other special purpose software to enhance your overall security rather than detract from it. This section is a catchall for special programs you may use or want to use that require special considerations.

Part IV: Security auditing

The chapters in Part IV cover monitoring your system, from configuring what is logged where to reading those logs afterward. You'll also learn how the bad guys check you out so you can use the same tools. Finally, you learn how to keep up with the bad guys, and counter new exploits before they can be used against you.

Appendixes

In addition, the book contains two appendixes. The appendixes contain a listing of security utilities you may want to test (some of which are included on the CD-ROM), and a listing of programs on the CD-ROM.

Conventions

The following conventions are used in this book to make the material easier to understand:

- ◆ Key combinations such as Ctrl+P are joined by plus signs.
- ◆ *Italics* are used for emphasis or first reference.
- ◆ **Bold** indicates text that you type.
- ◆ `Monotype text` indicates code and Internet addresses.

The icons used for the special features are shown below.

 The On the CD-ROM icon refers to an evaluation program that can be found on the CD-ROM at the back of this book.

 The Tip icon gives you insider information to help you make the best use of the information in the chapter.

 The Note icon is used to inform you of special cases or exceptions to the normal way that a feature works.

The Caution icon warns you about possible problems that you may encounter.

The Cross-Reference icon refers to a related topic in another chapter of the book, or sometimes elsewhere in the same chapter.

What is a sidebar?

Topics that appear in sidebars provide in-depth hints on technical issues

Acknowledgments

First, I thank my wife, Silvia, who, despite an arduous schedule of her own working in the morgue as a Doctor of Forensic Medicine and with a total ignorance of computers and my attraction to them, supports my Linux habit, and the writing of this book. Second, I thank my children, who pester me to stop being so wrapped up in my work and play with them and just enjoy life. I also thank the Linux developers, particularly those who've been kind enough to answer my e-mails and respond to my (often obscure) questions through the years, including Ted T'so, Dan Becker, Alan Cox, and many others whose names are too numerous to list. Without their devotion to programming, Linux would not be what it is today. I'd like to also thank Kurt Wall for his good work on the technical edits, and ensuring I didn't slip into technobabble without explaining what it meant first. Also to the folks at IDG Books for their hard work making sure that what I wrote actually made sense to someone other than myself. Finally, thanks to the growing community of Linux users the world over, without whom this book would not be necessary, and Linux would not be where it is today.

Contents at a Glance

Contents

Introduction: Why this book is important

Every day, more individuals and businesses are discovering Linux. Every day, more and more people are connecting to the Internet, and more and more frequently it is via a dedicated connection. And while we can wish it weren't so, the supposed anonymity of the net brings out the worst in many folks. Until something changes and these social misfits are hunted down and jailed for their crimes (and make no mistake about it, breaking into someone's system or denying someone bandwidth, be it via a deliberate Denial of Service attack or unsolicited commercial e-mail are — or should be — felonies the world over).

In the meantime, as inexpensive, dedicated connections become more abundant, newcomers to Linux need a no-nonsense book about security. If you bought a new house, and it came without locks on any of the doors, you wouldn't hesitate to call a locksmith to install some. So why build a server on the Internet and not find out how to secure the front door?

Some of you may have picked up this book thinking that by reading it and applying some magic formulas, you could bulletproof (or crack-proof) your system. Unfortunately, no silver bullet, no medieval chants, no magic potions can prevent someone, somewhere, sometime from breaking in, any more than the best lock can hold off a determined lock-pick forever. But like a good lock, it keeps honest men honest. One of Murphy's sayings for soldiers is: "If the enemy can't get in, you can't get out." Murphy may have known nothing about the Internet or computers, but he called this one right. What it will take on your part is a little vigilance. Someone will probe your system. Someone will try to get in. The information in this book will make the job more difficult and perhaps this someone will just move on.

In the summer of 1999, Microsoft put an IIS server on the Internet and dared folks to break in. It lasted less than three hours. Another challenger put a PowerPC with Linux up. He took it down a week later because the attempts were taking a toll on the provider's system, and some folks were trying to break into nearby boxes to backdoor the system, which was not part of the bargain (those were the ISP's systems). The box was not broken into (rooted) while it was on the Internet. But it was armored against such attacks. The only service running (available from the outside) was the Apache Web server. You'll learn how to make your system just as difficult to enter.

Today, all of us have a greater and greater dependency on computers. Just as man once discovered fire and became dependent on it, many are dependent on their computers and communications. No one will argue that some businesses depend entirely on the Internet (Amazon.com comes immediately to mind). And since the Internet is nothing more than a collection of connected computers, many livelihoods depend on these systems and keeping them secure. Computers are becoming as indispensable to individuals as to businesses.

 This book includes, and speaks primarily to, the Caldera OpenLinux distribution. However, most of the book applies to Linux in general. Where information applies only to Caldera or only to a few distributions, that information is noted.

What security is (an attitude)

System and network security begins one person at a time, and boils down to an attitude. Murphy was mentioned above in the context of soldiers at war. Make no doubt about it, from the instant you connect your system to the Internet, you have become either friend or foe to the rest of the networked community. You have brought this electronic war into your home or business, and your system or network is the battlefield.

You can approach security in many ways. Ignoring it should not be an option. Closing your eyes and hoping it will go away won't work. But don't worry, security really isn't a black art. It takes a little knowledge mixed with a lot of curiosity about what works and how and why, and imagining yourself in the part of the bad guy. How would you get in? What would you do once you were in? You know more about what's valuable on your system than those trying to get in.

Assessing your security needs (a simplified approach)

Assessing your risk is probably the hardest part of all. First, determine what is at risk. You can think of your information infrastructure in several ways, but one way is to consider your information systems as broken down into three parts: the hardware, the software, and the data. Each of these will be vulnerable in three different ways: outright destruction, unauthorized alteration, and unauthorized use. These vulnerabilities will be discussed along with each of the three elements.

Your hardware is anything you can physically touch, such as the monitor and CPU, but will also include any network devices you might have, such as routers, cable, etc. It will also include one thing you cannot touch, bandwidth. Bandwidth is considered here because it doesn't fit well anywhere else.

Your hardware is susceptible to destruction, not just from someone physically breaking it, but some programs are capable of damaging monitors, and on occasion graphics cards. The eeprom can be erased. While Linux does not have a version of the CIH virus that Windows does, someone who gains root access can run a program that would have a similar effect.

Similarly, a cracker does not need to gain physical access to your system to alter it. Changes can be made that put the Ethernet card into promiscuous mode or prevent the system from properly rebooting. This can also include altering the routing table, thus changing the way your network works.

Unauthorized use of the hardware not only denies you access to resources you've paid for (CPU cycles, memory, bandwidth), it also makes you vulnerable to being blacklisted, or having your service provider pull the plug on you if activities from your system violate the provider's terms of service. Having domains reject your mail because your site has been used by a spammer, or ftp or Web sites blocking you because a script kiddie has used your system to scan or attempt to break into other systems is a major inconvenience at best, and can result in a court appearance at worst.

Considering each of the three vulnerabilities with regard to software is much simpler. The programs can be erased, causing you loss of use until you can replace them. Programs can also be altered to allow access they shouldn't or capture passwords. Unauthorized use is the final vulnerability to software, and applies mainly to use of proprietary programs with license restrictions that you are responsible for enforcing on your systems. Unauthorized use also denies you CPU cycles that program is using.

Your data is the most vulnerable, and most difficult to replace, of the three elements. Its destruction will cause at least some loss of time until it can be retrieved from backup, and that part that wasn't backed up recreated. Alterations to data can cause undesired results depending on how the data is altered. Unauthorized use can include loss of proprietary or personal information to someone who has no right to the data. Just think of your data in the wrong hands.

While considering each of the above, think in terms of both insiders and outsiders. Insiders are those who have legitimate, authorized access to your systems. They may exceed their authorizations, either accidentally or intentionally. Be sure to remember that most actions by insiders will be unintentional. Good security awareness will reduce the number of problems you encounter from insiders. And while it is difficult to isolate a single incident and determine whether it was intentional or unintentional, a pattern of abuse will make it apparent that you may have a problem.

Developing a security policy

After you've determined what is at risk in your system, you can then determine an overall policy and develop it from there. An overall policy for a system would be very simply either open or closed. Put more succinctly, it would be either: Permit that which is not explicitly denied, or deny that which is not explicitly permitted.

You will see in the subsequent chapters how to implement this policy. You'll understand users and groups, and be able to decide between using a default group or user private groups. You'll understand about networks and services. You'll know how to turn off services you don't need, and make sure the ones you are running are set up properly. You'll learn how to look at your system from the outside and see what the bad guys can see. You'll also learn how to detect an intrusion and what to do to recover your system and resecure it. An assessment of what the attack cost you is beyond the scope of this book, but you should always keep in mind the consequences of any unauthorized entry, both in lost time and lost information.

You will learn how to use packet filters to drop, reject, or, where wanted, accept packets. These packet filters are Linux's firewall software. I will say it here, and I will say it again: a firewall is not foolproof, and will not prevent entry. What it will do is give you time – time to detect and subsequently react to an attack. If a cracker who knows his business gets in, the attack will be very difficult to detect until it is too late. In fact, you may never detect the penetration after a certain period despite the intruder's continuing usage of your system. Time is both your friend and your enemy.

But beyond the solely technical aspects in the above paragraphs, you'll need to deal with some very difficult questions. This book won't pretend to give you legal advice; for that you should consult a lawyer with some experience with computer crimes. But you'll need to determine what damages you suffered. Do you want to prosecute? Do you have sufficient evidence to pursue that avenue? Remember, logs can be tampered with, so logs on a compromised system must also be assumed to be compromised.

If you do decide to pursue a legal remedy, do you have the authority to call the police? If not, do you know who in your organization does? How do you or your management want to handle this? How about the possible ensuing publicity?

You should also have some kind of emergency response in mind. Do you immediately secure the systems, or do you permit the activity to continue, confining it to the current system in hopes of tracing the intruder back to his own system? Do you have the time to do this?

Your policy should also address more mundane things like your password policy (change interval, etc.), and e-mail policy (do you archive company e-mail or mandate destruction after a certain period of time?). Obviously, for the home user, you only need to consider these things. But every company with a network should have a network policy that covers this and more. For more information on this topic, refer to RFC-2196 and RFC-2504 on the CD-ROM.

Part I

Your host

Chapter 1

Users, groups, and security

IN THIS CHAPTER

- ◆ Understanding users
- ◆ Understanding privileged versus non-privileged users
- ◆ Understanding login files
- ◆ Understanding /etc/passwd
- ◆ Understanding /etc/shadow
- ◆ Understanding /etc/group
- ◆ Understanding /etc/gshadow
- ◆ Understanding /etc/login.defs
- ◆ Changing password aging information
- ◆ Understanding PAM

AS WITH MANY THINGS Linux, there is more than one way to do things. Few of them are wrong; most are just a matter of personal choice. Some will ease your administrative burden, which will directly affect the security of your system. If you are spending all your time administering your user accounts, you'll have less time to focus on security issues.

Understanding users and groups is central to understanding Linux security. All decisions about what users are permitted or not permitted to do is based on who the kernel thinks they are when they log in to the system.

User administration in general

Linux is a multi-user, multi-tasking system. This means that it was designed to be used by many users, and these users can all access the system at the same time. Obviously, they won't all be able to access the same keyboard and monitor at the same time, but a large number of users can be logged in via telnet, ftp, http, etc., simultaneously, and the operating system isolates and protects one user from another. The system tracks users to determine whether they are permitted access to files or are able to run programs based on who they are.

When a new user is created, that user is given a unique name. Many folks mistakenly believe that this unique username is how the system tracks the user and determines privileges. But this is inaccurate. You'll see later on in the chapter that while the username is important, the userid number is even more important.

 The user ID (UID) is what the system uses to determine what privileges a user has. While the UID need not be unique to a user, be aware that all translations from UID to username will stop with the first username/UID match.

As new users are added to the system, they are provided certain things. This normally includes a home directory and a shell. Think of the home directory as a room. This room is theirs to do with as they wish. This is not true for them regarding the rest of the house. As guests, they need to be given permission by the operating system (the owner of the house) to either clutter or clean any other rooms.

Understanding privileged versus nonprivileged users

When a new user is added to the system, they are provided with user identification numbers (UIDs). Under Caldera Systems OpenLinux, a UID given to a new user on the system begins at 500. Numbers available for use go up to and include 65534. Numbers below 500 are reserved for use by system accounts. This may be different on other distributions; they may opt to start ordinary users at 1000 vice 500. Where the system users end and ordinary users begin is a matter of personal preference.

There is nothing special about most of the numbers below 500. In fact, the numbers from 1 to 65534 have no special significance. The fact that numbers below 500 are reserved for system use is just a convention. It assures distributors like Caldera Systems that those numbers will more than likely be available if needed for whatever purpose. Often, programs require a special user with complete access to all files in order to properly use the program, so these UIDs are available for that purpose. Database programs come to mind here. These numbers belong to accounts that are nonprivileged. These UIDs signify that no special privileges are available.

But available UIDs go from 0 to 65535. The UID 0 is very special. Any process that is started with the UID of 0, or any user with the UID of 0 is privileged. This means that that person or process has the power to do anything. Nothing is sacred. Going back to the house analogy, root (UID 0) is, if not the owner of the house, then at least a trusted agent. UID 0 has the power to break windows, knock down walls, or burn down the entire house — no questions asked. Most longtime administrators, and all good ones, know that they become a user with this UID only when absolutely necessary, and only for as long as necessary to accomplish whatever task. We'll revisit this issue throughout the book.

That leaves the UID of 65535. This UID is also special. This UID belongs to the user nobody. But before everyone e-mails me to tell me that I'm clueless, permit me to explain. If you look (and you will shortly if you haven't already), you'll see that under OpenLinux, nobody is UID 65534. The UID 65535 is considered by the operating system to have absolutely no privileges. Try creating the user "noone" with the useradd program:

```
useradd -m noone
```

When you create this user with its own home directory, the first thing you should notice is that the home directory, rather than being owned by noone, is owned by root (when the useradd program creates a users home directory, it is always chown'd (change owner) to the new user, so something is obviously different here). If you "su - noone", you can read the dot files in the directory, but you can't create or remove any file because noone doesn't own them. So, to avoid the complications of this userid, nobody is 65534, and 65535 remains unused. (Don't forget to remove the user noone and the noone home directory: `userdel noone;rm -Rf /home/noone`.)

Once upon a time, one exploit was to create a user with UID 65536, which would give that user root privileges. If you look at UIDs in binary form, you can see that all contain a combination of 1's and 0's except root, which is zero (all zeroes), and of course our friend nobody as the UID of 65535 (all ones – 16 of them – 1111111111111111). So what happens when we make a UID with 17 binary digits – 10000000000000000? Theoretically, since this value only has space for 16 binary digits, the one in position 17 would be said to wrap (effectively dropping the one), and you'd be back to all zeroes, since the lone one would overflow the space allotted for this value. This would give you root's UID and privileges. But this exploit is old, and programs in Linux won't permit this UID (65536) to be set, nullifying this exploit. So what good is it? A lot, if you can replace the program that won't permit you to set this UID with one that will. And the same type of exploit can be used in other situations, as we'll see later in the book.

 You can create users with UIDs greater than 65536, but unless /bin/login is replaced, these UIDs cannot be used.

The ultimate objective of anyone with malicious intent is to become the user root. If that should happen, you are then at this person's mercy. The worst part is not that this person will simply trash your system – this is probably the best that you could hope for. Often, you'll hear about high-visibility Web pages being trashed, but this is just one game. Rather, malcontents will in all likelihood use your system to cause problems elsewhere that will be traced back to your system, and you. In how many languages can you say "lawsuit"? Why do you think the authorities rarely catch the folks who actually did the damage? It's because they didn't do it from their own systems and leave a trail. Often, they used a compromised system to do their foul deeds, and erased their tracks before leaving.

Understanding the /etc/passwd file

When someone logs on to the system, he or she inputs a username and a password. These are checked against a database of users maintained in the /etc/passwd file. This database contains a password (or, in the case of a shadowed system, points to another database that contains the password). If the password the user enters corresponds to the password maintained by the system for that user, the system permits access. Or, more specifically, the specified program in the password file is executed. If that file is a shell, the user is permitted to enter commands.

To understand how all this works, you're going to look at the passwd file. Located in /etc, this file is world readable. It has to be for some programs to be able to verify usernames and UIDs. Once upon a time, passwords were maintained in this file, hence its name. Look at Listing 1-1. This is an old-style passwd file. Let's go through the fields one by one to see what their purposes are.

Listing 1-1: An old-style /etc/passw

```
fileroot:1iDYwrOmhmEBU:0:0:root:/root:/bin/bash
bin:*:1:1:bin:/bin:
daemon:*:2:2:daemon:/sbin:
adm:*:3:4:adm:/var/adm:
lp:*:4:7:lp:/var/spool/lpd:
sync:*:5:0:sync:/sbin:/bin/sync
shutdown:*:6:11:shutdown:/sbin:/sbin/shutdown
halt:*:7:0:halt:/sbin:/sbin/halt
mail:*:8:12:mail:/var/spool/mail:
news:*:9:13:news:/var/spool/news:
uucp:*:10:14:uucp:/var/spool/uucp:
operator:*:11:0:operator:/root:
games:*:12:100:games:/usr/games:
gopher:*:13:30:gopher:/usr/lib/gopher-data:
ftp:*:14:50:FTP User:/home/ftp:
man:*:15:15:Manuals Owner:/:
majordom:*:16:16:Majordomo:/:/bin/false
postgres:*:17:17:Postgres User:/home/postgres:/bin/bash
mysql:*:18:18:MySQL User:/usr/local/var:/bin/false
silvia:1iDYwrOmhmEBU:501:501:Silvia Bandel:/home/silvia:/bin/bash
nobody:*:65534:65534:Nobody:/:/bin/false
david:1iDYwrOmhmEBU:500:500:David A. Bandel:/home/david:/bin/bash
```

The passwd file has a very strict structure. As with several tables in UNIX, the passwd file is delimited by colons, so colons cannot be used in any field. The table itself comprises seven fields: username, password, UID, group ID (GID), GECOS field (aka comment field), home directory field, and login shell field.

Dissecting /etc/passwd

The first field is the username. This field must be unique – no two users on the system may have the same username. If you try to make the field unique by directly editing this file (the useradd, coastool, and LISA programs will not allow it), any program searching by username will fail to find the second occurrence of the name and so will match the first username and ask for that corresponding password and assign that user's UID. So the duplicate entry could just as well not exist. This is the only field required to be unique.

The second field is the password field. This is a hashed password. The term "hash" refers to an encrypted field. In the case of Linux, this hash is created with DES (Data Encryption Standard). This field, if it contains a valid password, will contain exactly 13 characters. Some characters, such as the colon and a single quote (among others) will never be found here (see "Understanding /etc/shadow" below for more details). Anything other than a legal hashed 13-character password here will prevent someone from logging in – with one very important exception: a null field (that is, if you see an entry like this):

```
david::500:500:David A. Bandel:/home/david:/bin/bash
```

where the second field has nothing at all, not even a space, will allow a user to log in with *no password*. Obviously, this is probably not what you want. So one thing you should always check for is a null password field. If the field has a password in it and you change this field, such as by adding a single quote to the front of the hashed password, you've effectively locked the user out without changing the password. This is an old trick, and not of much use today. Now that modern systems use /etc/shadow (discussed below), better methods exist to lock an account without changing the actual password. But system administrators before shadow files who administered systems with large numbers of users (and as long as there have been users, there have been wannabe system crackers) would often lock the root password by putting a single quote mark as the first character. With the quote, the 14-character field with the illegal character is locked. Another account, sometimes called "toor" or "tuber" would be used in place of root for system administration.

A password can currently be up to eight characters in length. A user can enter a longer password, but all characters beyond the first eight will not be used. The first two characters of the hashed password are actually a salt. (A salt is a number fed to the encryption algorithm to initialize it, and this salt is randomly chosen at each password change.) This permits a large number of permutations, so that if two or three or even more users have the same password, a simple inspection of the hashed password field will not reveal this. The actual hashed password is a lot like a scrambled egg. That is, while you can scramble an egg and compare it with another scrambled egg, you can't unscramble the egg. For that reason, dictionary attacks against hashed password fields are the common ways to crack passwords.

A dictionary attack uses a dictionary and the salt in a brute-force attempt to crack the password by encrypting every word in the dictionary with the known salt. Good password crackers will also perform several variations of each word, changing the password to all upper case, first letter only capitalized, and also adding numbers (usually just 0–9) on the end to all these combinations. Many easily guessable passwords can be cracked this way.

Looking at Listing 1-1, you can see that the hashed password field for root, silvia, and david are the same. This is deliberate on my part and would not occur in practice. I will tell you that this is only one hash of the password "silvia" (not a real password used on any of my systems). This password is as bad as no password, particularly for the user silvia. Any cracking program will nail this password in about 3 nanoseconds, but I'll save you the computing time.

You'll learn about password security in Chapter 2.

The third field is the UID. You learned a lot about this field earlier in this chapter, so no recap will be given here. Despite what some believe, this field does not have to be unique. That is, a user other than root can have a UID of 0, and will be given all the privileges of root. So in the example I gave three paragraphs back of substituting another user to do system administration, this was done by giving that user – be it toor, or tuber, or any other username – a UID of 0 as well.

But this approach is not without its problems. Suppose that you decide to take this approach. You lock root with an impossible hash after creating a new user with a UID of 0. Then you log in using this new account to do system administration. Without thinking, you lock the terminal you are using because you need to step away for a minute and don't want to log out. When you return, you'll find you can't unlock the terminal. This happens because the locking program looks at the UID of the user who locked the terminal. This is UID 0. The first occurrence of UID 0 belongs to the locked user root. But the terminal locking program doesn't know that and doesn't look further; it prompts for root's password and – you're locked out. So this approach has its pitfalls. Be sure you understand how this works. We'll revisit UIDs and username relationships in NFS security in the second part of this book.

The fourth field is the GID. This is the user's login or primary group. A user can belong to any number of groups, but one is, and must be, the primary group. You'll look more at groups in this and the next two chapters.

The fifth field is now referred to as a comment field, but its original name was the GECOS field, for "GE consolidated operating system field." When you try to access information about a user via finger or other program, the information in this field is now returned as the user's true name. An entry in this field is optional.

The sixth field designates the user's home directory. All users should have their own home directory. If the home directory doesn't exist, the user can still log in, but he or she will be dropped into the root directory (system root "/", as opposed to the user root's directory "/root"). You'll want to be careful with some entries. For example, the user ftp should have the anonymous ftp root directory as a home directory.

The seventh and final field is the user's login shell. Not just any shell can be entered here. Depending on how the system is set up, this shell must come from a list of valid shells. By default, OpenLinux lists the permitted shells in the file /etc/shells (see discussion of PAM below).

As mentioned earlier, the passwd file used to contain passwords. Even several years ago, computers were capable of running a hashed dictionary file against a copy of the passwd file and breaking many passwords, often including root, in a matter of days or even hours. Today, that procedure can be accomplished in a matter of minutes. To prevent this, a way was needed to deter folks from downloading the hashed password. Enter the shadow file.

Understanding /etc/shadow

The shadow file is owned by and is readable only by root. You create the file by copying the username from the passwd file, and then moving the hashed password to the shadow file and replacing it with an x. If you look at your /etc/passwd file, you'll see that it contains an x in every password field. This tells the system to look in the /etc/shadow file for the password. To convert from a shadowed system to nonshadowed, you have three utilities at your disposal. First, to create a shadowed system, you should run pwck. This will check the passwd file for any anomalies that could cause the next step to fail or, worse, loop endlessly. Once pwck has done its work, run pwconv to create /etc/shadow. You may find you need to do this if the passwd file is updated by hand. The utility to convert back to a standard UNIX file is pwunconv.

The shadow file is similar in many respects to the passwd file. Its structure is similar — the two fields from the passwd file are the same. But when the shadow file was designed, some additional security information was incorporated. Listing 1-2 shows the contents of a typical shadow file.

Listing 1-2: A shadow file

```
root:1iDYwrOmhmEBU:10792:0::7:7::
bin:*:10547:0::7:7::
daemon:*:10547:0::7:7::
```

```
adm:*:10547:0::7:7::
lp:*:10547:0::7:7::
sync:*:10547:0::7:7::
shutdown:U:10811:0:-1:7:7:-1:134531940
halt:*:10547:0::7:7::
mail:*:10547:0::7:7::
news:*:10547:0::7:7::
uucp:*:10547:0::7:7::
operator:*:10547:0::7:7::
games:*:10547:0::7:7::
gopher:*:10547:0::7:7::
ftp:*:10547:0::7:7::
man:*:10547:0::7:7::
majordom:*:10547:0::7:7::
postgres:*:10547:0::7:7::
mysql:*:10547:0::7:7::
silvia:1iDYwrOmhmEBU:10792:0:30:7:-1::
nobody:*:10547:0::7:7::
david:1iDYwrOmhmEBU:10792:0::7:7::
```

Dissecting /etc/shadow

The first field in the shadow file matches exactly that of the passwd file.

The second field is the hashed password field. The implementation of shadow under OpenLinux allows this hashed field to be any number of characters from 13 to 24. However, the crypt program that OpenLinux uses returns only 13 characters as noted above. The available characters that the crypt program can return as a hash are the 52 letters of the alphabet (upper and lower case), the numbers 0–9, a period, and the forward slash (/). These 64 characters constitute the legal values for this field.

The salt, then, still the first two characters, has 4096 possible combinations (64 × 64). (The number 64 is derived from the fact that 1 character equals 1 byte, and 1 byte equals 8 bits. Since a bit can be either 0 or 1, this combination of 2 possible numbers raised to a power of 8, 28, equals 64.) The total key space is based on the DES 56-bit encryption key, so is 256 (2 raised to a power of 56) or approximately 72,057,590,000,000,000. While this number, 72 quadrillion, may seem large, an exhaustive search of this keyspace can in fact be accomplished in a very short period of time. In the last DES challenge (a contest using distributed computing to test the strength of the DES algorithm) before this book went to press, a computer broke the 56-bit code in under 24 hours. While I'm on the subject, let me note that programs like crack search that portion of the keyspace generally used by humans (comprising dictionary words and their permutations) and can do so with amazing speed. So the only thing that really keeps your passwords secure is the fact that only root can read the hash.

The third field begins the password aging information (see "Changing password aging information," below) and is the number of days elapsed since Jan. 1, 1970, that the password has been changed. Table 1-1 will give you a quick reference for numbers that will show up on the first of the month for the years 2000–2005.

TABLE 1-1 FIRST-OF-THE-MONTH VALUES FOR SHADOW FIELD THREE.

Month/Year	2000	2001	2002	2003	2004	2005
Jan (31)	10957	11323	11688	12053	12418	12784
Feb (28/29)	10988	11354	11719	12084	12449	12815
Mar (31)	11017	11382	11747	12112	12478	12843
Apr (30)	11048	11413	11778	12143	12509	12874
May (31)	11078	11443	11808	12173	12539	12904
Jun (30)	11109	11474	11839	12204	12570	12935
Jul (31)	11139	11504	11869	12234	12600	12965
Aug (31)	11170	11535	11900	12265	12631	12996
Sep (30)	11201	11566	11931	12296	12662	13027
Oct (31)	11231	11596	11961	12326	12692	13057
Nov (30)	11262	11627	11992	12357	12723	13088
Dec (31)	11292	11657	12022	12387	12753	13118

The fourth field is the minimum number of days that must pass before a password may be changed. Password changes may not be made until this number of days has elapsed.

The fifth field is the maximum number of days a password may be used before it must be changed. If this field contains a positive value, then the first time a user logs in after this many days since the last password change, the password command will be run forcing a password change.

The sixth field is the number of days in advance of field five that a user will begin receiving a warning that the mandatory password change date is approaching. This permits a user to begin formulating a password that is both secure and easy to remember.

The seventh field is the number of days after field five that a user account is disabled. That is, if a user has not logged in and changed his or her password before this number of days has elapsed after the password expired, then the account will be disabled.

The penultimate field merely records the day an account has been disabled.

The final field is not used and is reserved.

Final notes

One last thing before you move on. You may see in the passwd and shadow files, fields that look like this:

```
+:x:0:0:::
```

or

```
+:*:0:0::-1:-1::
```

These entries should be the very last ones in the passwd and shadow files respectively. If you are not using NIS (Network Information Services, formerly known as the "Yellow Pages," but changed due to a trademark claim by British Telecom), these entries should be removed. If you feel a very strong desire or need to use NIS, understand that it is an extremely unsecure protocol and suffers from insufficient system authentication. NIS+ is somewhat better, but Linux does not (yet) have a NIS+ server implementation. You run NIS at great risk to your systems. Its intricacies and security problems will not be discussed in this text, but are left to a book devoted to NIS.

Understanding /etc/group

The group file is similar in nature to the password file. You'll see in subsequent chapters more about the significance of groups. For this chapter, you will only be concerned with the format of the group file. You can see an example group file in Listing 1-3.

Listing 1-3: A sample group file

```
root::0:
wheel::10:
bin::1:bin,daemon
daemon::2:bin,daemon
sys::3:bin,adm
adm::4:adm,daemon
tty::5:
```

```
disk::6:
lp::7:daemon,lp
mem::8:
kmem::9:
operator::11:
mail::12:mail
news::13:news
uucp::14:uucp
man::15:
majordom::16:
database::17:
mysql::18:
games::20:
gopher::30:
dip::40:
utmp::45:
ftp::50:
silvia::501:silvia
nobody::65534:
users::100:david,silvia
david::500:david
```

Dissecting /etc/group

The file /etc/group contains four colon-delimited fields. The first field is the group-name field. Like the username field, it provides an easy reference for system users.

The second field is blank. This is because it is not usual to have security on the groups. If the field contains a password, any user can join that group by issuing the `newgrp` command and when prompted for a password, giving the correct one. I can hear one or two of you out there saying, "Ha – caught you, look, the group root has no password, so anyone can join it without a password." Not quite. If there are no passwords on a group, only those users listed as group members (see field four below) can join the group.

The third field is the GID number. This is used the same way the UID is used. While not required to be unique, it is a good idea.

The last field is a comma-separated list (with no spaces) of all those users who belong to it (leading and trailing spaces are generally ignored, but may confuse some programs). A user does not need to be listed as a group member of his login group specifically, but it doesn't hurt and could save some confusion later. The login group is specified (mandatory) in the passwd file and so will be assigned. But if the passwd file is changed, the user will no longer be able to be part of that login group.

Understanding /etc/gshadow

By default, OpenLinux is not set up with group shadow passwords. This is because passwords are discouraged. The reason is simple: Group passwords are not protected. If you implement group passwords, you can rightly assume that everyone knows them. The importance of protecting one's personal password is easy to impress on users. But the importance of protecting a password "everyone knows" is easily lost on them. Combine that with the need for a common password to be easy for everyone to remember, and you have a system that is as unsecure as it can be.

But if you insist on throwing caution to the wind, and you want to invoke group passwords, you may want to use group shadow passwords for the same reason you use shadow passwords with the passwd file (though this is not necessary).

If you wish to use group shadow passwords, you will need to create gshadow. Converting between using the group shadow file and having the hashed password stored in the standard UNIX group file is a similar procedure to that outlined for the passwd file above. As a precaution, you should run grpck first to ensure the group file is consistent and will not cause the next step to fail or loop endlessly. Then run grpconv. This will put the familiar x in the password field of the /etc/group file and create a file /etc/gshadow. This file (gshadow) consists of four comma-separated fields. The first field is the group name, the second, the hashed password (information regarding the hashed password field above applies). The third field is reserved. The fourth field is a comma-delimited list of group members. Remember though, if the group has a password assigned to it, anyone with the password can join that group. As with the shadow file, the gshadow file can be merged back into the group file with the utility grpunconv.

Understanding /etc/login.defs

When you need to add users to the system, you can use one of a number of programs to do so. The three common programs on OpenLinux include the new coastool, the older LISA program, or the useradd program. Any one will do. COAS has its own file and you'll look at that below, but useradd and LISA use the information stored in /etc/login.defs to put default information into the passwd and shadow files. The definition file for creating new users via useradd is the /etc/login.defs file. See Listing 1-4.

Listing 1-4: A condensed /etc/login.defs file

```
# Maximum number of days a password may be used:
# (-1 = no password changes are necessary)
PASS_MAX_DAYS    -1
# Minimum number of days allowed between password changes:
```

```
PASS_MIN_DAYS    0
# Number of days warning given before a password expires:
PASS_WARN_AGE    7
# Number of days till account is closed after password has expired:
PASS_INACTIVE    -1
# Force expiry at given day: (in days after 70/1/1, -1 = don't
force)
PASS_EXPIRE      -1
###
# Default values for useradd
# default group:
GROUP            100
# user's home directory: (%s = name of user)
HOME             /home/%s
# default user shell:
SHELL            /bin/bash
# directory where the home directory skeleton is located:
SKEL             /etc/skel
# Min/max values for automatic gid selection in groupadd
GID_MIN          100
GID_MAX          60000
```

The values in the file in Listing 1-4 constitute default values. These values are plugged in when not overridden on the command line. They make a good starting point, although if you want to implement password aging, you'll need to change these values. The seemingly nonsensical values of -1 in the top section mean no limit. Feel free to adjust the values to fit your needs. You will get a better understanding of what constitutes good values for these fields later in this chapter and in Chapter 2.

Caldera's COAS program uses a graphical interface for system administration. Under "System Administration/Account Administration" you can administer user and group accounts. The pull-down menus allow you to change everything, including the defaults for preferences of user groups.

Changing password-aging information

If you want to change password aging information on only one or two users, you can use the command `chage`, for change aging. The chage command can be run by non-privileged users only with the -l option and their own username. This will allow them to check their own password aging information. When chage is invoked,.at least the username must be specified. If only the username is specified, chage will be invoked interactively for the specified user and each parameter prompted. If invoked with the -1 option, chage will list aging information for the specified user. All other options require an argument. Invoking chage with no arguments will net you a usage message.

See Listing 1-5 for an example. Remember that values are given in days.

Listing 1-5: Password aging information on user david

```
# chage -1 david7
Minimum:          2
Maximum:          90
Warning:          7
Inactive:         14
Last Change:              Aug 11, 1999
Password Expires:         Nov 09, 1999
Password Inactive:        Nov 23, 1999
Account Expires:          Never
```

What Listing 1-5 shows is that user david must wait at least two days after changing his password before he can change it again. The maximum number of days he can go before being forced to change passwords is 90 days. He'll get a warning seven days in advance. If he doesn't log in (and successfully update his password) during the 14-day period following password expiration, the account will become inactive, and he won't be able to change it (or log in).

If you get summer help, you can set an account expiration date for them. Then you can set the minimum days to password change greater than the maximum password age. This will not allow them to change passwords while they have the account. Setting the warning to 0 won't bother them with warnings they can do nothing about. So you can see that with a little imagination, you can set up accounts to handle many different situations with password aging.

You'll learn more about why you should institute password aging in Chapter 2.

You can also use COAS to change aging information on an account-by-account basis. Values are in days. The GUI is self-explanatory.

The expiry command can be used to check or force expiration of a password on a user if required.

Understanding Pluggable Authentication Modules

One of the problems with the shadow file is that every application that needs to perform some kind of login validation has to be recompiled to understand shadow passwords. But Sun Microsystems came up with a solution, first used in Solaris 2.3, that was adapted by Linux developers. The system is called PAM (Pluggable Authentication Modules), and consists of modules and libraries. Applications built with PAM libraries don't have to understand the ever-changing authentication system in use. Instead, they ask PAM to mediate the authentication process for them. This permits a lot of flexibility in your system.

What PAM does is allow anyone to write a new security module, then have this security module interface with the file or device that is going to give the SUCCESS, FAILURE or IGNORE to authentication. PAM will then pass either SUCCESS or FAILURE to the service requesting the information. What this means is that you can have either a regular password file or a shadowed password file, and by using PAM, you can be authenticated. It also means that you can easily add more security. Let's say you want to add a voice recognition device to compare someone's voice to a voiceprint file. All you need is a module that will return a SUCCESS, IGNORE, or FAILURE. This module will talk to the voice recognition device, which will make the determination. This can be any biometric authentication, smartcard, etc. As long as a pluggable authentication module exists, this authentication can be added. Modules can be "stacked," requiring more than one type of authentication, or allowing any one of several. So a number of things can be considered all at once: kerberos, password expiration and successful change of the password, or more extravagant authentications, such as retina scan and smart card, and so on. A FAILURE returned to the service will result in a login failure.

To get an idea of how PAM works, take a look at Listing 1-6. This is the PAM login service file included with OpenLinux 2.3. If you look in the /etc/pam.d directory, you'll see a number of services including login, su, passwd, other, and more depending on what you've installed. Every restricted service will have its own file. Any restricted service that doesn't have a file will default to "other." (A restricted service is any service or program that requires some form of authentication to use – that is, if, under normal conditions, a service asks you for a username and password, it's a restricted service.)

Listing 1-6: The login service

```
auth        required        pam_securetty.so
auth        required        pam_pwdb.so
auth        required        pam_nologin.so
#auth       required        pam_dialup.so
auth        optional        pam_mail.so
account     required        pam_pwdb.so
session     required        pam_pwdb.so
session     optional        pam_lastlog.so
password    required        pam_pwdb.so
```

Looking at the login service file, you see three columns. In fact, there are four columns, but the last column is optional and not used in this instance. The last column would consist of any optional arguments. You'll see this in another example below. Lines that begin with # are ignored. So in Listing 1-6, the pam_dialup module (fourth line) will not be evaluated. As you read through the rest of this section, it may help you to follow the PAM flow chart in Figure 1-1. Note the multiple auth lines and multiple lines containing pam_pwdb.so. The technique of using multiple lines for any given check is called stacking modules, and can be used to enhance security by forcing several different checks at each portion of the login process.

Understanding PAM types

The first column is the type column and will contain one of four entries: *auth, account, session,* or *password.* Note that all entries in this file are case-sensitive.

◆ The *auth* (short for authentication) type is used to establish that users are who they claim to be. This is normally accomplished by performing the username/password comparison or, if the proper module is used, can be via smartcard or some biometric comparison (modules for these last two would need to be written).

◆ The *account* type verifies whether the user is permitted to use the service, under what circumstances, and whether or not a password has expired, etc.

◆ The *password* type is used to update authentication tokens. For example, if the expiration information in /etc/shadow shows the password as expired, the passwd module would launch the chauthtok (change authentication token) and would return SUCCESS with a successful password change.

◆ The *session* type performs actions when a user is logged in or out. This can include performing logging actions, mounting and unmounting directories, or just preparing the environment for the user, etc.

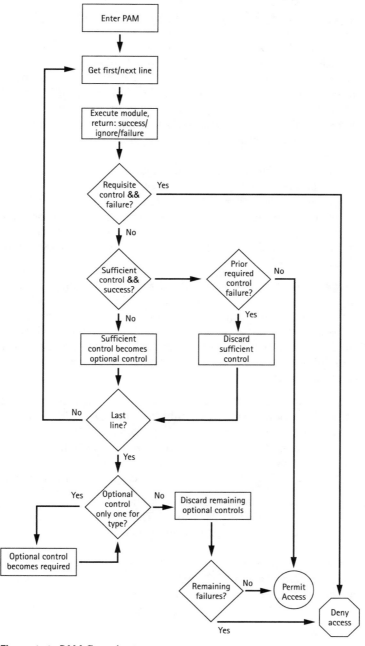

Figure 1-1: PAM flow chart

Understanding module controls

The second column is the control field and indicates what will happen should the module return SUCCESS, IGNORE, or FAILURE. This field can contain one of the following: *requisite, required, sufficient,* or *optional*. The values used on any given line in the control field affect other lines. For example, a line with *sufficient* that returns success will terminate the PAM process and log the user in. Similarly, a line with *requisite* that returns failure will immediately terminate the login process. In either case, no further lines will be processed. Normally, though, all lines are processed.

- The *requisite* control is final. Any line marked *requisite* will immediately terminate and return FAILURE back to the service if it receives a FAILURE from the module. No other modules will be evaluated. You will not normally want to use this control; required (see next entry) is better. This is because if requisite is the first control in the file, modules below it won't be evaluated, including ones to log an attempted access. (See "Modules explained" below.)

- The *required* control will be combined with all other lines. That is, regardless of the status (SUCCESS, IGNORE, or FAILURE) the rest of the modules will be evaluated. The required control is the most often used, since its status is not returned to the service until final status is received from all modules, meaning if one of the modules is to log an access attempt (successful or not), you'll get a log entry. You'll look at how this works more closely below.

- The *sufficient* control will pass SUCCESS back to the service immediately upon being encountered (successfully terminating the login process) as long as no prior required control field passed FAILURE. If a prior required control field passed FAILURE, the sufficient control field is ignored. If the sufficient control field passes back IGNORE or FAILURE, then it is treated as an IGNORE or FAILURE of an optional control (see next paragraph).

- The *optional* control matters only if it is the only module for any given type. Otherwise, a FAILURE is ignored. This control should be used if the user should be allowed to log in even if this control fails.

In order for a user to be permitted access to the system, then, no *requisite* or *required* module may return a FAILURE. As long as it doesn't, the user is permitted access. Remember that an *optional* control becomes required if it is the only one for any given type.

The modules themselves

The third column is the full filename of the module to be used. Modules may be located anywhere you wish to put them, but if the module resides in the compiled-in module directory, then only the name is required. Otherwise, the full path to the module must be specified. The compiled-in module path for OpenLinux is /lib/security.

The fourth column would contain any applicable options that you might want to pass to the module. Not all modules have options, and options are not always needed, but are used to modify the module's behavior in some way. You'll look at the options in conjunction with the modules below.

Available pluggable authentication modules provided with OpenLinux include those in Listing 1-7.

Listing 1-7: List of PAMs available on OpenLinux

```
pam_access.so
pam_cracklib.so
pam_deny.so
pam_dialup.so
pam_env.so
pam_ftp.so
pam_group.so
pam_lastlog.so
pam_limits.so
pam_listfile.so
pam_mail.so
pam_nologin.so
pam_permit.so
pam_pwdb.so
pam_radius.so
pam_rhosts_auth.so
pam_rootok.so
pam_securetty.so
pam_shells.so
pam_stress.so
pam_tally.so
pam_time.so
pam_unix_acct.so
pam_unix_auth.so
pam_unix_passwd.so
pam_unix_session.so
pam_warn.so
pam_wheel.so
```

First you'll take a look at some of the more common modules, then you'll look at examples of how they are used so you can understand module stacking, starting with the login service.

Modules explained

The `pam_access.so` module specifies the use of the file /etc/security/access.conf to determine whether or not to permit access. Access is permitted (or denied) based on matches made within this file. Each line in the file has the format:

```
permission:user(s):origins
```

- ◆ `permission` will be either + (permitted) or - (denied).
- ◆ `user(s)` will be one of ALL, username, or user@host, where host is the name of the local machine (otherwise the entry is ignored).
- ◆ `origins` will be one or more tty names (without the /dev/), hostnames, domain names (begin with a "."), IP network numbers (end with a "." as in 192.168.0. allowing all of the network 192.168.0.X), ALL, or LOCAL (matching any string without a ".").

OpenLinux does not include a sample file by default, but the above should allow you to create one and test this module if desired. This module takes no options.

The `pam_cracklib.so` module checks the password against dictionary words. This module applies some sanity checks to a password as the user tries to change it to see if it can be easily guessed, such as use of a dictionary word (or derivative), repeated letters, length (too short), and a few others. Options are not required, but three are provided for: `debug`, `type=`, and `retry=`. The debug option is verbose and logs the session. The `type=` option permits you to change the default "New UNIX password:" prompt, substituting the string after `type=` for UNIX. And retry will prompt the user the specified number of times in case of failure before returning an error (default is 1).

Listing 1–8: The other restricted service file

```
auth        required      pam_deny.so
auth        required      pam_warn.so
account     required      pam_deny.so
password    required      pam_deny.so
password    required      pam_warn.so
session     required      pam_deny.so
```

As you can see, *auth*, *account*, *password*, and *session* all list a control of *required* and call the `pam_deny.so` module. This prevents a rogue restricted service from starting. So if you don't want anyone to use the FTP service, you can easily deny this by temporarily renaming /etc/pam.d/ftp to /etc/pam.d/ftp.orig or another name.

The `pam_dialup.so` module checks the /etc/security/ttys.dialup file to see if a dailup password is required on any one or all of the dialup terminals. Note that this may apply to any tty, not just ttyS terminals. If applicable, the password is checked against the one in /etc/security/passwd.dialup. The passwd.dialup file is changed via the dpasswd program (do not attempt to change passwd.dialup manually). A related file is the /etc/security/ttys.dialup file. This file is related to the passwd.dialup file and is used when specific terminals require an additional password for access. This file will be used by dpasswd as appropriate.

The pam_group.so module requires a check on the /etc/security/group.conf file. This file specifies the groups a listed user can belong to under certain conditions, those conditions being that the service, tty, and time all correspond on one line with the user's name. These would be additional groups the user doesn't belong to at login, and would belong to only under specific conditions. A sample group.conf file is provided in /etc/security/ in the OpenLinux distribution with instructions on its use. This module takes no options.

The `pam_lastlog.so` module creates an entry in the lastlog if the user is logged in – normally a module for type session and control optional. The lastlog tracks the last time and place a user logged in from.

The `pam_limits.so` module can be used to set limits on logged-in users. These limits do not apply to root (or any account with UID 0). A sample /etc/security/limits.conf file is included in OpenLinux for those who need to limit users in some fashion. Limit settings are per login, and are not global or permanent – they are session-oriented.

The `pam_listfile.so` module checks an item against a list in a file and takes actions based on its findings, returning a SUCCESS or FAILURE. This module requires the following options:

- `item=[tty|user|rhost|ruser|group|shell]`

- `sense=[allow|deny]` (status to return; if the item is not listed in the file, then the opposite status is returned)

- `file=/full/path/and/filename`

- `onerr=[succeed|fail]` (if an error occurs, what status is returned?)

- `apply=[user|@group]` define the user or group to which the restriction applies. Note that with `item=[user|ruser|group]` this option doesn't apply, but for `item=[tty|rhost|shell]` it does.

The `pam_nologin.so` module is used by the auth type as a required control. This module checks for the existence of a /etc/nologin file. If one doesn't exist, it returns SUCCESS; if it does exist, it returns FAILURE and displays the contents of the file to the user. This module is often used to keep users out until the system has come up completely or when the system is taken down for maintenance, but is still connected to the network.

The `pam_permit.so` module complements the pam_deny.so module. It always returns SUCCESS. This module ignores all options.

The `pam_pwdb.so` module provides an interface to the passwd and shadow files. This module takes a number of options, but you should understand them before use. Available options are as follows:

- `debug` — log debugging information

- `audit` — log more debugging information than anyone needs

- `use_first_pass` _ take password from previous modules; no password prompt

- `try_first_pass` _ do not prompt for password unless authtok is unset

- `use_authtok` _ return FAILURE if pam_authtok has not been set; no password prompt (only intended for stacked password modules)

- `not_set_pass` — don't set other PAMs with password from this module

- `shadow` — try to maintain shadow password system

- `unix` — put password in /etc/passwd file

- `md5` — use md5 hash at next passwd change

- `bigcrypt` — use DEC C2 algorithm at next passwd change

- `nodelay` — avoid 1-second failed authentication delay

As of this writing, OpenLinux does not support the use of md5 or bigcrypt passwords, so these should not be used. Likewise, unless you've converted your shadow files and gone back to the old style UNIX passwd file, you should not use the UNIX option. Note that some options preclude use of their contrasts.

The `pam_rhosts_auth.so` module allows or disallows use of .rhosts and hosts.equiv files. It also allows or disallows use of "dangerous" entries in those files. Options include:

- `no_hosts_equiv` _ ignore this the /etc/hosts.equiv file

- `no_rhosts` _ ignore these /etc/rhosts or ~/.rhosts files

- `debug` — log debugging information

- `nowarn` — do not print warnings

- `suppress` — suppress all messages

- `promiscuous` — permit the "+" wildcard in any field (a real bad idea)

The `pam_rootok.so` module returns SUCCESS for any user with UID 0 (root). Used with the *sufficient* control, it will allow access to a service with no password.

Be careful with this one, as the first *auth* line with a *sufficient* control in the login service will allow root to log in with no password, which is probably not what you want — you've been warned. It takes one option: debug.

The pam_securetty.so module applies only to root. It reads the file /etc/securetty and permits only root (UID 0) to log in from the consoles listed in this file. If you are in a very secure environment and want root to be able to log in via telnet (which will be psuedo-tty's, ttyp designations) then either add lines for ttyp0-255 or comment out the pam_securetty.so line in the login service. Note that disabling this module is not recommended. The module checks to ensure /etc/securetty is not world writable.

The pam_shells.so module returns SUCCESS if the user's shell as listed in /etc/passwd is also listed in /etc/shells. If /etc/passwd has no shell listed, then the user is logged in with /bin/sh. Any shell listed in /etc/passwd that is not listed in /etc/shells returns FAILURE for that user. The file /etc/shells must not be world writable.

The pam_stress.so module is used for password management. This module has a large number of options, including debug, but under normal circumstances only two will be of interest:

♦ rootok — allows root to change a users password without being prompted for the old password

♦ expired — tells the module to act as if the user's password has expired

Other options will cause first or second (where applicable) functions to fail, to use a passwd from another module or pass a passwd to another module (or not), etc. While PAM is very flexible, if you need these specialized functions you should read the PAM documentation on this module.

The pam_tally.so module is not used by OpenLinux in any service file by default. However, it is sufficiently important to merit discussion. This module will maintain a count of attempted accesses. The count can be reset by a successful login, or can deny access after a predetermined number of failures. The default tally file is /var/log/faillog (cannot be world writable). Global options are:

♦ onerr=[succeed|fail] — what to do if on an error, such as cannot open file

♦ file=/full/path/and/filename — if not using defaultThe following option applies only to the *auth* type:

♦ no_magic_root — normally root (UID 0) doesn't increment the counter on failure, but this option forces that to happen. If you permit root telnet/r-commands, this is a good idea (although telnet/r-commands in general are a very bad idea)

The following options apply only to the *account* type:

- deny=n — deny access after n login attempts. Changes default reset /no_reset behavior from no_reset to reset except for user root (UID 0) when no_magic_root is not specified

- no_magic_root _ don't ignore deny for access attempts by root. When combined with deny= above, reset behavior is as for normal users

- even_deny_root_account _ can lock out root when combined with no_magic_root above. You've been warned. Root can bypass as long as no_magic_root is not specified, but normal users will be locked out

- reset _ reset counter to 0 on successful login for all users (including magic root)

- no_reset _ do not reset counter; default unless deny= is set and the user is not magic root

The pam_time.so module allows you to restrict access based on time to designated services. A sample time.conf file is provided in /etc/security/ in the OpenLinux distribution for your convenience. The file is well-documented for those requiring this type of access control. It takes no options: everything is included in the configuration file.

The pam_unix module is four separate modules that handle basic UNIX authentication. The modules are: pam_unix_auth.so, pam_unix_session.so, pam_unix_acct.so, and pam_unix_passwd.so. The name basically tells you which module belongs to which type. The *account* and *auth* type modules don't recognize any options. The passwd module recognizes one option to restrict its behavior: strict=false. This prevents the module from checking passwords against the dictionary, allowing users to input unsafe (easily guessed/broken) passwords. The session module allows to options: debug and trace. Debug is logged to the debug log as specified in syslog.conf, and trace to the authpriv log due to the sensitivity of the items being traced.

The pam_warn.so module logs a message to syslog when invoked. It recognizes no options.

The pam_wheel.so module will permit only members of the wheel group to become root. The wheel group is one of the system groups in Linux. This group is often given privileges via user, group, and file permissions that are beyond those given an ordinary user, but less than root's. This can add an extra layer of security to those systems where a number of users have been given the root password. If root can only log on at the terminal, this could be used to prevent users from exercising root privileges via telnet by denying them access unless they are also members of the wheel group. This module is also very flexible and can combine its options in some interesting ways. Options include:

- debug — logs debugging messages

- use_uid — uses the current UID rather than the login UID to determine eligibility

- ◆ `trust` — will return SUCCESS rather than IGNORE if the user belongs to the wheel group

- ◆ `group=xxx` — uses the GID xxx group rather than the wheel group for authentication

- ◆ `deny` — reverses sense (returns FAILURE). When used with group= can deny access to users in this group

 If you haven't noticed, the /etc/security directory is related to /etc/pam.d, which contains all the supplementary security files referred to by the various PAM modules.

Some examples

Now that you've seen what the modules do, look back at Listing 1-6, the login service. First, you see an auth type with required control calling the securetty module. This only allows root access from secure terminals as listed in /etc/securetty. The second line will check the /etc/passwd file to verify the user and UID. The third auth line will look for a file called /etc/nologin. If it doesn't exist, SUCCESS is returned. The fourth auth line is commented out, but can be easily changed if you want to check dialups using a password and authorization as defined in /etc/security tty.dialup and passwd.dialup, but this is not required to allow dialin access. The last auth line is optional, but may be needed if the system is only used by some for e-mail access.

The account type line checks the user's password contained in the shadow file. If it matches with what the user inputted, SUCCESS is returned.

The two session types are standard. The user is checked by the pwdb module to see if he can use the service, and the module to put an entry in the lastlog is optional, because you want to let the user enter even if the lastlog can't be written to. So here, you can get SUCCESS, IGNORE, or FAILURE, and still log in.

The password type is required and will be sued to update the authentication tokens should a password change be required.

Some of the files in /etc/pam.d will be very vanilla. The chfn, for example, uses only the `pam_pwdb.so` module, and it is required for type auth, account, and password. The chsh service is identical. The two mail services, imap and pop, also include the session type module for pwdb, and the nologin module for the type auth. Shadow is included, although not required, but is a good idea to ensure that a password change won't be entered in the /etc/passwd file. And while probably not a good idea, nullok means null passwords (no password) are acceptable.

You've looked at the other service file, and it contained no surprises. Looking at one or two files that may need some explanation, you see the ftp service. Its first line uses the listfile module. Here, you'll look in the file /etc/ftpusers for a username, and if it is listed, you're going to deny them ftp service (in this case it's easier to say who can't than who can use this service). If the file doesn't exist or is world writable, act like the user entry isn't there.

The rlogin file may also require some explanation. The first line checks to make sure root (UID 0) is only logging in from a secure terminal, usually one on the local system (we don't want root passing a clear text password over an untrusted network). So check /etc/securetty. The next line says that if a /etc/hosts.equiv or ~/.rhosts file exists, then that is sufficient to allow access (and of course the file is read-only for that user). If these files do not exist, then you'll have to go through all the rest of the modules successfully. Notice that by default, the line containing the `cracklib.so` module is commented out (contains a # at the beginning of the line). You may want to uncomment this cracklib.so line so that users can't change to unsafe passwords.

The last service you'll want to note is the su service. The first line:

```
auth    sufficient pam_rootok.so
```

with the control *sufficient* permits root to su to anyone without a password, as you've probably noticed from working on the system.

As you can see, by using the modules and stacking them, you can do just about anything you might want to, from restricting certain users by time of day or day of week, or by means (local versus remote access). If you decide to alter any of these to fit your own purposes, I suggest one thing: test several scenarios to ensure that the modules you've selected are acting the way you want them to, and not permitting access to those you don't want in. Test a user that should return a SUCCESS and a FAILURE, and don't forget to check root, for both passwords and nulls.

Tracking PAM log entries

You can view the results of authentication with restricted services via the syslog daemon. Messages coming from PAM will be entered into the /var/log/secure log file (see Listing 1-9).

Listing 1-9: PAM entries from /var/log/secure

```
Jan 11 16:45:14 chiriqui PAM_pwdb[30022]: (su) session opened for
user root by david(uid=0)
Jan 11 16:45:25 chiriqui PAM_pwdb[30022]: (su) session closed for
user root
Jan 11 17:18:06 chiriqui login[13217]: FAILED LOGIN 1 FROM (null)
FOR david, Authentication failure
Jan 11 17:18:13 chiriqui login[13217]: FAILED LOGIN 2 FROM (null)
FOR david, Authentication failure
Jan 11 17:18:17 chiriqui PAM_pwdb[13217]: (login) session opened for
```

```
user david by (uid=0)
Jan 11 17:18:06 chiriqui login[13217]: FAILED LOGIN 1 FROM (null)
FOR david, Authentication failure
Jan 11 17:18:13 chiriqui login[13217]: FAILED LOGIN 2 FROM (null)
FOR david, Authentication failure
Jan 11 17:18:17 chiriqui PAM_pwdb[13217]: (login) session opened for
user david by (uid=0)
Jan 11 17:18:17 chiriqui  -- david[13217]: LOGIN ON tty1 BY david
Jan 11 17:18:20 chiriqui PAM_pwdb[13217]: (login) session closed for
user david
```

Glancing through the various entries, you see the date, time, and hostname. Then you see PAM_pwdb. This is the password database authentication module followed by the process ID number (PID). After that, in parenthesis, is the name of the restricted service. In Listing 1-9 this will be either su or login and will state "session opened" or "session closed."

The line following a "session opened" line will be a LOGIN message. This tells you where the user finally logged in to (tty1, etc). If you have several login attempts, but cannot get logged in, you might want to check /var/log/secure to see why and where the login is failing.

Summary

This chapter explained in some detail about users and logins. You learned first about the /etc/passwd file and its role, both historically and currently. Then you learned how /etc/shadow brought some added security for users and eased the administration burden with several additional fields for password aging. You also became acquainted with the /etc/group file.

The next file you learned about was the /etc/login.defs file, what was in it, and how it affected the useradd program and the defaults for the system.

Finally, you learned what PAM is, how it works, and about a number of security related files used by PAM, such as /etc/securetty, /etc/shells, and files in /etc/security/. You also saw how modules are stacked to perform a number of different things or to allow restricted services to behave differently under varying conditions.

You'll learn more about groups in the next chapter, and about user/group interactions at the file level after that. You can begin to understand how important the user/group/permissions relationships are from this chapter, and you'll gain an ever-deeper understanding as you progress through the next few chapters.

Chapter 2

User and group security

IN THIS CHAPTER

◆ Understanding default user and private user groups schemes

◆ Changing user/group

◆ Understanding how changing user/group impacts your GUI

◆ Understanding user security

◆ Understanding password security

◆ Protecting your password

◆ Choosing good passwords

◆ Cracking passwords

YOU HAVE ONLY ONE way to manage users, and that is by the unique username assigned to every user. But with groups, you have your choice of two different schemes. Some thought should be given to this, because you'll want to set it up only once (particularly on a system with many users). The two schemes are default group, and user private groups. Each has its advantages and disadvantages.

Understanding the default group

Historically, all UNIX and UNIX-like operating systems (including Linux) used a system whereby all new users on a system belonged to one group by default. The system administrator could change this during account setup if desired, but often it was left this way. This was because a user could belong to only one group at a time. So all users were created with a default group that anyone could safely belong to. When users needed to be part of another group for a project, they could issue the newgrp command. They would join the new group, leaving their old group behind (assuming they had rights to join the new group).

Today, this limitation of belonging to one group at a time no longer exists. Users can belong to as many groups as are necessary. So there's a lot of flexibility. Under OpenLinux, whether you are using the default group or private user groups (discussed below) you can belong to as many groups as you need. When a user joins a group by using the newgrp command, this group becomes the login group (the user still belongs to all other groups previously held). The significance of this is that unless overridden by a directory setting, the login group is the group ownership the file will be given.

 See Chapter 4 for more information on directory settings.

The difference between default and user private groups is "openness." With the default group scheme, anyone can read (and often write) a file created by anyone else. With the private groups, no one can read or write a file another user creates unless the owner explicitly changes permissions to allow another to read or write to that file.

If a requirement exists for a special project that users will join and leave, and the project leader doesn't want to involve the system administrators beyond the setup, then a group can be set up with a password. Remember, one of two conditions must exist before you can exercise the privileges of a particular group: You must either belong to the group, or join the group. In order for a user to join a group he doesn't belong to when he logs in, the group must have a password assigned to it (via the /etc/gshadow file).

By default, OpenLinux does not use passwords, so it does not have /etc/gshadow. Chapter 1 outlines how to implement this feature.

Under OpenLinux, whether you have default groups or not depends on several settings. The default setting if you use useradd or LISA is default group. But under COAS, the default is user private groups. Either may be changed, but if they aren't and you alternate between using these different programs, you'll have a mishmash of default and user private groups. So you need to change either /etc/login.defs or COAS. Alternately, you can use one program exclusively, make changes on the command line, or create the new user and change it later. But the less work you need to do and the less time spent on administrative trivia, the more time you'll have for security tasks.

 By habitually using useradd, LISA, or COAS to perform routine user administration, you will find your user setups more consistent and easier to maintain.

The advantage to using a default group is that users can more easily share files without worrying about questions of file ownership. The use of the default group suggests an open approach to the system along the lines of "that which is not prohibited is permitted."

Chapters 3 and 4 provide more information about file ownerships and how they affect the ability to read and change files.

While the default group scheme is often a boon to users, on larger systems with users who are not totally trusted, you should consider user private groups. An open approach can enhance file sharing, but result in loss of privacy and also loss of data. Users probably will not know or care to know about permissions. So erring on the side of privacy and security is often in the user's best interests. Caldera uses the group "users" as the default group.

Configuring user defaults should be a high priority immediately after a new system is installed.

Understanding user private groups

User private groups are implemented simply by creating a group with the same name as the user. The group is made the user's login group and therefore the group name that files are saved as by default unless changed by directory permissions. As a result, the user "david" has a group "david," and files are saved this way.

The advantage to user private groups is that users don't need to think about whether other users have access to their files; by default they normally won't depending on overall file and directory permissions. Under OpenLinux, when user private groups are used, one user will not be able to read or change files belonging to another user. Users also will not be able to save files to other than their own home directory. Obviously, these defaults can be overridden by either the system administrator or the user at the file level or at the directory level (permissions permitting).

At this point it should be noted that the default user umask, a variable that determines the default mode of a saved file, is set so that newly created files will be read-write for both the owner and the group.

Chapter 3 discusses umask in detail.

Use of user private groups does not change the basic system of group membership. So a user who belongs to several groups can access files belonging to any of those groups. How this works is made clearer in the next two chapters.

TIP

If you have several systems, consider using one as the master and copy /etc/passwd, /etc/shadow, /etc/groups, and if applicable, /etc/gshadow to the others.

Changing user/group

Several commands exist with which users can manipulate the user and/or group to which they belong, or the user or group under which a program runs. One such program has already been mentioned above, newgrp.

As stated earlier, any user can issue the newgrp command. This command enables a user to join a group to which he was not formerly a member. In order for this to work, the group must have a password assigned to it. Groups with no password may not be joined by a user not already in that group.

The newgrp command may also be used by any user who is already part of a group. In this case, the newgrp command merely changes the "login group" to the one the user specified. User groups come in two flavors — a login group, and any other group to which the user belongs. The reason for the differentiation is that, while a user may belong to several groups, any files the user creates will normally be saved with the group name of the login group.

XREF

Chapter 4 provides you with a way to change this on a directory-by-directory basis.

Given the two methods you are currently familiar with (using newgrp or using the chown or chgrp commands), using newgrp is preferable over changing the group name of files either individually or *en masse*. The latter method introduces the possibility of error. For example, the user silvia wants to create a number of gif files. This user's login group is silvia, but the files will be used not only by silvia, but also by other members of the gifs group (and only by members of the gifs group). If silvia forgets to issue the newgrp command, the only alternative is to chown or chgrp the files to group gifs. Doing so one by one, silvia could forget one or more files. Using a wildcard would solve the problem, unless some gif files in the directory were deliberately not shared before. The user silvia could also use the sg command on the command line to start the program. The sg command is a link to newgrp. Called as sg, it is designed to leave the user's environment unchanged even as it allows the called program to run in a slightly modified environment – that being the new group. In case you're wondering, sg stands for substitute group. You'll learn more about a user equivalent below.

If you belong to login group "you" and are also a member of group users, then programs will normally execute and save files as group "you". If you want the files saved as group user, you can call the sg command to start the program. Assuming you want to run "xv" and save the files as group users, use the following command:

```
sg - users -c xv
```

If the command will take an argument or option(s), you must surround it with quotes:

```
sg - users -c "xv my.gif"
```

Also note, that if you're working in a graphical environment (X), you'll need to use the xhost command to permit use of the display.

In an X Windows environment, the newgrp command applies only to the xterm the user ran the command in, and of course any programs started from that xterm. This suggests that the user is locked into the login user group for programs started from the window manager. If the user always wanted to run a particular program as the same secondary group, then a script could be created that would handle starting the program as the new login group for the user.

More on the X environment

The X environment always brings with it some challenges. The challenges are not completely related to X; some are a result of the way /etc/groups and /etc/gshadow work. If you have not implemented shadow passwords for group, not much changes. You won't be able to change to a group requiring a password from a simple script in X, but if the user belongs to a secondary group, no password prompt is required, so all will go as expected. A simple script follows:

```
#!/bin/bash
sg - gifs -c /usr/X11R6/bin/xv &
```

The above two lines, implemented as an executable script and used to start XV, will change the user's login group for this program to "gifs." This file just needs to be called instead of directly calling xv.

However, if you have implemented gshadow, you'll get an ugly error message, because when you implement group shadow passwords, the list of groups passes to /etc/gshadow. When the group list exists in /etc/group, users in the list will be a part of that group when they log in. But if the list is transferred to /etc/gshadow by grpconv, then the user will not be part of the group at startup but will be able to add that group via the newgrp command, or run a command as that group via the sg command. The problem is that X believes this user (which isn't exactly the same one who started the X session) isn't authorized to connect. So as long as no password exists for the group to be added, the above script can be modified as follows:

```
#!/bin/bash
xhost +localhost
sg - gifs -c /usr/X11R6/bin/xv &
```

What this does is allow the new group (gifs) access to the screen. This does not pose any significant security problem for most workstations since you're only allowing logins from the localhost to access the screen. (For more information on xhost and X, see a good Linux administration manual.)

Use of an X server (particularly with xdm or kdm), brings with it a special set of considerations, particularly when an application is graphical, because it is often started from an icon and not from a command line.

Changing user

One aspect of system security that cannot be emphasized enough is never, never, ever log in as root unless it is absolutely necessary. Why? Because as a normal user, you can do a lot with the system. You can become root to perform those one or two tasks you can't perform except as the system administrator, and then revert to being a normal user.

As a normal user you are unable to unintentionally wipe out the system or any important files. As root, if you mistype one thing, more than just a few minutes' work can become history; in some companies, *you* can become history.

When you need to become another user, just use the su command. This command stands for "substitute user," but since it is primarily used to become the system administrator (root), people often believe it stands for "super user." To effectively use the su command, you should understand a few things about it and how it works.

The su command, with no arguments, will prompt you for, then log you in as root (if you provided the correct password). Because su is a restricted service, you can modify user's ability to use the service in the /etc/pam.d/su file. You can even arrange it so that select users don't need to know the root password to become root, but that is a very unsafe idea.

See Chapter 1 for more information on the /etc/pam.d/su file.

Invoked with no argument, you can become root. Invoked with an argument of a valid username, you become that user (root won't need to know the password). This can be a very effective way to troubleshoot problems with a user's login. But you'll most likely want to call su with a hyphen (-) between the su command and the username. This hyphen tells su that you want not only to become that user, but you want to do so as if you just logged in as that user, picking up the user's environment. Without the hyphen, you retain your own environment while becoming that user. So your PATH will be used instead of the new user's PATH. Perhaps not what you need.

If su is called without a username (with or without the hyphen), the program assumes you want to become root.

But as convenient as su is, no more than six users should know the root password or you've lost control of it. So how can you give users root permissions without giving them the root password? You can do this in any one of several ways, but the one most favored is sudo. The sudo program allows select users to run certain programs as root asking them for their own password to authenticate them rather than the root password. This program is used in the same way as sg is. The users just type sudo <command_to_run_as_root>, are prompted for their password, and if permitted, run the program as root.

While six users may seem like an arbitrary number, try remembering after six months the people you gave the root password to. You'll probably remember around six. Also, if these users know that only six have the password, it will be better guarded than if they know that 16 have it. Besides, how often do you want to change that password because someone has moved on? Still, less is better.

The configuration file is maintained in /etc and is very simple. While this is the best way, it is not the only way. Another way is to use groups and file permissions to accomplish restricting the program, while allowing it to run as root. You'll look at this in detail in Chapter 4.

Understanding user security

One thing you must always remember is that user security is an oxymoron. The only time I've seen a user concerned about security is after he's had a security problem. Users trust that their files are secure. So if you work under the assumption that a user is his own worst enemy where security of his own files is concerned, you will be safe.

Do not expect that users will be interested in anything except how to log in and start those programs they need to run. At least not until they lose some files. Then, it will only be enough to secure what they have, and they will promptly forget.

The system administrator's job then, is to decide how to implement a security policy. This policy may or may not have been drawn up with the administrator's knowledge or advice. The policy may or may not be realistic when compared to the assessed risk. These factors should influence security policy implementation.

You will hear that the greatest risk to a system generally comes from within. It can come from disgruntled users, particularly in a larger setting. But don't make the mistake of attributing something to a malicious user that can be attributed to simple user ignorance. And by understanding and putting to use the concepts in the first section of this book, you can keep users from doing too much inadvertent damage to their own or others' files. But regardless, the average user should be incapable of harming the system. You need only worry about users astute enough to figure out how to cause system or network chaos on purpose. These users are few and far between, but will generally come to your attention, particularly if you are watching for the signs. The dangerous ones are those who have or can obtain root access, by virtue of their position or their connections. These signs will become evident as you progress through this book.

By default, users get full control of their own home directory. If you institute a default user group, all users will belong to the default user group and will have access to each other's home directories and the files located therein. If you institute user private groups, users will not have access to others' home directories.

I recommend that if users need to access each other's files, you create a public directory somewhere, make sure all users belong to one group (it can be the group users or any other group you care to create), and have sufficient permissions within the directory. As long as all the files in this directory belong to the same group as the one all the users belong to, they will be able to access those files.

 See Chapter 4 for details on how to implement use of a directory by a group for projects, etc.

Some users will want or need to run programs themselves that are not part of the OpenLinux. Most will also have documents and other files to track. As time goes on, users will inevitably accumulate files. Helping users develop directory structures for themselves to organize files is not a strong point in Caldera's OpenLinux. Much is left to the administrator. So let me suggest a few things, and leave it to you and a good administration book to determine if this is good for your situation or not.

Implement as a standard structure, one installed by default when new users are created (under /etc/skel), something like the following:

- ◆ /bin

- ◆ /src

- ◆ /docs

- ◆ /misc

Often, programs can have default entries set to save things below these structures. Once users have their own default file structure explained, because they know it's there, they will tend to use it. You'll also want to make sure that ~/bin is included in their PATH statement, as one of the last entries. Again, a good system administration book will explain this in detail.

Understanding password security

The adage that a chain is only as strong as its weakest link certainly applies in a discussion of password security. Your security chain consists of a number of links, including the services offered. User passwords are another link. And user security practices yet another. But as stated earlier, the average user neither knows nor cares about security. The way to change that is to make security both easy and understandable. The "easy" part is the most difficult. As you explore what makes up secure passwords and practices, you'll see that it is anything but easy, and most people take the easy way out when it is presented. After all, users are on the system to get work done, not to create more work for themselves. So normally, I find it more effective to explain why good password security practices are important and make it personal, more than just that some unauthorized individual may read or destroy important files.

 Explaining why good password security is in the user's own best interests (without belaboring the issue) is the best way to gain his or her cooperation in choosing "secure" passwords and safeguarding them correctly.

Most users understand the importance today of e-mail. What they don't realize is that anyone who can log in to the system as them can become them and use their e-mail against them. Ask the user if he corresponds via e-mail with anyone and depends on that e-mail in any way. Normally, the response will be yes. Then ask if important business is transacted via e-mail. Fewer and fewer people will tell you no, and even if they do, some of the businesses they deal with consider business transacted via e-mail as binding as business conducted over the telephone.

Then explain to them that their e-mail will become (if it isn't already) as important as their signature. And while e-mail headers, just like signatures, can be forged, this constitutes a crime in most places. But if someone has another's password, no matter how obtained, and can log in to the system as that person, that other person effectively has the other's signature. Any e-mail sent will not be forged because it will come from the login used. Companies should strongly discourage providing anyone with the ability to log in as anyone else (except administrators who need to test a user's setup, but they won't need a user's password). Logging in as another user (even authorized to do so by the other user) should also be strongly discouraged. How strong this discouragement should be is left to the discretion of those responsible for approving the policy.

But users must understand that other ways exist for someone to gain access to their accounts. The most common is that users, afraid of forgetting their passwords, either create passwords that are too easily guessed by another, or are written down (often on a note taped to their monitor). Password security depends on two things: something held (a username), and something known (a password). Most people will guard a PIN to enter their bank account, but will not as zealously safeguard their user password. But unlike a bank account, where the "something held" is a physical item — the bankcard itself — everyone (at least anyone inside the company, and anyone with whom the user has exchanged e-mail) knows that "something held" part — the user name. So if the "something known" part is written down or is easily guessed or "cracked" by a program that searches the keyspace, then the login is not secure.

Finally, users need to be aware of a method to obtain passwords known as "social engineering." Most of us can think of at least one person we know whom we consider "slicker than snake oil." This person can convince most others, via seemingly plausible explanations, to provide him or her information. But this is not always how it is done. The person can sometimes just watch. For example, have you ever entered a username and password, looked up, and found that something had happened during the process (the prompt hadn't come back immediately, you had only hit Enter at the username prompt, given your username as a password, then entered your password at the login prompt, or something similar) and that your password was visible on the screen? Well, your password may just have been compromised.

The answer to compromises of this nature is to change your password regularly. The word "regularly" deliberately leaves a lot of latitude. You can change your password regularly every ten years, but I would discourage such a large interval, just as I would discourage changing your password regularly on an hourly basis. One interval is too long and the other too short — one invites compromise, and the other invites either forgetting your password, or being tempted to write it down.

Your concern about an outsider's being able to log in as a normal user will transcend simple compromise of a user's data, because the more someone knows about your system, the easier it is for that person to find and exploit a weakness.

That still leaves a lot of leeway. This book cannot perform a risk assessment for you, but the answers to a few questions should help you determine what constitutes a good interval for you. RFC 2196 in Appendix C covers some basics of risk assessment and provides other sources for information on this important topic.

♦ Is your work area free from prying eyes? That is, even if your password is displayed on the screen for a few seconds, can/will anyone see it?

♦ Is your network itself secure? If you have two systems connected to your local network, and the second is used only by your spouse or children, your network is probably very secure (unless your children are themselves "script kiddies").

♦ Is anyone ever logged in to your local system while you are logging on?

♦ Do you use the same password to remotely access other machines on your network using unsecure (non-encrypted) protocols? If so, might other systems be listening (their Ethernet cards in promiscuous mode)?

Once you've settled on what constitutes a "regular" basis for you, be it every week, every month, every three months, every six months, or every year, it can be easily enforced via password aging, which you learned about in the first chapter. But you also need to come up with a password that is both difficult to crack, easy to remember (so it's not written down), and difficult to guess for someone who might know you.

So what makes up a good password? A good password looks as much like a random string of characters as possible. It is from six to eight characters in length — six being an arbitrary minimum, although even five will work well under most circumstances. Anything longer than eight will be truncated, and can pose problems for some software, so is discouraged.

Inventing good passwords is difficult, but can be done. However, I highly recommend the following.

1. Install a copy of `makepasswd` on your system. (It can be obtained from `http://tech.ilp.physik.uni-essen.de/www.debian.org/Packages/stable/admin/makepasswd.html`.)

A copy of makepasswd is included on the CD-ROM that accompanies this book.

2. Use makepasswd to generate several passwords for you, then pick one that looks easy for you to remember.

3. Change your password.

4. Log out and log in a dozen times immediately. Then, later in the day, log out and log in perhaps half a dozen times more. This will help you remember your password. After about 20 logins, your fingers should have the keystrokes memorized.

But if you don't want to use makepasswd to generate passwords, how can you tell if a password is good or bad? The following is a list of good and bad passwords. Good passwords:

◆ Words with "special" characters (!@#$%^&* and/or numbers along with letters) in two or more positions

◆ Mixed-case words

◆ Words six to eight characters in length

◆ Anything unintelligible, or a combination of words separated by special characters

Bad passwords:

◆ Dictionary words or derivatives (including foreign words): *party*, *fiesta*, *party5*, *fi3sta*, and so forth

◆ Proper nouns, especially spouse's or children's names: silvia, etc.

◆ Dates: 610930 or 300961, etc.

◆ Anything closely related to you: Social Security numbers, phone numbers

◆ Anything related to hobbies, etc., that you may have. That is, if it is something personal that you know very well and is related to you or the company you work for, it is very prone to blind guessing. Dictionary words for obvious reasons are always easily broken, as are characters or places from books.

It goes without saying that passwords shouldn't be written down.

In places where common passwords that were easily remembered, yet difficult to crack were desired, I normally picked a theme, then used that theme to create a set of passwords. For example, let's take the theme "plants." Using combinations of plant names (like rose, oak, ivy, etc.) and combining them with something like colors (red, blu, blk, etc.) and joining them with special characters, I can create passwords that are secure yet easy to remember:

◆ blk*ros3

◆ blu!ivy

◆ red#oak4

To ensure the password scheme you've created is secure against cracking, you'll want to try to run a password-cracking program against it. See below for more information.

But again, the best way to create truly random passwords, or to create a number of accounts in a short time is by using the makepasswd program. Called without arguments, it will return a six- to eight-letter password that will be extremely computationally intensive to crack. Unfortunately, these are the very passwords users will write down, and it will be obvious to anyone that these are passwords. So impressing on users the importance of safeguarding them is paramount.

The makepasswd program is a very simple perl script that will output a password, and if necessary also an encrypted version of the password. For example:

```
# makepasswd --char 8 --count 8 --crypt
ecuraCdK    aFP4Fy.p/K9bY
dLeiVWVd    Flqcui.9L3xQI
7FSBjEFH    MkHjkpOId8mLc
ORA2vLsv    1QYuK3Fw5Ih8U
DuSbFxDj    bB.thDEpz7Zi.
wCPOIX6v    Xe3ntRWjABCnM
8owKUgvg    Z485y6UQyMEdE
xPViT6AU    X9gm2NtZc.hK6
```

The beauty of the makepasswd script is that it can easily be integrated into a shell script that can do everything necessary to make a large number of secure accounts. A simple loop through a list of new usernames (like student1 through student100) to create an account, a password for the account, and merge the account name and password into a file to later provide to students.

ON THE CD On the CD-ROM is a crude script for taking a file of usernames you want added to the system, and creating good eight-character passwords for them. The script creates a group, then the user (both with the same UID/GID number) encrypts the password created for him and inserts it into the /etc/shadow file.

Some cautions: The script does perform some test, such as whether or not you're root, whether the UID already exists (but not the GID), and so on. However, it does not test for everything. One thing it does not test for is whether or not someone is updating her password at the time.

Some things are hard-coded — the use of eight characters for the password, for example. If this is changed, then you'll need to change a cut value further down. If you are good with scripts and would like to improve it, feel free. This script wasn't meant to be anything other than a demonstration of one way to tackle a problem with which I've had a number of requests for help. A better way would have been through the use of an expect script, but I'm not an expect guru. The expect scripting language is used where interactive responses are *expected* by a program, but you want to use a script instead to automate the process. So I wrote this script for one reason: The available programs were not convenient to use for adding a large number of users quickly and efficiently.

```
 1   #!/bin/bash
 2   # Written by D.Bandel - 3 Sep 99; released under the GPL
 3   # script to take a list of usernames and create secure logins
 4   # then to put the encrypted passwds into /etc/shadow
 5
 6   prog=/usr/bin/makepasswd
 7   names=/root/newusernames
 8   logins=/root/newlogins
 9   tmpshadow=/root/shadow.tmp
10   startid=1000
11
12   if [ $UID != 0 ] ; then
13       echo "You must be root to run $0"
14       exit 1
15   fi
16
17   if [ ! -e /etc/shadow ] ; then
18       echo "You don't have a shadowed system"
19       exit 2
20   fi
21   if [ ! -x $prog ] ; then
22       echo "You don't have $prog installed"
```

```
23      exit 3
24   fi
25   if [ `grep ":${startid}:" /etc/passwd` ] ; then
26       echo "Please change startid (beginning UID/GID) and try
again"
27       exit 4
28   fi
29   echo ; echo "working ... "
30   for i in `cat $names`
31   do
32   j=`$prog --char 8`
33   echo "${i}:${j}" > $logins ; echo " . "
34   done
35
36   k=$startid;cp /etc/shadow /etc/shadow.orig
37   echo ; echo "continuing . . . "
38   for i in `cat $logins`
39   do
40   j=`echo $i | cut -d : -f 1 -`
41   l=`echo $i | cut -d : -f 2 -`
42   groupadd -g $k $j
43   useradd -m -u $k -g $j $j
44   k=$[$k+1]
45   m=`$prog --clear=$l --crypt | cut -b 12- -`
46   sed "s|$j:\*not set\*|$j:$m|" /etc/shadow > $tmpshadow
47   mv $tmpshadow /etc/shadow ; echo " . "
48   done
49
50   exit 0
```

The script is simple enough. All you need to do is create a file called
/root/newusernames with the names of all the users you want to add (three to eight
characters, no spaces). Then run the script.

- ◆ Lines 6–10 set up a few variables. I deliberately used root's home directory
  for the temporary files, because of the nature of the information in those
  files. Make sure no one except root can read files in root's directory. You
  may want to change the name of the input file (names) as well as the
  starting UID/GID.

- ◆ Lines 12–28 just perform a few very simple tests. Not everything is tested
  for, but the really important things are.

- ◆ Lines 30–34 take the new usernames and create passwords for them. These
  username/password pairs will be used later in the script.

◆ Lines 38–48 actually do all the work of creating a user private group, a user, then encrypting the user's password and inserting it /etc/shadow.

Note that it may take a while for the script to run. The makepasswd program takes some time to create the random passwords and also to generate the encrypted password from the clear text.

Password "cracking"

One way systems administrators and security auditors can assist in ensuring the network and systems are secure is to think like a bad guy and do what the bad guys would do. This means wandering around to users' areas and looking for passwords taped to their monitors, or "dropping by" in the morning when they're about to log in (to see if they need to grab a crib sheet to log in with).

It may also mean looking at the orientation of a user's monitor if he or she works with sensitive information to see if that information is visible to just anyone wandering by. And do these users turn on locking screen savers or log out when they leave their desks (especially if they have access to sensitive material)?

 But the best way to assess a user's education vis-a-vis password security is to attempt to crack his or her passwords. Performed on a routine basis, cracking programs can provide a good measure of the strength of the passwords link in your security chain.

A number of good cracking programs exist, and more sophisticated ones are created all the time. But cracking passwords is a time- and resource-intensive application, so I recommend you do it at night on a relatively secure system with little processing going on while the crack program is running.

Summary

In this chapter you continued to learn about security with regard to users and groups. First you learned about the two group schemes, default user group and private user groups. Then you learned about changing the login group and user. Next you learned about user security, and how to best protect users, both from themselves and each other, while providing them the access they need. Finally, you learned about password security and what constitutes a good password versus a poor password. This chapter continued to build on the information covered in the first chapter. These two chapters are the basis for the information that will be covered in the next two chapters.

Chapter 3

Files and permissions

IN THIS CHAPTER YOU'LL look at files in general and file permissions in particular. Chapters 1 and 2 deal with users and groups. Now, you'll expand that knowledge to see how users and groups affect files and permissions.

Linux: A file system

Linux is a file system. As such, everything Linux knows about – your printers, your floppy disk drives, your hard disk drives, and so on – is represented by files. Anything you can do with a file, you can do with your peripherals. You can send information to them via programs or pipes, and you can get information from them in the same way. This doesn't, however, make a lot of sense for a peripheral like a printer that only receives files to print. But the screen you are looking at, and other things (the modem, printer, hard disk, disk partitions, and so on), are all represented by files.

The Linux kernel acts as a manager over all the things it knows about. It bases requests for access on specific permissions the file has, and compares those permissions one group at a time to the identity (UID/GID) of the requestor.

Understanding file types

Linux has a number of different file types. You're going to look at how to identify each. Then you'll look at these files from a security perspective.

Performing a long listing of a directory, you can get a better idea of file types. Shown below is a listing of an imaginary directory containing files of various types:

```
drwxr-xr-x  24 root      root          2048 Sep  4 00:01 .
drwxr-xr-x  20 root      root          1024 Aug 26 19:09 ..
drwxr-xr-x   3 root      root          1024 Jul 22 22:17 .civctp
crw-rw-r--   1 root      root    29,     0 Aug  5 09:12 fb0
brw-rw-rw-   1 root      root     2,     0 Jul 27 19:14 fd0
-rw-r--r--   1 root      root           694 Sep  2 21:02 foo
srwxrwxrwx   1 root      root             0 Sep  3 19:18 mysql.sock
prw-------   1 root      root             0 Sep  3 19:14 initctl
lrwxrwxrwx   1 root      root             4 Aug  5 08:49 sh -> bash
```

For the moment, concern yourself only with the first column, with the items marked d, d, d, c, b, -, s, p, and l. Each of these characters tells you and Linux what type of file you're dealing with (see also Table 3-1 below). The "d" stands for directory. While it is still a file to the operating system, some operations just make no sense and will not return the expected results. The two called "." and ".." in the final column are special. The former points to the present directory, the latter to the parent directory. In the root (/) directory, the ".." points to the "." instead of the name of the parent directory. This is why, when you use the command "cd .." you move up one level in the directory hierarchy. Think of these as links, because they are. In fact, because they are links, they can be "unlinked" so that calling 'cd .' will leave you where you are. If you have need to perform low-level work on the disk that cannot be performed with ordinary tools, you can look at the documentation for debugfs, but be aware that many programs and people rely on this link, so use with caution.

Unlinking a directory has very profound effects. Do not do this unless you know exactly what you are doing.

Looking at the listing again, you can see another directory, but this one starts with a ".". Any filename that starts with a ".", aka a dot file (they're normally files, many are startup files found in a user's home directory), isn't normally seen in a directory listing unless the -a switch has been used. This is not so much a security matter as a matter of convenience. Many programs (including the bash shell) use dot files so users don't see them unless they need to. So don't use dot files to hide things. You'll want to change the permissions to keep those who have no need from reading them.

TABLE 3-1 FILE TYPES

File designation	File type	Examples
-	regular file	data files, ASCII text, programs
d	directory	/bin
b	block special device	/dev/hda (first IDE hard disk)
c	character special device	/dev/ttyS1 (DOS com2 equivalent)
s	socket	/dev/log
p	named pipe	/dev/initctl (named equivalent to "|")
l	symbolic link	/dev/modem -> /dev/ttyS1

The next two files are device files. The first is a character device, the second is a block device. These files are normally found in the /dev directory along with all other device files. But there is nothing significant about the location of these files. They can reside anywhere. They can even reside on a floppy disk or in memory (on a ramdisk). When the kernel is directed to use one of these files, it reads the file information, then uses the driver appropriate to that piece of hardware (often a module) and uses it in accordance with the permissions given to the device file. The difference between a block device and a character device is that a character device sends information character by character in a stream, while a block device sends information in parallel, usually 8 bytes at a time, and in blocks or large chunks.

The above information should make alarm bells go off in your head. If the only thing that Joe User needs to do to access hardware that he shouldn't have access to is to create a device either in his home directory or on a floppy and mount it, then he can access anything he wants. True. And to permit an ordinary user to arbitrarily create or mount devices to use is not very secure for a relatively "secure" operating system, either. But it's not quite that easy. Devices are recognized to be special. So the mknod program that creates device files can be used only by root (or anyone with UID 0), at least under normal circumstances. What you must ensure is that no one is able to mount a partition (floppy disk or otherwise) with active device files on them, either under the /mnt/floppy (or other) mount point, or over top of /dev. But a good security check is to look through /home for device files. These two lines should do that fairly quickly:

```
find /home -type b -print
find /home -type c -print
```

See Chapter 5 for more on mounting file systems.

Why any user would need device files in his or her home directory is highly questionable. In fact, you *will* want to talk to any user with his or her own device files.

The next file, of file type "-", is a regular file. Regular files constitute the large majority of files found on a Linux system. These can be executable files, data files, or text-based files (pure ASCII text files, shell scripts, etc.).

The next file, of file type "s", is a socket. This is the mysql listening socket. If you look at the output of `netstat -a`, you'll see it listed:

```
unix   0     [ ACC ]     STREAM     LISTENING     12210   /tmp/mysql.sock
```

So you can see that this is, indeed, an active listening socket. You'll look more at sockets in other chapters.

The output of netstat is discussed in detail in Chapter 10.

The next file is a named pipe. A named pipe acts exactly like any other pipe. It is used to funnel the output of one program into the input of another program.

The final file listing is that of a soft link (or symlink for symbolic link). This file is just a pointer that points to another file or directory as the target. Soft links are always created with completely open permissions. They take on the final permissions of the file they are pointing to. A symlink does not hold a copy of the contents of the file. If the target is removed, what remains is called a dangling symlink. It points to nothing. A Macintosh alias or Windows shortcut is roughly equivalent to a symlink in Linux.

An inode is an information node, a small block that contains information about a file that it points to. A directory listing points to the inode. The inode contains all important information about the file, such as: inode number, file type, file mode, version number, user and group IDs, file size, atime (last access date-time), ctime (date-time created), mtime (modification date-time), block number(s) containing the file, and more. The inode can be viewed with the debugfs command.

One file type that isn't listed differently is a hard link (or just a link). Looking at another directory listing, but this time with the -i option included with the -l, you see this:

```
20512 -rwxr-xr-x   3 root      root        49280 Jul 27 19:37 gunzip
20512 -rwxr-xr-x   3 root      root        49280 Jul 27 19:37 gzip
20512 -rwxr-xr-x   3 root      root        49280 Jul 27 19:37 zcat
```

Here, you see almost the same information, but this time with another number out front (20512). This first number is an inode number. The name you see as the directory listing points to an inode. This inode contains a significant amount of information. In fact, it contains all the information you see in the directory listing and more. The significance of the three identical inode numbers is that the three names you see are in fact the same file. If you look across at the file size (49280), you can see they are all the same. As long as any one of these filenames remains, the file will remain. Only after the last filename is deleted is the information pointed to by the inode lost. So if the contents of a file are meant to be deleted irretrievably, the last filename pointing to that inode must be deleted. Looking at the output above again, you can see a number just before the first iteration of "root". That number indicates the number of links to the inode. If you removed zcat, you would still see gunzip and gzip, but the link count would be two. A directory always starts out with two links. Each file is a link unto itself, and a directory holds two files within, one called ".." that points up to the name of the directory, and thus is the second link. If a directory has a link count of one, then the ".." has been unlinked.

While a symlink can cross file systems and disk partitions, a hard link cannot since the directory listing is pointing to an inode number. A symlink will be owned by the user who created it, but the file permissions will still be those of the file itself, so while anyone can symlink to a file, the permissions are those of the target when the link is followed. If the user following the link does not have permissions to access the file, he still cannot access it. A hard link will pick up the ownership and permissions stored in the inode for display in a listing.

Understanding "normal" file permissions

Look at another listing:

```
-rwxr-xr-x   1 root      root          3164 Jul 27 20:27 arch
-rwxr-xr-x   1 root      root        317504 Jul 27 22:22 bash
-rwxr-xr-x   1 root      root        464564 Jul 28 02:54 bash2
-rwxr-x---   1 root      root         34236 Jul 28 09:37 box
-rwxr-xr-x   1 root      root         11856 Jul 28 09:37 build_menu
lrwxrwxrwx   1 root      root             5 Aug  5 08:50 bunzip2 -> bzip2
```

```
lrwxrwxrwx   1 root      root            5 Aug   5 08:50 bzcat -> bzip2
-rwxr-xr-x   1 root      root        57404 Jul  27 20:11 bzip2
-rwxr-xr-x   1 root      root         7152 Jul  27 20:11 bzip2recover
-rwxr-xr-x   1 root      root         9240 Jul  27 21:12 cat
-rwxr-xr-x   1 root      root        11692 Jul  27 21:38 chgrp
-rwxr-xr-x   1 root      root        11820 Jul  27 21:38 chmod
-rwxr-xr-x   1 root      root        12164 Jul  27 21:38 chown
-rwxr-xr-x   1 root      root        28204 Jul  27 21:38 cp
-rwxr-xr-x   1 root      root        47448 Jul  27 19:32 cpio
lrwxrwxrwx   1 root      root            4 Aug   5 09:02 csh -> tcsh
-rwxr-xr-x   1 root      root        38132 Jul  27 22:59 ctags
```

You know the first column (in this example a "-" or an "l") tells you that you are looking at regular files or symlinks to files. The next nine columns can be split into three groups of three. These correspond to owner, group, and others. So in reading across, most of the files are rwx for read, write, and execute for the owner, read and execute for the group, and read and execute for the world (all other users). What is happening at the inode level is that each file has three octal numbers assigned to it. Octal numbers range from 0–7 (or in binary, they occupy three places 000–111). So a bit is either turned on or turned off for each of these permissions. The first bit (on the right) corresponds to execute, the second bit to write, and the third to read. So starting with all permissions turned off, you add 1 for execute, 2 for write, and 4 for read. Adding that up gives you numbers from 0–7. Doing that for each of the three places and you can see that the permissions (also called the mode) can be anything from 000 to 777. The scheme shown above is common for many utilities available to all users: a mode of 755. To change the mode, simply use chmod 755 filename. (See Table 3-2.)

To the right of the permissions columns comes first the link count column, then the owner name followed by the group name (subsequent columns are the file size, date and time of modification, and filename). When Linux is asked by a shell or program to access a file, it looks at the requestor's UID. If the UID of the requestor matches the UID (not the name) of the owner of the file, it looks across at the first three permissions bits and grants the requestor the permissions shown. If the UIDs do not match, then it compares the requestor's GID to the GID the file belongs to. A match here and the permissions corresponding to the group are used. If neither the UID nor GID match, then the requestor falls into the category of "other" or the world. For example, look at the fourth line in the example above. The permissions are owner: read, write, execute; group: read, execute; world: no permissions (note this line has been modified for the sake of this example). So you are looking at a file with mode 750. If a request for access to the file "box" comes from the user with UID 0 (root), then that requestor is given read, write, and execute access for that file. If the requestor's UID is not 0, then the GID is compared. If the requestor's GID is 0, then read and execute permissions are granted. If neither the requestor's UID nor GID match, then the requestor is denied access because the of the mode of the file.

TABLE **3-2** CHMOD OCTAL EQUIVALENTS

Permissions	Octal equivalent	Comments
- - - - - - - - -	000	Numbers correspond to each group of 3 permissions
- - x - - x - - x	111	You can mix and match permissions numbers to achieve the desired result
- w - - w - - w -	222	rwxr-x--x = chmod 751
- wx - wx - wx	333	
r - - r - - r - -	444	
r - xr - xr - x	555	
rw - rw - rw -	666	
rwxrwxrwx	777	

 A UID-to-permissions mapping stops with the first match.

This comparison stops at the first match. That is, if the UID is root, and the mode is 055, meaning no read, write, or execute permissions are granted to the owner of the file, even though the owner also belongs to the same group, the group permissions are never tested, so access is denied. The owner can be denied access to her own file.

In actuality, what happens is that if an owner of a file does not have write access to a file, but tries to delete that file, the kernel forces a query: Delete file overriding mode 0055? (y/n). If the owner answers yes, the file will be removed. But it will not be removed without answering unless the owner answers "y" to the query. The owner would also not be able to execute the file if permissions were so set.

A shell script file, in order to be executed, must have both the read and execute bits set. But a compiled program only need have the execute bit set. This is because the kernel executes the compiled program and the user cannot run it any other way. But the user must be able to read the instructions in a shell script in order to execute the file. If a shell script can be read but does not have the execute bit set, it can still be executed by preceding the script name with the particular program required to run it:

```
perl myperlscript.pl
```

or

```
sh myshellscript.sh
```

 The filename does not need to end in .sh for a shell script or .pl for a perl script any more than an executable in Linux must end in either .exe or .com. This is just a convention the author uses to distinguish that a file is a perl or shell script.

You can tell what kind of file is a compiled program and which is a script by using the file command. This command uses the file /usr/share/misc/magic to determine what kind of file it is looking at. If you wish to add your own definitions for files, you should add them to /etc/magic.

Directory permissions are different from other file permissions, but not much. Like other files, directories have owners and groups. The difference lies in the read-write-execute permissions. A set permission bit of read allows the contents of the directory to be read by the usr/group/other for whom it is set. This does not mean any individual file within the directory can be read. It means that the filenames within that directory can be read. The files themselves may be read-only.

A set permission bit for write means that the user/group/world (as applicable) can write to that directory. Permissions may not be sufficient to overwrite what is already there, that will depend on the specific permissions of the file to be overwritten or deleted. But a file can be created.

A set permission bit for execute means that the user/group/other to whom it applies can cd into the directory. If the bit is not set for a particular user, then that user might be able to read files in the directory, even write to or create files in the directory, but cannot actually enter the directory.

An example of a directory where all bits (or at least the read and execute bits) are not both set is the anonymous ftp incoming directory. The permissions on this directory normally look like this:

```
drwx-wx-wx   2 root      ftp          1024 Jul  8 12:47 incoming
```

This set of permissions allows the group ftp and the world to cd into the directory and write files. But regardless of the permissions set on the file, the files in this directory cannot be seen or read by anyone other than root. This allows you to permit uploads without the problems created by anonymous abuse (using the server to upload and subsequently download proprietary software, etc.).

This text is not meant to be legal advice. However, the system's owners, administrators, and/or users (if they can be identified) may be held liable for illegal activity occurring on the system. This can, at the least, cause considerable embarrassment.

Implementing default permissions (umask)

Every user, including root, has default permissions that are assigned to every file that user creates. You know that every file has an owner and group assigned to it. When a user creates a file, under normal circumstances that file is owned by the user creating it and is assigned the user's login group. Further, the file is given read-write-execute permissions based on the user's umask.

The umask is an octal number that is logically ANDed with either 0777 or 0666 to arrive at the initial file permissions. For those of you unfamiliar with Boolean arithmetic, this means that you subtract the umask from either 0777 or 0666 to arrive at the initial file permissions.

If the file command returns a value specifying the newly created file as a binary executable, then the permissions 0777 minus the umask will be applied to the file. All other files will use 0666 minus the umask to arrive at the initial permissions.

Under OpenLinux, when a user logs in, a file in /etc/config.d/shells is sourced (normally bashrc) and a umask is assigned. The umask will be either 022 if the user is root, or 002 for any other normal user. So in the example above, files created by root will have a mode of 755 (rwxr-xr-x) for binaries, and 644 (rw-r--r--) for all other files. Normal user's files are created with a mode 775 (rwxrwxr-x) or 664 (rw-rw-r--). The umask can be verified by calling umask with no arguments, and changed by providing the appropriate information (e.g., umask 222).

Remember that using the standard COAS tool, the default is user private groups, so the owner name and group name will be the same unless the user has used the newgrp command to change the login group.

Changing file permissions

File permissions are changed using chown and chmod to change the ownership and mode of the file. In order to change either of these, you must have permissions sufficient to both the directory and the file. If you cannot write to the file or to the directory, you can't use chmod or chown to modify the file.

The chown command takes as an argument the owner and/or group names followed by the file or directory name to be changed. The group name is preceded by a period, which is used to separate it from the owner name. For example, if the file foo has as its owner silvia and group ownership silvia and you want to change that to owner root and group gifs, then the following command is used:

```
chown root.gifs foo
```

Either of root or .gifs can be used alone if only one is to change.

The chmod command is used to change the mode of the file. Again, if you can't write to the directory or file, you can't change the mode. You've already learned how the octal numbering system works regarding the mode. But just to review, if you have a shell script you created and your umask was 002, then the file was created with permissions 664. But attempting to execute this file directly results in an error message: permission denied. Remember, this file is not a binary; it, as all shell scripts are, is basically a text file with calls to executable commands or built-in shell routines. So to change it to mode rwxr-xr-x (755), you issue the command

```
chmod 755 filename
```

But assume for a moment you want to change only one bit. This too can be done. This method is effective for changing a large number of files at one time. The chmod command is still used, but substituting a letter, and operator, and another letter for the octal numbers.

The system works this way: Call chmod with an argument of any one or more of ugoa, standing for the owner, group, others, and all respectively, then an operator, one of +=-, and the bit to turn on or off (rwx). So using the example above, now that your shell script is 755, you've decided it really needed to be 775. But you want to change it without affecting any other permissions:

```
chmod g+w filename
```

Using this method, you can easily turn just one bit on or off. The + operator turns on the bit, the - turns off the bit, and the = turns off all bits except what is specified by the command. The argument following the operator is the bit to be turned on or off.

Summary

In this chapter you've learned the basics about file security and how it is achieved on a Linux system. You learned about file types, file permissions, and how to change them. You learned where default permissions come from for new files, and how that can be changed.

In the next chapter, you'll finish learning about file permissions as you explore some more advanced file and file system properties.

Chapter 4

SUID/SGID settings (files/directories)

IN THIS CHAPTER

- ◆ Understanding SUID and SGID files and directories

- ◆ Understanding SUID/SGID dangers

- ◆ Controlling SUID/SGID files

- ◆ Changing permissions

- ◆ Understanding ext2-specific permissions

- ◆ Using chattr

- ◆ Using lsattr

THIS CHAPTER DISCUSSES SPECIAL settings for files and directories beyond the ordinary read, write, and execute. You'll look at the different settings available via chmod, what they do, and any dangers inherent to using them.

Then you'll look at some settings that are only available under the ext2 file system and how to change and control those attributes.

Understanding SUID/SGID

Remember back in Chapter 1 where you looked at the /etc/shadow file that contained passwords for all the user accounts on the system? Recall also that that particular file had permissions such that only root could read or write the file to prevent just anyone from getting the hashed passwords to try to crack? Also in that file were settings that could be used to force a user to change his or her password. But how can a user change her password if she's not root? Simple. The passwd program runs as root and has complete access to the file.

A special setting exists that will allow any program you desire to run as the owner of the file. Under normal circumstances, an executable file runs as the user who invoked the command with whatever privileges or limitations that user has. But if a special bit, called the SUID (set user ID) bit, is set, the program will run as the owner of the file regardless of who invoked it.

When most folks talk about running a program SUID, they are talking about SUID root. This is the most common use for setting the SUID bit, to allow a user to run a program as root so that she can perform some action she otherwise wouldn't be able to.

But this can also be used by users who have set up a special program that only they can run to allow others to use that program. This may include personal database type programs that the user wants to allow others to access.

One note: Setting the SUID on a script will not work. The script will not execute as the user, it will only execute normally. Only compiled binaries can be executed SUID. If running a script SUID is required, the recommendation is to either make those programs called by the script SUID that need to be run SUID, or write a wrapper program in C to call the other programs and set the wrapper program's SUID bit.

Another way to do this is to make the program SGID. The SGID bit acts in exactly the same way, forcing a program to run as a particular group. Often, this will be a better response for a user who wishes others to use a personal program.

On a directory, the SUID and SGID bits have different meanings. The most common use is for a public directory where users can share files, allowing others to update those files. The directory is set SGID, and all files created or modified will be saved under the groupname of the group the directory belongs to. So if a number of users are working on gifs, the directory may be SGID, and if the group is owned by the group gifs, then all files will be saved as with group ownership gifs. Assuming "others" have no rights in this directory, then all files will be accessible only to users belonging to the group gifs.

One final bit of importance is a bit known as the "sticky" bit. Below, you'll see how to set the SUID and SGID bits. The sticky bit is set in the same manner. On executable files, this bit tells the operating system to save text on the swap device instead of keeping it in memory. On directories, it prevents users other than the owner from making changes to the file. Others may read the file, but cannot change it. You'll look at how and where this bit it used below.

Understanding SUID/SGID dangers

Having SUID programs scattered around the system invites trouble. As stated earlier, some programs must be SUID for ordinary users to be able to use them. But the list of those programs must be scrutinized.

Any program that allows a user to execute arbitrary commands or shell out to a command prompt is not a candidate for SUID status. But this should not be used as a guide. If no good reason can be found for a particular file to be SUID, then it shouldn't be. Also, no good reason exists for a user to have a SUID root program in his/her home directory.

Running the following command:

```
find / -perm +u+s -exec ls -l {} \;
```

yields the following output:

```
-r-sr-xr-x   1 root     root     2105164 Aug 30 07:25 /usr/local/bin/vmware
-rws--x--x   1 root     root      606031 Jul 22 20:07 /usr/local/bin/ssh1
---s--x--x   1 root     bin      1647592 Jul 25 13:34 /usr/local/bin/xlock
-rwsr-xr-x   1 root     root      285151 Aug 21 17:23 /usr/local/sbin/mtr
-rwsr-xr-x   1 root     root       17134 Aug 27 10:55 /usr/X11R6/bin/cardinfo
-rws--x--x   1 root     root        7150 Jul 27 20:25 /usr/X11R6/bin/Xwrapper
-rwsr-xr-x   1 root     root      177280 Jul 28 00:32 /usr/bin/lpq
-rwsr-xr-x   1 root     root      235672 Jul 28 00:32 /usr/bin/lpr
-rwsr-xr-x   1 root     root      171060 Jul 28 00:32 /usr/bin/lprm
-rwsr-xr-x   1 root     root       14576 Jul 27 19:17 /usr/bin/rcp
-rwsr-xr-x   1 root     root       10512 Jul 27 19:17 /usr/bin/rlogin
-rwsr-xr-x   1 root     root        7840 Jul 27 19:17 /usr/bin/rsh
-r-sr-xr-x   1 root     bin         8703 Jul 27 19:16 /usr/bin/passwd
-rws--x--x   2 root     root      556924 Jul 28 03:05 /usr/bin/suidperl
-rws--x--x   2 root     root      556924 Jul 28 03:05 /usr/bin/sperl5.00502
-rwsr-xr-x   1 root     root       38752 Jul 27 20:15 /usr/bin/chage
-rwsr-xr-x   1 root     root       28244 Jul 27 20:15 /usr/bin/expiry
-rwsr-xr-x   1 root     root       32268 Jul 27 20:15 /usr/bin/gpasswd
-rwsr-xr-x   1 root     root       28320 Jul 27 20:15 /usr/bin/newgrp
-rwsr-xr-x   1 root     root       13872 Jul 27 20:27 /usr/bin/chfn
-rwsr-xr-x   1 root     root       13712 Jul 27 20:27 /usr/bin/chsh
-r-sr-sr-x   1 uucp     uucp      125852 Jul 27 20:53 /usr/bin/cu
-r-sr-xr-x   1 uucp     uucp       91568 Jul 27 20:53 /usr/bin/uucp
-r-sr-sr-x   1 uucp     uucp       38492 Jul 27 20:53 /usr/bin/uuname
-r-sr-xr-x   1 uucp     uucp       99656 Jul 27 20:53 /usr/bin/uustat
-r-sr-xr-x   1 uucp     uucp       92720 Jul 27 20:53 /usr/bin/uux
---s--x--x   1 root     root       23420 Jul 27 19:18 /usr/bin/crontab
-rwsr-xr-x   1 root     root      173920 Jul 28 00:32 /usr/sbin/lpc
-rwsr-xr-x   1 root     root       12544 Jul 27 20:48 /usr/sbin/ppplogin
-rwsr-xr-x   1 root     root       17212 Jul 27 19:18 /usr/sbin/sliplogin
-r-sr-xr-x   1 root     root       21146 Jul 27 19:22 /usr/sbin/traceroute
-r-sr-xr-x   1 uucp     uucp      221348 Jul 27 20:53 /usr/sbin/uucico
-r-sr-xr-x   1 uucp     uucp      101852 Jul 27 20:53 /usr/sbin/uuxqt
-r-sr-x---   1 news     uucp      101368 Jul 27 23:22
/usr/libexec/inn/bin/rnews
-r-sr-x---   1 root     news       51732 Jul 27 23:22
/usr/libexec/inn/bin/startinnfeed
-rwsr-xr-x   1 root     root       16700 Jul 27 21:30
/usr/libexec/sendmail/mail.local
-r-sr-xr-x   1 root     mail      317628 Jul 27 21:30
/usr/libexec/sendmail/sendmail
-rwsr-xr-x   1 root     majordom    8268 Jul 27 19:55
/usr/lib/majordomo/wrapper
```

```
-rwsr-sr-x  1 root    root         91140 Jan 10  1995 /usr/lib/svga/demos/3d
-rwsr-xr-x  1 root    root         14576 Jul 27 19:19 /bin/ping
-rwsr-xr-x  1 root    root         14000 Jul 27 20:32 /bin/su
-rwsr-xr-x  1 root    root         54112 Jul 27 20:27 /bin/mount
-rwsr-xr-x  1 root    root         27804 Jul 27 20:27 /bin/umount
-rwsr-sr-x  1 root    root          6644 Jul 27 23:57 /opt/kde/bin/kcheckpass
-rwsr-xr-x  1 root    root        371796 Jul 28 00:59 /opt/kde/bin/kppp
-r-sr-sr-x  1 root    tty          38044 Jul 27 19:24 /sbin/dump
-r-sr-sr-x  1 root    tty         397068 Jul 27 19:24 /sbin/restore
-rwsr-xr-x  1 root    root         13959 Aug 27 10:55 /sbin/cardctl
```

Looking though the list of files, you can see that most are standard fare for having the SUID bit set. Several services considered "restricted" must have the bit set or non-privileged users cannot execute them, for example the programs that allow a user to change his or her own password. Some are programs (like vmware) that require that the user have access to devices and the like.

Note that several uu* programs are SUID, but the owner is uucp. These programs will run as UUCP because if they don't, they won't work. Most systems are not using uucp any more because the Internet is so pervasive. But for those who still do, you have extra considerations. These include dial-up login prompts, etc. But for the most part, the security around this part of the system is the same as for other parts of the system. So if you manage uucp, consider it as you read about login prompts, etc.

As an occasional quick check, run the above find command and save the output to floppy. Then, if you suspect problems, you can do a quick check by comparing (using diff) the old output versus the new output. If you create a script to run this job via cron on a daily basis and mail it to you, it will help you keep an eye on things. Better programs exist to help you do this, like tripwire, but this is a good quick and dirty check. As with many things in the security world, the results are only as good as their interpretation. Running rpm -V to verify files is another check that will do essentially the same thing, assuming of course that the database hasn't been altered or the attacker didn't install an insecure version on top of yours.

Controlling SUID/SGID files

Maintaining control of SUID/SGID files should go without saying. Ensuring that no new ones have shown up, or that you have replaced those that have, are only two of three checks you should perform on your system(s). How often you perform these checks depends on your own risk assessment.

Remember that users can have SUID or SGID files and directories for their own use, but should not have SUID root files.

More important than checking for new or changed SUID files is checking for newly discovered vulnerabilities in programs you have on your system. Normally, known vulnerabilities are corrected within hours of being discovered, but until then, recommendations for workarounds are released immediately by the distribution vendor or an agency like CERT (Computer Emergency Response Team) until new binaries can be obtained.

 Caldera has a mailing list to warn users of vulnerabilities discovered in products it has released. Please go to `http://www.calderasystems.com` and look for the security advisories mailing list.

Changing permissions

Permissions for SUID, SGID, and the sticky bit work exactly the same as for regular file permissions (as explained in Chapter 3). The chmod command is used to change these file permissions. The specific octal numbers used to make these changes are: 4 for SUID, 2 for SGID, and 1 to set the sticky bit. This octal number becomes the fourth number at the beginning.

Here's an example. A normal file permission is: chmod 755 *filename*. In actuality, this is chmod 0755 *filename*. But now, you'll change the leading 0 to any number from 1–7 to accomplish what you need. If you need to set the sticky bit, as used for the /tmp directory so only the owner can change or delete the file, it is done as follows:

```
chmod 1777 /tmp.
```

If you want to specify a directory as SGID so that all files saved into that directory are saved as the group name assigned to the directory, then you would use something like: chmod 2775 *dirname*. The same goes for making a file SUID: chmod 4755 *filename*. Setting both SUID and SGID on a file (as is the case with the cu program, part of UUCP), the command is

```
chmod 6755 cu
```

This is the addition of SUID (4) and SGID (2).

After you make a change, you'll see under a long listing that the "x" part of rwx for file permissions has changed to an "s". This is true for both the SUID and SGID bits. The "s" will occupy a place in either the owner portion or the group portion. The sticky bit is a little different, it puts a "t" in place of the "x" in the world permissions section.

Seeing what changes and how in the permissions, you should be able to guess what will be placed in the chmod command if you use the letter masks. Here, you can simply make a program SUID by calling chmod as follows: chmod u+s *program*. Similarly, g+s will make the file or directory SGID (and a minus operator will remove it in both cases). And the sticky bit is added or removed with a + or - "t". Table 4-1 is an expanded version of Table 3-2, which includes the various special permissions bits.

TABLE 4-1 EXPANSION OF TABLE 3-2, CHMOD OCTAL EQUIVALENTS

Permissions	Octal equivalent	Special permissions	Octal equivalent	Comments
- - - - - - - - -	000	- - x - - x - - x	0111	Leading "0" may be omitted, chmod only requires three octal numbers
- - x - - x - - x	111	- - - - - - - - t	1001	t = sticky bit
- w - - w - - w -	222	- - - - - s - - -	2010	s = SUID bit
- w x - w x - w x	333	- - - - - s - - t	3011	You can mix and match permissions numbers to achieve the desired result
r - - r - - r - -	444	- - s - - - - - -	4100	rwxr-x--x = chmod 751
r - x r - x r - x	555	- - s - - - - - t	5101	Special Permissions show minimum permissions — where you have a "1", it is mandatory that you have at least a one in that column
r w - r w - r w -	666	- - s - - s - - -	6110	
r w x r w x r w x	777	- - s - - s - - t	7111	

Understanding ext2-specific permissions

The ext2 file system currently in use by Linux as its native file system has several other security features of interest. While this file system may be replaced in the 2.4 kernel or later (more likely later) with the SGI file system, ext2 remains viable, its primary drawback being that it is not a journaling file system.

The ext2 file system has eight additional attributes. By default, all bits are turned off, that is, none of the attributes are active. The system administrator must activate those she wishes to use. The attributes are stored in the inode under the heading "flag," and stored as a hex number.

◆ The A attribute will prevent modification of the atime (access time) for a file that is modified. This is designed to reduce disk I/O. However, this feature is not currently implemented.

◆ The S attribute tells the operating system to write asynchronously to disk all file modifications. This mimics the DOS file system and is tantamount to issuing the sync command after each file modification.

◆ The A attribute designates the file for append operations only, so the file will not be clobbered by a redirect. This is one of the attributes that only the system administrator can set.

◆ The C attribute specifies that the file is to be compressed when written to disk. It will be automatically uncompressed when read from disk.

◆ The D attribute tells dump to ignore the file, do not back up.

◆ The I attribute makes the file immutable. When set, the file cannot be deleted, modified, renamed, or even linked to. This attribute prevents even root from performing any modifications to the file. Only the system administrator can set this attribute.

◆ The S attribute tells the kernel to zero its blocks and write it back to disk when deleted. This "secure" bit makes recovery of any of the file's data extremely difficult if not impossible.

◆ The Uattribute is designed to allow a file to be undeleted. But this particular attribute should not be depended on. Often, this will allow recovery of a file, but only the first block (normally 4096 bytes). A better bet for a safe remove is a function that moves the file to a "holding" directory for a period where cron will delete it permanently after a given amount of time.

Using chattr

The chattr program sets the specific attributes outlined above. In this case, chattr is used in a manner very much like the chmod command, using the letter attributes preceded by an operator. The operator performs one of three actions: The + operator adds the particular attribute to any existing attributes; the - operator subtracts the attribute, leaving other attributes intact; the = operator makes the attribute(s) following it the only attribute, removing all other attributes.

The chattr command also understands the -R option, which works recursively through subdirectories, and the -V option, which prints the version number of the chattr program and is verbose while it works.

One other option that can be used is the -v option, which is followed by a number. This is a versioning number that can be used as the user sees fit. The version number is a version number for the inode, and has nothing to do with the file itself. So for example, any file that is created gets an unused inode number from the pool of available inodes, and by default, it is version number one until the user changes that number. So if you perform a mv foo foo2, then foo2 will have the inode number that belonged to foo (the inode is reused). If a file foo2 already existed, its inode (and version number if unique) would have been replaced. But if you did a simple cp foo foo2, if foo2 existed, it would retain the version number it had originally, or if it didn't exist would have version 1. Caldera uses this number, and stamps each file present during initial Lizard installation with a unique number. All files created since the original installation will not have this unique number. If you replace a package using RPM (via the -U switch), the new files will not have the unique version number, just the version one. More on this below.

Using lsattr

The lsattr program is very similar in some ways to the ls program. It will list the filenames, and show the attributes of the files.

Like the chattr program, lsattr understands the -R option to recurse through subdirectories. The -V shows the program version as the first line. The -a option lists all files, including dot files. The -d option will only list directories, but not files. The -l option show the listing in a long format, spelling out each attribute the file has. Finally, the -v option lists the file's version.

Following is a highly modified directory listing using lsattr. You can see each bit that's set for each file:

```
-------- ./conf.messages
-ucS-a-A ./uid
s---i-d- ./userbatch
```

The file conf.messages above is a normal file (no attributes set). The uid and userbatch files both have various attributes set. Each position corresponds to a number, and the total is stored in the inode under flags as noted previously. So the flags will contain a number from 0x0 to 0xff (0–255 in hex) depending on which attributes are set.

Below is another highly edited listing of the /bin directory:

```
1883578780 -------- ./nisdomainname
1883578780 -------- ./domainname
1883580320 -------- ./ps
1883596959 -------- ./ex
1883596959 -------- ./rview
1883596959 -------- ./rvim
1883596959 -------- ./vi
1883596959 -------- ./view
1883596959 -------- ./vim
1883602714 -------- ./zsh
1883587488 -------- ./csh
1883587488 -------- ./tcsh
         1 -------- ./ksh
         1 -------- ./pdksh
```

Here you have the same files as above, but this time show via ls -li:

```
20538 -r-xr-xr-x  2 root      root        6764 Jul 28 01:03 nisdomainname
20538 -r-xr-xr-x  2 root      root        6764 Jul 28 01:03 domainname
20539 -r-xr-xr-x  1 root      root       77428 Jul 27 19:31 ps
20564 lrwxrwxrwx  1 root      root           3 Aug  5 08:59 ex -> vim
20565 lrwxrwxrwx  1 root      root           3 Aug  5 08:59 rview -> vim
20566 lrwxrwxrwx  1 root      root           3 Aug  5 08:59 rvim -> vim
20567 lrwxrwxrwx  1 root      root           3 Aug  5 08:59 vi -> vim
20568 lrwxrwxrwx  1 root      root           3 Aug  5 08:59 view -> vim
20569 -rwxr-xr-x  1 root      root      470696 Jul 27 22:59 vim
20571 -rwxr-xr-x  1 root      root      366344 Jul 27 21:03 zsh
20572 lrwxrwxrwx  1 root      root           4 Aug  5 09:02 csh -> tcsh
20554 -r-xr-xr-x  1 root      root      265516 Jul 27 20:21 tcsh
20573 -rwxr-xr-x  1 root      root      170768 Apr 30 12:14 ksh
20574 lrwxrwxrwx  1 root      root           3 Aug  5 23:52 pdksh -> ksh
```

The nisdomainname and domainname files have the same lsattr version number because they are links — they have the same inode number. You also have a direct correlation between symlinks and their targets.

The pdksh and its symlink ksh were added after the system was up and running. Notice that they do not have unique version numbers. All files added after the initial Lizard install have a version number of 1 unless you modify it.

Do not rely on the unique versioning numbers because they can be noted, and any sabotaged replacement can have the same versioning number placed on it. However, if a file like /bin/login has a versioning number of 1, you can be sure it is a replacement.

Is there any reason not to make whole unchanging parts of the file system immutable? None. In fact, this is one way to ensure that root doesn't accidentally delete large portions of the file system. If you want to do this, the major sections to change would include /usr (less local/ and src/), /bin, /sbin, /lib, and perhaps a few others.

Directories not to make immutable include /var, /etc, /tmp, /home, and any other subdirectories containing files that change on a regular basis.

Summary

This chapter covered a wide range of topics from SUID and SGID to some not too well known or easily understood ext2 file system attributes, including what the SUID/SGID bit does for executable binaries as well as for directories. It also included the "sticky bit" and what it means for directories. The material covered how to set these bits, and why they should or shouldn't be set.

Then you looked at the chattr and lsattr commands, what they could do, and how to set such attributes as immutable, and inode versioning numbers.

Chapter 5

File system layout

THIS CHAPTER WILL COVER some of the security aspects involved in the layout of a file system. Many considerations, such as disk space, need to be taken into account. But security concerns should not be forgotten. This chapter discusses some of those security concerns.

Understanding mounts

Mount points are directories where one may mount a second disk partition to a first to make the second appear as part of the first. That is, the tree receives a "graft," another branch, at that point, and the tree thus becomes that much larger. In fact, this is the only way to add to the existing file system's volume, by adding another partition to it. This additional partition could just as easily be an NFS (network file system) mount from another host across the network, but would obviously only be available when the network and the remote host were.

Under OpenLinux, the most common file system type as of this writing is ext2, Linux's native file system. The ext2 file system has certain attributes, some of which you learned about in Chapters 3 and 4. You learned that, unlike DOS, ext2 uses a system of inodes that contain a lot of information. In fact, every operating system uses different file systems, so a large number of file systems are in existence. Linux can read many of them.

Mount points must necessarily be directory names. But the directories don't need to be empty. No directory is truly empty, it contains at a minimum the "." and ".." files. But it can contain a lot more. If a partition is mounted over an existing directory, the contents of the existing directory become unavailable. They can't be seen or used, and the disk space used by those files is lost. The files in the disk partition mounted over it replace the original. So if someone were to mount a floppy disk with some modified binaries over top of /bin or /sbin, the modified binaries would be used instead of the originals, with rather obvious security implications.

But those of you who've tried to mount something as someone other than root know, you can only mount what is permitted by /etc/fstab — non-root users cannot specify devices or options. Take a look at a sample fstab:

```
/dev/hda1    /             ext2      defaults                 1  1
/dev/hda     /home         ext2      defaults                 1  2
/dev/hda4    swap          swap      defaults                 0  0
devpts       /dev/pts      devpts    gid=5,mode=620           0  0
/proc        /proc         proc      defaults                 0  0
/dev/fd0     /mnt/floppy   msdos     defaults,users,noauto    0  0
/dev/hdc     /mnt/cdrom    iso9660   ro,user,noauto           0  0
```

The fstab file consists of six columns delimited by white space. Column one refers to specific devices, normally disk devices, either sd, hd, or fd entries. The one exception shown above is devpts, which are psuedo-terminal devices. Your kernel is compiled by default with up to 256 of these unless you changed that (this is the CONFIG_UNIX98_PTYS and CONFIG_UNIX98_PTY_COUNT kernel configuration options). The second column shows the mount point. This is where the devices in column one will be mounted. If you list the directory /dev/pts, it will show different files at different times. The files are numbered and correspond to a pty as shown in the process list. Telnet sessions and xterms, etc., open up a pty. Console logins will not show a pty; they use a tty.

For those who are thinking about these /dev/pts files from a security standpoint, note in the fstab that the mode is specifically listed as 620, or owner read-write, group write, and world nothing. Let's take a look at what's in /dev/pts:

```
drwxr-xr-x   2 root      root            0 Sep 13 07:06 .
drwxr-xr-x   4 root      root        11264 Sep 13 08:52 ..
crw--w----   1 david     tty       136,  0 Sep 13 09:18 0
crw--w----   1 david     tty       136,  1 Sep 13 09:11 1
crw-------   1 david     tty       136,  2 Sep 13 09:13 2
```

Look first at the permissions and ownerships on the ptys. They are owned by the user who opened them, and they are opened rw. The group is tty, and has permissions to write only, but only for pty0 and pty1. Notice that pty2 is read-only. Now list the write and wall commands:

```
-rwxr-sr-x   1 root      tty        8356 Jul 27 20:27 /usr/bin/write
-rwxr-sr-x   1 root      tty        6748 Jul 27 19:22 /usr/bin/wall
```

The permissions for write and wall include SGID tty, the same group that owns the ptys. Apparently, write and wall can write to the first two ptys, but not the last. It is important that only the user be able to read these ptys or you have a serious security problem, since someone could then monitor the ptys in hopes of gaining knowledge of any passwords passed through them.

Remember the mesg command? If you were to issue the mesg command on all of david's pty's, you'd find that two would return y, and one would return n. This prevents anyone from writing to user david on that one pty. So 'mesg y' would make the pty writable by the tty group, and 'mesg n' would remove that permission.

Just as a refresher, examining the pty line further, following the group owner-ship you see the device major and minor numbers; in this case, major is 136 and minors are 0, 1, and 2. The date is when the user last wrote to that pty. So the date will change as commands are issued via that pty.

You might review the contents of /dev/pts and compare that to either "w" or "who", cross-referenced to a "ps aux | grep pts". You should have no "stale" pts' in /dev/pts (pts' with old dates on them), pts' with processes not associated with an active user, or pts' using processes you know nothing about. Any of these could (but do not necessarily) indicate a security breach.

The third column in /etc/fstab indicates the file system type that is mounted by default. This can be any file system name including nfs, vfat, etc., or swap, devpts, or ignore. This must be the name the file system is known as to the kernel.

The fourth column is the options column. Here, you're looking at the options for fstab as opposed to those options that are command line options. Command line options are more numerous and are slightly different from the options that follow the -o switch. For example, in fstab you'll see ro for read-only. On a command line you may see -o ro or just -r. All are synonymous. This text will not be concerned with all the command line options, just the options that may be used in the fstab file.

Any user with UID 0 may mount any file system on any mount point — basically, on any directory. As explained above, this then makes anything below that on the origi-nal file system inaccessible. It may be desirable to do this under some circumstances. For example, one distribution had put a required library in /usr/lib, so during bootup before the /usr partition was mounted to /usr, certain actions could not take place. The solution was either to relocate the library, or simply to make sure a copy of the library existed in /usr/lib on the root partition and on the /usr partition. Either solution would work. But since the RPM wanted this critical library in /usr/lib, for upgrade purposes, the better solution was the latter. So approximately 40k worth of disk space was lost from the root partition while /usr was mounted, but this is small by today's standards.

From a security standpoint, only root can mount file systems not listed in /etc/fstab, and even then, only file systems specifically designated as user mount-able. Users cannot specify options, they can only mount file systems as listed in /etc/fstab if the particular mount contains the option user or users.

Only options that will affect security will be discussed here. Since UID 0 is trusted, any user with this UID can do anything. But others can't, and all for security reasons. However, you must understand how the mount command works in order to understand the ramifications of changing the default behavior and why you might or might not want to do that in certain situations.

Allowing users to mount file systems presents some risks. Ensure that you understand what those risks entail, and use appropriate options in /etc/fstab.

For purposes of this text, you will see both the cdrom and the floppy mounted. Look back at the sample fstab earlier in this chapter. Make note of the differences in the lines for the cdrom and the floppy, particularly the difference in user versus users. The mount command with no options will read the mtab and display the mounted partitions. Output of the mount command:

```
/dev/hda1 on / type ext2 (rw)
/dev/hda3 on /home type ext2 (rw)
devpts on /dev/pts type devpts (rw,gid=5,mode=620)
/proc on /proc type proc (rw)
/dev/hdc on /mnt/cdrom type iso9660 (ro,noexec,nosuid,nodev,user=david)
/dev/fd0 on /mnt/floppy type msdos (rw,noexec,nosuid,nodev)
```

For comparison's sake, this is what the /etc/mtab file looks like at this moment:

```
/dev/hda1 / ext2 rw 0 0
/dev/hda3 /home ext2 rw 0 0
devpts /dev/pts devpts rw,gid=5,mode=620 0 0
/proc /proc proc rw 0 0
/dev/hdc /mnt/cdrom iso9660 ro,noexec,nosuid,nodev,user=david 0 0
/dev/fd0 /mnt/floppy msdos rw,noexec,nosuid,nodev 0 0
```

The mounted file systems are also listed in /proc/mounts and look exactly the same as /etc/mtab. However, it would be unwise to make /etc/mtab a link to /proc/mounts, since this could cause problems if you use loopback devices.

Differences are that mtab shows a white space-delimited file of all mounted file systems (or at least those not mounted with the -n option), including the relevant dump and fsck columns from /etc/fstab (but also note all entries are 0 0). The mount command doesn't show the last two columns, and shows the options set apart in parentheses, which is slightly easier for many people to read.

If a file system is mounted with the "-n" command (no mtab entry), then neither the df command nor the mount command will show the file system. However, if /proc is in use, the file system will show under /proc/mounts. The -n is used to prevent mount from trying to write an mtab entry while the file system is mounted read-only and is not meant for general use.

Both listings show the floppy and cdrom mounted. The cdrom line shows user=david. The floppy line has no such listing. The difference is in the user vs users entry in /etc/fstab. When the entry specifies user, any user may mount the specified file system on the specified mount point, but only that user may unmount it. When the users option is specified, any user may mount the specified file system, and any user may unmount it. The example is a deliberate transposition of the user and users entries from the recommended practice. Notice that the floppy file system is mounted rw, and the cdrom ro. Another user can swap diskettes and capture a file someone else is saving to disk, then swap them back again. So this may not be such a good idea. However, with the cdrom mounted ro, no one will be writing a file, so no such problem exists. If you're wondering about a CD-R (writable CD), most CD-ROMs lock the tray closed while they are mounted, so the problem is not as prevalent.

The options (in no particular order) are the following:

- async/sync — I/O to mount will occur asynchronously/synchronously
- atime/noatime — inode access times on the mount will/won't update
- auto/noauto — the -a option to mount will/won't include this mount point
- dev/nodev — character or block special devices will/won't be interpreted on the mount
- exec/noexec — binaries will/won't execute on the mount
- suid/nosuid — SUID/SGID bits will/won't take effect on the mount
- nouser/user(s) — users are allowed/are not allowed to mount file system
- rw/ro — file system will mount read-write/read-only
- remount — file system should be remounted if possible (normally used to change root file system from ro to rw or vice versa)
- default — most entries will be default, which implies: rw, suid, dev, exec, auto, nouser, and async

Examining the default entry gives rise to some questions. If the option `user(s)` is specified, and the default mount is suid, dev, exec, then what prevents someone other than root from mounting a floppy containing a binary SUID root with malicious code? Simple. When the option `user` (or `users`) is specified, the defaults are changed to `noexec`, `nosuid`, and `nodev`. If, for some reason, you want binaries to be available for use without copying them out and setting their executable bit, then you can explicitly put `exec` as an option. But for this option to have effect, it must come after the `user` option. Ditto for the `dev` and `suid` options. The mount command reads the options from left to right, changing them as it goes down the line, the last one overriding previous option. So if you put `users` followed by `defaults`, it would be the same as putting `nouser` on the line after `user` (or omitting `user` entirely). The last option takes precedence. So a user could not mount anything. All options are sensitive to order, later ones overriding earlier ones.

The fifth column in /etc/fstab is the dump column and will be a 1 for yes or a 0 for no. The sixth column is used by fsck to specify the order to check the file systems. The root file system should be 1, all others 2, with a 0 specifying don't check (for those file systems where an fsck doesn't make sense, which would be almost any non-ext2 type file system). Blank entries for either columns five or six are interpreted as 0 (however, note that if column six contains an entry, so must column five).

Mount point permissions

The preceding options apply to all file systems that you can mount. File system-specific options are also available and vary from file system to file system. This is mostly due to the nature of the information (or lack thereof) contained within each file system for the files and directories that reside on it.

Linux is capable of mounting a myriad of different file systems, and the number is increasing. Very likely, a new kernel source will have yet another file system it can support. In some cases, you're on your own, so you'll need to check the man and info pages. Some of the more common ones are outlined below. The greatest number of options will generally be for non-UNIX file systems – that is, those that are principally from single-user systems like DOS and Macintosh. The discussion will center specifically on security-related options available to these file systems. Some file systems will have no entry below – not because they are unknown or because they have no options but because they have no options of interest from a security standpoint. These include: coherent, ext (no longer in use), minix, ncp, nfs (covered in Chapter 12), romfs, smbfs, sysv, ufs, xenix, xiafs (use not recommended), and loopback devices (covered under the specific file system type mounted).

See Chapter 12 for a discussion of nfs.

Amiga affs

The Amiga affs file system has a number of security-related settings. These can be set from the command line (UID 0 only) or in /etc/fstab. The first one of interest is: `uid=` and `gid=`. These options do exactly what they say they do, set the uid and gid of the root of the file system (which sets all files and directories below it) to the designated ID. The default for affs is uid=gid=0. However, if you put the `uid=` and/or `gid=` option without a value specified, it will take the uid/gid of the process doing the mounting. That is, if a user calls mount, that user's uid/gid will be used to set the file system's root. This may be exactly what you want, but be sure that it is.

The next option of interest is `setuid=` and `setgid=`. This option specifically sets the owner and/or group of all files. This differs from `uid=gid=` in that the former sets the files permissions specifically on the file system, while the latter sets the root (and therefore ownership of the entire file system) to the specified IDs.

The next two options, `mode=` and `protect`, go hand in hand but may be used individually as needed. Using `mode=`, you can set the mode of all files and directories on the file system regardless of what the permissions were originally. The `protect` option will not allow a user to change any permissions on the file system regardless of ownership. This may be necessary if you want to force the file permissions from having the execute bit set and keeping the owner from changing them back. See also `noexec`, in the global options above.

The final option of interest for this text (an administration text will cover others) is the `usemp` option. This option is used on other file systems as well, though it is certainly an odd option. This option says to mount the file system based on the uid and gid assigned to the mount point at mount, but then clear this option on unmount.

Linux ext2

The first of two options of interest is `grpid` (aka `bsdgroups`) and its antonym `nogrpid` (synonym `sysvgroups`). The default is `nogrpid`. Setting the `grpid` option is the same as setting the SGID bit on the directory: The newly created files will be group ownership of the group the directory is set to. Setting `nogrpid` will set the group ownership to the owner of the process (or user) creating the file.

BSD and SysV differ slightly in the way they handle group IDs on directories. Linux tries to take the best from both worlds, and in this case, the SysV way won out. In other ways, such as command line utilities, BSD is favored. So saying Linux is one or the other is only partially correct.

The second option of interest is the `resgid=` and `resuid=`. Under ext2, a percentage of the file system is reserved. By default this is 5 percent, but may be changed using tune2fs, or during creation of the file system. Setting these determines the user and/or group this reserve is available to for use.

The file system reserve normally belongs to root. Allowing a file system to become full will deny use of the file system to all users until the file system can be repaired (files removed) surgically — that is, this will often require use of tools such as debugfs. This is not a desired outcome.

FAT, MSDOS, UMSDOS, VFAT

The FAT is not a file system unto itself, but a common part of the MSDOS, UMSDOS, and VFAT file system. But given its status as an integral part of those file systems, it is convenient to consider them together. Differences will be noted in the text below.

The first option of interest is the uid= and gid= options. The default is the uid and gid of the user or process mounting the file system. All FAT file systems will mount as the particular user mounting them. If this is not desired, then you'll need to specifically assign the uid and gid in /etc/fstab.

The second option is umask=. Default is the umask of the current process (normally the user's shell).

The third option is the check= option. The default is normal. This option can take three values: r for relaxed, n for normal, or s for strict. The security aspect of this option is that under Linux, the normal value allows some special characters that MS-DOS cannot accept (the files will therefore be unavailable), such as +, =, spaces, and more. If your users exchange data between MS systems and Linux, you will probably want to set this value to s.

The fourth option is conv=. The default is b. The three values that are available are b for binary, t for text, and a for auto. This option allows conversions between DOS's line terminations (carriage-return line-feed) and Linux's terminations (newline). The "t" option performs kernel translations on all files. The a option performs translations on all files except "well-known binaries" as listed in /usr/src/linux/fs/fat/misc.c. The b option performs no translations.

 Use of the a option is very likely to damage files beyond repair. Use of translation programs such as unix2dos/dos2unix or fromdos/todos (or the translation capability built into vi) is highly recommended.

The next option is fat=, with a specification of either 12 or 16. The kernel has an autodetection routine, but this will override that routine. Specifying the wrong option will make your data unreadable. Use of this option is highly discouraged.

The fat system also has a number of options that should not be used. They are attempts to brute-force UNIX or DOS conventions onto a FAT file system, and you may have varying degrees of success with them. These include sys_immutable, showexec, dots, nodots, dotsOK=[yes|no] (this last option is specifically killed by both umsdos and vfat).

An additional option for VFAT is posix. This allows filenames that differ in case only.

OS/2 HPFS

The options of interest for HPSF are similar to those for DOS. They include the uid=, gid=, umask=, and conv=. These work exactly the same as their DOS counterparts. Changing the conv= option from its default of b to either t or a is discouraged.

CD-ROM ISO9660

A normal CD-ROM (no extensions, ISO9660) uses the standard DOS 8.3 filename convention in all upper case. No file ownerships, permissions, etc., are present. Most CD-ROMs today use either Rock Ridge extensions or Joliet extensions. Only the Rock Ridge extensions apply to ISO9660 CD-ROMs. This extension provides a system of files that map names in the present directory to long filenames as used in Linux, and include file ownerships and permissions. By default, use of Rock Ridge extensions is turned on, but can be turned off as an option. Given the fact that CD-ROMs are mounted read-only by default, some options are not as great a security problem as with writable file systems.

ISO9660 file systems will mount by default as uid=gid=0. This is in contrast to the AFFS, FAT, and HPFS file systems that mount as the uid=gid=current process, and can be changed with the uid= and gid= options, and will override the information found in the Rock Ridge extensions.

The mode= and conv= options are also available (see the FAT file system above for details).

The unhide option allows hidden and associated files to show.

PROC

The /proc file system isn't a true file system at all (the next chapter will look at it in more detail). Only one option is available for proc, the uid= and gid=. However, as of this writing, these particular options have no effect on the author's system (kernel version 2.2.12). No valid reason would exist for changing these values even if the option worked.

 Default options, particularly for non-ext2 file systems, don't need to be specified /etc/fstab, but doing so ensures that future changes to the mount command defaults don't compromise security.

Summary

This chapter looked at file systems and mount points and explained the security implications of permitting users to mount file systems. Despite these risks, it is often necessary to permit the practice, but understanding what happens when users mount file systems and how to change the behavior of the mount is important to overall system security.

Allowing users other than root requires a specific entry in /etc/fstab, and that entry will be used exactly as is. Users are not permitted to override options found in /etc/fstab. So once the entry is set, the system administrator can relax.

Chapter 6

The /proc file system

IN THIS CHAPTER

◆ Understanding /proc

◆ Understanding /proc/sys

◆ Understanding /dev/pts

◆ Examining special security considerations for /proc

THE /PROC FILE SYSTEM is unlike any other file system. With the exception of devpts (the pseudo-terminal devices, discussed later) all other file systems are just that, regular file systems of some type. This includes swap (which is used exclusively by the operating system), and loopback and encrypted file systems. They all physically exist, even the pseudo-terminals. But /proc exists only because the operating system is running. And although the pseudo-terminals go away when the system shuts down normally, if power is pulled, the files remain (to be cleaned up when the system restarts). This is not true of /proc.

The /proc file system

Think of the /proc file system as a window you can look through to see the state of the operating system. For the most part, that's all it is. It allows you to see in. While this chapter is short, the concepts about what is happening here are very important.

It is possible to build a kernel without the /proc file system, but it makes little sense to do so. The /proc file system is used by a number of utilities that would then either not work or have to get their information elsewhere in the system. These other sources of information aren't nearly as accurate or complete. In order to ensure the /proc file system is included in the kernel, go to the File systems menu during the kernel configuration process and choose the /proc file system support option (this is enabled by default). The .config file option appears as:

```
CONFIG_PROC_FS=y
```

This option is not available as a module.

Once compiled in, the system is ready to make use of the /proc file system. But as with all things Linux, the system may be turned on and off — in this case, in

/etc/fstab. In order for the system to create and use the /proc file system, it must be "mounted" just like any other file system. What the mounting process does in this case is make the /proc file system available for use. Just as other file systems mount points (directory entries) exist on disk whether they are mounted or not, the /proc file system cannot be used until it is "mounted" because a path must exist to the file system to make use of it. Therefore, if you removed the /proc directory entry in the root file system, there'd be no place to mount /proc, and you'd get an error and not /proc file system. The appropriate line in /etc/fstab appears as follows:

```
/proc /proc proc defaults 0 0
```

The file system is /proc and has no corresponding device file allocated to it because it isn't a device. The mount location is /proc, the file system type is proc, it uses defaults to mount, and is neither checked in any way nor dumped. It doesn't make much sense to check or dump dynamic memory variables, since you can't correct or change them, except the files in /proc/sys, discussed below. Also, you won't be restoring /proc, since altering this system by forcing a restore on top of /proc would make the system unstable.

The /proc file system is very dynamic. A number of entries will be changing almost all the time depending on system activity. If you look at the /proc file system, you see a snapshot in time. Listing 6-1 shows the /proc root file system.

Listing 6-1: The /proc root file system

```
dr-xr-xr-x  58 root    root           0 Nov 15 19:01 .
drwxr-xr-x  21 root    root        1024 Nov 15 12:02 ..
dr-xr-xr-x   3 root    root           0 Nov 16 07:46 1
dr-xr-xr-x   3 root    root           0 Nov 16 07:46 1076
dr-xr-xr-x   3 root    root           0 Nov 16 07:46 1079
dr-xr-xr-x   3 dns     dns            0 Nov 16 07:46 1088
dr-xr-xr-x   3 root    root           0 Nov 16 07:46 1092
dr-xr-xr-x   3 bin     root           0 Nov 16 07:46 1094
dr-xr-xr-x   3 root    root           0 Nov 16 07:46 1176
dr-xr-xr-x   3 root    root           0 Nov 16 07:46 1181
dr-xr-xr-x   3 root    root           0 Nov 16 07:46 1190
dr-xr-xr-x   3 root    root           0 Nov 16 07:46 1202
dr-xr-xr-x   3 root    root           0 Nov 16 07:46 1263
dr-xr-xr-x   3 root    root           0 Nov 16 07:46 1270
dr-xr-xr-x   3 root    root           0 Nov 16 07:46 1271
dr-xr-xr-x   3 root    root           0 Nov 16 07:46 1284
dr-xr-xr-x   3 root    root           0 Nov 16 07:46 1286
dr-xr-xr-x   3 root    root           0 Nov 16 07:46 1287
dr-xr-xr-x   3 root    root           0 Nov 16 07:46 1288
dr-xr-xr-x   3 nobody  nobody         0 Nov 16 07:46 1317
dr-xr-xr-x   3 nobody  nobody         0 Nov 16 07:46 1318
dr-xr-xr-x   3 nobody  nobody         0 Nov 16 07:46 1319
```

```
dr-xr-xr-x   3 nobody   nobody          0 Nov 16 07:46 1320
dr-xr-xr-x   3 nobody   nobody          0 Nov 16 07:46 1321
dr-xr-xr-x   3 root     root            0 Nov 16 07:46 1363
dr-xr-xr-x   3 root     root            0 Nov 16 07:46 1371
dr-xr-xr-x   3 root     root            0 Nov 16 07:46 1372
dr-xr-xr-x   3 root     root            0 Nov 16 07:46 1373
dr-xr-xr-x   3 root     root            0 Nov 16 07:46 1374
dr-xr-xr-x   3 root     root            0 Nov 16 07:46 1375
dr-xr-xr-x   3 nobody   nobody          0 Nov 16 07:46 1618
dr-xr-xr-x   3 nobody   nobody          0 Nov 16 07:46 1619
dr-xr-xr-x   3 nobody   nobody          0 Nov 16 07:46 1620
dr-xr-xr-x   3 root     root            0 Nov 16 07:46 1741
dr-xr-xr-x   3 root     root            0 Nov 16 07:46 1800
dr-xr-xr-x   3 david    david           0 Nov 16 07:46 1892
dr-xr-xr-x   3 root     root            0 Nov 16 07:46 2
dr-xr-xr-x   3 root     root            0 Nov 16 07:46 3
dr-xr-xr-x   3 root     root            0 Nov 16 07:46 4
dr-xr-xr-x   3 root     root            0 Nov 16 07:46 4856
dr-xr-xr-x   3 david    david           0 Nov 16 07:46 4858
dr-xr-xr-x   3 david    david           0 Nov 16 07:46 4914
dr-xr-xr-x   3 david    david           0 Nov 16 07:46 4915
dr-xr-xr-x   3 david    david           0 Nov 16 07:46 4917
dr-xr-xr-x   3 david    david           0 Nov 16 07:46 4963
dr-xr-xr-x   3 david    david           0 Nov 16 07:46 4964
dr-xr-xr-x   3 david    david           0 Nov 16 07:46 4965
dr-xr-xr-x   3 root     root            0 Nov 16 07:46 4967
dr-xr-xr-x   3 root     root            0 Nov 16 07:46 4968
dr-xr-xr-x   3 root     root            0 Nov 16 07:46 5
dr-xr-xr-x   3 root     root            0 Nov 16 07:46 5038
-r--r--r--   1 root     root            0 Nov 16 07:46 apm
dr-xr-xr-x   4 root     root            0 Nov 16 07:46 bus
-r--r--r--   1 root     root            0 Nov 16 07:46 cmdline
-r--r--r--   1 root     root            0 Nov 16 07:46 cpuinfo
-r--r--r--   1 root     root            0 Nov 16 07:46 devices
-r--r--r--   1 root     root            0 Nov 16 07:46 dma
-r--r--r--   1 root     root            0 Nov 16 07:46 fb
-r--r--r--   1 root     root            0 Nov 16 07:46 filesystems
dr-xr-xr-x   2 root     root            0 Nov 16 07:46 fs
dr-xr-xr-x   4 root     root            0 Nov 16 07:46 ide
-r--r--r--   1 root     root            0 Nov 16 07:46 interrupts
-r--r--r--   1 root     root            0 Nov 16 07:46 ioports
-r--------   1 root     root    134221824 Nov 16 07:46 kcore
-r--------   1 root     root            0 Nov 15 19:01 kmsg
-r--r--r--   1 root     root            0 Nov 16 07:46 ksyms
-r--r--r--   1 root     root            0 Nov 16 07:46 loadavg
```

```
-r--r--r--    1 root      root          0 Nov 16 07:46 locks
-r--r--r--    1 root      root          0 Nov 16 07:46 meminfo
-r--r--r--    1 root      root          0 Nov 16 07:46 misc
-r--r--r--    1 root      root          0 Nov 16 07:46 modules
-r--r--r--    1 root      root          0 Nov 16 07:46 mounts
dr-xr-xr-x    3 root      root          0 Nov 16 07:46 net
-r--r--r--    1 root      root          0 Nov 16 07:46 partitions
-r--r--r--    1 root      root          0 Nov 16 07:46 pci
-r--r--r--    1 root      root          0 Nov 16 07:46 rtc
dr-xr-xr-x    2 root      root          0 Nov 16 07:46 scsi
lrwxrwxrwx    1 root      root         64 Nov 16 07:46 self -> 5038
-r--r--r--    1 root      root          0 Nov 16 07:46 slabinfo
-r--r--r--    1 root      root          0 Nov 16 07:46 stat
-r--r--r--    1 root      root          0 Nov 16 07:46 swaps
dr-xr-xr-x    9 root      root          0 Nov 16 07:46 sys
dr-xr-xr-x    4 root      root          0 Nov 16 07:46 tty
-r--r--r--    1 root      root          0 Nov 16 07:46 uptime
-r--r--r--    1 root      root          0 Nov 16 07:46 version
```

The first thing you should notice is that almost all files and directories have size 0. The file self is a symlink, so it has a size, and kcore, the system's memory, also has a size.

Notice too, that all entries are read-only, even for the owner (in most cases root). That's because, with few exceptions, this file system cannot be manipulated.

Examining the listing more closely, it can easily be split into two sections, one section of numbered entries, the other of named entries. Looking quickly down the list of numbers, most are owned by user root, but a few others are not. These numbers are actually PIDs (process IDs). If you looked at a `ps aux` listing side by side, you'd see the permissions in /proc corresponded to owner and group of the process listing. Listing 6-2 shows what one of the /proc PID subdirectories contains.

Listing 6-2: A /proc pid subdirectory

```
-r--r--r--    1 root      root          0 Nov 16 08:23 status
-r--r--r--    1 root      root          0 Nov 16 08:23 statm
-r--r--r--    1 root      root          0 Nov 16 08:23 stat
lrwx------    1 root      root          0 Nov 16 08:23 root -> /
-rw-------    1 root      root          0 Nov 16 08:23 mem
pr--r--r--    1 root      root          0 Nov 16 08:23 maps
dr-x------    2 root      root          0 Nov 16 08:23 fd
lrwx------    1 root      root          0 Nov 16 08:23 exe -> /usr/sbin/klogd
-r--------    1 root      root          0 Nov 16 08:23 environ
lrwx------    1 root      root          0 Nov 16 08:23 cwd -> /
-r--r--r--    1 root      root          0 Nov 16 08:23 cmdline
dr-xr-xr-x   58 root      root          0 Nov 15 19:01 ..
dr-xr-xr-x    3 root      root          0 Nov 16 08:23 .
```

All the PID subdirectories contain exactly the same information (see Table 6-1). Each of these entries points either somewhere on the system itself (the symlinks) or contains information about the running process. This is the information you see nicely formatted and with appropriate headers in various utilities, such as ps, top, etc. Anything you could want to know about what is going on with any given process is contained in these "files."

TABLE 6-1 PROCESS SUBDIRECTORIES

Name	Function
cmdline	command line arguments
cwd	link to the working directory (where the command was issued from)
environ	environment variables
exe	link to the executable file for this process
fd	directory containing file descriptors; links to other files, e.g.,
	lr-x------ 1 root root 64 Dec 13 08:56 0 -> /dev/null
	l-wx------ 1 root root 64 Dec 13 08:56 1 -> /var/log/xdm-errors
	l-wx------ 1 root root 64 Dec 13 08:56 2 -> /var/log/xdm-errors
	lrwx------ 1 root root 64 Dec 13 08:56 3 -> socket:[1556]
	lrwx------ 1 root root 64 Dec 13 08:56 5 -> socket:[573]
maps	memory maps (pipe that will show executable/shared libraries in use)
mem	memory held by this process
root	link to root directory for this process (normally /)
stat	process status
statm	memory status for process
status	human readable status information (which stat and statm are not)

Examining the root /proc directory again, this time focusing on the named entries, you'll notice a large number of familiar files or subdirectories, at least by name. The interrupts "file" contains a list of all used interrupts and what they are assigned to. In fact, each file contains exactly what its name infers, whether you understand the reference or not. The directories also contain certain information. All systems with /proc are nearly identical. Directories may be empty, but they are created for standardization. For example, this system has no SCSI devices, yet a SCSI directory exists. It is, however, empty. A SCSI-based system with no IDE devices will still have an IDE directory, albeit empty as well.

A number of subdirectories exist under these directories as needed.

The actual structure of the /proc file system is contained in /usr/src/linux/ include/linux/proc_fs.h. This file contains sufficient comments for those who understand something about /proc and have a basic knowledge of C structures and variables. Feel free to look it over. The listing is too long to include in this chapter, but it contains all the structures to create the directory tree you see in /proc and dynamically create the inode structure needed to support this virtual file system. Also, /usr/src/linux/Documentation/proc.txt, while not completely up to date, is also a good source of basic information for the technically inclined.

While directories are created, files are created only as supported by the kernel. That is, if a particular capability is built into the kernel – sound, for example – it will appear as a file in the /proc tree. If you build sound as modules, the sound file will not exist until you load the appropriate sound modules. If sound is completely modular and you load the sound modules, the file /proc/sound will be created (the window to look into the kernel at the sound configuration will appear). Now, if you load the sb module (the soundblaster module – assuming you have a SoundBlaster card), you will be able to cat /proc/sound and see the loaded module and the parameters you passed or that it autoprobed.

This is true also for other subsystems like ppp, slip, etc. While the directory structure will be found under /proc, the files may be absent. As another example, assume you have a SCSI CD-ROM that you built as modules (ditto for the iso9660 file system). This is an Adaptec aha154x module. Before it is loaded, nothing exists under /proc/scsi. After you load the aha154x module, you will see two entries under scsi: scsi0 and sda (or sdb/c/d depending on the CD-ROM drive settings). By looking in the created files, you will be able to see all details about the CD-ROM. If you then mount a CD, you will get additional entries under /proc/filesystems, etc.

Taking this a step further, assume that for whatever reason, you've brought the system into single-user mode (runlevel 1), unmounted all file systems, and then remounted the root file system read-only and remounted /proc. Then you wanted to mount a vfat floppy read-only. Because the root file system is read-only, the mount command cannot create the /etc/mtab file that mount relies on to tell you about mounted file systems. (You can accomplish the same thing by mounting systems with `mount -n`, which will not write the mount to /etc/mtab.) Now, if you use df or mount to identify mounted file systems, the floppy will not show up. However, since /proc is mounted, you can look in /proc/file systems and see that vfat support has been installed in the kernel via the vfat module (assuming vfat was built as a module) and look in /proc/mounts to see what the kernel knows to be mounted.

The /proc/sys directory

One directory in particular is very special within /proc. This directory is the sys directory. When you rebuild your kernel to take advantage of Linux's packet filter firewall software (be it for building a firewall or just masquerading hosts behind your Linux system), you'll need to include support for something called sysctl or system control. This particular option is listed under the kernel configuration "General Setup" and is called Sysctl support. It is enabled by default.

CONFIG_SYSCTL=y

When this option is built into a kernel with /proc file system support (and /proc is mounted), a sys directory will appear with entries in it. Unlike the rest of the /proc file system, which is read-only, the sys subdirectory contains writable files.

 In newer kernels with mtrr support, the mtrr "file", located in the /proc root, is also writable. It is also the only file besides symlinks and kcore to have a file size, and so is another anomaly.

The files in /proc/sys are used to alter the state of the running kernel. This allows you to change compiled-in defaults for certain variables and alter the system's behavior. Many programs will deliberately alter variables. For example, when the XFree86 X server starts, you may have noticed that you can no longer shut down the system by using the Ctrl+Alt+Del key sequence (unless you change first to a VT). This is because as long as you are on an active X screen, the X server writes a "0" to /proc/sys/kernel/ctrl-alt-del. VTs write a "1" to this location, thus enabling and disabling the use of this key sequence to shut down the system.

You will also need to change variables within /proc/sys manually. Where you feel you know better than a compiled-in default, you may make changes to many subsystems, including virtual memory (paging, etc.), the kernel, and file system parameters, but mostly to various networking subsystems. For instance, you will need to change /proc/sys/net/ipv4/ip_forward from "0" to "1" to enable IP forwarding. This is turned off by default. Obviously, if you omit support for sysctl or /proc in the kernel config, you won't be able to do this. The defaults are configured during the kernel build. While you could simply change the kernel source so that forwarding is enabled by default, and then omit sysctl and/or /proc, this doing so is not a good idea. The kernel defaults are "safe" defaults decided on so that the majority of systems would run properly. If you altered the virtual memory subsystem in the kernel source files and compiled the kernel, you could end up with an unusable kernel for many systems.

 It is possible to change the values in some /proc/sys files (particularly under vm) to values that would make the system unstable. Before proceeding, make sure you read and understand the information contained in /usr/src/linux/Documentation directory describing the subsystem you wish to alter.

Changing the values after you have a safe, stable, running kernel, by altering those values from a file when a daemon or process subsystem that requires the changes is started, is infinitely wiser than altering the kernel source.The /proc file system will not be changing significantly in the new 2.4x kernel. Some files will change names,and some default values may change, but these are only indicative of improvements in the kernel and not indications of design or security problems in /proc, but just structural or name changes in the kernel itself. Since the kernel is changing, the view of the internals will necessarily change with it.

The dev/pts file system

The /dev/pts file system is another improvement added to the Linux kernel during the 2.1x development series. This is a change from using the BSD-style /dev/pty? devices and fixes some of their shortcomings. Use of /dev/pts is an all-or-nothing affair, the two styles may not be mixed and matched. By default, Caldera OpenLinux comes with the devpts file system.

To ensure the /dev/pts file system is used by the system, two kernel configuration options and one file entry must be in place. The first kernel config option is found on the Character devices menu, labeled Unix98PTY support. This option also allows you to configure the number of available PTYs for use. By default 256 are available, but this may be changed within the range shown on the configuration page, generally up to 2048 on an Intel architecture system.

```
CONFIG_UNIX98_PTYS=y
```

The second kernel configuration option is found on the File systems menu and is listed as /dev/pts file system for Unix98PTYs. If neither option is selected, the system will fall back to using the older BSD-style pty terminals.

```
CONFIG_DEVPTS_FS=y
```

Once these two are configured, it is important to ensure that /etc/fstab have a line that looks like the following:

```
devpts /dev/pts devpts gid=5,mode=620 0 0
```

If an older /etc/fstab from a 2.0.x kernel is overlaid on the newer /etc/fstab installed by CSOL 2.2 or higher, you won't be able to access the system because it won't be able to create the necessary devices. These devices are created on the fly in /dev/pts/ and are numbered.

The line above in fstab shows the file system device as devpts, the mount point as /dev/pts, and the file system type as devpts, with a gid of 5 corresponding to the system user tty, mode of rw--w----. The 620 allows others to send messages to this particular terminal and is equivalent to mesg=y. This may be changed by the command mesg=n or by changing the mode to 600.

As telnet and xterm, etc., sessions are opened on the system, you'll see devices dynamically created in this subdir. The maximum number of terminals were built into the system by the configuration above. As users log out, the pts devices are dynamically destroyed.

Special security considerations for /proc

The /proc file system provides a look at the entire system. Anyone with access and proper permissions can look at this and find out anything she wants about the system, and also alter the system via /proc/sys.

But if you look closely, you'll also notice that except for the user who owns a process, non-privileged users can find out very little via /proc that isn't otherwise accessible to them on the running system. The system designers understand the need to secure these files, and those files that contain sensitive information cannot be read by non-privileged users. If any unauthorized person gains root access, the least of your worries will be those regarding the /proc file system, since he or she will have the power to do anything anyway, so gaining information here is of little concern.

The /proc/sys file system is similarly designed to prevent those without need from changing system variables. Eliminating either or both /proc or /proc/sys does nothing to enhance security, but can cause major inconveniences for the system administrator. These virtual systems are there for you and system utilities to use.

The /proc file system should be excluded from tape backups for a number of reasons, not the least of which is that it will never be restored from tape (without dire consequences). It makes little sense to waste time and tape backing this up. Tapes should always be safeguarded since they will contain files such as /etc/shadow, etc., that could be read onto another system.

The devpts file system is another file system that has the potential for compromise. You must ensure that no one but the owner can read from these files (the mode=620 does that by default). Someone who can read from a /dev/pts file will be reading keystrokes sent from the keyboard buffer. This includes unencrypted passwords that are not displayed on the screen. This danger exists with numerous device files, but by default all are created with correct permission to prevent this type of abuse.

Summary

In this chapter you learned that the /proc file system is important both to system utilities and to you as the administrator as a "window" into the kernel and its operation. You also learned about the sys subdirectory and its importance in the overall scheme for changing important kernel parameters on the fly.

You then took a quick look at the one other unusual file system in Linux, the devpts file system that provides Unix98 PTYs. Despite its potential to "leak" information, setting the proper mode in /etc/fstab will promote a good security posture.

Chapter 7

Bootup process

IN THIS CHAPTER

- ◆ Understanding the boot process
- ◆ Understanding what init is
- ◆ Understanding /etc/inittab and SysV initialization
- ◆ Understanding how rc scripts work

IN ORDER TO UNDERSTAND what vulnerabilities exist during bootup, you must understand the bootup process. It's one of a system's most vulnerable times if a knowledgeable person has physical access to the system. The next chapter specifically addresses console attacks. This chapter provides the background and prepares you to assess your own system and how changes may impact security during system initialization.

Caldera OpenLinux uses the System V (SysV)-style system initialization as opposed to BSD-style initialization. These are the two primary methods of performing system initialization in the UNIX and Linux worlds. BSD uses a few large scripts to handle all system initialization. SysV makes use of runlevels and a group of initialization scripts. The initialization scripts are run to start and stop *daemons* (background processes) depending on the *runlevel* (also referred to as the *system state,* or just *state*). One script per daemon or process subsystem is kept in a centralized directory you'll examine in detail later. System V runlevels range from 0 to 6 by custom, with each runlevel corresponding to a different mode of operation, and often, even these runlevels are not all used. While SysV initialization seems more complex, particularly to those coming from the world of DOS and Windows, this appearance belies a flexibility not seen with BSD-style initialization.

BSD, on the other hand, uses a few large scripts to handle all system initialization. This style initialization is a characteristic of Slackware. While currently not as popular as SysV, it performs the same task. Despite BSD's use of just two modes, S, for single user mode, and M, for multiuser mode, the init binaries used by Slackware are the same as those used by Caldera. The difference is in init's configuration table (inittab).

Understanding the boot process

All x86 type computers boot similarly. The details are unimportant for the purposes of this text, and so will be skipped. When a system is powered on, a chain of events occurs that is referred to as "booting" the computer. The term comes from an old saying: "to pull yourself up by your bootstraps." Most computers (but not all), after the initial power on, receive a power good signal from the power supply. The system then begins a self-check process known as the POST (Power On Self Test). This test looks for any system problems that would make the computer nonfunctional, such as bad memory, etc. An acceptable POST normally terminates in one beep from the built-in speaker. Two or more (usually a maximum of eight) beeps indicate a specific problem, and the number of beeps gives an indication of where to look for the problem.

On successful POST completion, a very small loader program runs. This loader program runs another, larger loader that looks at all the acceptable places for other code to load and run. Normally, the boot program will look in the boot sector of the first floppy disk, the boot sector of the first hard disk, and possibly the boot sector of the first CD-ROM, depending on your particular computer. This may be changed in the computer's setup program, generally accessible by pressing a key (such as Delete, Insert, or F2) during the POST process. Older systems required a setup disk to change the setup. See your motherboard of system users manual for details.

If the system finds executable code in one of the boot sectors of the bootable disks (the system will use the first one it finds), it will load and run it. In the case of most Linux systems, this would be LILO (Linux Loader). LILO is a boot loader that can present a user with a selection of operating systems or different Linux kernels to run. Optional arguments may also be passed to the kernel or init.

 This text discusses Intel architecture specifically. Other architectures, such as Sparc or Alpha, etc., use similar boot loaders but with different names, like SILO (Sparc) or MILO (Alpha), etc.

LILO then loads the kernel. A detailed discussion of the Linux kernel-loading process is beyond the scope of this book, so suffice it to say that it is a multi-stage process. On disk, a Linux kernel image is compressed. This image is uncompressed as it loads into memory. It is customary within the Linux community to use a "z" in the name of the kernel image to designate that an image is compressed, as in vmlinuz, zImage, or bzImage. This should tell you that, unlike DOS, this image is only read once during bootup. After bootup, the kernel image on the disk is never read again, so if the kernel image is altered or removed it will not affect the running kernel. In order for someone to make a change to the running system that involves the kernel image on the disk, the system must be restarted for the changes to take effect. Also, the size of the kernel image on disk is not representative of the amount of RAM memory it will occupy.

init: Where system installation begins

Once the kernel is loaded into memory, you have a running Linux system. But it isn't very usable, since the kernel doesn't interact directly with the user. The kernel runs one (and only one) program: init. The program is responsible for everything else, and is referred to as the "parent of all processes." The kernel, then, becomes the system manager, handling kernel space and all requests for resource access.

Kernel space refers to that memory and those functions that belong exclusively to the kernel. This memory is protected. User space is the complement to kernel space, where programs started by users (including root) run.

When init starts, it reads its configuration from a file called 'inittab' (which stands for *initialization table*) located in the /etc directory. Any defaults in inittab are discarded if they've been overridden on the command line. The inittab file describes how to will set up the system. See Listing 7-1 for the default OpenLinux inittab that comes with OpenLinux 2.3.

The *tab* ending on a file, as in inittab, fstab, mtab, and so on, indicates the file is a table, normally a configuration table. In the case of inittab, it contains system initialization information, much as config.sys does in DOS.

Listing 7-1: The /etc/inittab File with line numbers added

```
 1  #
 2  # inittab        This file describes how the INIT process should
set up
 3  #               the system in a certain run-level.
 4  #
 5  # Author:        Miquel van Smoorenburg,
<miquels@drinkel.nl.mugnet.org>
 6  #               Modified for RHS Linux by Marc Ewing and Donnie
Barnes
 7  #               Modified for COL by Raymund Will
 8  #
 9
10  # The runlevels used by COL are:
11  #   0 - halt (Do NOT set initdefault to this)
```

```
12  #   1 - Single user mode (including initialisation of network
interfaces,
13  #      if you do have networking)
14  #   2 - Multiuser, (without NFS-Server und some such)
15  #      (basically the same as 3, if you do not have networking)
16  #   3 - Full multiuser mode
17  #   4 - unused
18  #      (should be equal to 3, for now)
19  #   5 - X11
20  #   6 - reboot (Do NOT set initdefault to this)
21
22  #
23  # Default runlevel.
24  id:5:initdefault:
25
26  # System initialization.
27  s0::sysinit:/bin/bash -c 'C=/sbin/booterd; [ -x $C ] && $C'
28  si::sysinit:/bin/bash -c 'C=/etc/rc.d/rc.modules; [ -x $C ] &&
$C default'
29  s2::sysinit:/bin/bash -c 'C=/etc/rc.d/rc.serial; [ -x $C ] &&
$C'
30  bw::bootwait:/etc/rc.d/rc.boot
31
32  # What to do in single-user mode.
33  ~1:S:wait:/etc/rc.d/rc 1
34  ~~:S:wait:/sbin/sulogin
35
36  l0:0:wait:/etc/rc.d/rc 0
37  l1:1:wait:/etc/rc.d/rc 1
38  l2:2:wait:/etc/rc.d/rc 2
39  l3:3:wait:/etc/rc.d/rc 3
40  l4:4:wait:/etc/rc.d/rc 4
41  l5:5:wait:/etc/rc.d/rc 5
42  l6:6:wait:/etc/rc.d/rc 6
43  # Normally not reached, but fallthrough in case of emergency.
44  z6:6:respawn:/sbin/sulogin
45
46  # Trap CTRL-ALT-DELETE
47  ca:12345:ctrlaltdel:/sbin/shutdown -t3 -r now
48
49  # Action on special keypress (ALT-UpArrow).
50  kb::kbrequest:/bin/echo "Keyboard Request--edit /etc/inittab to
let this work."
51
```

```
52  # When our UPS tells us power has failed, assume we have a few
minutes
53  # of power left.  Schedule a shutdown for 2 minutes from now.
54  # This does, of course, assume you have powerd installed and
your
55  # UPS connected and working correctly.
56  pf::powerfail:/sbin/shutdown -h +5 "Power Failure; System
Shutting Down"
57
58  # If battery is fading fast -- we hurry...
59  p1::powerfailnow:/sbin/shutdown -c 2> /dev/null
60  p2::powerfailnow:/sbin/shutdown -h now "Battery Low..."
61
62  # If power was restored before the shutdown kicked in, cancel
it.
63  po:12345:powerokwait:/sbin/shutdown -c "Power Restored; Shutdown
Cancelled"
64
65
66  # Run gettys in standard runlevels
67  1:12345:respawn:/sbin/getty tty1 VC linux
68  2:2345:respawn:/sbin/getty tty2 VC linux
69  3:2345:respawn:/sbin/getty tty3 VC linux
70  4:2345:respawn:/sbin/getty tty4 VC linux
71  5:2345:respawn:/sbin/getty tty5 VC linux
72  6:2345:respawn:/sbin/getty tty6 VC linux
73
74  # Run kdm in runlevel 5
75  kdm:5:respawn:/opt/kde/bin/kdm -nodaemon > /var/log/kdm 2>&1
```

Since the /etc/inittab file in Listing 7-1 is specific to Caldera OpenLinux 2.3, unless you are running OpenLinux 2.3, yours will almost certainly be different. You will find fewer differences between Caldera and Red Hat (or SuSE or Mandrake or Debian) than you will between any of those distributions and Slackware. But because the init binary is the same on all Linux distributions (compiled from the same source code), the difference is strictly in the inittab file. Examining the differences will help you understand how init works.

inittab specifics

Reading inittab, this text will skip those lines that begin with a #, since these are ignored by init as comments. You should read those comment lines, since they will provide you additional information regarding the inittab author's thought process or examples and explanations. The uncommented lines used by init are formatted similarly to other typical configuration tables, with each column separated by a colon and reads from left to right as follows:

- ◆ id: This first column is a unique identifier for the line. It may be up to four alphanumerics long, but is typically two digits. Older systems had a two-alphanumeric limitation, and most distributions (all I'm aware of) haven't opted to use the extra digits available.

- ◆ runlevel: The second column indicates the runlevel(s) this row is executed for. If null, it is executed for all runlevels. See line 60 in Listing 7-1 for an example of a null field in column two.

- ◆ action: This field can contain any of a predefined range of keywords. The most common is "respawn", but it can also be any one of the following: boot, bootwait, ctrlaltdel, initdefault, kbrequest, off, once, ondemand, powerfail, powerokwait, powerwait, and sysinit.

- ◆ process: The specific process or program to be run.

Each row in inittab has a unique identifier. Traditionally, this is an identifier that is easily associated with the specific action performed. For example, an entry to spawn a getty on the first serial port might use the identifier s1.

The runlevels are identified as 0–6 and A–C (or a–c) by default. Runlevels 0,1, and 6 are special and should not be changed lightly. These correspond to system halt, maintenance (or single user) mode, and system reboot, respectively. Changing runlevel 1, for example, can have far-reaching consequences. Within the init binary, the arguments 1, s, and S are all synonymous. So that if you passed any one of these to init, the effect would be the same. Runlevels 2–5, though, can be customized as desired.

Using telinit is the traditional method to pass commands to init, but it is perfectly acceptable to call init directly. In OpenLinux, telnint is symbolically linked to init. Other distributions may create a hard link. Either way, the same binary is run.

In some distributions, the command "runlevel" (normally installed in /sbin) will give you information about the current and previous runlevels. Output is in the form of previous runlevel and present runlevel: N 3. The N indicates no previous runlevel, as might occur following a reboot. If you make a change to state 2, then reissue the `runlevel` command, you'll see: 3 2. On distributions where the runlevel command is not available, a process status (ps ax) listing will normally show an entry for init with the current runlevel as its argument.

Runlevels are always given as numbers, but you also have several letters that may be passed to init. The Q argument is discussed in the next paragraph. The letters A–C (or a–c, which are functionally equivalent) are used only with the action "ondemand", and "ondemand" is only used with runlevels A–C. An entry in inittab using runlevel A–C with action ondemand can be used by root (only root can call inittab) to spawn a process as required.

The Q (upper or lowercase, they are equivalent) is used to tell init to reread inittab. The inittab file may be changed as often as required, but will be read only under certain circumstances:

- An init spawned processes dies (respawn another?)

- A power daemon sends init a powerfail signal (or the signal is sent from the command line)

- When told to change state by telinit

- When told to reread inittab by root via the Q (uppercase or lowercase) argument to init.

The inittab file from top to bottom

Follow along with the discussion by referring to Listing 7-1.

You already understand the format for inittab (id:runlevel(s):action:process), but examining a few lines will reinforce how it works in practice.

Skip down to line 24 and look at the identity id. Normally, this line would only be executed for runlevel 5. However, the action field, which is initdefault, tells init to take that value as its default runlevel (unless overridden on the command line). In Caldera OpenLinux (and several other distributions), starting in runlevel 5 presents you with a graphical login. So if you don't want to be presented with a graphical login screen, this runlevel should be changed to 3. This is also true of Red Hat Linux, but under Debian, the default runlevel is 2,and the graphical login is not related to a runlevel, but to whether or not the xdm rc script is configured and run.

 Since this text deals with Caldera's OpenLinux, this inittab is specific to OpenLinux and may not reflect your system's setup. If you are running older versions of OpenLinux, your inittab will also differ. But the concepts remain the same.

Below the default runlevel line (line 24 in Listing 7-1), on lines 27 through 30, are the system initialization script calls. From the names of the scripts, you can surmise that these scripts load modules, set up the serial ports, and perform other boot-time-only functions. Line 30's action is bootwait, where the system stops and waits until this script has completed before continuing. That is, the four lines

(27–30) will run simultaneously, but the system will wait to run anything else until it completes the bootwait action. This allows certain preparations to complete before the system starts to spawn daemons and logins.

Lines 33 and 34 call two scripts that will run whenever the system enters runlevel 1, the maintenance (single user) mode. The 'sulogin' program is a special program to make your system a little more secure by preventing just anyone who can gain physical access to the machine from rebooting into single user mode and gaining access to the system without knowing the root password. Without this line, booting into single user mode would present a root shell to the user without prompting for a password. However, this will not prevent a sophisticated user from breaking into the system if she has physical access to the machine. In fact, one of the ways to bypass 'sulogin' is discussed in the next chapter.

Lines 36 through 42 run whenever you change to the runlevel. Each runlevel change will run the rc script using as an argument the particular runlevel (by number) being entered (this does not happen for changes to runlevels A–C). So a change from runlevel 5 to runlevel 3 would force execution of line 39.

Line 44 is a safety net designed to present a root password prompt in case a machine doesn't properly reboot when it enters runlevel 6. This is only precautionary.

Line 47 traps the keyboard sequence Ctrl+Alt+Del and performs a shutdown and reboot. If desired, this line may be modified to change the -r to a -h to halt the system; or you can just remove the -r to bring the system into single user mode with a root prompt.

Line 48 traps the keyboard sequence Alt+Up arrow. Currently it will echo the notice that this needs to be configured before use. On a default Caldera setup with bash, this particular command sequence will be ignored. (This is also true of most other distributions that use the bash shell as their default shell.) So first the key mappings will need to be changed so bash passes the key sequence without interpreting it. Once that is done, change the process portion of the line (the column with the echo command) substituting the command you want to run for the echo command.

Lines 56, 59, 60, and 63 will be of interest to those who have a UPS compatible with powerd, the power daemon. The power daemon can monitor the serial port and perform the actions as documented in inittab. The power daemon isn't distributed with Caldera OpenLinux. The problem is that few UPSs currently work with the power daemon, no matter which distribution you have. If you have or buy a Linux-compatible power daemon, you'll want to take advantage of this feature in inittab.

Lines 67 through 72 spawn gettys to the virtual terminals (VT)s. Note that in single user mode only one VT is available. If you want to save some memory, you can run fewer VTs (I suggest one) in runlevel 5; they are seldom needed with the graphical login. You can increase the number of VTs simply by adding more lines (with unique IDs, of course).

Notice that ca, kb, pf, p1, p2, and po run regardless of the runlevel (note the null values in the second column in Listing 7-1, lines 50, 56, 59, and 60). When the runlevel column is null, then the process is run in every runlevel.

Finally, runlevel 5 spawns KDM (the KDE Display Manager) as listed in Listing 7-1 on line 75. On Red Hat systems this may be XDM or gdm. On Debian systems, they have always used runlevel 2 and spawned xdm as a separate process package like any other server.

If your system has a default runlevel other than 1, but your system boots into maintenance mode, then the rc.boot script has detected a problem with a hard disk that requires you to manually run fsck. When finished, the system will reboot and try to enter multi-user mode again.

The rc scripts, part one

Under OpenLinux, you'll find all the system initialization scripts in /etc/rc.d. This subdirectory has more subdirectories — one for each runlevel: rc0.d - rc6.d, and init.d. Within the /etc/rc.d/rc#.d subdirectories (where the # is replace by a single digit number) are symbolic links to the master scripts stored in /etc/rc.d/init.d (see Listing 7-2). The scripts in init.d take an argument of start or stop, and occasionally reload or restart. While restart/reload arguments are not difficult to implement, at least one daemon (dhcp) does not properly reread its configuration file with a simple SIGHUP (hangup signal, which means: Reread your configuration files and continue to work but with the new configuration).

Signals are used to tell running processes to perform a certain action. The most common use is to tell a process running in the background to exit. Available signals range from 1–31. The most commonly used ones are SIGTERM (terminate), which correspond to a signal 15. Others are SIGKILL (signal 9), SIGHUP (signal 1), and so on. See `man 7 signal` for a complete list. These signals may be sent to a process' PID (process identification number) in one of two formats, via the signal name or the signal number as follows: kill -SIGHUP <PID> or kill -1 <PID>. If no signal is given, the SIGTERM (signal 15) is assumed.

Listing 7-2: Directory listing starting at /etc/rc.d/ (partial)

```
drwxr-xr-x   2 root      root       1024 Aug 30 07:25 init.d
-rwxr-xr-x   1 root      root       5336 Aug 16 22:45 rc
-rwxr-xr-x   1 root      root       8930 Jul  7 08:55 rc.boot
-rwxr-xr-x   1 root      root        478 Aug 27 08:48 rc.local
-rwxr-xr-x   1 root      root       2809 Jul 14 16:45 rc.modules
-rwxr-xr-x   1 root      root       5586 Aug 16 22:45 rc.orig
```

```
-rwxr-xr-x   1 root      root       10903 Mar 12  1999 rc.serial
drwxr-xr-x   2 root      root        1024 Aug 11 23:04 rc0.d
drwxr-xr-x   2 root      root        1024 Aug 11 23:04 rc1.d
drwxr-xr-x   2 root      root        1024 Aug 11 23:04 rc2.d
drwxr-xr-x   2 root      root        1024 Aug 11 23:04 rc3.d
drwxr-xr-x   2 root      root        1024 Aug 11 23:04 rc4.d
drwxr-xr-x   2 root      root        1024 Aug 30 07:25 rc5.d
drwxr-xr-x   2 root      root        1024 Aug 30 07:25 rc6.d
-rwxr-xr-x   1 root      root         846 Jun 29 11:02 unconfigured.sh
init.d/
-rwxr-xr-x   1 root      root        2144 Jul 14 16:56 bigfs
-rwxr-xr-x   1 root      root         864 Jan 28  1999 cron
-rwxr-xr-x   1 root      root        1364 Apr 13 13:38 dhcpd
-rwxr-xr-x   1 root      root        6920 Jul 14 16:55 functions
-rwxr-xr-x   1 root      root         833 Jul 14 22:46 gpm
-rwxr-xr-x   1 root      root        1296 Aug 16 22:45 halt
-rwxr-xr-x   1 root      root         983 May 11 11:24 httpd
-rwxr-xr-x   1 root      root        1243 Jul 14 15:52 inet
-rwxr-xr-x   1 root      root         978 Jul  7 05:30 keytable
lrwxrwxrwx   1 root      root          11 Aug  5 12:35 local -> ../rc.local
-rwxr-xr-x   1 root      root         804 Jul 14 23:09 logoutd
-rwxr-xr-x   1 root      root         931 Nov  4  1998 lpd
-rwxr-xr-x   1 root      root        1720 Jul 14 22:04 mta
-rwxr-xr-x   1 root      root        1294 Jul 27 23:16 named
-rwxr-xr-x   1 root      root        2260 Jul 14 16:05 netmount
-rwxr-xr-x   1 root      root        2072 Jul 14 16:23 network
-rw-r-xr-x   1 root      root         791 Jul 27 23:22 news
-r-xr-xr-x   1 root      root        1863 Jun 22 07:57 nfs
-rwxr-xr-x   1 root      root        1232 Jan  7  1998 nis-client
-rwxr-xr-x   1 root      root         831 Jan  8  1998 nis-server
-rwxr-xr-x   1 root      root        1489 Apr  3 00:26 ntp
-r-xr-xr-x   1 root      root        3157 Aug 27 10:55 pcmcia
-rwxr-xr-x   1 root      root         649 May 26  1998 ppp
lrwxrwxrwx   1 root      root           4 Aug  5 12:35 reboot -> halt
-rwxr-xr-x   1 root      root         238 Oct  2  1997 rmnologin
-rwxr-xr-x   1 root      root         780 Oct  2  1997 rstatd
-rwxr-xr-x   1 root      root        1130 Jul 14 22:06 rusersd
-rwxr-xr-x   1 root      root        1130 Jul 14 22:05 rwalld
-rwxr-xr-x   1 root      root        1130 Jul 14 22:06 rwhod
-rwxr-xr-x   1 root      root        1211 Jul 15 03:10 samba
-rwxr-xr-x   1 root      root         969 Nov 25  1997 single
-rwxr-xr-x   1 root      root        1159 Apr  9  1998 skeleton
-rwxr-xr-x   1 root      root         607 Apr 29 04:15 skipped
-rwxr-xr-x   1 root      root        1714 Jul 14 20:08 squid
```

```
-rwxr-xr-x    1 root      root          1147 Mar 25 06:28 syslog
-rwxr-xr-x    1 root      root          1060 Mar 16  1999 urandom
-r-xr-xr-x    1 root      root          6949 Aug 30 07:25 vmware
-rwxr-xr-x    1 root      root           259 Jul 21 09:27 webmin
-rwxr-xr-x    1 root      root           990 Aug 10 17:48 xdm
-rwxr-xr-x    1 root      root           948 Mar 25 07:53 zap
rc2.d:
lrwxrwxrwx    1 root      root            14 Aug  5 12:35 K05news -> ../init.d/news
lrwxrwxrwx    1 root      root            15 Aug  5 12:35 K09samba ->
../init.d/samba
lrwxrwxrwx    1 root      root            15 Aug  5 23:51 K12squid ->
../init.d/squid
lrwxrwxrwx    1 root      root            13 Aug  5 12:35 K25gpm -> ../init.d/gpm
lrwxrwxrwx    1 root      root            15 Aug  5 09:01 K25httpd ->
../init.d/httpd
lrwxrwxrwx    1 root      root            17 Aug  5 12:35 K30logoutd ->
../init.d/logoutd
lrwxrwxrwx    1 root      root            16 Aug  5 12:35 K39rwalld ->
../init.d/rwalld
lrwxrwxrwx    1 root      root            16 Aug  5 12:35 K40rstatd ->
../init.d/rstatd
lrwxrwxrwx    1 root      root            15 Aug  5 12:35 K44dhcpd ->
../init.d/dhcpd
lrwxrwxrwx    1 root      root            17 Aug  5 12:35 K47rusersd ->
../init.d/rusersd
lrwxrwxrwx    1 root      root            15 Aug  5 12:35 K48rwhod ->
../init.d/rwhod
lrwxrwxrwx    1 root      root            13 Aug  5 12:35 K50mta -> ../init.d/mta
lrwxrwxrwx    1 root      root            13 Aug  5 12:35 K60nfs -> ../init.d/nfs
lrwxrwxrwx    1 root      root            13 Aug  5 12:35 K70ntp -> ../init.d/ntp
lrwxrwxrwx    1 root      root            17 Aug  5 12:35 K73ipxripd ->
../init.d/ipxripd
lrwxrwxrwx    1 root      root            20 Aug  5 12:35 K79nis-client ->
../init.d/nis-client
lrwxrwxrwx    1 root      root            20 Aug  5 12:35 K80nis-server ->
../init.d/nis-server
lrwxrwxrwx    1 root      root            14 Aug  5 12:35 K85inet -> ../init.d/inet
lrwxrwxrwx    1 root      root            15 Aug  5 21:25 K90named ->
../init.d/named
lrwxrwxrwx    1 root      root            17 Aug  5 12:35 S01network ->
../init.d/network
lrwxrwxrwx    1 root      root            16 Aug  5 12:35 S01pcmcia ->
../init.d/pcmcia
```

```
lrwxrwxrwx   1 root      root           16 Aug  5 12:35 S05syslog ->
../init.d/syslog
lrwxrwxrwx   1 root      root           17 Aug  5 12:35 S05urandom ->
../init.d/urandom
lrwxrwxrwx   1 root      root           18 Aug  5 12:35 S20netmount ->
../init.d/netmount
lrwxrwxrwx   1 root      root           13 Aug  5 09:02 S26ipx -> ../init.d/ipx
lrwxrwxrwx   1 root      root           13 Aug  5 12:35 S35lpd -> ../init.d/lpd
lrwxrwxrwx   1 root      root           14 Aug  5 12:35 S40cron -> ../init.d/cron
lrwxrwxrwx   1 root      root           13 Aug  5 12:35 S41atd -> ../init.d/atd
lrwxrwxrwx   1 root      root           18 Aug  5 12:35 S75keytable ->
../init.d/keytable
lrwxrwxrwx   1 root      root           15 Aug  5 12:35 S98local ->
../init.d/local
lrwxrwxrwx   1 root      root           15 Aug  5 12:35 S99bigfs ->
../init.d/bigfs
lrwxrwxrwx   1 root      root           19 Aug  5 12:35 S99rmnologin ->
../init.d/rmnologin
lrwxrwxrwx   1 root      root           17 Aug  5 12:35 S99skipped ->
../init.d/skipped
lrwxrwxrwx   1 root      root           13 Aug  5 12:35 S99zap -> ../init.d/zap
```

The files in the /etc/rc.d/rc#.d directories all begin with either an S or a K for start or kill, respectively, a number that indicates a relative ASCII order for the scripts, and the script name – commonly the same name as the master script found in init.d to which it is linked. For example, you might see S35lpd. This is a symbolic link to ../init.d/lpd, and is used by rc? to run the lpd script in init.d with the argument start, which starts up the line printer daemon. The scripts can also be called from the command line:

```
/etc/rc.d/init.d/lpd start
```

The nice part about SysV initialization is that it is easy for root to start, stop, and, in some cases, restart or reload a daemon or process subsystem from the command line simply by calling the script in init.d with the appropriate argument. Only root can perform this action. If you are using a BSD-style initialization process you must know how to start the daemon or process subsystem from a command line, which isn't always as easy as just executing the daemon.

When not called from a command line with an argument, the /etc/rc.d/rc script determines what to run and how based on the previous and current runlevel. For example, if we are in runlevel 3 and change to runlevel 2, the /etc/rc.d/rc script uses the runlevel command and notes differences in the two directories corresponding to the two runlevels to determine what to do. Any process subsystems that are running that need to be stopped are stopped by calling the appropriate kill script, and any that are not running that need to be started, are started by the execution of the corresponding start scripts. The rc script will always run the Knn scripts from lowest to highest, and then the Snn scripts also in ascending order. This ensures that the correct daemons are running in each runlevel, and are stopped and started in the correct order. For example, you shouldn't start sendmail (mta) or the Apache Web server (httpd) before you start networking. By the same token, you'll want to stop sendmail and Apache before you stop networking.

The above is somewhat Caldera-centric, since Red Hat and others don't compare directories, they just run the kill and start scripts found in the subdirectory corresponding to the new runlevel.

The rc scripts, part two

Now you understand how basic system initialization works, from the kernel to init. This section will extend your knowledge to the process packages that init executes for each runlevel via lines 36–42 in Listing 7-1. Because the kernel starts init, init runs as root. Because init runs as root, the scripts that start process packages also run as root. So unless the process packages are written to run a particular process as a different (usually non-privileged) user, everything started as part of the process package will run as root. If a malicious user managed to insert a command to start a program that captured keystrokes to a file and periodically mailed that file to himself, he would eventually have every active username and password on the system. If a user could create a link in one of the /etc/rc.d/rc[1–5].d/ directories to a file anywhere on the system (including her $HOME directory), that linked file would be run as root during system initialization.

 All files below /etc/rc.d/ run as root during bootup (on Debian systems, these would be the rc.boot/, rc[0–6].d/, and init.d/ subdirectories directly under /etc). Links that are followed, whether they remain within /etc/rc.d/ or not, will execute programs as root. Any new scripts or changes to existing scripts would run at the next system restart or runlevel change. Ensure the directories and files used during system initialization cannot be written to by anyone except root.

Following is a very brief overview of some key scripts including one start-stop script. This text is not intended to teach script reading. For more information, please refer to a book on shell scripting. But a look at these scripts will give you a idea of just how easy it would be to make an inappropriate change and start a malicious program. The first key script is /etc/rc.d/rc (see Listing 7-3). The line numbers don't appear in the actual script; they are for reference.

Listing 7-3: The rc script (with line numbers included for reference)

```
1 #!/bin/bash
 2 #
 3 # rc   This file is responsible for starting/stopping
 4 #      services when the runlevel changes.
 5 #
 6 #      Temporary feature:
 7 #      If the action for a particular feature in the new run-
level
 8 #      is the same as the action in the previous run-level, this
 9 #      script will neither start nor start that feature, since
that
10 #      would have no effect except to thrash the system for no
reason.
11 #      Once all scripts are converted to use start-stop-daemon
12 #      to _start_ their daemons (most of them only use it to kill
13 #      them), this feature can be removed.
14 #
15 #      $Id: rc,v 1.7 1999/07/14 21:36:04 ray Exp $
16 #
17 #      Author: Miquel van Smoorenburg, <miquels@drinkel.ow.org>
18 #      Hacked to bits by Bruce Perens <Bruce@Pixar.com>
19 #      Modified for COL by Raymund Will <ray@lst.de>
20 #
21
22 export RC_DEBUG=false
23 export RC_VERBOSE=true
24 LOG=/dev/tty12
25
26 true() { return 0; }
27 false() { return 1; }
28 Echo() {
29   local a=$1; shift
30   local o=$1; shift
31   local i
32
33   echo -n "$a" > $LOG
34   for i in "$@"; do
35     echo -n " '$i'" > $LOG
36   done
37   echo "$o" > $LOG
38 }
39
40   # check for new-style boot-logger
41   export SVIBooter=/sbin/booter
```

```
42    [ -x $SVIBooter ] || SVIBooter=false
43
44    if $SVIBooter test; then
45      export SVIuseBooter=true
46      CMDS="add start"
47
48      # redirect STDOUT and STDERR
49      exec - > $LOG 2>&1
50
51      #DEBUGGING
52      Booter() {
53        local c=$1; shift
54        local s
55        local i
56
57        case "$c" in
58         add)
59           s="$1"; shift
60  eval "$s" $c
61  ;;
62         start)
63           s="$1"; shift
64           eval "$s" $c "$@"
65  case $? in
66    0) $SVIBooter ok;;
67    1) $SVIBooter fail;;
68    2) $SVIBooter skip;;
69    *) $SVIBooter "N/A";;
70  esac
71  ;;
72         stop)
73  s="$1"; shift
74  Echo "# Booter " "." "$s" $c "$@"
75           eval "$s" $c "$@"
76  ;;
77         *)
78           $SVIBooter $c "$@"
79  ;;
80        esac
81      }
82      [ -z "$PREVLEVEL" ] && {PREVLEVEL=N
83    else
84      SVIuseBooter=false
85      CMDS="start"
86
```

Continued

```
 87     # Set onlcr to avoid staircase effect.
 88     stty onlcr 0>&1
 89
 90     Booter() {
 91       local c="$1"; shift
 92       [ "$c" != "start" -a "$c" != "stop" ] && return 0
 93       local s="$1"; shift
 94       Echo "# eval " "." "$s" $c "$@"
 95       eval "$s" $c "$@"
 96     }
 97     fi
 98
 99     # Now find out what the current and what the previous runlevel
are.
100
101     runlevel=$RUNLEVEL
102     # Get first argument. Set new runlevel to this argument.
103     [ -n "$1" ] && runlevel=$1
104
105     previous=$PREVLEVEL
106
107     Echo "runlevel=$runlevel previous=$previous" "."
108     export runlevel previous
109
110     RCD=/etc/rc.d
111     # Is there an rc directory for this new runlevel?
112     if [ -d "$RCD/rc$runlevel.d" ]; then
113       avoid="" # A list of start scripts I don't have to run.
114
115       # First, run the KILL scripts.
116       if [ "$previous" != N ]; then
117         for i in $RCD/rc$runlevel.d/K[0-9][0-9]*; do
118           # Check if the script is there.
119           [ -f "$i" ] || continue
120
121           suffix=${i#$RCD/rc$runlevel.d/K[0-9][0-9]}
122
123           # Generate the name of the start script corresponding
124           # to this stop script, the start script in the previous
125           # level, and the stop script in the previous level.
126           # Check these files, and see if the previous level's
127           # files are links to the ones for this level.
128           # If they are, this level treats this feature the same
129           # as the previous level, and I don't have to run these
130           # files.
```

```
131          stopIt=true
132          start=$RCD/rc$runlevel.d/S[0-9][0-9]$suffix
133          previous_start=$RCD/rc$previous.d/S[0-9][0-9]$suffix
134          previous_stop=$RCD/rc$previous.d/K[0-9][0-9]$suffix
135
136          if [ -f $previous_stop ] && [ $i -ef $previous_stop ];
then
137            stopIt=false
138            if [ -f $start ] || [ -f $previous_start ]; then
139              if [ -f $start ] &&
140                 [ -f $previous_start ] &&
141                 [ $start -ef $previous_start ]; then
142              stopIt=true
143              else
144                 avoid=$avoid" "$start
145              fi
146            fi
147          fi
148
149          # Kill it.
150          $stopIt && Booter stop $i
151        done
152     fi
153
154  Booter list "RUNLEVEL Run-level change..."
155  Booter add_menu "BLANK4"
156  Booter add_menu "T4 Entering run-level $runlevel:"
157  for cmd in $CMDS; do
158
159    # Now run the START scripts for this runlevel.
160    for i in $RCD/rc$runlevel.d/S*; do
161      # Check if the script is there.
162      [ -f "$i" ] || continue
163
164      startIt=true
165      case " $avoid " in
166        *\ $i\ *) startIt=false;;
167      esac
168      if $startIt; then
169        suffix=${i#$RCD/rc$runlevel.d/S[0-9][0-9]}
170        previous_start=$RCD/rc$previous.d/S[0-9][0-9]$suffix
171        stop=$RCD/rc$runlevel.d/K[0-9][0-9]$suffix
172        if [ -f $previous_start ] &&
173           [ $i -ef $previous_start ] &&
174           [ ! -f $stop ]; then                    Continued
```

```
175              startIt=false
176         fi
177      fi
178
179      $startIt && Booter $cmd $i
180    done
181
182    if [ "$cmd" != "add" ]; then
183       Booter complete RUNLEVEL
184    else
185       Booter end
186       Booter activate RUNLEVEL
187    fi
188  done
189  fi
190
191 [ $SVIuseBooter = false ] && exit 0
192
193
194 if [ $runlevel != 5 ]; then
195   sleep 1
196   /usr/bin/chvt 1
197 else
198   /sbin/booter list "FINAL"
199   /sbin/booter add_menu "BLANK5"
200   /sbin/booter add "KDE Starting KDE"
201   /sbin/booter end
202   /sbin/booter activate "FINAL"
203   /sbin/booter item "KDE"
204   sleep 1
205   ( trap "" SIGHUP
206     sleep 10
207     echo -e "\n\nPlease switch to a different virtual console
for login!\n\n"
208   ) > /dev/tty7 &
209 fi
210
211 Booter quit
212 # eof /etc/rc.d/rc
```

Lines beginning with # are remarks (except the first line, which designates the program used to interpret the script) and will be ignored when the script runs. Lines 2–117 initialize variables, determine the current and previous runlevels, and compare the start-stop scripts in each of these corresponding /etc/rc.d/rc{runlevel}.d subdirectories.

Then Lines 119 through the end first execute those kill scripts to stop running process subsystems not needed for the new runlevel. Then, the script starts any needed process subsystem(s) for the new runlevel that aren't already running.

The next script we'll look at is a typical shell script found in /etc/rc.d/init.d used to start a process subsystem. These scripts are linked to from the various runlevel directories. The script in Listing 7-4 is representative of others in init.d/.

Listing 7–4: The named init script

```
 1 #!/bin/sh
 2 #
 3 # named          This shell script takes care of starting and
stopping
 4 #               named (BIND DNS server).
 5 #
 6
 7 NAME=named
 8 DAEMON=/usr/sbin/$NAME
 9
10 # Source function library.
11 . /etc/rc.d/init.d/functions
12
13 # Source networking configuration.
14 . /etc/sysconfig/network
15
16 # Check that networking is up.
17 [ ${NETWORKING} = "no" ] && exit 0
18
19 [ -r /etc/sysconfig/daemons/$SUBSYS ] || ONBOOT=Yes
20 [ ! -r /etc/sysconfig/daemons/$SUBSYS ] || .
/etc/sysconfig/daemons/$SUBSYS
21 [ "$ONBOOT" = "no" -a "$PROBABLY" = "booting" ] && exit 0
22
23 [ -x $DAEMON ] || exit 0
24
25
26 # See how we were called.
27 case "$1" in
28  start)
29   [ -e /var/lock/subsys/$SUBSYS ] && exit 1
30
31   [ -f /etc/named.conf ] || exit 0
32
33   # Start daemons.
34   echo -n "Starting BIND DNS server: "
35   start-stop-daemon -S -n $NAME -x $DAEMON -- $OPTIONS
```

```
36    echo "."
37    touch /var/lock/subsys/$SUBSYS
38    ;;
39
40  stop)
41    [ -e /var/lock/subsys/$SUBSYS ] || exit 0
42
43    # Stop daemons.
44    echo -n "Stopping BIND DNS server: "
45    start-stop-daemon -K -p /var/run/$NAME.pid -n $NAME
46    echo "."
47    rm -f /var/lock/subsys/$SUBSYS
48    ;;
49
50  restart)
51    [ -e /var/lock/subsys/$SUBSYS ] || exit 0
52
53    echo -n "Re-starting BIND DNS server: "
54    start-stop-daemon -K -s 1 -p /var/run/$NAME.pid -n $NAME
55    echo "."
56    ;;
57
58  *)
59    echo "Usage: named {start|stop|restart}"
60    exit 1
61  esac
62
63  exit 0
```

Again, when the script runs it will ignore lines beginning with "#". But you should read them as they will provide insight into the operation of the script so that you can better understand what is going on.

Lines 7 and 8 initialize some variables, and lines 11 and 14 read in (source) some global variables from the system configuration directory (not found on all distributions). Line 17 ensures that the network has started and exits the program if it hasn't (there's not much sense running a name server without a network). Lines 19–21 check to see if the system configuration files want named started during system initialization, and line 23 ensures that the program exists and is executable. In each case, a false reply will terminate the script.

Then the argument passed to the script is checked. If it is "start", then lines 29–38 execute. If it is "stop", then line 41 checks that the daemon is running and if so executes lines 44–48. If the argument was "restart", line 51 checks to see if the daemon is running, and if so, executes lines 53–56 which send a signal 1 (SIGHUP) to the daemon to restart it (have it reread its configuration file and continue running).

Finally, if the argument was not one of the above (or no argument was provided), a usage message is displayed on the screen.

The above outline will hold true for all rc scripts in all SysV using distributions. The details will vary from distribution to distribution, but each will normally offer a skeleton for those who need to write their own SysV initialization scripts. But a good generic script will run on any system. BSD style systems like Slackware were not covered, but they also use scripts for system initialization. A handful of larger scripts do the job of the multitude of SysV scripts, but without the start/stop/restart/reload flexibility. These BSD scripts will start a number of daemons or process subsystems at once the way DOS does with config.sys or autoexec.bat.

Summary

This chapter covered how System V initialization works. While it concentrated on Caldera OpenLinux 2.3, the information is applicable to a large extent to all distributions that use SysV initialization. You learned how the system gets everything set up and enters the default init runlevel, and that a runlevel is a software-implemented way to organize groups of process subsystems. You also learned where to look for the daemons or process subsystems that are stopped and started in each runlevel.

You also learned that if the bad guys can put a script into the initialization directories, change a script already there, or put in a link in one of the runlevel directories, they can start any program they want during system initialization.

Chapter 8

Physical security and console attacks

IN THIS CHAPTER

- ◆ Understanding pre-boot vulnerabilities
- ◆ Understanding LILO
- ◆ Understanding emergency boot options
- ◆ Recovering the root password
- ◆ Backing up your system
- ◆ Protecting your network

AFTER READING THE LAST chapter, you should have a good idea of where and how someone who can gain physical access to a machine can compromise it. This chapter will show you just how to do that (in case you missed one or two vulnerabilities). Given the ease with which it can be gained, you'll see why it's true that anyone who has physical access to a system "owns" it.

Pre-kernel boot

Your system is vulnerable to a console attack at any time, even before the system boots. All that is required is for the system to restart. Restart could be precipitated by a normal shutdown or by someone throwing the BRS (Big Red Switch). Kicking the power cord will produce the same result. So it isn't very difficult to get a system to shut down. Once the system is down, it is normally a trivial matter to reboot the system using a floppy disk or CD-ROM.

I hear you you can simply go into the BIOS and make the only bootable option the "c:" drive (/dev/hdc) MBR. Then, to prevent a change to that parameter, password-protect the Setup screen. Now, it will take someone with the setup password to enter the system, change the setup, and boot the system.

Choosing a password for setup is not the same as choosing one for root. Making it the same as root's password is probably a good idea, since the setup password will rarely, if ever, be used, so is prone to be forgotten. However, if you do this, be sure to change the setup password when you change root's password, or you'll find yourself several changes behind.

If you find, after several months (or years), that you've forgotten the password to enter the system setup, don't worry. You'll want to consult your motherboard's documentation (if you still have it), but look for a jumper that will allow you to clear the setup password (or initialize the entire CMOS setup). Most newer motherboards include that feature. Older ones won't. So failing that, you'll need to disconnect the power to the system and remove the CMOS battery and wait about 20 minutes (30 minutes if you want to be sure). This will return the CMOS (where the password is kept) to its factory settings. This also means that all other custom CMOS settings will be lost. But remember, if you can do it, anyone else who has physical access can too.

Keep a screen print of the CMOS setup screens locked away somewhere safe in case you lose the CMOS setup. Apart from your having to deliberately reset the CMOS, the CMOS battery could die and take the CMOS settings with it the first time you have to take the system down for any length of time.

LILO

After the system finishes its POST, it will look for a system to boot. If you've told setup to look only to the "c:" disk, then it will access the master boot record of that disk for code to load. This text will continue under the assumption that Linux is the only operating system on the host and is using the native LILO software. Most operating system boot loaders work in a similar manner and have similar options. Those with dual-boot system (Linux and Windows, Solaris, BeOS, OS/2, etc.) will normally have a choice of systems presented during boot either by LILO or another boot manager. For more information on these, please see the instructions that come with your boot manager, or in the case of LILO, a good system administration guide.

By default, when LILO is configured on the MBR, your /etc/lilo.conf will contain a couple of standard lines in the global section:

```
prompt
timeout = 50
```

These two options serve two functions: They ensure that you can access your choice of boot images (OS kernels) and/or they put boot time options on the command line. The first lilo.conf option (prompt) tells lilo you want a "LILO:" prompt at bootup. Without this option, no prompt is shown. The second option tells lilo how long (in tenths of a second) to wait before booting the default kernel. This allows an unattended reboot for your system. Once this time passes (in the example above, five seconds), the default kernel image boots.

If you use the prompt option in /etc/lilo.conf and forget to add (or remove) the timeout= option, your system will not be capable of an unattended re-boot.

If you remove both lines, the system will simply boot directly into the default kernel image. You will not get the chance to select a kernel image or pass any boot-time parameters in. So all desired boot-time parameters must be in the "image" section of lilo.conf.

If you do make lilo boot directly into the default kernel image, when you change your kernel be sure to change this option (or have a boot disk with the old kernel ready) until you're sure this new image will boot properly.

If removing these two options is not possible, perhaps because you have a dual-boot system (be it multiple Linux kernels or different operating systems), you can password protect, on an image-by-image basis, any kernel images you want to.

By default, /etc/lilo.conf is world readable. If you password protect one or more kernel images, you'll probably want to `chmod 600` this file. Alternately, after you run lilo, you can move the /etc/lilo.conf file onto a floppy for safekeeping because it is not required to boot the system. Remember that if the default kernel image (the first listed in lilo.conf) is password protected, the system will not be able to boot unattended, so you may want to only password protect non-default kernel images.

Emergency boot options

Sometimes, during even the most careful kernel rebuild or editing of initialization files, something will prevent the system initialization procedure from finishing. Editing inittab or any of the rc scripts requires some degree of caution. But even the best tests cannot simulate a complete system reboot, and a script that may appear to function properly after a system initialization may fail to execute, or worse, hang, during system reboot. The possible reasons are diverse, but usually involve getting things out of sequence.

For example, a script created to start the kerneld process early in the boot sequence on a system that ran a 1.2.13 kernel with modules. When I upgraded the system to a 2.0.25 kernel, I used the same script. Unfortunately, the boot process hung loading the newer kerneld required by the upgraded kernel. I found out that with the newer kerneld, it needed to know the hostname of the system, which the system did not yet know. Putting the hostname discovery process early in the initialization sequence (in /etc/rc.d/rc.boot) solved the problem.

But things like this can happen to anyone. Something as simple as fat-fingering a key or forgetting to full-path programs without declaring a PATH variable in a script can leave you in the lurch.

 Not all apparent system "hangs" are true hangs. One thing you'll want to do before you panic and hit <reset> or power off is give the system time for IP to timeout. This is generally 2 minutes, but could be a little longer. If you remove the vga=274 line, you'll see each rc script as it runs. Note the last one listed for later troubleshooting.

Fortunately, if you have the `prompt` and `timeout` options in lilo.conf, you can pass boot-time parameters to init. When the system boots and you see LILO:, you can hit the <Shift> key and then the <Tab> key to see the kernel labels available for booting. You can then type a kernel label and follow it by any parameters you need to boot the system. Any parameters the kernel needs are used and discarded: for example if you have 128MB of RAM installed, but only want the system to use 96MB of it, you need to pass that to the kernel in the form mem=96MB (or however much RAM you want). But if you pass the `-b` switch, the kernel won't use this, and will pass it on to init. The same goes for any single-digit number or the letters s or q in either upper or lower case.

 Use the `-b` option to boot into maintenance mode without running any rc scripts. For use when scripts may hang the system.

By passing any legitimate runlevel number or letter to init, you are overriding the defaults in inittab. Most of these numbers or letters do exactly what they would do if passed from a command line on a running system. But the -b argument is special. It is the emergency boot parameter. The -b parameter tells init to read the inittab, but not execute any rc scripts. It also forces init to put the system into runlevel 1 (maintenance mode). So no rc scripts will be executed. You may mount the system read-write and fix it. One exception to not executing any inittab commands is any process id starting with ~, such as the two id's ~~ and ~1. If you add or change any script with an id beginning with ~, it would be a good idea to check it as another id first. You won't find this feature in the man pages: it's undocumented.

If you look back at the default inittab in Chapter 7, Listing 7-1, you'll see the following two lines:

```
~1:S:wait:/etc/rc.d/rc 1
~~:S:wait:/sbin/sulogin
```

Regardless of the -b option, these lines will be executed. The second line makes the system present a root password login prompt. But you're still not completely safe.

 This next paragraph is about booting directly to a shell. Performing this procedure can cause irreparable corruption to the file system. This is a last-resort option only!

If, however, despite your best efforts, you find that the boot process hangs even with the -b option to LILO, or you've forgotten the root password, don't despair. At the LILO prompt, you may pass the parameter init=/bin/sh. This argument will be used by the kernel itself. Remember the kernel runs one and only one program before it goes into the background: init. If you pass the above argument to lilo, the kernel will run a shell as its only program. This is very dangerous, but will allow you to mount the root file system read-write (mount -n -o remount,rw /), change /etc/inittab or /etc/shadow, then sync and reboot. In this case, I recommend calling sync twice, then rebooting. The calls to sync flush the dirty buffers to disk, ensuring the changes you made to any files are written to disk. This method of fixing a critical file should be used as a last resort before a reinstall, because it could corrupt your disk making a reinstall inevitable.

Root password recovery

Before you attempt the above, your best bet is to use the Caldera OpenLinux boot disk (or boot disk from your distribution) or the install CD-ROM (most are bootable) and allow it to boot up. Once you get to the screen that asks you to choose a disk to install Linux to, stop. Continuing on that screen will run fdisk – not what you want to do. Consult your distribution's guide for specifics, but they should be similar. Basically, you want to boot into your distribution's install disk, but then get to a command prompt and continue as below.

Instead, at this point, press <Ctrl>+<Alt>+<F2> (Caldera-specific, your distribution may vary) and log in as root (no password will be needed). Caldera (other distributions as well) uses a ramdisk and it contains a complete root file system, including a directory call "target". If you mount your old root file system on "target", cd to target/etc, you can then edit the shadow password file. For now, just remove the hashed password (leaving nothing, not even a space, between the two colons that separate the fields). Then cd back up to "/", unmount the file system you mounted on /target (very important), and reboot the system into your old file system. You will be able to log in as root without a password.

 Your system is very vulnerable without a root password. When you perform this procedure you should be disconnected from the network (unplug the Ethernet cable) and should immediately reset the root password.

Remember that anyone who has physical access to your system can do all the things that are outlined above.

Backups

Perhaps the most overlooked area of system security is backup. If you follow any Linux list at all, you'll see the phrase "You do have a backup, don't you?" or similar at some point. Backups are recommended for everyone, even home users. But not everyone has a tape drive. A good tape backup can still be the most expensive part of the system. Often, only companies have them.

Some of you may be tempted to use Zip drives, spare hard drives, or even recordable CD-ROMs for backup. While they can be used, they suffer from several severe shortcomings. The Zip drives are lossy devices that don't do proper error detection, reporting, and correction like a hard disk. If you use a Zip drive for backups, expect to lose data. Using a spare hard drive, while it may seem like a good expedient, is subject to the same voltage spikes that may fry your main drive. And recordable CDs are very slow and have a limited capacity (660MB).

Recommendations for backups range from a full-system backup performed nightly, to only weekly with optional daily or three times weekly incremental backup. Many firms will also opt for off-site storage of weekly or monthly backup tapes as a backup to the tapes stored on-site. For this, you should choose a reputable firm, without actual physical access to the tapes.

At many locations you might visit, though, you'll see backup tapes left in systems or sitting out. If other than authorized personnel (those with the root passwords) have access to the area, the backup tapes should be protected even better than the systems themselves.

A backup tape, especially a full-system backup tape, will contain a complete image of the system. These tapes can be used to re-create that system. In fact, a good, complete backup tape of a system is better than being able to physically access the system. This is because these tapes can be loaded on almost any system if the backup utility used is known (and many graphical commercial backup utilities are just front-ends for common Linux backup utilities like tar, cpio, or dump).

The ability to grab one single file, /etc/shadow, off onto another system would compromise not only all the data in the system (since the backup tape contains those files) but also future data. All passwords, including root's, should be considered compromised. The thief, with all the time now on his side, could leisurely run any number of cracking programs against the file. Most passwords will quickly be known. But the most important one is the root password.

TIP If you suspect that a backup tape has been compromised (removed by an unauthorized person), either by theft or by copying, all passwords on that system should be changed, and all systems that trust that system (see Chapter 12) should be considered compromised as well.

Safeguarding a Linux network

Considering the foregoing information, the need to protect different systems in different ways becomes more evident. While networks and networking vulnerabilities will be discussed in depth in the next part of this book, physical access to client systems will be discussed here.

If you are running a network of any size, you'll probably have a few different system classifications. You'll have client systems where most users will work. You'll have a server or two for file and print sharing (likely with all user's home directories NFS mounted to the clients, along with mail, etc.). If you have Internet access, you likely also will have a firewall system that can also server as a masquerading system.

For now, let's consider some vulnerabilities to any Linux clients you may be running, and how those vulnerabilities can extend to the servers.

Depending on your network model, different accounts may be on Linux clients. That is, usually an abbreviated /etc/password will be on client machines. But regardless of whether you're using NIS, only using the clients with complete password accounts, or using xdm so that clients are logging in directly on a server, the /etc/shadow on all client machines should be considered compromised. That is, you *must* have a root account as the first entry, but the root password on client machines should be different from the root password on a server, which should be different from the root account password on your firewall, which again, should be different from the root password on any systems you have sitting on the Internet.

Also, you'll want to make sure that while the clients trust the servers, the servers do not trust the clients. There's no real reason for the server to trust the clients, and it should be assumed that the client systems can be or have been compromised.

Summary

This chapter rounded out the preceding chapter, where you learned about how the system boots. You learned just how vulnerable a system is during the boot process, and how any knowledgeable individual can help himself to anything on the system, even those things normally only available to root, including the root account itself.

This extends beyond the system to include backup media, which is not protected in any way. As you'll learn, the more information you give someone, the easier it is for that person to gain complete access.

Part II

Your network

Chapter 9

Network primer (how things work and why)

IN PART II OF THIS BOOK you'll learn about your network and its vulnerabilities. Most attacks will be network-based, since it is unlikely your system is sitting on a street corner somewhere where just anyone can access it. If you do have your systems in a publicly accessible place, read Chapter 8 to understand your vulnerabilities to a console attack.

Some years ago, it took a true systems engineer, someone who truly understood how the system works, to attack that system with any real probability of gaining access. As the number of systems engineers grew, a number with questionable ethics appeared on the scene and coded programs to exploit vulnerabilities. These programs are easily accessible to anyone with access to the Internet. Many can be found at http://www.rootshell.com/ and similar sites. They are put there ostensibly for security engineers. But since anyone can access them, a fair number have fallen into the hands of even more folks with fewer ethics than the program's coders.

Enter the script kiddies. These are often teenagers with an overabundance of time and a total lack of respect for anyone, particularly authority figures, and who believe they are acting anonymously on the Internet. These social outcasts who don't actually understand what they are doing have become the scourge of the Internet. The media and other misfits mislabel themselves as "hackers," when in

119

fact they are only wannabe crackers, criminals, and are incapable of anything constructive enough to be deemed "hacking."

This chapter will explain some basics of the medium in which they work. An in-depth understanding is not necessary, but the basics should be understood. You will learn a little about the current system in use today, the Internet Protocol version 4, IPv4, or just IP for short. The Linux kernel also has support for other protocols, including IPv6, the proposed (and still experimental) successor to IPv4, but it is not in widespread use as of this writing.

Understanding the basics

In order to understand how networks work, it is easiest to start small and work up. Everything in computers works on the basis of 1 and 0, on and off. These two states describe everything that a computer knows about. But these two numbers by themselves are rather limiting. That is, you can describe only two states, on or off.

 The singular numeric place that this on or off can occupy is called a bit. It forms the foundation for what is to come.

A bit describes just one place marker. To be really useful, though, you're going to deal principally with groups of eight (octets) called bytes. Do not confuse bits and bytes, although it is easy to do given their similarity. Modems often reference bits because it makes the numbers much bigger. When you are transmitting data, the modem will tell you it is capable of 56k. This number is in bits, not bytes.

In most other instances, you will use bytes. An octet (8 bits) can hold a number from 0–255 in decimal terms — that is, two numbers, a 0 or a 1, can occupy 8 spaces, and 2 raised to a power of 8 equals 256. For a computer that uses base 16, or hexadecimal, this works out very nicely to a number from 00–FF. In counting in hex, the numberline goes from 0–9, but continues by using the letters a–f before becoming 10 (decimal 16). Table 9-1 shows the numbers from 0–16 in decimal and hexadecimal.

TABLE **9-1 DECIMAL TO HEXADECIMAL CORRELATION**

0	1	2	3	4	5	6	7	8	9	10	11	12	13	14	15	16
0	1	2	3	4	5	6	7	8	9	A	B	C	D	E	F	10

Hex numbers are normally distinguished by preceding the number with 0x. This text will use the same connotation where required for clarity, but the reader may assume that the number FF is hex and equal to 255 without use of the 0x.

That said, you will normally see decimal numbers used for the convenience of humans (computers translate to hexadecimal for themselves), though you will see hex numbers occasionally. The system chosen for presentation of the numbers appears to be up to the author of the particular utility used, but this text will attempt to make it clear which system is in use.

Understanding IP

RFC 791 defines the Internet Protocol (IP). It is the IP protocol, used as an envelope, which carries a number of other protocols inside, such as TCP and UDP. The IP header contains all the information needed for the packet to get to its destination. IP is not the only protocol used on the Internet, but it is by far the most common. Other packets that traverse the network may include RIP (routing information protocol), BGP (border gateway protocol), ICMP (Internet Control Message Protocol), GGP (gateway to gateway protocol), and ARP (address resolution protocol). With the exception of ICMP and ARP, this text will not deal with these routing protocols, but leave them to a book on advanced networking.

As a general guide, when an application wants to communicate with a server on another system, a chain of events occurs. First, the application uses an IP address to decide which system to communicate with, using DNS (domain name service) to translate a system name into an IP address if necessary. The application also will specify whether to use TCP or UDP, and also specify a port to connect to on the remote system.

For more information on ports and how they work, see Chapter 10, "Common (well-known) services."

The information to be sent is packaged as specified by the application into a UDP or TCP packet. This packet is then inserted into an IP packet. The kernel, based on information in a routing table, passes the IP packet to the appropriate interface device (this may be an Ethernet card, a modem, a token ring card, etc.). The interface device may need to further package the packet. In the case of an Ethernet card, the card finds out the destination on the local network. This will be either the receiving system or the gateway. With this information, it requests, via ARP, the MAC address of the card that is to receive the packet and, if it can communicate with that card, sends the packet on its way.

An Ethernet card assumes all communications will be on the local network, and that they will be directly connected via a wire so that it can "see" the destination card. Ethernet cards identify each other via the MAC address, a unique number burned into the card by the manufacturer. The system uses ARP to build an IP to MAC table for the Ethernet card. All IPs that are not on the local network map to the MAC address of the gateway. So at the lowest level, Ethernet cards set up communications based on a MAC address. When a packet arrives at a local destination, the IP headers are processed by the receiving system, and if not destined for that system are handed back down to the Ethernet card to go back out. In the case of the gateway, the packets will arrive on one interface and go out on another. While a second system (not the gateway) could also resend the packets, normally it will not because forwarding will be disabled (the default in Linux). So guessing what system is a gateway will usually not work.

IP packet headers

Based on the foregoing discussion, you can surmise that an IP packet consists of two parts: the header, and the data. This header portion has a very strict format. This format is checked each time the packet is handled. The header is also modified each time it is handled. Each system the packet passes through examines the header for integrity. The system determines the integrity of the packet via the checksum. If the checksum is not correct, the system assumes the packet has been mangled in transit (normally via a collision with another packet) and drops the packet. The packet may also be dropped for other reasons: host unreachable, network unreachable, packet too large for the next network segment to accept and has the DNF (do not fragment) bit set, etc. When a packet is dropped for any reason except that it was mangled, the system that dropped the packet sends an ICMP message back to the packet's source (as found in the dropped packet) with the reason.

If you examine the IP header diagram shown in Figure 9-1, you can see that is has been broken into sections for two reasons: First, it is too long to portray as one continuous stream of bits (which is what it would look like on the wire); and second, it is easier to read and explain in 4-byte groupings.

 The diagram is deliberately broken into 32-bit segments. Pentium systems are capable of transmitting and receiving 32 bits on their bus. This four-byte grouping is referred to as a word. So Pentium systems have a four-byte word, while older 286 systems use a two-byte word (as do 386SX systems on their bus, although the CPU processes four-byte words).

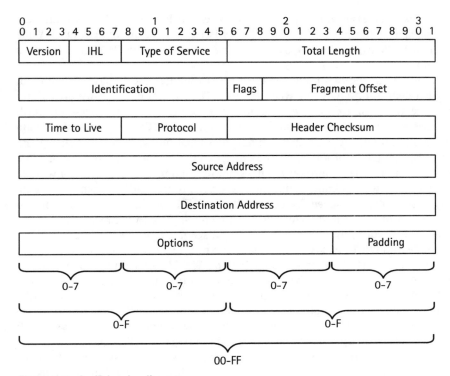

Figure 9–1: An IP header diagram

Examining the IP diagram in Figure 9-1, you can see that almost all fields consist of multiples of four bits. Those that are only four bits are located next to another four-bit field. This is deliberate, since systems most commonly work with a byte, which is eight bits. The one exception is the flags and fragments fields, which individually are not even multiples of four bits, but which, when combined, are 16 bits (two bytes). The focus of this chapter will be on the Source and Destination fields. But knowledge of the other fields will come in handy in Chapter 16.

While the header contains a lot of information, the most important is where it came from (source address) and where it's going to (destination address). After all, that's what IP is all about — routing messages.

IP data packet

The portion of the packet behind the IP header is the data packet, also known as the payload. The payload can be just about anything, but most commonly contains either a TCP packet or a UDP packet. Less commonly, the payload may contain a

NetBIOS packet, or even another IP packet. When an IP data packet contains another IP packet as the payload (IP in IP), this is referred to as tunnelling. A Wide Area Network (WAN) is created by tunnelling an unroutable IP packet inside a routable one.

When looking at the two protocols most often found as the IP payload, you will find a great deal of difference between the two. The first, TCP, the transport control protocol, creates a connection. This requires several packets to flow back and forth between two systems in order to establish this connection. TCP is used wherever data integrity is important, such as when copying files from one system to another (FTP). UDP, the user datagram protocol, on the other hand, is connectionless. One or more packets are sent, but the remote system does not respond to the sender in any way, so the sender has no way to know if the packets arrived or not. UDP is used where data integrity is secondary to speed. Voice over IP uses UDP, because even if one or two packets are lost or dropped, the voice will still be intelligible to the receiver.

If you look in your /etc/services file, you will see most ports have both UDP and TCP listed. Although both are listed, most services use one or the other but not both. Services that use UDP specifically include SNMP (the simple network management protocol), TFTP (the trivial file transfer protocol), RLP (the resource location protocol), and a few others. FTP (the file transfer protocol), telnet, SMTP (the simple mail transport protocol), and many others use TCP. DNS (the domain name service), will use both. If the DNS query is small, the response will come as a UDP packet. However, for larger queries, such as zone transfers, TCP is used.

As mentioned before, TCP sets up a connection between two systems. This connection ensures data integrity. The connection is established via a three-way handshake that works like this:

1. The client contacts the server and requests a connection (the SYN bit is set).

2. The server, sitting on the wait queue, sends a packet back to the client with the SYN and ACK bits set. This server will wait on the wait queue for a response, but cannot respond to any request except that of the original client.

3. The client answers the server's packet by sending a packet with the ACK bit set. When the server receives this confirmation packet, the server moves off the wait queue so another server process can listen for more connection requests and the connection is complete. The original server communicates only with the client that contacted it.

The above is a rather simplified look at how the connection process works. Omitted from the above are details such as the use of packet sequence numbers (incremented by one with each packet) to keep track of the connection, and the negotiation of a random return port to compete the connection on. The server will send data to the upper port, which the client is now binding waiting for responses.

You will learn more about ports and services in Chapter 10.

A lot can happen while a connection is being established. Packets can get lost or mangled and dropped; packets can be dropped because they're too big; the random port the server chose may not be available, etc. The server will wait a short interval and try again. Eventually, the connection will complete.

One attack, the SYN DoS attack, takes advantage of the fact that the server waits on the wait queue for a reply. See Chapter 13 for more information.

Understanding ICMP

The Internet Message Control Protocol (ICMP), unlike TCP and UDP, doesn't travel inside IP packets. ICMP has its own header. You are probably familiar with ICMP because of the ping packet, but ICMP is much more than just ping. The ping packet is actually two separate packets. As defined by RFC 792, the Echo Request message (ping) is an ICMP Type 8 packet. The reply to a ping (sometimes called a pong) is an ICMP Type 0 Echo Reply message. A complete list follows:

```
ICMP Message Types and Codes
Type 0 Echo Reply Message
Type 3 Destination Unreachable Message
    Code
        0 = net unreachable;
        1 = host unreachable;
        2 = protocol unreachable;
        3 = port unreachable;
        4 = fragmentation needed and DF set.
        5 = source route failed.
Type 4 Source Quench Message
Type 5 Redirect Message
    Code
        0 = Redirect datagrams for the Network.
        1 = Redirect datagrams for the Host.
```

```
        2 = Redirect datagrams for the Type of Service and Network.
        3 = Redirect datagrams for the Type of Service and Host.
Type 8 Echo Message
Type 11 Time Exceeded Message
    Code
        0 = time to live exceeded in transit;
        1 = fragment reassembly time exceeded.
Type 12 Parameter Problem Message
    Code
        0 = problem with option.
Type 13 Timestamp Message
Type 14 Timestamp Reply Message
Type 15 Information Request Message
Type 16 Information Reply Message
```

If you've used computers on a network before, you've probably seen the host unreachable message when a system on the Internet was down. But the other messages are also used even though you'll never see most of them. ICMP is very important for the functioning of your system on the network. Linux uses ICMP to do MTU (maximum transmission unit) discovery. Ethernet cards transmit data in large blocks called transmission units. By default, these blocks are 1500 bytes. Using blocks this large speeds communications on fast networks. But slow networks will drop the MTU because it takes so long to transmit these large blocks that errors creep in requiring retransmission. MTU on a dial-up link is often around 296. To discover the optimum tranmission size for the connection, Linux sets the "DF" or don't fragment bit. If a link along the way cannot or will not pass such a large packet, it drops the packet and sends an ICMP Type 3 Code 4 "fragmentation needed and DF set" message. Linux drops the MTU and tries again. In this way, Linux self-tunes packet sizes to the optimum size for greatest speed.

Why is this important? System crackers will often probe networks first with ping packets to get a list of live systems. A firewall can be set up to drop ICMP packets. But you don't want to drop all ICMP packets or you risk not receiving important messages for proper MTU discovery and host unreachable messages. Unfortunately, most crackers these days know ICMP Type 8 (Echo Request) messages are dropped, and use other techniques to probe for live systems.

Network and Internet routing

Routing is the method by which ICMP and IP packets find their way from one computer to another. The packets travel from the interface device of one system to the interface device of another until they finally arrive at their destination — as long as nothing happens to the packets along the way. This text generally treats all interface devices as Ethernet cards. But an interface device can be any device used to pass packets from one system to another. Interface devices may be modems, token ring cards, etc. The important thing is that each interface device will have a unique IP address assigned to it. No two interface devices may have the same IP address if a route between them exists. Many IP addresses have a name assigned to them. The name can belong to more than one IP address, but care must be taken in the implementation of such a scheme.

Every Ethernet card has a unique number burned into it when it is manufactured. This hardware address, known as a MAC address, is a six hexadecimal number: 01:23:ab:cd:4e:5f. A host learns about the IP-address-to-MAC-address correlation of each system it needs to talk to via ARP, the Address Resolution Protocol. The system builds a table (and ARP cache) of IPs to MAC addresses when it needs to talk to another host. The system maintains this cache (typically for approximately two minutes) and uses it until it expires and is purged. Then it has to learn the IP to MAC address correlation again before it can talk to any host it doesn't have in its ARP cache. All IPs not on the local network will list the gateway as the IP/MAC to talk to.

IP addresses are assigned to communications devices. These are the devices that physically connect to the network, i.e., Network Interface Cards (NICs), modems, HP JetDirect printer spoolers, etc., not the computer. Each communications device (there may be several on one host) gets its own unique IP address.

ARP can also be used in reverse (RARP, reverse address resolution protocol) to enable a system to learn its IP address. HP Jet Direct cards in HP LaserJets and HP Jet Direct print spoolers by default listen on the network for a host to communicate with their MAC address and tell them what their IP address is.

By way of definition, when you talk about a host being on a local network, you are talking about a host that is directly connected to the same wire or network segment. If you have to go through another host to get to your destination (gateway or router), then the destination is not local, even if it is on the same wire. This also applies to machines that would appear to belong to the same Class C address, but when subnetted via variable length subnet masking (VLSM), are on a separate network, as explained under CIDR below.

An ARP cache, then, can grow to as many as 254 hosts in the case of a full "Class C" network, but is often less. So ARP caches normally don't grow very large, unless, of course, you are employing a host as a router with connections to several networks. Then the ARP cache can grow quite large.

Understanding CIDR

CIDR, Classless Inter-Domain Routing, allows you to maximize use of the limited address space under the current implementation of the Internet Protocol version 4 (IPv4). After reading this section, even if you've never configured a computer for network communications before, you should have a good understanding of these references to networking.

Background

CIDR is the current trend in routing and has been since the mid-1990s. This concept was introduced in 1993 to alleviate the shortage of Internet Protocol (IP) addresses until the next generation (IP version 6 – IPv6, aka IPng for "IP next generation") arrives.

Currently in testing, Ipv6 will significantly expand the IP address space by several orders of magnitude. Ipv6 will also come with its own security enhancements. Those who wish to participate in the future today may have the opportunity to do so, since Linux has kernel-level support for Ipv6. Until Ipv6 is deployed on a wide scale, making the best use of what we have is what CIDR is all about.

To help you understand why we need CIDR at all, let's journey back in time to the late 1980s. IPv4, the protocol used by computers to find each other on a network, was in use then, but there really weren't many connections to the Internet or machines needing Internet connections. In fact, a good number of systems still relied on uucp, the UNIX-to-UNIX copy protocol, where machines called each other at predetermined times and exchanged e-mail traffic. At that time, the IP-address pool seemed unlimited. That was before Mosaic, the first Web browser, appeared. Since Mosaic, the Internet has been growing dramatically, and the demand for IP addresses has grown with it.

IP routing basics

Those who consider themselves well-versed in classful routing may wish to skip ahead to the next section. Computers understand base two numbers (ones and zeroes), and most humans understand base ten (0–9), so engineers worked out a compromise to give computers numbers while keeping things simple for use by humans. All computers on the Internet have a unique IP address which can be represented by a string of ones and zeroes (bits). If that string is divided up into four sets of eight bits (octets), you get four numbers that range from 0 (eight zeroes) to 255 (eight ones), and are written in the form XXX.XXX.XXX.XXX. This arrangement is called *dotted decimal notation* and makes understanding the significance of each unique IP address a little easier for us humans. These addresses were then further broken down into arbitrary classes A–D. Looking at the first half of the first octet, you can see below how the classes are divided:

- ◆ Class A = 0–127 (0000) – 16,777,216 hosts per network
- ◆ Class B = 128–191 (1000) – 65,534 hosts per network
- ◆ Class C = 192–223 (1100) – 254 hosts per network
- ◆ Class D = the rest (1110) – No default number of hosts

The numbers above provide for a maximum of:

- ◆ 127 Class A networks of 16,777,214 hosts each
- ◆ 64 Class B networks of 65,534 hosts each
- ◆ 32 Class C networks of 254 hosts each

The positions beginning from the left represent 128, 64, 32 and 16, respectively. Furthermore, Class A uses only the first number as the network number, e.g., 10.XXX.XXX.XXX; Class B uses the first two numbers as the network number, e.g., 172.32.XXX.XXX; Class C uses three numbers as the network number, e.g., 192.168.1.XXX; Class D is reserved for testing purposes. A network address can be thought of as having a network and host portions represented by numbers and XXXs respectively. For a Class C address, the network portion consists of the first three octets with the host portion as the final octet.

As a refresher, eight bits equal one byte. In decimal, a byte represents 0–255. In hexadecimal, a byte represents 00–FF, the hexadecimal numbering system running from 0–F: 0, 1, 2, 3, 4, 5, 6, 7, 8, 9, A, B, C, D, E, F.

It's important that you understand the following concepts. The technical definitions are useful only to those who already understand the concepts, but confusing to others. The definitions here are expanded for understanding, but are factually correct.

- ◆ *host address*: A unique address assigned to a communications device in a computer. If a computer has multiple communications devices (e.g., Ethernet cards or modems), each of these devices will have its own unique address. This means that a host (computer or router) can be multi-homed, i.e., have multiple IP addresses. This can also be artificially created by assigning different IP addresses to the same device via IP aliasing.

◆ *network address*: The base (lower) address assigned to a network segment, depending on its netmask. This is the first host IP number on a subnet. For example, on the Class C network that extends from 192.168.1.0 to 192.168.1.255, the network address would be 192.168.1.0.

◆ *broadcast address*: The upper address assigned to a network segment. In the example above, this address would be 192.168.1.255. All hosts on the net should listen to packets sent to this IP address.

◆ *netmask*: A mask consisting of that portion of the IP address where all greater bits consist of ones (in base two) and all lower bits consist of zeroes — in other words, ones represent the network portion of the address, and zeroes represent the host portion. For the example above, this mask would be 255.255.255.0. If we wanted the netmask for a class B address, it would be 255.255.0.0. That is, the portion of the IP address that doesn't change from host to host on the network is replaced by ones in binary.

With this introduction to IP addressing, and remembering that a decade ago almost no PCs participated in networking, it is easy to see why during the 1980s IPv4 seemed to have an endless supply of addresses, even though not all addresses could be assigned. Theoretically, if you could make use of all the usable IP addresses available, you'd have a maximum of approximately 500 million addresses, but if even 100 million hosts have IP, that is extremely optimistic and insufficient for today.

The netmask defines the network. Two systems, even if they would normally be on the same network, but have different netmasks, will act as though they are on two separate networks.

Implementing CIDR with VLSM

The IP addressing scheme detailed above using class boundaries is obsolete. The terms used to describe them — Class A, Class B, and Class C — are also obsolete, but are still in widespread use because they are easy to understand. This text will use those terms as well for clarity. This text will also use the classful addressing as a stepping stone. But to implement CIDR, you'll also need to understand Variable Length Subnet Masking (VLSM).

Basically, with a Class address, you have a default subnet mask. For a Class C address, this default subnet is 24 bits long, so putting all ones in the first 24 bits (first 3 octets) and zeroes in the rest, you have 255.255.255.0 (hex: ffffff00). For classes A and B, this would be 255.0.0.0 and 255.255.0.0, respectively. This basically gives anyone assigned a full Class C address 256 unique addresses, of which two are reserved, one each for network and broadcast addresses. Under classful addressing, you are limited to providing full Class A, B or C addresses to those requiring IP addresses. With classless addressing, you can subnet these addresses quite simply. As stated above, the network portion of the address is equivalent to that portion of the IP address corresponding in base two to all ones, and the host address to all zeroes. This means that a Class C address looks like:

```
11111111.11111111.11111111.00000000 = 255.255.255.0
```

(128+64+32+16+8+4+2+1 in the first three positions and 0 in the last).

Again, note that this is 24 ones and eight zeroes, for a total of 32 positions.

By way of example, imagine that you have been allocated one Class C address (192.168.0.0). You have two geographically disparate office locations with 50 systems at each site you need to network. With classful addressing, you could use the same Class C address at each site, each using a unique set of IP from the Class C range. Unfortunately, these two offices could not communicate directly as a WAN because they are not sharing the same wire, but are sharing the same network address. Each set of systems believes the other set of systems is local (meaning they don't have to pass through a gateway to get to the others). You only need to go through a gateway to reach IP addresses that are not on your local network. This is not the case here.

A gateway is a machine (computer or router) that has two or more network addresses — at least one on the local network and one or more on other networks. A gateway sends any communications not destined for the local network to one of its other communications devices, depending on the information stored in its routing table. Under classful routing, you would need two (but less than half-used) Class C addresses for each office, which would be very wasteful of scarce IP addresses.

Under CIDR, you can split the Class C address up at any of several boundaries. By using VLSM, you change your subnet mask, thereby changing the boundaries that define the network. With Class C, you are using ones in the first 24 positions, or in dotted decimal notation you have 255.255.255.0 (11111111.11111111.1111111. 00000000). Suppose you change the first 0 in the last octet to a 1. You now have 25 ones and seven zeroes, or 255.255.255.128. If you use this netmask for both office locations, and use one half of the host range for one location and the other half of the host range for the other location, each will look for the other by first traveling to the gateway. So what you have is two networks, one extending from 192.168.0.0 to 192.168.0.127, and the other from 192.168.0.128 to 192.168.0.255. Remember that the first address from each half (.0 and .128) is your network address, and the last address is your broadcast address (.127 and .255)

In the same manner, you can continue slicing up your network into four networks, eight networks, 16 networks, 32 networks, and so on. In fact, starting at /8, you can slice and dice until you reach /30. Since you have 32 numbers to work with, a /32 represents just one address, and in this special case, there's no need for network or broadcast addresses. That also means a /31 would represent two addresses, but since one would be the network address and the other the broadcast address, this would leave you with no host addresses — almost certainly undesirable.

Under classful addressing, a network netmask always started with 255 and repeated the 255 until the first 0, which then repeated until the end of the four octets. Under CIDR, the first octet of the netmask would remain 255, but after that you can change any of the other numbers. Instead of being restricted to 255 and 0, you may find yourself replacing the first 0 in your netmask with any of 128, 192, 224, 240, 248, 252, or 254 (except in the last octet as noted above), and then terminating any remaining octets with 0. The network and broadcast addresses would bind each subnet. Now, any network can be referred to by its variable length subnet mask, or the number of ones in the host portion of the address from /8 to /32 (excepting /31). By extrapolation, each host can be referred to directly by its IP address and the VLSM notation, so that it is readily apparent what the network and broadcast addresses and netmask are.

For example, if someone told you to assign my machine 192.168.0.50/27, you should now know that the network address is 192.168.0.32, the broadcast address is 192.168.0.63, and the netmask is 255.255.255.224. For those of you who still have problems visualizing how this all translates, I've provided a table to assist you.

TABLE 9-2 CIDR TRANSLATION TABLE

mask	A	B	C	networks	divisions (multiples of)	hex
.0	/8	/16	/24	1	none	00
.128	/9	/17	/25	2	128	80
.192	/10	/18	/26	4	64	C0
.224	/11	/19	/27	8	32	E0
.240	/12	/20	/28	16	16	F0
.248	/13	/21	/29	32	8	F8
.252	/14	/22	/30	64	4	FC
.254	/15	/23	N/A	128	2	FE
.255			/32	0		FF

You will find more uses for classless addressing than this. CIDR can also give you a way to isolate departments in large organizations to provide better security (by implementing internal firewalls) and decrease traffic on any given network segment, reducing collisions and increasing response times.

Using ifconfig

The ifconfig utility is used to configure all communications interfaces on a host. But this will do more than just configure an interface; it will also provide you with details about that interface. All of these details can be changed, though not all drivers support changing all parameters. Some of the important details for security are discussed below the sample `ifconfig -a` output below. The -a option shows all interfaces, even those that are down.

Following is a sample ifconfig output:

```
eth0      Link encap:Ethernet  HWaddr 00:10:5A:8B:0C:FA
          inet addr:209.127.112.185  Bcast:209.127.112.191  Mask:255.255.255.192
          UP BROADCAST RUNNING PROMISC MULTICAST  MTU:1500  Metric:1
          RX packets:0 errors:0 dropped:0 overruns:0 frame:0
          TX packets:12 errors:0 dropped:0 overruns:0 carrier:12
          collisions:0 txqueuelen:100
          Interrupt:9 Base address:0x300

eth0:1    Link encap:Ethernet  HWaddr 00:10:5A:8B:0C:FA
          inet addr:207.199.127.84  Bcast:207.199.127.255  Mask:255.255.255.0
          UP BROADCAST RUNNING PROMISC MULTICAST  MTU:1500  Metric:1
          Interrupt:9 Base address:0x300

lo        Link encap:Local Loopback
          inet addr:127.0.0.1  Mask:255.0.0.0
          UP LOOPBACK RUNNING  MTU:3924  Metric:1
          RX packets:3615 errors:0 dropped:0 overruns:0 frame:0
          TX packets:3615 errors:0 dropped:0 overruns:0 carrier:0
          collisions:0 txqueuelen:0
ppp0      Link encap:Point-to-Point Protocol
          inet addr:208.143.150.16  P-t-P:208.143.150.9  Mask:255.255.255.255
          UP POINTOPOINT RUNNING NOARP MULTICAST  MTU:1500  Metric:1
          RX packets:3237 errors:5 dropped:0 overruns:0 frame:5
          TX packets:3354 errors:0 dropped:0 overruns:0 carrier:0
          collisions:0 txqueuelen:10

ppp1      Link encap:Point-to-Point Protocol
          inet addr:192.168.10.10  P-t-P:192.168.10.11  Mask:255.255.255.255
          POINTOPOINT NOARP MULTICAST  MTU:1500  Metric:1
          RX packets:0 errors:0 dropped:0 overruns:0 frame:0
          TX packets:0 errors:0 dropped:0 overruns:0 carrier:0
          collisions:0 txqueuelen:10

vmnet0    Link encap:Ethernet  HWaddr 00:50:56:80:00:00
          BROADCAST MULTICAST  MTU:1500  Metric:1
```

```
          RX packets:0 errors:0 dropped:0 overruns:0 frame:0
          TX packets:0 errors:0 dropped:0 overruns:0 carrier:0
          collisions:0 txqueuelen:100

vmnet1    Link encap:Ethernet  HWaddr 00:50:56:8A:00:00
          BROADCAST MULTICAST  MTU:1500  Metric:1
          RX packets:0 errors:0 dropped:0 overruns:0 frame:0
          TX packets:0 errors:0 dropped:0 overruns:0 carrier:0
          collisions:0 txqueuelen:100
```

Examining the interfaces one at a time, you can see that the eth0 interface is a link encapsulation type Ethernet. The hardware address is the MAC address referred to above. Despite the fact that these addresses are burned into the card, they can be overridden from the command line. So if you know another system's IP and MAC address, you can become that system. This is actually done in the case of failover systems. But clients should not be taking over a server address. You can find out a remote system's MAC address by looking in the ARP cache. The command `arp -a` will display the entire arp cache. If the system you want is not listed, ping it once, then run the arp command again (this is because stale ARP entries are flushed after a timeout period, that is, no contact with the remote host). This will work only for systems on the local network.

The second line in the ifconfig for eth0 just shows the dotted decimal notation for the IP address, netmask, and broadcast. The third line, though, is of interest. What's interesting here is the PROMISC entry. This means that the Ethernet card is in promiscuous mode. Unlike with humans, this just means it's reading everyone else's mail. Normally, a system only pays attention to packets destined for its own system. But this Ethernet card will receive all packets on the wire. Running some software, such as tcpdump, will force a card into this mode. This could indicate that a "sniffer," a program that eavesdrops, is running. If you are going to run this type of software on a network, you should be very careful. Some systems are still susceptible to attacks like the "big ping" attack. If a network card is in promiscuous mode and a big ping is sent over the network, even if it wasn't destined for this host, it will be received, and if the system is susceptible, it will probably crash. Some systems will crash even if only the last fragment of a big ping is received. You'll see how this is important in Chapter 16.

Most of the rest of the lines are just statistics. But look at the last line in the eth0 section. This tells you the base address and IRQ. While the ability to do so is driver dependent, you can change the I/O and IRQ. There really is little reason to do so, however.

The second interface entry, eth0:1, signifies that this particular interface has an alias. The alias is the second IP address. This particular entry reads exactly the same as the one above, but aliases do not carry all the stats. Those go only to the primary interface.

The third entry is lo. This is the localhost. All systems have a localhost entry that is defined by 127.0.0.1. In actuality, the entire Class A equivalent of 127.0.0.0-127.255.255.255 belongs to every system. So if you ever have reason to put a sniffer on your network and you see a 127.0.0.0/8 address, you'll know someone is "spoofing." That is, they are deliberately changing an address to make it look like it is coming from somewhere else (in this case from the localhost) in order to get access they would normally be denied. Often, this will take the form of an attack on a firewall where someone coming from the outside will "spoof" an address from the inside. More on this in the netfilter chapter as well.

The two pppX entries indicate that a modem (or two) is available for use. In this instance, you'll notice that ppp0 is up, and ppp1 is down. This would be a very interesting entry if policy were no unauthorized connections to the Internet and this machine were not authorized dial-up access.

The two vmnet interfaces are interesting from the standpoint that they don't actually exist. Yet you can see they have MAC addresses and everything else an Ethernet card would have. While they don't have one at the moment, when these interfaces are activated, they get IP addresses via DHCP (Dynamic Host Control Protocol). These exist only in software and in this case belong to a particular software package. Seen from the outside (on the network), when these interfaces are active, two separate systems are seen (note that normally two more exist for a total of four, but the list was edited for brevity).

Other interfaces could also exist — for example, ipppX for ISDN PPP, and trX for token ring. But these will show similar kinds of information to that described above.

Using route

From a security standpoint, route is of little interest, but is mentioned here because it goes with ifconfig. The default output for route is resolved names for the routing table, but overall, IP addresses are more informative, so the -n option should be used.

```
Kernel IP routing table
Destination     Gateway         Genmask         Flags Metric Ref    Use Iface
208.143.150.9   0.0.0.0         255.255.255.255 UH    0      0        0 ppp0
127.0.0.0       0.0.0.0         255.0.0.0       U     0      0        0 lo
0.0.0.0         208.143.150.9   0.0.0.0         UG    0      0        0 ppp0
```

The only column of interest is the Flags column, which shows the status of the route. The presence of a U indicates that the route is up. The H specifies a host, and a G a gateway. Not seen as often are R, D, and M, standing for reinstate, dynamic, and modified, respectively. Also seen from time to time is "!", which means reject. *This is not a firewall substitute.* What this does is set up a route that fails lookup. So if you try to send a packet from this host to the network or host specified as rejected, you'll get an error message that the route is down. It will not prevent incoming packets like UDP, it will only stop outgoing UDP and prevent a TCP connection.

Summary

This chapter provides a very brief overview of networks as they relate to security. You learned how systems communicate with each other. You also learned a little about ifconfig and what the parameters you learned about mean from a security point of view.

Chapter 10

Common (well-known) services

IN THIS CHAPTER

◆ Understanding services

◆ Understanding netstat

SERVICES ARE AN ESSENTIAL part of the networking picture. Without services, a computer could only run one program that clients could connect to remotely, and then only one at a time. Services implement the concept of ports for clients to specify in addition to the IP address. This allows a large number of clients to connect all at once and to various programs. Most users are not conscious of ports, because all clients have a built-in default. But an understanding of services is essential to understanding network security.

Understanding services

Imagine, if you will, a company at a single location (for the sake of simplicity) with a dedicated incoming phone number capable of handling many simultaneous calls. Imagine also that this company has several hundred extensions, all individual. When someone calls a particular phone number, a recording invites her to enter an extension. When she does so, she is connected either to an individual person or to a switchboard (unless the extension is not assigned, in which case she will be told the extension number entered is invalid). Your client software works this way, but has the default extension (port) programmed in, so you don't need to specify it explicitly, which is why most users are unaware of it.

This scenario is really not too far from how your computer accepts incoming requests from clients to use services. The phone number is the IP address of your system. The extension is a particular port. All calls to your system use this IP:Port system to communicate. All clients have a default port that they want to talk to, and if a server compatible with that client is listening on that port, initial communications will begin. The server may terminate those communications if authentication is required from the client and not received or is incorrect, but by that time, the client and server have already created a connection.

The ports/services implementation was designed so that you could run FTP, telnet, HTTP, etc., at the same time. Without the IP:PORT model, a single system could provide only one service.

Figure 10-1 shows graphically how this works.

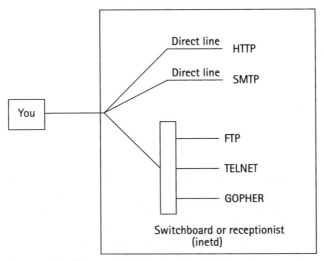

Figure 10-1: The ports/services implementation

When you want information from a company, you call that company. Using the analogy above, you enter the extension for the department you want to talk to. If you wanted to discuss purchasing a product or product pricing, you'd talk to sales, not the technical support department. Likewise, if you had a question about installation procedure, you'd call tech support, not sales. Each department has a particular function and probably doesn't know much about the others. Each probably also has its own jargon. The same concept holds true for different servers, but in the case of servers, the jargon would be their protocol.

With computers, the concepts are identical. You sit in front of your computer (now known as the client), open a Web browser, and put in the name of the company you wish to get information from. Let's say you input www.calderasystems.com. Your client will look up Caldera Systems's address. In this case it is an IP address. In reality, because you've opened a Web browser, when you go to the calderasystems address, you are also calling on a port. In this case, it is port 80. This particular port is assigned to Web servers as a Well Known Service (WKS). Because you are using a Web client, it would do you little good to talk to a telnet server or mail server because they do not use the same protocol, or set of rules for communication, so no communication would be possible (although later you will see that this is not completely correct). This is like talking to a salesperson about a technical problem. The "communication" will probably do you little good.

Now that you understand that ports are as much a part of the communications process as the IP address, take a look at a sample /etc/services file that shows a number of well-known services:

```
#       $NetBSD: services,v 1.18 1996/03/26 00:07:58 mrg Exp $
#
# Network services, Internet style
#
# Note that it is presently the policy of IANA to assign a single well-known
# port number for both TCP and UDP; hence, most entries here have two entries
# even if the protocol doesn't support UDP operations.
# Updated from RFC 1340, ``Assigned Numbers'' (July 1992).  Not all ports
# are included, only the more common ones.
#
#       from: @(#)services      5.8 (Berkeley) 5/9/91
#
tcpmux          1/tcp           # TCP port service multiplexer
echo            7/tcp
echo            7/udp
discard         9/tcp           sink null
discard         9/udp           sink null
systat          11/tcp          users
daytime         13/tcp
daytime         13/udp
netstat         15/tcp
qotd            17/tcp          quote
msp             18/tcp          # message send protocol
msp             18/udp          # message send protocol
chargen         19/tcp          ttytst source
chargen         19/udp          ttytst source
ftp-data        20/tcp          # default ftp data port
ftp             21/tcp
ssh             22/tcp
ssh             22/udp
telnet          23/tcp
#               24 - private
smtp            25/tcp          mail
#               26 - unassigned
time            37/tcp          timserver
time            37/udp          timserver
rlp             39/udp          resource        # resource location
nameserver      42/tcp          name            # IEN 116
whois           43/tcp          nicname
domain          53/tcp          nameserver      # name-domain server
domain          53/udp          nameserver
```

```
mtp              57/tcp                          # deprecated
bootps           67/tcp          # BOOTP server
bootps           67/udp
bootpc           68/tcp          # BOOTP client
bootpc           68/udp
tftp             69/udp
gopher           70/tcp          # Internet Gopher
gopher           70/udp
finger           79/tcp
www              80/tcp          http            # WorldWideWeb HTTP
www              80/udp          # HyperText Transfer Protocol
link             87/tcp          ttylink
kerberos         88/tcp          krb5            # Kerberos v5
kerberos         88/udp
#                100 - reserved
hostnames        101/tcp         hostname        # usually from sri-nic
rtelnet          107/tcp         # Remote Telnet
rtelnet          107/udp
pop2             109/tcp         pop-2 postoffice  # POP version 2
pop2             109/udp
pop3             110/tcp         pop-3           # POP version 3
pop3             110/udp
sunrpc           111/tcp
sunrpc           111/udp
auth             113/tcp         authentication tap ident
sftp             115/tcp
uucp-path        117/tcp
nntp             119/tcp         readnews untp   # USENET News Transfer Protocol
ntp              123/tcp
ntp              123/udp                         # Network Time Protocol
netbios-ns       137/tcp                         # NETBIOS Name Service
netbios-ns       137/udp
netbios-dgm      138/tcp                         # NETBIOS Datagram Service
netbios-dgm      138/udp
netbios-ssn      139/tcp                         # NETBIOS session service
netbios-ssn      139/udp
imap2            143/tcp         imap            # Interim Mail Access Proto v2
imap2            143/udp
snmp             161/udp                         # Simple Net Mgmt Proto
snmp-trap        162/udp         snmptrap        # Traps for SNMP
xdmcp            177/tcp                         # X Display Mgr. Control Proto
xdmcp            177/udp
bgp              179/tcp                         # Border Gateway Proto.
bgp              179/udp
```

```
irc             194/tcp                         # Internet Relay Chat
irc             194/udp
at-rtmp         201/tcp                         # AppleTalk routing
at-rtmp         201/udp
at-nbp          202/tcp                         # AppleTalk name binding
at-nbp          202/udp
at-echo         204/tcp                         # AppleTalk echo
at-echo         204/udp
at-zis          206/tcp                         # AppleTalk zone information
at-zis          206/udp
z3950           210/tcp        wais             # NISO Z39.50 database
z3950           210/udp        wais
ipx             213/tcp                         # IPX
ipx             213/udp
imap3           220/tcp                         # Interactive Mail Access
imap3           220/udp                         # Protocol v3
#
# UNIX specific services
#
exec            512/tcp
biff            512/udp        comsat
login           513/tcp
who             513/udp        whod
shell           514/tcp        cmd              # no passwords used
syslog          514/udp
printer         515/tcp        spooler          # line printer spooler
talk            517/udp
ntalk           518/udp
route           520/udp        router routed    # RIP
timed           525/udp        timeserver
tempo           526/tcp        newdate
courier         530/tcp        rpc
conference      531/tcp        chat
# temporary entry (not officially registered by the Samba Team!)
swat            901/tcp        # Samba Web Administration Tool
#
#
# AppleTalk DDP entries (DDP: Datagram Delivery Protocol)
#
rtmp            1/ddp          # Routing Table Maintenance Protocol
nbp             2/ddp          # Name Binding Protocol
echo            4/ddp          # AppleTalk Echo Protocol

zip             6/ddp          # Zone Information Protocol
```

For the sake of brevity, the above services file has been edited. Be sure to use the services file that came with your distribution. The authoritative document is currently RFC 1340, but that will also change in the future.

 A copy of RFC 1340 can be found in Appendix C. Also, on the CD-ROM in the col/security directory is a program called rfc, which you can use to find the latest version of any RFC you need.

While you may add unique port numbers with identifying services, you should not add services that already exist. That is, you may want to use port 8080 for www, but the entry will not do any good, since www already has an entry at port 80. Any service told to bind "www" will do so to port 80, and not port 8080. At least this is what would happen assuming you put the second entry for www as port 8080 below that of the original entry. When Linux needs to reference a service name to a port, it will look in the /etc/services file and use the first entry corresponding to the service name that it finds. Subsequent entries with the same service name will be ignored.

 Do not delete WKS from your /etc/services file. Deleting or commenting the services out could pose problems because programs requiring them will not have access.

Deleting WKS from your /etc/services file is likewise a bad idea. This is a reference file for services. Changes to names of WKS or port numbers, etc., could result in an inability to bind those services when they are required. But adding unique services to unused ports is a good idea for two reasons: First, this will allow utilities like netstat to translate the port number into an identifiable service name, and second, some services will require the entry in /etc/services in order to work properly.

A very important point about services: Under Linux, all ports below 1024 are considered "privileged" ports. That is, only root (UID 0) can bind a service to those ports. Any unused port above 1024 can be used by anyone. Commonly, some unofficial "Well Known Ports" exist above 1024. That is because they are used by convention, not by mandate, and so will not be listed in the WKS RFC. One was listed above as 8080 and is commonly used as a user Web server port. A couple of exceptions to this generalization exist. The "X" protocol, the same one you see as a GUI on your system, uses ports 6000–6010. But this is because the X protocol is considered unsecure, so forcing it to bind a port below 1024 is unwise.

In all, some 65536 ports are available for use. Port numbers above 65535 should not be used. The same problem of wrapping mentioned for UIDs could present itself if modified binaries are used on the system. That is, since the port is above 1024, anyone can bind it, but if it is above 65535, it will wrap and map to a lower numbered port and, if the mapping falls below 1024, will be a privileged port. Again, this would require a modification to the system, but is a known attack.

 While we're on the subject of attacks, some ports are used by crackers as "markers." Typically, these will be ports such as 31337 or 31173 or some other similar combination. If you substitute *es* for the threes, *ls* or *is* for the ones, and *ts* for the sevens, you'll see that they spell some variation of the word "elite." You can be fairly certain, if a system shows one of those ports open for service, that it has been cracked.

You're probably thinking that 65,000 ports is a little excessive, but it's not. Remember in the previous chapter how the SYN-ACK sequence for establishing a TCP connection was described. Not emphasized in that explanation was the fact that the client requests that information be sent back to it on a randomly picked port above 1024. This will be explained in detail in "Understanding netstat" below. So each TCP connection will actually use two ports. If you have 30 simultaneous www connections to a system, you will have 31 ports in use, 30 randomly picked ports above 1024, and of course port 80. The randomly picked ports, along with sequence numbers on packets, are how the system tracks the 30 separate communications connections and keeps them separate. If you see a possible vulnerability here, you're starting to think like a cracker, which is the only way to keep up with them.

Identifying IPs and ports for connections between two systems is fairly easy. But for a cracker to insert himself between two systems to "hijack" the connection requires that the sequence code be guessed beforehand. On most UNIX systems, that is an extremely difficult proposition. However, some systems use a time-related function to generate the initial sequence number, which can make hijacking (also known as a *man in the middle* attack) a fairly easy affair. Fortunately, this is a fairly sophisticated attack, so generally beyond reach of the average script kiddie.

Understanding netstat

The best tool available for examining the state of the network on any particular host is netstat. netstat, with no options, will show you the state of network connections. By default, it will resolve both IP addresses and service names through the standard resolver routines and the /etc/services file.

Output

This section will look at some sample output from netstat so that you understand what the output means.

The first line of the netstat output will always remind you what you are looking at: Active Internet connections (w/o servers). This line will change depending on the option. The term "servers" in this line refers to programs binding a port and waiting for a connection; they are on the wait queue listening, but are not communicating with a client yet.

```
Active Internet connections (w/o servers)
Proto Recv-Q Send-Q Local Address         Foreign Address        State
tcp       0      0 ppp15.chi.pty.com:2034 209.207.224.222:www    ESTABLISHED
tcp       0      0 ppp15.chi.pty.com:2033 209.207.224.222:www    ESTABLISHED
tcp       0      0 ppp15.chi.pty.com:2032 209.207.224.222:www    ESTABLISHED
tcp       0      0 ppp15.chi.pty.com:2031 209.207.224.222:www    ESTABLISHED
tcp       1      1 ppp15.chi.pty.com:2030 209.207.224.245:www    CLOSING
tcp       0      0 ppp15.chi.pty.com:2026 mail03.dfw.mindspr:pop3 TIME_WAIT
Active UNIX domain sockets (w/o servers)
Proto RefCnt Flags       Type     State       I-Node Path
unix  1      [ ]         STREAM   CONNECTED   26740  @0000013f
unix  1      [ ]         STREAM   CONNECTED   652    @00000004
unix  1      [ N ]       STREAM   CONNECTED   27587  @00000162
unix  1      [ ]         STREAM   CONNECTED   26744  @00000140
unix  1      [ ]         STREAM   CONNECTED   642    @00000003
unix  1      [ ]         STREAM   CONNECTED   28666  /tmp/.X11-unix/X0
unix  1      [ ]         STREAM   CONNECTED   27588  /tmp/.X11-unix/X0
unix  1      [ ]         STREAM   CONNECTED   27527  /tmp/.X11-unix/X0
unix  0      [ ]         STREAM               27523
unix  1      [ ]         STREAM   CONNECTED   26760  /tmp/.X11-unix/X0
unix  1      [ ]         STREAM   CONNECTED   26754  /tmp/.X11-unix/X0
unix  1      [ ]         STREAM   CONNECTED   653    /dev/log
unix  1      [ ]         STREAM   CONNECTED   643    /dev/log
unix  1      [ ]         STREAM   CONNECTED   597    /dev/log
```

The second line is the headers for the first section. The first column is Proto, for protocol, normally tcp or udp, but may also be raw, etc., as defined in the /etc/ services file we looked at above. The second and third columns are the Revc-Q and Send-Q (Receive Queue and Send Queue), respectively. This shows the number of bytes not copied by the user program connected to the socket, or bytes not acknowledged by the remote hosts respectively. After a tcp socket closes, it is common to see one byte not acknowledged by the remote host. This is because the connection is closed, the connection has been torn down, and the final ACK could not be acknowledged.

The next two columns are local and foreign (remote) addresses, respectively. These are in the form of address:port. In the example, ppp15.chi.pty.com:2034 (the full domain name is often truncated to fit in the space provided) is connected to 209.207.224.222:www, which we know is port 80. Because tcp "connects" the server to the client, it sends on one port (in this case 80) and receives on another port (in this case 2034). The return port is not specifically set. This will be a random port above 1024 not currently in use.

On the first connection, the client will tell the server which port it picked, and will await the SYN-ACK packet from the server on that port. If the sever cannot use that port because it's busy, an ICMP type 3 code 3 "port unreachable" message will be sent back to the client, which will pick another port at random. When the client finally receives the SYN packet on the chosen port, it will return an ACK, the connection will be complete, and data will begin to be passed.

This is a good example because what has happened is that multiple connections have been made to a site. The fourth connection on client port 2030 was the first to be made, and subsequently redirected the connection. This particular site has a number of banner ads and makes multiple connection requests back, showing the sequence in the example (reading up). A similar disconnection sequence occurs when the connection is terminated. Which brings us to the last column: in this case it says CLOSING, but could just as easily be LAST_ACK. When the client sends the LAST_ACK, and the server receives it, the server drops the connection. Since no connection exists, no reply is possible.

The last column, the state of the connection, can be any of the following:

```
ESTABLISHED
SYN_SENT
SYN_RECV
FIN_WAIT1
FIN_WAIT2
TIME_WAIT
CLOSED
CLOSE_WAIT
LAST_ACK
LISTEN
CLOSING
UNKNOWN
```

Some of these correspond only to the server side, others to the client side, but a few to both sides.

Upon our adding the -e switch to netstat, one more column called "User" would appear and give us the UID number of the user running the process that created this connection.

Starting the next section, we see Active UNIX domain sockets (w/o servers), then a header line. Note that this portion of the output has been severely edited. The header line includes Proto, RefCnt, Flags, Type, State, I-Node, and Path.

Let's examine each of the columns.

◆ The Proto column is for Protocol, as we saw above. Only this protocol will normally be UNIX, for UNIX-type sockets.

◆ The RefCnt column is a reference count of the number of attached processes and will normally be 1, but may be 0.

◆ The Flags column will normally be blank, but if the RefCnt is 0 and the corresponding processes are awaiting a connect request, the flag may be ACC for SO_ACCEPTON, meaning the socket is ready to accept a connection. On occasion, other flags may show up, such as W for SO_WAITDATA or N for SO_NOSPACE.

◆ The Type column will normally be STREAM, but also be DGRAM, RAW, RDM, SEQPACKET, PACKET, or UNKNOWN. These correspond to a stream (connection) socket, datagram (connectionless) mode, raw socket, reliably delivered message, sequential packet, raw interface access packet, or unknown mode (for future expansion).

◆ The State column shows the state of the socket and may be any of: FREE, LISTENING, CONNECTING, CONNECTED, DISCONNECTING, or blank (no entry), or UNKNOWN. The final state (UNKNOWN), should not occur.

◆ The I-Node column is not of general interest. It shows the I-Node that corresponds to the connection. However, this I-Node exists in /proc only when the connection is in use, so a search for this I-Node will not give the expected result.

◆ The final column is Path and shows the process attached to the socket.

The foregoing examples have not shown one of the most common connection states: LISTENING. This particular state will be shown by `netstat` only when accompanied by the `-a` switch. Using this switch will change the first line in each of the section headers. Where before we saw Active Internet connections (w/o servers), we now see Active Internet connections (including servers). Likewise for the second section, which will now read Active UNIX domain sockets (including servers). This will show us a much longer list of servers because it includes those listening for connections as shown below. Again, the output is edited for brevity.

```
Active Internet connections (servers and established)
Proto Recv-Q Send-Q Local Address           Foreign Address         State
tcp        1      0 208.143.150.24:2034     209.207.224.222:80      CLOSE_WAIT
tcp        1      0 208.143.150.24:2033     209.207.224.222:80      CLOSE_WAIT
tcp        1      0 208.143.150.24:2032     209.207.224.222:80      CLOSE_WAIT
tcp        1      0 208.143.150.24:2031     209.207.224.222:80      CLOSE_WAIT
tcp        1      1 208.143.150.24:2030     209.207.224.245:80      CLOSING
tcp        0      0 0.0.0.0:6000            0.0.0.0:*               LISTEN
tcp        0      0 0.0.0.0:51966           0.0.0.0:*               LISTEN
tcp        0      0 0.0.0.0:3306            0.0.0.0:*               LISTEN
tcp        0      0 0.0.0.0:80              0.0.0.0:*               LISTEN
tcp        0      0 0.0.0.0:1024            0.0.0.0:*               LISTEN
```

```
tcp        0        0 0.0.0.0:10000          0.0.0.0:*              LISTEN
tcp        0        0 0.0.0.0:25             0.0.0.0:*              LISTEN
tcp        0        0 0.0.0.0:111            0.0.0.0:*              LISTEN
tcp        0        0 0.0.0.0:901            0.0.0.0:*              LISTEN
tcp        0        0 0.0.0.0:79             0.0.0.0:*              LISTEN
tcp        0        0 0.0.0.0:143            0.0.0.0:*              LISTEN
tcp        0        0 0.0.0.0:110            0.0.0.0:*              LISTEN
tcp        0        0 0.0.0.0:21             0.0.0.0:*              LISTEN
tcp        0        0 0.0.0.0:37             0.0.0.0:*              LISTEN
tcp        0        0 0.0.0.0:19             0.0.0.0:*              LISTEN
tcp        0        0 0.0.0.0:13             0.0.0.0:*              LISTEN
tcp        0        0 0.0.0.0:9              0.0.0.0:*              LISTEN
tcp        0        0 0.0.0.0:7              0.0.0.0:*              LISTEN
udp        0        0 0.0.0.0:1025           0.0.0.0:*
udp        0        0 0.0.0.0:177            0.0.0.0:*
udp        0        0 0.0.0.0:37             0.0.0.0:*
udp        0        0 0.0.0.0:19             0.0.0.0:*
udp        0        0 0.0.0.0:13             0.0.0.0:*
udp        0        0 0.0.0.0:9              0.0.0.0:*
udp        0        0 0.0.0.0:7              0.0.0.0:*
raw        0        0 0.0.0.0:1              0.0.0.0:*              7
raw        0        0 0.0.0.0:6              0.0.0.0:*              7
Active UNIX domain sockets (servers and established)
Proto RefCnt Flags       Type       State        I-Node Path
unix  0      [ ACC ]     STREAM     LISTENING    593    /dev/log
unix  1      [ ]         STREAM     CONNECTED    26740  @0000013f
unix  1      [ ]         STREAM     CONNECTED    25943  @00000137
unix  0      [ ACC ]     STREAM     LISTENING    3864   /tmp/.axnetipc
unix  0      [ ACC ]     STREAM     LISTENING    670    /dev/gpmctl
unix  0      [ ACC ]     STREAM     LISTENING    17104  /tmp/.X11-unix/X0
unix  1      [ ]         STREAM     CONNECTED    25957  @0000013a
unix  0      [ ACC ]     STREAM     LISTENING    1032   /tmp/mysql.sock
unix  1      [ N ]       STREAM     CONNECTED    27526  @00000160
unix  1      [ ]         STREAM     CONNECTED    26753  @00000142
unix  1      [ ]         STREAM     CONNECTED    652    @00000004
unix  1      [ N ]       STREAM     CONNECTED    27587  @00000162
unix  1      [ ]         STREAM     CONNECTED    26744  @00000140
unix  1      [ ]         STREAM     CONNECTED    642    @00000003
unix  1      [ ]         STREAM     CONNECTED    28666  /tmp/.X11-unix/X0
unix  1      [ ]         STREAM     CONNECTED    27588  /tmp/.X11-unix/X0
unix  1      [ ]         STREAM     CONNECTED    27527  /tmp/.X11-unix/X0
unix  0      [ ]         STREAM                  27523
unix  1      [ ]         STREAM     CONNECTED    26760  /tmp/.X11-unix/X0
unix  1      [ ]         STREAM     CONNECTED    653    /dev/log
unix  1      [ ]         STREAM     CONNECTED    643    /dev/log
unix  1      [ ]         STREAM     CONNECTED    597    /dev/log
```

As you examine the list, if you compare the output to a list of running processes on your system, you can determine that some of the processes listening for requests do not have a daemon spawned to bind the port. This is because the inetd metadaemon is listening and ready to spawn a daemon for those ports on demand, such as the telnet port.

inetd is discussed further in Chapter 11, "inetd, inetd.conf, and network attacks (rooting the box)."

If netstat is called with the -v switch, you could find out about unsupported protocols on the system. The last few lines of output give you this:

```
netstat: no support for `AF IPX' on this system.
netstat: no support for `AF AX25' on this system.
netstat: no support for `AF NETROM' on this system.
```

These lines show that this particular system does not have support for IPX, AX25, or NETROM compiled in.

By examining the output of `netstat -a`, you can quickly determine which ports are ready to respond to queries on the system. Any ports without a corresponding entry in /etc/services will have a process in the process table listening specifically on that port. An entry in /etc/services is not required for all services but helps prevent contention for a port if you know it is already allocated. If a port is already bound, another service cannot start up there.

So if you find open ports and don't know what they are or what is binding them, you might want to find out, since remote control or other Trojans will bind arbitrary high ports.

Any port that is closed (not connected and not listening) is one less way for someone to enter the system. If no port is listening for a connection, no connection will occur, and an attacker will have to move on.

But the answer is not to stop all services—many are either needed or desired. Options for handling these ports will be examined in later chapters.

Summary

This chapter briefly covered well-known services, what ports are, how they relate to services, and why they are needed. Then, it examined the output to netstat to determine ports in use and ports listening for connections. These are needed for a connection to occur to a system. These ports are the means outsiders use to communicate with the host.

Chapter 11

inetd, inetd.conf, and network attacks (rooting the box)

IN THIS CHAPTER

- ◆ Understanding inetd

- ◆ Working with inetd.conf

- ◆ Defending against network attacks

- ◆ Understanding honey pots

UNDERSTANDING HOW YOUR system spawns servers that aren't started during system initialization or found in the process table (until someone connects to them) but are still available is a mystery to many newcomers to Linux. But you need to know how this happens and how to change it so you aren't running services you don't want to offer. The first part of this chapter will cover how services not started at system initialization are started and how you can prevent that.

The second part of the chapter discusses network attacks. The Internet is a cross-section of society, and is as friendly or unfriendly as society. But you need to think global society, not just what's within 100 or even 1,000 miles of you. This includes unfriendly governments as well as unfriendly people.

inetd

To understand about inetd, examine the output from netstat -a. Listing 11-1 is an abbreviated output from netstat -a to illustrate the points discussed in this section.

Listing 11-1: Partial netstat -a output

```
Active Internet connections (servers and established)
Proto Recv-Q Send-Q Local Address          Foreign Address       State
tcp      0      0 *:6000                  *:*                   LISTEN
tcp      0      0 *:3306                  *:*                   LISTEN
tcp      0      0 *:www                   *:*                   LISTEN
```

tcp	0	0	*:10000	*:*	LISTEN
tcp	0	0	*:smtp	*:*	LISTEN
tcp	0	0	*:sunrpc	*:*	LISTEN
tcp	0	0	*:swat	*:*	LISTEN
tcp	0	0	*:finger	*:*	LISTEN
tcp	0	0	*:imap2	*:*	LISTEN
tcp	0	0	*:pop3	*:*	LISTEN
tcp	0	0	*:ftp	*:*	LISTEN
tcp	0	0	*:time	*:*	LISTEN
tcp	0	0	*:chargen	*:*	LISTEN
tcp	0	0	*:daytime	*:*	LISTEN
tcp	0	0	*:discard	*:*	LISTEN
tcp	0	0	*:echo	*:*	LISTEN
udp	0	0	*:xdmcp	*:*	
udp	0	0	*:sunrpc	*:*	
udp	0	0	*:time	*:*	
udp	0	0	*:chargen	*:*	
udp	0	0	*:daytime	*:*	
udp	0	0	*:discard	*:*	
udp	0	0	*:echo	*:*	
raw	0	0	*:icmp	*:*	7
raw	0	0	*:tcp	*:*	7

Examining first the lines with service numbers and not names, you have 6000, 3306, and 10000. The reason these are numbers is that they are not listed in /etc/services. Because they are not listed in /etc/services, they have their port number rather than a name associated with them.

Going through the list, you should try to identify which servers belong to the numbered services. The first one is 6000. Remember, though, as mentioned in the previous chapter, ports 6000–6010 are used by the X server, so this listing is of no concern since you know an X server is running. The 3306 port is used by mysql. Since mysql will always use this, you could list this port in /etc/services and always know at a glance what you're looking at. The final one is 10000. This port is in use by a program called webmin. Again, if you've allocated that port for use by webmin, you could just list it in /etc/services, and not wonder what it is the next time you look at it.

Only one process may bind any given port at any one time. So each listed port has one and only one process associated with it.

The rest of the services in Listing 11-1 are shown by their names because all are listed in /etc/services. But if you compare the list of servers awaiting connections with the list of servers in the process table, you come up short on servers. You will be able to find a server for port 80, the www server, which is listed in the process table as httpd. In fact, you'll see a number of httpd processes. You will also find sendmail running and binding port 25 (smtp). Several others are also obvious. But what appears to be missing from the process list is a list something like the following: swat, finger, imap2, pop3, ftp, and others. Looking these up in /etc/services, you see that they are exactly what they say they are. So if they are not running, how is it that the ports they service are bound? If you open an ftp client and ftp to local-host, an ftp server will greet you. Once that server has greeted you, you can look in the process list (while that client is active) and find a listing for an ftp server.

httpd processes are discussed in detail in Chapter 20, "Installing and running a secure Apache Web server."

What is happening is very simple. A program called inetd is running and bind-ing these ports based on a list it has of which ports you want it to listen to. This saves resources because you aren't running dozens of servers all the time — just one small program. When a request for a service comes in on a particular port, inetd looks in /etc/inetd.conf for the program to start. This is why you will notice a very short delay between requesting a connection and receiving a login prompt, at least the first time. Subsequent delays should be much shorter.

Not all services can or should be run via inetd. Some services require a lot of time to load and initialize. You risk losing the connection on these services if you run them from inetd. Check the server documentation for guidelines regarding the use of inetd for any particular service.

Because not all services can or should be run from inetd, those that are recom-mended are already set up. You will look at this list below. Many of these services are neither required or desired in many cases, and can simply be disabled.

Working with inetd.conf

In order to run services from inetd, you need to understand how /etc/inetd.conf works. This is the configuration file you will use to enable or disable services on a port not bound by a running server, and specify what actions to take for a connec-tion request to any listed port.

The /etc/inetd.conf file shown in Listing 11-2 is a fairly complex configuration file with seven fields.

◆ The first field is the service name. This name must correspond to a service name listed in the first field of the /etc/services file.

◆ The second field is the socket type and will correspond to one of stream, dgram, raw, rdm, or seqpacket, depending on the socket type the server requires: stream, datagram, raw, reliably delivered message, or sequenced packet socket. In general, tcp packets will be stream, and udp packets will be datagram. When setting up a service in inetd.conf, these values should be used unless instructions accompanying the software state differently.

Listing 11-2: Default Caldera (2.3) /etc/inetd.conf file

```
#
# inetd.conf    This file describes the services that will be available
#           through the INETD TCP/IP super server.  To re-configure
#           the running INETD process, edit this file, then send the
#           INETD process a SIGHUP signal.
#
# Version: @(#)/etc/inetd.conf   3.10   05/27/93
#
# Authors: Original taken from BSD UNIX 4.3/TAHOE.
#          Fred N. van Kempen, <waltje@uwalt.nl.mugnet.org>
#
# Modified for Debian Linux by Ian A. Murdock <imurdock@shell.portal.com>
#
# Modified for RHS Linux by Marc Ewing <marc@redhat.com>
#
# Further modified by Olaf Kirch <okir@caldera.com> for Caldera Open Linux
#
# <service_name> <sock_type> <proto> <flags> <user> <server_path> <args>
#
# Echo, discard, daytime, and chargen are used primarily for testing.
#
# To re-read this file after changes, just do a 'killall -HUP inetd'
#
# Note: builtin UDP services now silently drop packets from ports < 512.
echo       stream   tcp    nowait    root    internal
echo       dgram    udp    wait      root    internal
discard    stream   tcp    nowait    root    internal
discard    dgram    udp    wait      root    internal
daytime    stream   tcp    nowait    root    internal
daytime    dgram    udp    wait      root    internal
chargen    stream   tcp    nowait    root    internal
chargen    dgram    udp    wait      root    internal
time       stream   tcp    nowait    root    internal
time       dgram    udp    wait      root    internal
```

```
#
# These are standard services.
#
ftp        stream  tcp    nowait  root     /usr/sbin/tcpd in.ftpd -l -a
#telnet    stream  tcp    nowait  root     /usr/sbin/tcpd   in.telnetd
#gopher    stream  tcp    nowait  root     /usr/sbin/tcpd   gn
#
# do not uncomment smtp unless you *really* know what you are doing.
# smtp is handled by the sendmail daemon now, not smtpd.  It does NOT
# run from here, it is started at boot time from /etc/rc.d/rc#.d.
#smtp      stream  tcp    nowait  root     /usr/bin/smtpd   smtpd
#nntp      stream  tcp    nowait  root     /usr/sbin/tcpd   in.nntpd
#
# Shell, login, exec and talk are BSD protocols.
#
#shell     stream  tcp    nowait   root    /usr/sbin/tcpd   in.rshd
#login     stream  tcp    nowait   root    /usr/sbin/tcpd   in.rlogind
#exec      stream  tcp    nowait   root    /usr/sbin/tcpd   in.rexecd
#talk      dgram   udp    wait    nobody.tty   /usr/sbin/tcpd   in.talkd
#ntalk     dgram   udp    wait    nobody.tty   /usr/sbin/tcpd   in.ntalkd
#dtalk     stream  tcp    wait    nobody.tty   /usr/sbin/tcpd   in.dtalkd
#
# Pop and imap mail services et al
#
#pop2      stream  tcp    nowait  root     /usr/sbin/tcpd ipop2d
pop3       stream  tcp    nowait  root     /usr/sbin/tcpd ipop3d
imap       stream  tcp    nowait  root     /usr/sbin/tcpd imapd
#
# The Internet UUCP service.
#
#uucp      stream  tcp    nowait  uucp     /usr/sbin/tcpd   /usr/sbin/uucico -l
#
# Tftp service is provided primarily for booting.  Most sites
# run this only on machines acting as "boot servers." Do not uncomment
# this unless you *need* it.
#
#tftp      dgram   udp    wait    root     /usr/sbin/tcpd   in.tftpd
#bootps    dgram   udp    wait    root     /usr/sbin/tcpd   bootpd
#
# cfinger is for GNU finger, which is currently not in use in RHS Linux
#
finger     stream  tcp    nowait  nobody   /usr/sbin/tcpd   in.fingerd -u
#cfinger   stream  tcp    nowait  root     /usr/sbin/tcpd   in.cfingerd
#
# Finger, systat and netstat give out user information which may be
```

```
# valuable to potential "system crackers."  Many sites choose to disable
# some or all of these services to improve security.
#
#systat    stream    tcp    nowait    nobody    /usr/sbin/tcpd  /bin/ps    -auwwx
#netstat   stream    tcp    nowait    nobody    /usr/sbin/tcpd  /bin/netstat --inet
#
# Authentication
#
#auth     stream   tcp      nowait  root    /usr/sbin/tcpd in.identd -t120
swat     stream   tcp      nowait.400 root    /usr/sbin/tcpd swat
#
# End of inetd.conf
```

♦ The third field is the protocol type and may include any of tcp, udp, rpc/tcp or rpc/udp. This field will also correspond to the protocol type listed for the service in /etc/services.

♦ The fourth entry will be either wait or nowait. Generally, udp will be wait, and tcp will be nowait. One exception to this is tftp, which, although it is a udp packet, creates a psuedo-connection, and so must use nowait in order to avoid a race condition. The nowait allows a process to intervene because it does not die immediately and continues to run as a privileged process, a condition which must be avoided (see sidebar). The wait forces each new request to authenticate because the psuedo-connection dies immediately. Otherwise, the process still waiting on the queue may pick up this psuedo-connection as the previous user. The wait and nowait tell the server how to respond to packets received on the port. The wait services are single threaded and remain on the wait queue until they terminate. The nowait services establish a connection and move off the wait queue while they continue communications so another server can bind to the port. This entry may also have an optional numeric argument appended following a decimal point, as in: nowait.400. This specifies the maximum number of servers that may be spawned within a 60-second period. Without this option, the default is 40.

♦ The fifth field specifies the user the server will run as when invoked by inetd. This permits the flexibility to run a service as a less privileged user than root. The user field can also optionally specify a group in the form *user.group*. If no group is specified, the primary group of the specified user is used.

♦ The last two fields are the program and program arguments. The flexibility of having two fields for the program is what makes it possible to invoke the tcp wrappers program with the actual server as the argument. The default entries in our example use tcpd, the tcpwrappers deamon to call the actual daemon.

Race conditions

You've probably heard or seen the term "race condition" before. If not, you will. A race condition depends on two things: commands that take place over time, and commands where the effective user ID changes to 0 during execution.

When working with a file system, commands, such as the mkdir command, internally change effective user ID to 0 in order to create a directory. This must happen whenever a file (directory) is created because the command is working directly with the file system, and the file system is owned by root. So when the directory is created (this is a multi-step process), it happens as the effective UID of 0. Once the directory is created, it must have the ownership changed to that of the user calling the program. These are two separate, easily distinguishable processes that occur when mkdir runs.

Now assume the system is under a heavy load, and the user called mkdir with nice to slow the process down even more. Assume also that directly following the mkdir command in the shell script was a command to remove the directory and create a link to /etc/shadow. If the bad guy could create a condition whereby the directory was removed and the link established between the time mkdir created the directory and performed the ownership change, then /etc/shadow would now be owned by the user running the program.

So a race condition depends on a process with a chain of events, with those events occuring as the effective UID 0, and whose chain occurs over time and may be intervened. In other words, process A calls process B, which modifies the result of process A, but which allows a window of opportunity between the processes. Other conditions are also required to be able to exploit the race, but the details are beyond the scope of this text.

See Chapter 15 for more details on TCP Wrappers.

Looking at the example, you'll see that the line starting `ftp` is in use. If you want to deny use of ftp, you simply put a "#" sign as the first character on the line and restart your inetd server. Frequently, newcomers to Linux will be confused by the difference between the /etc/inetd.conf file, which tells inetd what services to run, and the /etc/services file. Remember, though, that you don't want to comment out services from the /etc/services file, but you will want to comment them out of the /etc/inetd.conf file. While commenting out or removing an entry from either file will have the same result (you won't run that particular service), other programs may use /etc/services and may need the entry.

You can restart a server in several different ways. Most texts recommend sending a SIGHUP, or hangup signal, to the server. Two easy ways to do this are:

```
kill -1 $(pidof inetd)
kill -HUP $(pidof inetd)
```

Or, you can just restart the server:

```
/etc/rc.d/init.d/inet stop ; /etc/rc.d/init.d/inet
start
```

One thing to note is that any servers already running will not be stopped. That is, if someone is already logged in to the system via telnet, that session will not be killed. But no one else will be able to log in.

Defending against network attacks

Right up front, understand that for an attacker to enter your system over the network, you must have one or more services running and accessible on the interface the attacker has access to.

You are vulnerable to attack (your box being cracked) only through services you offer. Shut down or block access to services, and you deny entry.

That said, having a server isn't much good if it doesn't serve anything. It also does not prevent someone from denying you access to your network, but that is a different story. The rest of this book will be dedicated to maintaining a secure system that offers network services. Be advised that doing so will require some effort on your part. If you are unable or unwilling to "keep an eye" on your system (either manually or via scripts that mail you information), then you should either not run network services or block them to all but trusted connections. Even then, you may not be completely safe.

What is the object of an attack? Many of the crackers on the Internet are script kiddies. They tend to be young, rebellious, sometimes anti-social, but all start out wanting to see if they can do it. But be aware that this is only a percentage of the attackers on the Internet today. A number of much more highly sophisticated crackers are also loose. Their eventual targets are much bigger, but they will want to cover their tracks. So any system they can use as a "cut-out" to get to their eventual target may be the reason they're interested in your system.

The following will be repeated a number of times in the course of this section of the book: Time is both your friend and your enemy. Some of the information in this book is designed to help buy you time — time with which to discover and react to attempted cracks or actual breaches. But once a cracker successfully enters your system, time becomes your enemy. Given only a short amount of time, most crackers can delete any trace of the crack attempt and replace your binaries with ones that will allow them continued access undetected.

A network works because at some level there is trust. Trust can be given to a user, and/or a system. The system trusts root. You trust your binaries. This is why a cracker will almost always replace a key, trusted binary. This is why the attempt to gain access to your system will almost always be as root. If a cracker is to eradicate all traces of entry and activity, it must be as root. If a cracker is to assure himself continued access, he will install one or more sabotaged binaries or alter the /etc/passwd and /etc/shadow files.

TIP You can only do so much to protect your trusted system. After that, you need to set up audit trails. The more difficult these audit trails are to detect, the better your chances of detecting an intruder. And several audit trails are better than one.

So what can you do? How will you know? As I said at the outset, time is your friend. Before an attempt on your system is made, in most (but not all) cases, you will get some kind of warning. The attacker must know something about your system to be able to identify possible vulnerabilities. This can be accomplished in any number of ways, but the most common is simply to scan your systems. By scanning your systems, an attacker can learn what services you are offering (much as you did with netstat -a). In most cases, he will also know what operating system you are running, even to within a few version numbers. Once he has this information, he can look over OS vulnerabilities and vulnerabilities of services. The specific service may or may not be guessed. That is, often, an attacker who wishes to know more about a particular service may simply connect to it and ask the server for information about itself (which many either provide for the asking, or provide up front without asking).

Each step narrows the list of possible vulnerabilities. This is an important point: The more an attacker knows about your system, the more vulnerable it is. For example, several FTP server packages are available for Linux: wu-ftpd, ProFTP, etc. Each server has a different set of vulnerabilities. The vulnerabilities of any one will be different from the vulnerabilities of another. In most cases, an attempt to gain root access to a system ("to root a box" using the root user name as a verb to describe the action) comes via a buffer overflow.

TIP

Once in, an intruder will often bring a "root kit" with her to expedite continued access.

A buffer overflow is a condition whereby more information than is expected is passed to a variable. So if the variable is expecting eight bytes of information or fewer, and it receives 16 bytes, if the programmer forgot to check for this invalid condition, 16 bytes would be passed to the registers. These extra bytes would overflow into other memory, and depending on what they are, could be executed.

By way of an example, an old attack on a Web server consisted of exploiting an untrapped buffer overflow in a program called phf (no longer in use, but often still found on older systems). The exploit was to send a particular sequence to a www URL on a vulnerable server – for example:

```
http://www.yourserver.org/cgi-bin/phf?Qname=x%0a/bin/sh+-s%0a
```

Notice the "/bin/sh" sequence? The attacker is attempting to trick phf into spawning a shell onto a port. Since this phf script would run as root, this would provide the cracker a root prompt.

But will you always see a scan before an attack? No. If you offer services, such as www to the world, expect that any attacker out there knows that. He doesn't need to scan if he wants to attack the www server. He can simply attempt the attack in the above paragraph hoping that some server, somewhere, is still vulnerable. I have no doubt that if this particular malfeasant were not caught and prosecuted by his ISP (very unlikely) or one of the systems he compromised, he has root access to a system somewhere at this time. In fact, it appears that this attack came from a "rooted" box (the attack appeared to come from two different educational institutions at the same time, almost certainly from compromised systems at each location).

What other means can a cracker use to gain access? Several, but one favorite seems to be to obtain access to a system and simply listen for any traffic traveling on the local wire, capturing any and all username password pairs traveling that wire. For example, a script kiddie on Road Runner (a cable modem service available in some areas in the United States) could simply listen for all traffic on the local network segment. If the local segment has 200–500 users, he could potentially get over 1,000 username password pairs in just a few days. Many folks will log in to their company, either using telnet, ftp, or just picking up mail. Under most circumstances, passwords are sent unencrypted. Now, this cracker will have hundreds of systems and legitimate username password pairs to use to attempt access. A quick look around on one of these systems is all it will take. With a legitimate login, files can be ftp'd in, and a "root kit" installed on the system. If this is not caught, this cracker will own that system and can glean even more username password pairs.

Some operators have caught on to this particular trick and have implemented a more secure means for cable modem users to access the Internet without compromising passwords so easily. Basically, their connection has a tunnel directly to the server, and systems on the same wire cannot see each other's traffic. But this is not universal (yet).

Once a cracker is inside a system, all the buffer overflow tricks still work, and in fact, there are even more binaries available (any that run as SUID root) to try to get to overflow. But another set of vulnerabilities is also present. One is creating an exploitable race condition. A race condition exploit is a special set of circumstances a user tries to induce to get a non-privileged system call to execute with root privileges.

On a Linux system, some processes, such as creating a directory, involve the kernel in the process through a system call. The process of creating a directory has two phases, one of creating the directory entry, and another of chowning the directory to the correct user. Each of these processes will take some unit of time. The chowning process involves the kernel, so at some point has root privileges.

Other vulnerabilities involve tricking root into running a process for the user, or taking advantage of a "secure" directory, such as /tmp, where root may place a file by a known name. The cracker who can know in advance the name of the file can put one there ahead of time for root to use in place of the one root would create.

Considering the information in the foregoing paragraphs, it is easy to become paranoid. And while the amount of malicious activity on the Internet is increasing daily (thanks mostly to inexpensive, dedicated 24-hour access), the benefits most decidedly outweigh the risks. The problem comes in ensuring that your system remains safe from the script kiddies and system crackers on the Internet today.

Understanding honey pots

A honey pot is a system designed to entice "flies," in this case crackers, to attempt to break into a system. This system is booby-trapped such that all attempts against it are logged, because it offers no legitimate services. At least, it has no content of any interest to anyone. Its sole purpose in life is to watch and record all attempts against it. This includes programs like tcpdump to record all network traffic sent to the Internet-connected interface.

Several security outfits run honey pots to learn more about the anatomy of a crack. They do not do this lightly, and they know what to look for. Running a honey pot, especially if the cracker learns what it is, could net you all kinds of grief. Many of the script kiddies these days have a very anti-authoritarian streak, and if they find a "trap," they will come after you with a vengeance. You can expect attempts on any box they can identify as part of your network, and failing any success there, they will likely run Denial of Service attacks. Running a honey pot is very bad idea for all but advanced security administrators.

Summary

This chapter expanded your knowledge of how Linux offers a large number of services without using excessive resources to do so. By using the Internet metadaemon, you can efficiently handle a number of small, fast services. You also learned how the configuration file, /etc/inetd.conf, dictates those services to be offered via inetd.

You also gained an understanding of the consequences of offering services to the world and how crackers may attempt to take advantage of these services. You learned that, in general, some warning would be present to alert you to the fact that someone may attempt to crack your security. You also learned some basics of how this can be accomplished, and what the cracker must know or do to gain entry.

Chapter 12

Vulnerable services and protocols

IN THIS CHAPTER

◆ Understanding network services

◆ Understanding vulnerabilities

◆ Demystifying servers

IF YOU LOOK AT ALMOST any distribution as it is installed by default, you will see a number of services running (see "Understanding netstat" in Chapter 10). What you see running may be influenced by a number of things, including which packages you chose to install, etc. For the most part, if you told the install program to install a particular service, then that service is most likely running and with a default configuration. This is fairly standard for most distributions. The Debian distribution will walk you through a configuration on some services, but not all. So if you install a service, expect to see it running. It's up to you to ensure that it is properly configured. If you don't want to offer that service, remove the package.

The problem with running a large number of services is that each one introduces a potential security problem. Each network service, even services you might not think of as network services, normally have a listener on either a tcp port, a udp port, or an rpc port. Here you'll learn about several common services and their potential for problems.

 TIP Network security vulnerabilities can be exploited only via services offered. Services that are not running cannot be exploited. If you see a service offered that you don't understand, turn it off or block its use by any but localhost (more on this in Chapter 16). This will reduce your risks significantly.

Services run on ports below 1024 are considered "privileged." That is, only root may bind a port below 1024. So any service on any port below 1024 is being run by root. Unless some precautions are taken, this can compromise your system. While ports above 1024 can be bound by anyone, they can also be bound by root. So just because a service binds to a port above 1024 doesn't mean it's necessarily safe. This chapter, however, will consider only those services run on privileged ports.

FTP, port 21 and 20

The file transfer protocol (FTP) is used to exchange files between two machines. For FTP, a server is not usually running. A listener is placed on TCP port 21 by inetd and a server is spawned on demand (connection by a client). If you are using tcpd, actions dictated by tcpd will be carried out, and if the client isn't blocked, he will be connected and provided a login prompt.

When discussing FTP, most talk is about a client or server application that provides one side of a service or the other. But FTP is a protocol. That is, each server application, be it ftp, telnet, etc., has its own protocol.

 A protocol is a set of rules that dictates how two systems will communicate (*protocol* means rules). So each different service has its own communications protocol.

FTP is unusual as far as servers go in that it will open a second port in addition to the connection on port 21, but only when requested. The entire transaction starts as follows:

1. Client makes a connection request to port 21.

2. The SYN-ACK sequence takes place, and (if applicable), tcpd performs its functions.

3. If the connection request is not rejected by tcpd, an FTP server is started to answer the port 21 query.

4. Client and server exchange information and begin a session.

An active FTP session (called "active" only to differentiate it from "passive") will use this port 21-port 1024+ (a random port above 1024 to complete the connection) for passing login data and other commands between the client and server. But once the server has been asked to provide information back to the client (a directory listing or the contents of a file), a second channel is opened. This is where the ftp-data port, port 20, comes in. The server contacts the client on port 20 (and completes the connection via a random port above 1024) and begins sending the client the requested data. The status of the transfer is sent via port 21.

Binding a port

This and many networking texts will tell you that a service binds a port. What this means is that the program offering the service makes a connection to that port. It does this by creating a socket and listening on that socket to network traffic. A system can have only one socket per port. So two programs (or two separate instances of the same program) cannot bind the same port. But one program can service multiple connections to the one socket by spawning child processes and passing each incoming connection off in turn to a new child process. The parent process is the only process binding the port; the child processes just service the requests. Some services can also bind multiple ports (Apache, for example).

If you try to start a separate instance of a program, or a different program designed to bind a port that is already bound by another program, you will receive an error message that the port is already bound. The same port can show up as bound for a TCP or a UDP connection or both. Ports are generally bound to offer a service, but some ports are bound by the bad guys as markers that a system has been rooted. A complete list of ports used by Trojans and markers can be found at http://www.simovits.com/nyheter9902.html.

Some of you may be saying, "Oh, so that was why I had problems using ftp and had to use Netscape to ftp in some files." A lot of firewall software, and especially software that performs masquerading (aka Network Address Translation — NAT) will allow connections on port below 1024 outbound, but not permit inbound connections. Since the FTP server is trying to contact the client on port 20 (that is, the client puts a listener on port 20), the firewall is blocking that connection, or in the case of a masquerading firewall, may not know who the requesting client is; it only knows it (the firewall) didn't request the connection, so it drops the packets on the floor.

Firewalls and masquerading are discussed more extensively in Chapters 16 and 18, respectively.

Netscape uses a form of transfer for ftp known as passive mode. That is, instead of the server opening a separate channel to contact the client to send data, it waits passively for the client (in this case Netscape) to get the data on port 21. This can also be done by using a program provided in OpenLinux called pftp, for passive ftp. Some clients also have a passive mode that may be invoked on command.

To give you a better understanding of the basics, you're going to use telnet, which uses a different protocol, to connect to ftp and issue a few commands. Follow along with Listing 12-1 and feel free to try this yourself:

Listing 12-1: A connection to an FTP server from a telnet client

```
[david@volcan david]$ telnet chiriqui 21
Trying 192.168.0.2...
Connected to chiriqui.pananix.com.
Escape character is '^]'.
220 chiriqui.pananix.com FTP server (Version wu-2.5.0(1) Tue Jul 27
18:42:33 MDT 1999) ready.
user david
331 Password required for david.
pass mypasswd
230 User david logged in.
help
214-The following commands are recognized (* =>'s unimplemented).
    USER    PORT    STOR    MSAM*   RNTO    NLST    MKD     CDUP
    PASS    PASV    APPE    MRSQ*   ABOR    SITE    XMKD    XCUP
    ACCT*   TYPE    MLFL*   MRCP*   DELE    SYST    RMD     STOU
    SMNT*   STRU    MAIL*   ALLO    CWD     STAT    XRMD    SIZE
    REIN*   MODE    MSND*   REST    XCWD    HELP    PWD     MDTM
    QUIT    RETR    MSOM*   RNFR    LIST    NOOP    XPWD
214 Direct comments to root@localhost.
pasv
227 Entering Passive Mode (192,168,0,2,214,43)
stat
211-chiriqui.pananix.com FTP server status:
     Version wu-2.5.0(1) Tue Jul 27 18:42:33 MDT 1999
     Connected to volcan.pananix.com (192.168.0.1)
     Logged in as david
     TYPE: ASCII, FORM: Nonprint; STRUcture: File; transfer MODE:
Stream
     in Passive mode (192,168,0,2,214,43)
     0 data bytes received in 0 files
     0 data bytes transmitted in 0 files
     0 data bytes total in 0 files
     45 traffic bytes received in 0 transfers
     1113 traffic bytes transmitted in 0 transfers
     1208 traffic bytes total in 0 transfers
211 End of status
quit
221-You have transferred 0 bytes in 0 files.
221-Total traffic for this session was 1319 bytes in 0 transfers.
221-Thank you for using the FTP service on chiriqui.pananix.com.
```

```
221 Goodbye.
Connection closed by foreign host.
```

By examining the above connection, you can see a lot of what is going on. The first line is starting a telnet session, but it is pointed not at its default port of 23 but at the ftp port 21. As part of the initial connect, the server tells the client something about itself. Here is where you can usually find out about the server and version the remote system is running. Here, the remote host "chiriqui" is running the Washington University wu-ftp server version 2.5.0(1) built on Tue, 27 Jul 1999 at 6:42 pm Mountain Daylight Time. This is a significant amount of information. The wu-ftp server has some known bugs in some versions that are exploitable. A quick search of cracker sites will turn up any known information about this server and its vulnerabilities, and often a program to exploit those vulnerabilities.

The next few lines contain 'user david'. Normally an ftp client would ask you for a username as part of the connection process. Since this isn't an ftp client, you need to tell the ftp server what it is you're sending. This is followed by a notice that you need to send a password, so just below that is 'pass mypasswd'. Note that this password will appear just as it is in the text. Within the ftp client, the code runs a system call (in a manner similar to you running `stty -echo`) that turns echoing to the screen off. Once the user inputs the password and hits return, the password is transmitted and the equivalent of the `stty echo` command returns screen display to normal.

The commands that you are typing and the return information you are seeing are exactly as they would appear on the wire if you were watching the transaction with a program like tcpdump. This should give you an indication of how vulnerable you are if someone can run tcpdump or a similar program on a system on your network. In fact, you will find that if the upstream router you are connected to "leaks" packets onto your network (packets not destined for machines on your network) that you can see a good many username/password pairs traversing the wire.

The help command above shows commands the server knows about. You should take care when using these since they often require arguments or other transactions with the client you may not be able to provide. Finally, you can get some stats and quit the session.

 Should you connect with a telnet client to a non-telnet server and find you are "stuck" — that is, you can't get a command prompt — press Ctrl+]. (That's what the note about "Escape character is '^]'." is all about.) You will receive a telnet prompt and can type **quit** to end the session.

By default, anonymous FTP access is provided by an FTP client for "anonymous" or "ftp" user access. The user anonymous is a synonym for ftp. When anonymous access is provided, the system will perform a chroot to the ftp home directory. A chroot forces the user into a "jail" so to speak, not allowing her to leave. As far as that user is concerned, she is seeing the entire system. She cannot cd up out of that subdirectory. Symlinks pointing to other parts of the system are not followed. But this chroot jail must contain all the pieces the system root requires in order to function properly. (More on this in Chapter 14 on mitigating vulnerabilities.) Several services can or do use a chroot jail to limit where a user can go and the damage any cracker can cause.

Providing too many services on one system can open security holes that any one service wouldn't. In this sense, allowing FTP access and HTTP access to the same system could pose a problem. One exploit calls for ftp'ing in some file that is then accessed via an (albeit misconfigured) http server such as Apache. Likewise, permitting both anonymous and user FTP access is also questionable unless the machine is dedicated to only FTP. Chapter 3 discussed appropriate permissions for an FTP server's incoming directory. Your best bet is to use two separate systems, one to provide ftp and another to provide http access. Using http only to provide download capability is one way around the problem, but you will lose upload capability with this solution.

Another way to reduce your vulnerabilities is to ensure that your /etc/pam.d/ftp file has the best options for your situation. The OpenLinux /etc/pam.d/ftp default file appears in Listing 12-2.

Listing 12-2: Default /etc/pam.d/ftp file

```
auth       required     /lib/security/pam_listfile.so item=user
sense=deny file=/etc/ftpusers onerr=succeed
auth       required     /lib/security/pam_pwdb.so shadow nullok
auth       required     /lib/security/pam_shells.so
account    required     /lib/security/pam_pwdb.so
session    required     /lib/security/pam_pwdb.so
```

The first line forces a lookup in /etc/ftpusers (file=/etc/ftpusers). Because the file contains usernames (item=user), those users are denied system access (sense=deny). If the file doesn't exist, or the username isn't listed, then no one will be denied.

The second line requires a username/password match (although null passwords are acceptable). The third line just verifies that the users shell is one of the shells listed in /etc/shells. The last two lines are stacked as explained in Chapter 1.

telnet, port 23

Another common protocol is the telnet protocol. You saw in the previous section how a telnet client could be used to connect to any port. The telnet client is an extremely powerful tool for use in debugging services, particularly those where the protocol of the server is known.

But make no mistake about it, the telnet server is one of the most dangerous servers to have running. It is a totally wide-open protocol in the sense that anyone can use it to access a system. The connect stream is simple and unencrypted. This server is bad news even on a private network. A much safer (and easily more flexible) remote login protocol is provided by ssh, the Secure Shell client and server.

If you are running a telnet server, I highly recommend turning it off. If you feel the urge to find out who is looking for open telnet ports (most wannabe crackers and script kiddies do), you can booby trap port 23 via the TCP Wrappers program (see Chapter 15) then deny the service or just use netfilter to log and drop the packets (see Chapter 16). Your call. Like all things UNIX, there's more than one way to solve any given problem. Just make sure it fits your policy.

TIP Not included in this book, but of great value in tracking IP addresses back to their source is 'dig'. By using `dig -x <unknown.ip.address.here>` you can find out who owns the IP. Copying your logs with a complaint may get action. If it doesn't, blocking the IP or subnet is also effective.

smtp, port 25

Caldera's OpenLinux by default installs sendmail, the undisputed king of Internet mail back ends. This server is extremely powerful and flexible. It can handle hundreds of simultaneous connections both sending and receiving. A discussion of its proper configuration could fill a book. As configured by Caldera, it will suite most common user needs. You do need to have an smtp server running, but others are reputed to be more secure and easier to configure. They include qmail and a few others. These are not provided by Caldera, so would require a search on the Internet.

NOTE Mail programs have three classifications. The back end, or smtp server, used to transfer mail between system, is the Mail Transport Agent (MTA). The front end, or mail client, used to read and send mail to the MTA, is the Mail User Agent (MUA). Often there is a local delivery agent (sometimes referred to as the Mail Delivery Agent — MDA) between the two, such as procmail, etc., which will take mail from sendmail and hand it off to a local mailbox.

Because sendmail is a large and powerful program, crackers have shown resourcefulness in abusing it. Fortunately, sendmail has a few tricks of its own. They include forking a process to specific users — normally those sending or receiving a message to limit the amount of damage should the message contain executable code (a Trojan horse — more on Trojan horses in Chapter 14).

Many folks on various Usenet newsgroups will recommend replacing sendmail. This book will not do that. Despite its power and complexity, it can be used safely. Shown in Listing 12-3 is the output from a mail connection in verbose mode.

Listing 12–3: A mail connection

```
[david@volcan david]$ mail -v root@chiriqui
Subject: test
this is a test.
.
EOT
root@chiriqui... Connecting to chiriqui.pananix.com. via esmtp...
220 chiriqui.pananix.com ESMTP Sendmail 8.9.3/8.9.3; Fri, 8 Oct 1999
09:52:50 -0500
>> EHLO volcan.pananix.com
250-chiriqui.pananix.com Hello volcan.pananix.com [192.168.0.1],
pleased to meet you
250-EXPN
250-VERB
250-8BITMIME
250-SIZE
250-DSN
250-ONEX
250-ETRN
250-XUSR
250 HELP
>> MAIL From:<david@volcan.pananix.com> SIZE=49
250 <david@volcan.pananix.com>... Sender ok
>> RCPT To:<root@chiriqui.pananix.com>
250 <root@chiriqui.pananix.com>... Recipient ok
>> DATA
354 Enter mail, end with "." on a line by itself
>> .
250 JAA06968 Message accepted for delivery
root@chiriqui... Sent (JAA06968 Message accepted for delivery)
Closing connection to chiriqui.pananix.com.
>> QUIT
221 chiriqui.pananix.com closing connection
```

By using the "mail" program, and invoking it in verbose mode, you can watch what happens during a normal sendmail transfer. This can be used effectively to troubleshoot remote mail problems. Note that, doing this from any but a valid sendmail host may get you rejected, but will give you a good indication of whether or not the remote system insists on accepting mail only from a valid sendmail host.

Now, do this same thing via telnet. This connection will come from host volcan (192.168.0.1) to host chiriqui (192.168.0.2). Refer to Listing 12-4. As installed, sendmail will require the connecting host to resolve, but after that, it is very trusting, and not because the host volcan is on the same subnet because this can be done to any selected host on the Internet. Those hosts not requiring reverse resolution are particularly vulnerable. (This particular sendmail mta has anti-relaying turned on, but in this case, chiriqui is configured to allow it to relay for volcan.)

Listing 12-4: A telnet to sendmail connection

```
[david@volcan david]$ telnet chiriqui 25
Trying 192.168.0.2...
Connected to chiriqui.pananix.com.
Escape character is '^]'.
220 chiriqui.pananix.com ESMTP Sendmail 8.9.3/8.9.3; Fri, 8 Oct 1999
09:59:39 -0500
EHLO localhost
250-chiriqui.pananix.com Hello volcan.pananix.com [192.168.0.1],
pleased to meet you
250-EXPN
250-VERB
250-8BITMIME
250-SIZE
250-DSN
250-ONEX
250-ETRN
250-XUSR
250 HELP
MAIL From:<root@localhost>
250 <root@localhost>... Sender ok
RCPT To:<root@localhost>
250 <root@localhost>... Recipient ok
DATA
354 Enter mail, end with "." on a line by itself
I see you.

You can't hide.


.
250 KAA07061 Message accepted for delivery
QUIT
221 chiriqui.pananix.com closing connection
Connection closed by foreign host.
```

TIP You can always issue the "help" command to find out about commands the mta will recognize. But be aware that the mta may refuse some commands, such as vrfy or expn, which can be used to verify or expand a mail address.

The first difference you should notice between the first and second exchanges is the loss of the >> sign to signal who is talking. This one is signed by root@local-host, which it's supposedly from. But you know it's really from david@volcan. In fact, you don't need to provide the from address at all; you can just do as shown in Listing 12-5.

Listing 12-5: Connection from a null host

```
MAIL From:<>
250 <>... Sender ok
```

and as indicated by the second line, that's perfectly OK with sendmail.

But looking at the mail message including full headers, you can expect what is shown in Listing 12-6.

Listing 12-6: Full mail message headers from connection in Listing 12-4

```
Received:  from localhost (volcan.pananix.com [192.168.0.1]) by
chiriqui.pananix.com (8.9.3/8.9.3) with ESMTP id KAA07263 for
root<root@localhost>; Fri, 8 Oct 1999 10:15:07 -0500
           Date:  Fri, 8 Oct 1999 10:15:07 -0500
      Message-ID:  <199910081515.KAA07263@chiriqui.pananix.com>
          Status:
  X-Mozilla-Status:  0000
 X-Mozilla-Status2:  00000000
           X-UIDL:  37fd305900000706

I see you.

You can't hide.
```

The above is viewed with Netscape, so includes a few Netscape-specific lines. Since the From line was blank, it doesn't show up. Standard headers would also include a Subject: line, a To: line, and a From: line.

Examining the first line (which actually covers three lines on the page) tells you that volcan.pananix.com at IP 192.168.0.1 calling itself "localhost" sent a message to chiriqui's sendmail server version 8.9.3 via the extended SMTP protocol with message id KAA07263 to root on Fri, 8 Oct 1999 at 10:15 am local time which is five hours behind GMT. The id KAA07263 will appear in the mail logs and gives the information shown in Listing 12-7.

Listing 12-7: Mail log listing for mail transaction in Listing 12-4

```
Oct  8 10:15:45 chiriqui sendmail[7263]: KAA07263: from=<>, size=29,
class=0, pri=30029, nrcpts=1,
msgid=<199910081515.KAA07263@chiriqui.pananix.com>, proto=ESMTP,
relay=volcan.pananix.com [192.168.0.1]
Oct  8 10:15:46 chiriqui sendmail[7264]: KAA07263: to=david,
delay=00:00:39, xdelay=00:00:00, mailer=local, relay=local,
stat=Sent
```

Each line starting with a date is a separate entry. So two entries appear. The first is the entry accepting the message for further delivery. The second shows whom it was delivered to. The reason you see `to=david` is that all root's mail is forwarded to a specific user to read.

This trick is used by script kiddies to frighten novice administrators. But now that you know how this is done (by spammers as well), you'll see that it is just a trick and no special privileges have been given to the user sending the mail. You also have a complete audit trail.

In a large majority of cases of abuse with sendmail, attackers have taken advantage of inappropriate permissions. Sendmail accesses a number of directories and files. If permissions on these files are too "loose," abusers can take advantage. Most directories and files belonging to sendmail should be read-only if that for anyone other than the user sendmail runs as. Users .forward files should be in directories with group and world write permissions turned off. The .forward file itself should be read-write for the user only.

What you also need to be careful of is the user you are when you read the mail. Mail should never be read by root. Instead, all mail destined for root should be redirected, preferably via sendmail's aliases file, to a non-privileged user. Some e-mail clients can be tricked into running code attached to a mail message. Rather than worrying about whether a particular e-mail client might be vulnerable, it is simply easier to always have a non-privileged user read the mail. Linux doesn't have the problem that other platforms do with viruses, but all systems are vulnerable to Trojan horses.

domain, port 53

Port 53 is the port the Domain Name Service (DNS) runs on. Under normal conditions — that is, requesting the specific IP address of one host — the information is passed via UDP over IP. But on occasion, DNS uses TCP — for example, when doing zone transfers or the like. This is because a zone transfer can easily exceed the size of a UDP packet.

The DNS daemon (a.k.a. BIND, for Berkeley Internet Nameserver Daemon), which runs as named (for name server daemon), has been the subject of attacks and has granted root access to more than one attacker. Chapter 14 will deal strictly with a nameserver daemon and how to set up and run one in a change root (chroot) jail.

But other daemons can work in a similar manner to control what they can access and damage.

Some daemons, notably the Apache Web Server and the anonymous FTP server, create their own chroot jails, so this procedure isn't necessary for them. Users can also be put into chroot jails if required, but this will make administration much more difficult. An overall security policy using private user groups and restricting rights within the file system makes more sense and is more easily administered.

tftp, port 69

The trivial file transfer protocol may be trivial, but can be a very large headache and a security problem, which is the only reason it is mentioned here since it is not in widespread use. TFTP works via UDP but creates a psuedo-connection. Its original use was with ARP (address resolution protocol) or BOOTP (bootstrap protocol) and used to transfer the file system to a diskless workstation. If you have to set up a diskless workstation, use the kernel's BOOTP or RARP (reverse address resolution protocol) and NFS to mount the file system. This is a much safer method than using TFTP. Unless you have some very old systems that can use only tftp, tftp should be disabled in /etc/inted.conf. There is no way to adequately secure this protocol.

finger, port 79

The finger daemon is a constant source of information for script kiddies and crackers. OpenLinux includes a daemon called safe_finger. This can be used on the localhost without the port's being open. It can also be used to attempt to connect to a remote finger daemon. By default, even this utility is only available to root on an OpenLinux system. As mentioned several times, providing this information to remote hosts is not prudent from a security standpoint.

www, port 80

The Apache Web server and its security features will be discussed in detail in Chapter 20. The 2.4.x kernel also has a Web server, which may be built into the kernel or as a kernel module to allow small systems to run a small Web server for simple pages if there isn't enough room for Apache. A number of other Web servers are also available for Linux, depending on the intended use of the server. However, this kernel http daemon was not meant to replace an httpd server. Chapter 20 will address this new feature, which can provide increased security when used in conjunction with the Apache Web server.

pop2, port 109 and pop3, port 110

The post office protocol is a fairly secure protocol that can generally be provided safely. This is the protocol in widest use among ISPs for providing mail services to their clients. You should use pop3 rather than the older pop2, but neither has any glaring security holes beyond the use of clear text passwords going out over the network. This is another good case for not using the root account to read mail.

The pop service has a pam module, which contains by default (on OpenLinux) the information shown in Listing 12-8.

Listing 12-8: The default pop service pam module

```
auth        required     /lib/security/pam_pwdb.so shadow nullok
auth        required     /lib/security/pam_nologin.so
account     required     /lib/security/pam_pwdb.so
password    required     /lib/security/pam_pwdb.so shadow nullok use_authtok
session     required     /lib/security/pam_pwdb.so
```

No surprises in this file: four stacked modules that require username/password authentication, and one that checks for the presence or absence of /etc/nologin, denying or permitting access (respectively).

sunrpc, port 111

The Sun remote procedure call (sunrpc), developed by Sun Microsystems to level the playing field when it came to mounting file systems across a network, is used by the system to register all other RPC programs. An nfs client will contact an nfs server across a network on this port first. Depending on the particular application, this may be either a udp or tcp exchange.

You can see the sunrpc in action by running `rpcinfo -p *hostname*` against your systems. If running, you'll see at least the portmapper running as both tcp and udp on port 111. This may also list any other RPC services offered by the system as shown in Listing 12-9.

Listing 12-9: rpcinfo output

```
[david@chiriqui david]$ rpcinfo -p volcan
   program vers proto   port
    100000    2   tcp    111  portmapper
    100000    2   udp    111  portmapper
    300019    1   tcp    743  amq
    300019    1   udp    744  amq
    100021    1   udp   1024  nlockmgr
```

```
100021   3   udp   1024   nlockmgr
100021   1   tcp   1024   nlockmgr
100021   3   tcp   1024   nlockmgr
100001   5   udp    781   rstatd
100001   3   udp    781   rstatd
100001   2   udp    781   rstatd
100001   1   udp    781   rstatd
```

The RPC services are registered by program number. The version is important only so that the client can ascertain what the server's capabilities are. The third column, protocol, indicates which protocols are available for use. For the most part, both are offered. The port information is of use in determining which ports you may want to block via netfilter (or ipchains) to prevent access by third parties. Note that with the exception of the portmapper itself, most programs do not have any service registered in /etc/services for the port in use by portmapper.

The RPC services are more secure than services like tftp, but can be fooled through spoofing. These services do not check, but accept the client's word for their identity. For all systems that offer read-write access, the server should be set to perform a "root_squash" — that is, it should remap all requests for root (UID 0) access to the user nobody. Access to RPC services should be very closely controlled.

 RPC allows remote systems to use system calls across the network. Generally, these calls are system-specific. But all systems know how to perform reads and writes to file systems So these calls from the remote system are translated into equivalent calls on the local system, and if permitted, are then executed.

auth, port 113

The authentication service spawns the ident daemon (identd). This daemon has fallen out of usage with the increasing numbers of Microsoft clients, which do not offer the authentication service. Few, if any, remaining servers on the Internet will disallow a connection to a client that does not reply to this form of authentication, though many services still request it.

Several versions of Caldera OpenLinux have been plagued with a version of identd that doesn't properly terminate. This can result in a system with hundreds of running identd processes. Given the fact that this service is no longer required in most places, simply turning it off is an acceptable practice.

netbios, ports 137–139

Any systems that run the LanMan protocol on their systems, including Linux systems running Samba, will find that ports 137–139 are used by processes in the LanMan stack to find other systems. You will want to decide for yourself (if you're running Samba) if you want to permit these ports to answer connections, and if so, only on internal portions of the network or to external connections as well. These ports are what a Microsoft client uses to browse the Network Neighborhood.

On non-Microsoft systems (and even on Microsoft systems that have only a TCP stack and do not have NetBIOS loaded), all NetBIOS calls are carried via TCP. When NetBIOS is routed over TCP, it can reach further than it would as a purely NetBIOS call. NetBIOS is a broadcast protocol that is restricted to the local network – that is, the broadcasts are designed not to be passed by gateways and routers, so systems on other network segments normally cannot be reached. By using TCP, you can increase this reach. That is, messages can be directed to systems on other network segments, which gives crackers yet another open door. These ports should be blocked to all but local systems.

imap2, port 143; imap3, port 220

The Internet Mail Access Protocol (IMAP), aka Interim Mail Access Protocol and Interactive Mail Access Protocol, is another of the least secure server programs run on a system. Numerous vulnerability reports show that this particular daemon is not one to run lightly. It is much more powerful than POP (the Post Office protocol), but that power comes with some risk and is the reason many ISPs don't use it.

IMAP is installed as an RPM that includes imapd as well as popd. Removing the imap RPM will also remove popd – probably not what you want. Most e-mail clients can use either imap or pop, so the choice is yours to make. But if you run imapd (the version on OpenLinux is v2 and will be active on port 143), watch for attempts against this port. You may want to block large portions of the Internet, depending on where your users will connect from.

The imap service also has a corresponding pam.d/imap file. The default OpenLinux file containst the following information as shown in Listing 12-10.

Listing 12–10: Default /etc/pam.d/imap file

```
auth        required      /lib/security/pam_pwdb.so shadow nullok
auth        required      /lib/security/pam_nologin.so
account     required      /lib/security/pam_pwdb.so
password    required      /lib/security/pam_pwdb.so shadow nullok use_authtok
session     required      /lib/security/pam_pwdb.so
```

This particular PAM contains nothing unusual. Except for the second line, this module just performs a username/password check. The second line permits or denies login based on the absence or presence (respectively) of an /etc/nologin file. You can improve imap's security posture by stacking another auth line that requires the securetty.so module and removing the two instances of nullok from the pam_pwdb.so module (users shouldn't have null passwords). The securetty.so module prevents root from using this service (root's mail should be redirected to another user anyway). This can also be done for the pop service.

xdmcp, port 177 (udp)

When you run X on your system, you will open one or more ports in the 6000–6010 range. These are the normal ports with which users can connect to X remotely. But if you are running xdm, this service will bind port 177. Look for this as a udp socket. If an X server starts looking via xdm for a server to manage the display, port 177 is the default. If you don't want X servers to use a server running xdm to manage their display, you'll need to block UDP port 177.

printer, port 515

The printing deamon, lpd, as supplied in the LPRNG RPM, is installed and configured during the install process. Also installed is a file called /etc/lpd.perms, used to determine which systems/users have what permissions with respect to the lp daemon.

The default CSOL lpd.perms file is (relatively) wide-open. That is, anyone can print to your printer. See Listing 12-11.

Listing 12-11: Default /etc/lpd.perms permissions

```
ACCEPT SERVICE=C SERVER REMOTEUSER=root
ACCEPT SERVICE=S
REJECT SERVICE=CSU
ACCEPT SERVICE=M SAMEHOST SAMEUSER
ACCEPT SERVICE=M SERVER REMOTEUSER=root
REJECT SERVICE=M
DEFAULT ACCEPT
```

The various SERVICE values are P, printing; R, spooling; C, control; S, status; U, user allowed lpc operation; M, remove from queue; Q, queue information. According to Listing 12-11, the first line allows root to control the lpd service from the local server. The second line allows anyone to get the lpd server's status — including folks in other parts of the world. No IP checking is accomplished in the file above. The third line, however, rejects control or use of the lpc command from everyone not already granted access.

Lines 4–7 deal with removal of print jobs from the queue and is relatively sane, only root (UID 0) from the local server or the same user from the same host can delete print jobs, everyone else is rejected. But the last line, the default accept, means that what hasn't been prohibited is permitted. Anyone, from anywhere in the world who can reach out and touch your IP can print anything they want to your printer. Do you really want this?

The easiest way to block unwanted print requests is to simply block port 515 from anyone outside the local network. While no particular security risks are known (as of this writing) with LPRNG, most other folks probably have little reason to print to your printer.

The alternative method of blocking unwanted printer users is to learn the lpd.perms syntax and add new rules to the file. The LPRNG program has an extremely flexible and powerful set of rules for lpd.perms to control lpd access, but it is more than just a little difficult for newcomers to understand. A good administration book will cover this topic adequately, and in great detail.

TIP You can connect to any TCP-based service and talk to it via telnet as if your telnet session were a client. All you need to do is know what the service expects. UDP services are only slightly more difficult, but the same principle applies.

"r" commands (rsh, rexec, rlogin), ports 512, 513, 514

The "r" or remote commands were among the original services to provide remote shell, remote login, and remote execution of jobs. They were designed to supplement or replace telnet. Designed in times when more trust was placed in the security of the networks, these commands provide users a way to access other systems on the network without ever being challenged for a password. And therein lies one of their greatest dangers.

All the "r" commands trust the users and network implicitly. It is simply too easy today to take advantage of these trusts. And this trust isn't limited to normal users but also includes privileged users. Two files, located either in /etc or in users' home directories, will cause all manner of headache. An alternative to the "r" commands is ssh (Secure Shell).

XREF ssh is explained in detail in Chapter 21.

But unfortunately, despite the availability of the much more secure ssh program, a number of businesses prefer to stay with the "r" commands. If you find yourself in this position, you'll want to understand how to better secure these services. Just remember, all communications are passed in the clear — no encryption takes place — so passwords can be easily sniffed.

 Any tool or software program that reads packets traveling across a network is called a *sniffer*. These tools were designed to help network administrators troubleshoot connectivity issues, but are now used by others to snoop for username/password pairs on the network.

In the /etc/services file, these services are listed without the "r" prefix — that is, they are listed as shell, exec, and login. The /etc/inetd.conf file refers to these, but at the end of the line, you'll find rshd, rexecd, and rlogind. If these lines are commented out (which I strongly recommend) and the inet daemon sent a SIGHUP, then these services will no longer be available.

If you must permit these services, you may then want to look at the authentication services. Start by looking in /etc/pam.d/. Here, three separate files exist, rsh, rexec. and rlogin, corresponding to the restricted service by the same name. You can examine these three files in detail in Listings 12-12, 12-13, and 12-14.

Listing 12-12: Default /etc/pam.d/rsh

```
auth        required        /lib/security/pam_rhosts_auth.so
auth        required        /lib/security/pam_nologin.so
account     required        /lib/security/pam_pwdb.so
session     required        /lib/security/pam_pwdb.so
```

The first line of the /etc/pam.d/rsh file can have a number of options, which are explained in Chapter 1. The line, as it stands, permits use of rhosts files in the users' home directories.

Listing 12-13: Default /etc/pam.d/rexec file

```
auth        required        /lib/security/pam_pwdb.so shadow nullok
auth        required        /lib/security/pam_nologin.so
auth        required        /lib/security/pam_listfile.so
file=/etc/ftpusers item=user sense=deny onerr=succeed
account     required        /lib/security/pam_pwdb.so
```

The rexec is a little more secure, not permitting use of the rhosts file, but you could change that just by adding it as another line. Note, however, that rexec uses the

/etc/ftpusers file the same way ftp does to deny access to someone who shouldn't be using it over the net. Again, this can be added to the rsh file. For another option, see the /etc/pam.d/rlogin file in Listing 12-14.

Listing 12-14: Default /etc/pam.d/rlogin file

```
auth        required     /lib/security/pam_securetty.so
auth        sufficient   /lib/security/pam_rhosts_auth.so
auth        required     /lib/security/pam_pwdb.so shadow nullok
auth        required     /lib/security/pam_nologin.so
account     required     /lib/security/pam_pwdb.so
#password   required     /lib/security/pam_cracklib.so
password    required     /lib/security/pam_pwdb.so shadow nullok
use_authtok
session     required     /lib/security/pam_pwdb.so
```

In the /etc/pam.d/rlogin file, the first line prevents root (UID 0) from logging in on anything other than a local tty. The second line allows a login without password challenge if the user connecting has an rhosts file with appropriate entry (or an /etc/hosts.equiv).

If line 2 fails, then lines 3–8 (except any commented lines, like line 6) are tested. These modules have all been discussed earlier in this chapter or in Chapter 1.

The hosts.equiv file is a global file installed by the system administrator. This file is generally used to tell the local host that users on the remote systems listed (by hostname or IP address) are equivalent to the same username on the local system.

The user's .rhosts file does basically the same thing as the /etc/hosts.equiv file, only on a user-by-user basis. rhosts entries look like one of those in Listing 12-15.

Listing 12-15: Some rhosts entry options

```
<host>          Same user (hosts.equiv: all users) from <host>
permitted
<host> <user>   <user> from <host> is permitted
-<host>         No users from <host> permitted
<host> -<user>  <user> from <host> is not permitted
The following only apply when the "promiscuous" option is used:
   +            Allow anyone from any host to connect.
   + +          Same as above
   + <user>     Allow the user to connect from anywhere.
   <host> +     Allow any user from the host.
   + -<user>    Disallow the user from any host
```

With the exception of the last one, you shouldn't use wildcards (+) as they leave your system wide-open.

Other services

There are a lot of other services you can run on your system. Some things to watch for:

◆ Is the service running as a privileged user? Only root can bind sockets below 1024, so these will be run by root. Sockets above 1024 can be bound by any user, including root.

◆ Can the service run as a non-privileged user? If so, do it.

◆ Can you put the service in a change root jail? (See Chapter 14 for more information.)

◆ Can you block or otherwise restrict access to the port?

◆ Is the service needed? If not, or if you're not sure, turn it off.

Summary

This chapter examined a number of common services and their vulnerabilities. The text examined how a couple of select protocols communicates (although all work in a similar manner).

Chapter 13

DoS attacks and how they work

IN THIS CHAPTER

- ◆ Understanding denial of service attacks
- ◆ Understanding ping flooding
- ◆ Understanding the TCP SYN attack
- ◆ Understanding ping attacks
- ◆ Reducing the consequences of a DoS attack

A DoS ATTACK IS a denial of service attack. This kind of attack can take many forms, but comes down to the same thing: denying you access to a resource you have paid for. All computer-related resources are paid for by someone, there's no such thing as a free ride. It may not have been you directly, but someone is footing the bill. Denial of service attacks are generally perpetrated by angry or frustrated people who cannot find a better way to respond. This type of attack ranges from extremely low-tech to moderately technical, depending on the type of attack, and sophistication of steps taken to hide the author's identity. One very technical DoS attack also exists, but the number of engineers capable of performing a domain hijacking is very small.

A denial of service attack can take many forms, but regardless of the form, its effectiveness cannot be disputed. Some ISPs have gone out of business because angry former customers have mounted attacks on them. And when an ISP is unable to provide services, it's only a matter of time before all its clients go elsewhere. In the case of several small start-ups, this happened over the course of not much more than a weekend. The inability of most small- and even medium-sized operations to cope with this kind of attack can be debilitating. Knowing what to do can mean the difference between having and not having network and server availability.

Understanding ping flooding

Several types of attacks fall under the heading of *ping flooding attacks*. Under normal conditions, ping sends out one ping packet per second to the target host. But a ping flood occurs when ping attempts to feed ping packets as fast as the slowest link in the path permits. This means that on a fast connection so many packets will pass that other traffic will slow to a crawl. In fact, about the only more certain way to create traffic congestion would be through the use of spray, a program designed to measure bandwidth by filling it completely. This requires a client and server piece, so can be used only between configured hosts.

A ping flood is particularly simple, and tools are available on the Internet to do this under most operating systems. Under Linux, the ping command itself contains the switch to perform a ping flood, -f. But only a user with UID 0 can call ping with this option. Normal users are not permitted to use the flood option for obvious reasons.

Ping flooding affects not only the target, but also the client. What many of the converted programs do is rewrite the header and change the source address. Doing this allows an attacker to hit two systems at once, but he must continue to send the ping packets. The output of a ping flood might look like Listing 13-1.

Listing 13-1: Ping flood of an adjacent host

```
volcan# ping -f chiriqui
PING chiriqui.pananix.com (192.168.0.2): 56 data bytes
.....................
--- chiriqui.pananix.com ping statistics ---
7321 packets transmitted, 7299 packets received, 0% packet loss
round-trip min/avg/max = 0.4/3.3/21.6 ms
```

These results were obtained on a quiescent network between two systems connected on a 10-megabit circuit. Quite different results are obtained when the ping is directed to the localhost, as shown in Listing 13-2. You'll note the difference in packet loss and speed. Denial of service basically depends on packet loss.

Listing 13-2: Ping flooding localhost

```
volcan# ping -f localhost
PING localhost (127.0.0.1): 56 data bytes
...............................................................................
...............................................................................
.................
--- localhost ping statistics ---
5448 packets transmitted, 1022 packets received, 81% packet loss
round-trip min/avg/max = 0.3/122.3/342.1 ms
```

Another trick that may or may not work is to ping the broadcast address. I say "may or may not work" because most modern routers will not pass a ping packet destined for a broadcast address. It also depends on target systems whose IP stack conforms to the RFCs, as will become apparent in the next paragraph.

 The RFCs are documents that explain how things are supposed to work on the Internet (that is, they set the standard — non-compliance means that your software won't behave like everyone else's and may not be interoperable). That said, Linux is one of the few 100-percent compliant IP stacks.

By way of demonstration, if you have a network with multiple Linux systems running (or other UNIX systems – SCO OpenServer, HP-UX, AIX, and Solaris are known to be sufficiently compliant), and a few Microsoft systems (Win9*x* or NT 4) – you can easily test this.

On this network, run the following:

```
ping -c 2 <network_broadcast_address>
```

What you should get back will look like the returns in Listing 13-3.

Listing 13-3: Return from a pinging a broadcast address

```
64 bytes from 192.168.0.1: icmp_seq=0 ttl=255 time=0.3 ms
64 bytes from 192.168.0.2: icmp_seq=0 ttl=255 time=0.6 ms (DUP!)
64 bytes from 192.168.0.1: icmp_seq=1 ttl=255 time=0.2 ms
```

If you ping only once, you will see only one address, because the local system will always reply more quickly than another system. Since ping is waiting for only one reply, it will exit before receiving the reply from other systems. But with multiple pings, it will see all non-Microsoft hosts.

 Performing the above from a Microsoft host will return only the MS host's reply. Obviously, since only MS IP stacks respond this way (do not respond to broadcast messages), they do not conform to the RFCs. This is the most obvious way MS IP stacks are broken, but it also affects other aspects of IP interaction on the network. Do not expect a MS host to work properly on a network.

The above test will not work on a point-to-point network, and will not work through a router. So trying to find out what non-MS systems are on a network like @home should show only your own, since the cable modem is a router and should not pass a broadcast ping. But a misconfigured router, or one with the broadcast ping block turned off will work.

But a ping flood is not a particularly effective means of attacking someone's system. For one thing, it will usually be short-lived. The attacker must run the ping from a system that will then be unusable from a networking standpoint. That system can be easily identified, and a quick phone call can usually have it disabled. Even if the source address is altered, the original source address must continue to send these modified packets. It is difficult for the attacker to know if this attack is successful, and the attack will result in attention being drawn to the attacking system.

One exception to the above does exist, and does work. It is called a smurf attack, from a program of the same name that is easily obtained on the Internet. If other systems are used (systems that have been compromised) the attacker can simultaneously co-opt several of these to attack a site. And by using the source rewriting capabilities of smurf, the attacker can make a fairly effective attack that will also be difficult to trace.

Understanding and stopping the SYN DoS attack

A much more effective attack takes advantage of the fact that systems employ a SYN-ACK handshake sequence before moving a connection off the queue. This is an older attack, but still effective against a number of systems. On a standard OpenLinux system that is not heavily trafficked, this particular attack will be little more than a nuisance.

The attack worked because in the past (and the present for some other systems) the wait queue was small and would fill quickly. Connections were supposed to move off the queue, but this happened only after the SYN-ACK handshake was complete. It was only at this point that a TCP connection had taken place. An attacker could, by requesting a connection, then ignoring the return packet with the SYN bit set (or telling the server that the source was another system altogether, thus having the SYN packet sent to a system that could not answer), the server would wait for long periods holding this request on the queue. While waiting, no one else could connect, and the attacker would just keep up a barrage of requests, tying up the wait queue and denying others connections to the system.

 Rewriting a packet header and altering the source address is one form of "spoofing."

When this particular attack hit the Internet, a number of ISPs suffered. The only way to restore service was to stop and restart the affected service. For some of the hardest hit operating systems, it meant a complete reboot. And if the attack continued, legitimate service would again be denied.

The Linux kernel hackers developed several responses to this particular attack. The first consisted of using "SYN cookies" to detect an attack that attempted to tie up the wait queue. This particular method, while still available for use for those who suspect they have an ongoing SYN DoS attack, uses quite a few resources and is no longer necessary in light of other methods. The feature, even if compiled into the kernel, is turned off and must be deliberately turned on. This can be accomplished by the following line:

```
echo 1 >/proc/sys/net/ipv4/tcp_syncookies
```

What this does is cryptographically challenge each connection. You will receive notices for IP addresses suspected of flooding your server, but the source addresses logged are the source addresses provided in the packet, and may be spoofed addresses or addresses from compromised systems. So talk to those responsible for the addresses, but understand they may be innocent victims.

Since the addition of the SYN cookies, the wait queue size was increased to permit more waiting connections than in the past. This, in itself, prevented small-scale attacks or attacks from clients with slower connections. A determined attacker can still fill the wait queue and prevent a fair number of legitimate connections, but more legitimate connections are more likely than with tcp_syncookies enabled. As with the smurf attack discussed above, multiple compromised systems can still be used simultaneously to flood a target.

A third measure employed to thwart SYN DoS attacks is to change how long the system waits to complete the SYN-ACK sequence before dropping the request off the wait queue. Also buried in the code is an algorithm that will drop a stale connection request if the wait queue is full. This can happen even before the normal timeout if necessary (but it rarely is). Only an extremely heavily loaded server should need to respond in this manner.

If your server is heavily loaded and comes under SYN attacks, you can also alter several parameters in the kernel if necessary. This is not a task to be undertaken lightly. All the configurable parameters are found in the kernel sources in tcp.h (normally found in /usr/src/linux/include/net/tcp.h). Here are defined the number of open tcp connections available, the number of SYN retries, and the time between retries, etc.

Changing the defaults in tcp.h can have far reaching consequences. For example, the number of retries (TCP_SYN_RETRIES) is defined as 10 currently. If you reduce this too much, some clients may not be able to connect. This inability can be due to dropped packets (collisions, fragment too big and DNF — the do not fragment bit — set, etc.) or the random upper port chosen is not available so must be renegotiated, etc. Other problems may occur if the value is too big.

If you do take the opportunity to look at tcp.h, while you might feel lost, you will see a number of references to tcp connection states you've seen before, namely Fin Wait, Time Wait, Established, Listening, Closing, etc. You'll also find the code heavily commented.

 In C code, comments come between matching sets of /* and */, and may include lines with * only. Do not confuse this with the # sign used to delineate comments in shell scripts. The # sign precedes such things as includes, defines, etc., and must be included.

Older attacks (more than three years old)

Another old attack that some operating systems still have trouble with is a "big ping" attack, also known as "the ping of death." Remember from earlier chapters where you learned about bits and bytes. A byte is 8 bits and contains a number from 0–65535. By definition, ICMP messages will not exceed this size. So a number of systems didn't (and still don't) test to ensure that an ICMP packet is within the given limit. In practice, the only packet easily modifiable is a ping packet.

So attackers found a way to modify the code that creates a ping packet to permit padding to be added to it that exceeds the limit. An ICMP header will normally be 8 bytes. The header looks just like any IP header. A standard packet also has 56 bytes added as padding to bring the packet to a size of 64 bytes.

The size of the ping packet in Linux can be adjusted from the normal size of 64 bytes. The -s option can be used to specify the size of the padding to be added. However, not just any size can be specified on an unmodified ping binary. Legal values will go from 1 to 65468. Choosing values from 1 to 65454 should provide you with a normal looking return. Values from 65465 to 65468 may return no indication of progress, or a screen full of "packets." Values starting at 65469 will return a "packet too big" message. This prevents a system that has problems with big ping packets from receiving one that, after fragmenting and adding headers to the fragments, still won't exceed 64kb. But since Linux's ping binary is open source, anyone can alter the code to allow a larger packet to be built and sent.

At least one operating system in use today doesn't need to receive the entire big ping packet to crash the system; the last packet is sufficient. Obviously, these systems must be protected. As long as a Linux firewall is running, and CONFIG_IP_ALWAYS_DEFRAG=y is compiled into a 2.2.x kernel (the 2.4.x kernels forgo this option; this will be handled by netfilter), then fragments will not be passed and those systems will be safe from external attack.

Reducing the consequences of a DoS attack

Before you go to extremes or start seeing DoS attacks where none exist, it is important to get a feel for your network and traffic patterns. You might also want to be aware of others on your wire offering services. While you may suspect a DoS attack, the first thing to do is rule out other causes. These could include things like a sudden interest in yours or a neighboring site upstream (such as a new link from a popular site). Several companies have found out how overwhelmingly successful an ad campaign can be. When Victoria's Secret had its promotion in 1999, its site may have been able to handle the sudden surge in traffic, but the network it was connected to suffered greatly. While a denial of service from some standpoints, it was not deliberate.

 To get a feel for normal network traffic, a tool such as the Multi-Router Traffic Grapher (MRTG) is excellent. If you monitor the router that connects you to the Internet (and perhaps even one further upstream), you can get a good visual idea of your traffic pattern. Be sure to request permission if the routers don't belong to you. MRTG is available from: `http://ee-staff.ethz.ch/~oetiker/webtools/mrtg/mrtg.html`

You'll also want to make sure you aren't running some software yourself that is eating bandwidth. An unintentional, self-inflicted denial of service is embarrassing, but easily remedied. Also look for hardware problems, such as chatty network cards that need replacing.

Once you've ruled out all possible unintentional possibilities, you're faced with the problem of what to do next. Looking at any logs you have might give you some idea, but the logging from SYN cookies cannot be considered reliable. If the network is overloaded, SYN cookies may give some false readings. It also won't point to a site that is rewriting source addresses; it will only provide greater opportunity during an attack for more connections, but at a price in terms of server resource overhead.

Much of what you can do will depend on how you're connected to the Internet. Those of you using cable modems probably won't experience this particular attack per se. The cable modem companies do have it in their best interests to ensure sufficient bandwidth is available for their customers, and a denial of service attack, if brought to their attention, should be dealt with at that level.

If you have a DSL line, this provides a point-to-point type connection to your provider. Running a traceroute may show you whether the inconvenience also affects the point-to-point portion of the connection, or only upstream bandwidth (which you can likely have little effect on).

The best advice, though, is to continue operations as though the attack hadn't occurred (or wasn't effective). Why? First, because eventually the attack will stop. Second, an attacker who thinks the attack isn't effective may look elsewhere.

If the attack seems to be centered on one system and coming in via one route, you could try to shift some of the load for outgoing traffic to another system and point the default gateway to an alternate route to relieve some congestion on your primary route (if you're lucky enough to have that kind of backup available).

If only one service seems to be affected, stopping and starting the service will temporarily clear the queue. But it will begin to fill up again, so this will provide only temporary relief. If the packets seem to be coming from one address or network, you could try to simply drop all packets from that network (see Chapter 16).

Summary

In this short chapter you've taken a brief look at one of the most difficult problems on the Internet today. You've looked at a few types of DoS attacks and how they are perpetrated. You've gained some understanding of how easy this particular attack is, but also how ineffective it can be. You also looked at some measures to reduce the consequences.

Chapter 14

Mitigating your vulnerabilities

IN THIS CHAPTER

◆ Reducing vulnerability

◆ Reducing services

◆ Building a chroot DNS server

◆ Recovering from a breach

◆ Detecting an intrusion

◆ Recovering a file system

THIS BOOK STARTED BY providing you information regarding your system and the network you are connected to give you the basic information you need to make informed decisions about protecting yourself and your system. Now you will start to build on that knowledge, looking first to prevention, and then to detection of hostile activity aimed at your system.

Once again, remember that the only secure system is the one that's still packed in its original shipping container, with you sitting on top of it. But to get anything out of it, you'll need to have it running. Until it is connected to other systems, the only vulnerability comes from the console and any programs loaded into it. If you are particularly paranoid, you can grab source code for everything you want to run, comb the source code for Trojan horses, and only when you're happy that it's clean, compile and use it. But few are that paranoid.

What you will want to do is get a good copy of a reputable distribution (such as the one that comes with this book) and trust that that company has taken every step to ensure that what you have is free of Trojans. Every distribution maker starts with the source and builds the binary packages itself. Caldera's packages are self-hosted. That is, using a previous release, all packages are built new, then installed on the system and rebuilt to create the packages you receive. This is true for all except the packages in the contrib directory, which others built and provided to Caldera, and on this CD-ROM, the packages in the security directory, which were built by the author on a Caldera OpenLinux 2.3 system.

The CD-ROM that comes with this book includes a complete OpenLinux 2.3 binary distribution (source is available from the Caldera Systems ftp site) including a col/security directory provided by the author to assist with security tasks as outlined in this book.

The time to secure your system is *before* you connect to the outside world. After that, the system cannot be completely trusted.

After you have the distribution you want, you'll want to install it. At this point, you should not be connected to any network. Right after installation, your system is its most vulnerable. Go ahead and configure your network card, but don't connect a LAN cable to it (at least not one that connects to the world.) Be aware that in certain configurations (DNS loaded and pointed in /etc/resolve to 127.0.0.1 for the first nameserver) that some daemons, particularly amd, the automount daemon, will "hang" until it times out waiting for a response from DNS that can never come. If this two-minute wait annoys you, disable amd until after you're connected to the Internet to re-enable it. The same holds true for sendmail.

Once your system is up and running, use the information in this book and any other resources you have to ensure that your system is configured and as safe as practical within the constraints of your policy. Then you may connect to the Internet.

Limiting the damage

At this point (unless you've skipped ahead), you don't have a lot to work with as far as how to best protect your system. It's installed, and you've made sure no glaring holes exist. You've read about the network, and you've checked out what services you're offering (killing those you don't want to offer). Now you're down to those services you do want to offer.

So how do you ensure that what you're offering is a service and not a security exploit? As mentioned previously in this book, the objective of any cracker is to become root. Only root can bind privileged ports. It is through these ports the cracker will attempt to gain access to a root shell and subvert the system.

You have a couple of options. The first is to redirect all connections from a privileged port to a non-privileged port that is running as a non-privileged user. The second is to run any privileged process in a change root (chroot) jail. Note that not all services can be run as non-privileged. For example, the network time protocol daemon needs to be able to adjust the system clock, which may be done only by root. So understanding what the daemon needs to be able to do is part of the picture. But for services that only read static documents, making them non-privileged and redirecting any queries from their default port should not pose a problem. So if you have a daemon that does not need to write (or in any way change what is on the system), one option is to run the daemon as a non-privileged user that can only read the documents it needs to serve (the documents owned by root, but that can only be read by the user running the daemon). The daemon will have to bind a port above 1024, but you may then use a redirection program that intercepts connections to the standard port for that service and redirects them to the port the daemon is binding. See Chapter 18 for details on how to accomplish this redirection.

Some servers have built-in security in that they start as root, but then change identities and run as a non-privileged user. But this does not make them completely safe, since crackers will try to exploit those processes and subroutines that run as root.

In some cases, you're lucky in that the privileged process already knows how to run in a chroot environment as a non-privileged user despite being privileged. A couple of common examples are anonymous ftp, which, when connected to as the user ftp or anonymous run as the user ftp. The Apache Web server normally runs as the user nobody, and is restricted to the document root, so it also performs the equivalent of a chroot. But Apache is vulnerable, depending on the configuration.

The Apache server is discussed in Chapter 20.

For purposes of illustration, what is involved in creating a chroot jail will be illustrated here using the privileged DNS server. Fortunately, as of BIND version 8.1.2, this daemon understands how to work in a chroot environment. Unfortunately, this wasn't the case until after a number of boxes were penetrated because of vulnerabilities found in the named binary.

The specifics of the vulnerabilities are beyond the scope of this book, but the version of BIND that ships with OpenLinux 2.3 contains them. If the server has been compromised, you will find the file ADMROCKS in /var/named. You should obtain the updated package from `ftp://ftp.calderasystems.com/pub/OpenLinux/updates/2.3/current/RPMS/`. The three affected packages are called bind-8.2.2p4-1.i386.rpm, bind-doc-8.2.2p4-1.i386.rpm, and bind-utils-8.2.2p4-1.i386.rpm. Note that if a newer version is available, you should use it.

RPM package version numbers

To ensure that you have the latest packages, you can issue the following command:

```
rpm -qa | grep bind
```

This command will show you which binary packages installed on the system contain bind. Compare the output with the filenames packages available on the Caldera Systems site (or, if you're using another RPM distro, with the package name on your distribution's update site). RPMs will use the package name, software version number, rpm package revision number, and architecture:

```
<package_name>-<software.verion.number>-
<rpm_package_version_number>.<architecture>.rpm
```

As you look over the bind filename, bind-8.2.2p4-1.i386.rpm, then, the filename breaks out this way:

Package name: bind

Software version: 8.2.2p4

RPM package version number: 1

Architecture: i386

Possible architectures include: i386, sparc, alpha, arm, m68k, mips, ppc, s390, sparc64, and noarch. The noarch means that the package is architecture independent. A lot of Perl programs are like this as well as shell scripts. You may also see src in lieu of the foregoing architecture names.

The SRPMs, or rpms containing src.rpm as the final part of their name, are source rpms. They are installed on the system, but then must be built into binary RPMs. On a Red Hat system, you would install the rpm, then, as root, cd into /usr/src/redhat/SPECS (on a Caldera OpenLinux system the path would be /usr/src/OpenLinux/SPECS — your RPM-based distribution may vary). From this directory, issue the command:

```
rpm -bb <program_name>.spec
```

or

```
rpm -ba <program_name>.spec
```

substituting the appropriate program name. The first command will build a binary rpm file. The second will build both a binary rpm and a new src.rpm file. The second method would be used if you made changes to the particular spec file before rebuilding and wanted the newer src.rpm file. The binary rpm files will be locate in ../RPMS/i368/ or ../RPMS/noarch/. Many src.rpm files will build into multiple binary rpm files. The bind src.rpm is one package that will build the three binary rpm files listed in the text. The src.rpm files will be found in ../SRPMS.

BIND stands for Berkeley Internet Nameserver Daemon. The actual binary, the nameserver daemon itself, is called named (short for nameserver daemon). Moving and setting up this daemon as a chroot daemon will give you some idea of the complexity involved in creating a chroot environment. If you take a quick look at the anonymous ftp directory (/home/ftp), you'll get an idea of what lies in store.

Before you start, a little planning is in order. First, you'll need a file system with sufficient space to accommodate what you're about to undertake. For the purpose of illustration, assume that /home is on a partition of its own and has plenty of available space. If this is not the case for you, you may want to look at either /usr/local or /usr. Second, you'll need to decide on a username to run your daemon as. Consider creating a username indicative of the service. Also, think about the UID/GID number you want to assign. Caldera reserves IDs from 0–499 for the system and IDs 500 and above for ordinary users. The /etc/passwd file shows that by default, all system IDs fall below 100. That leaves plenty of room for you to grab some IDs for uses such as this. So if you reserve IDs 200–299, that will almost certainly be more than sufficient and shouldn't interfere with either the system IDs or the common IDs.

So using any administration tool of your choosing, do the following:

1. Create a UID/GID 200 for dns, with home directory /home/dns:

```
groupadd -g 200 dns
useradd -g dns -u 200 -m dns
```

   The above will accomplish what you need. Make sure this account is locked, since no one will actually log in as the user dns. You can lock the account in COAS (System Administration/Account Administration) by ensuring the account is disabled. The useradd command above locks the account when it is created. If you don't want to create the dns directory under /home, then omit the "-m" switch from the useradd command and put the correct path into /etc/passwd (/usr/dns, or whatever you choose) and create the directory by hand (be sure the directory is owned by the user dns).

2. Now cd down to /home/dns. Located in this directory are several files (mostly hidden dot files) that you'll want to remove just to clean things up. Once you've done that, the real work starts.

3. Whenever you create a chroot jail, everything required to run the programs (libraries, devices, binaries, configuration and data files, etc.) must be located below the changed root. They must also be located in relatively the same location as in the main operating system. So begin by creating the basic structure you'll need:

```
mkdir dev ; mkdir etc ; mkdir usr ; mkdir usr/sbin ; mkdir
var ; mkdir var/named ; mkdir var/run ; mkdir var/lock ;
var/lock/subsys ; mkdir lib
```

   That should be the basic structure.

4. Now you'll need to fill this structure with the files necessary to run named. You can guess that this will include the named binary and all associated configuration and data files. So copy the following files:

```
/usr/sbin/named
/usr/sbin/named-xfer
/etc/named.conf
/var/named/*
```

 If you're running a distribution other than Caldera OpenLinux, your binaries may be in other locations.

Copy all these files to their corresponding directories under /home/dns (e.g., /usr/sbin/named is copied to /home/dns/usr/sbin/named).

5. Then, cd /usr/sbin and run `ldd named`. This will return a list of libraries required by named as shown in Listing 14-1.

Listing 14–1: Results of ldd run against named

```
libc.so.6 => /lib/libc.so.6 (0x4001a000)
/lib/ld-linux.so.2 => /lib/ld-linux.so.2 (0x40000000)
```

This tells you what libraries are required to run named. This will be the same for named-xfer. So copy these two libraries to their corresponding location in /home/dns.

6. Then copy /etc/named.conf and /var/named/* to their respective directories below /home/dns. Look at the /etc/named.conf file and make sure you've copied all the pertinent zone files listed in that file. You may or may not have zone files in /var/named (you might not even have /var/named), but this is a good place to put new zone files.

If you want to have system logging (a good idea), then you'll also want to copy the time zone file into etc. If your system is properly configured, /etc/localtime should be a link to /usr/share/zoneinfo/.../<*yourtimezone*>. But if you just copy the /etc/localtime file into /home/dns/etc, you'll get the file at the end of the link and all will be fine:

```
cp /etc/localtime /home/dns/etc/localtime
Now cd to /home/dns/dev and create the null device:
mknod -m 0666 null c 1 3
```

You'll also need urandom:

```
mknod -m 0644 urandom c 1 9
```

Your basic structure is now complete. But before you rush off and start named, a few details need to be cleaned up. The first detail is sysloging. By default, syslog looks only at /dev/log. In order to tell syslog to look elsewhere, you need to add an option to tell syslog where else to look. On OpenLinux, this variable is added to /etc/sysconfig/daemons/syslog. You'll need to add the entry "-a /home/dns/ dev/log" to the OPTIONS_SYSLOG line. After you've done that, stopping and starting syslog will force syslog to start watching the additional log device that named will create in /home/dns/dev/. When you restart syslog, you should see a new socket called "log" in /home/dns/dev. If not, stop then restart syslog again. Sometimes, a reload doesn't successfully read the options.

While you're in /etc/sysconfig/daemons, edit the named file and change the OP-TIONS line to look like the following: `OPTIONS="-t /home/dns/ -u dns -g dns"`.

> **TIP** If you run into trouble, and your chroot daemon segfaults, run strace against it and look at the last few subroutines it tried to run. You'll get some clues about what to look at to correct the situation.

All that's really left to do is edit the scripts that control starting and stopping named. The two scripts are /etc/rc.d/init.d/named and /usr/sbin/ndc. Copy the initialization script to named.orig in case you need it later. Change the DAEMON line from /usr/sbin to /home/dns/usr/sbin. Then look for any references to /var/*anything* and add your /home/dns to the front. Finally, look for the section that says "# Start daemons.". Just below this is a line that should be changed from "start-stop-daemon -S -n $NAME -x $DAEMON" to "start-stop-daemon -S -n $NAME -x $DAEMON -- $OPTIONS (adding the -- $OPTIONS).

The ndc script is a little more complicated. Follow these steps:

> **NOTE** Check before trying to edit ndc. Newer versions use a compiled binary rather than a shell script. If the results of running file /usr/sbin/ndc returns "ELF 32-bit LSB executable, Intel 80386, version 1, dynamically linked (uses shared libs), not stripped" (or similar), then skip the steps outlining changes to ndc — you won't be able to use it.

1. Make a copy called ndc.orig, just in case.

2. Now add /home/dn/usr/sbin to the beginning of the PATH statement.

3. Next, change the PIDFILE to point into /home/dns/var/run/named.pid. Now find all occurences of /usr/sbin/named and change them to:

```
/home/dns/usr/sbin/named -t /home/dns -u dns -g dns ...
```

There should be two such lines.

Now you're ready to start. You can use either of ndc or /etc/rc.d/init.d/named to start or stop named. In fact, you should make sure both properly start and stop it. If you look in the process table, you should see that named is running as user dns with the -t /home/dns argument.

You'll want to test your setup, and you can use either nslookup, dig, or dnsquery. If your hosts resolve properly, you now have a working chroot dns server.

Similar procedures can be used for other servers but may require the use of the chroot command prior to invoking the server. You will need to follow the same basic steps locating a copy of all program-required files below the changed root.

Other measures

Running restricted services in a chroot jail is only one of the measures you can take to protect your system. Other measures include running IP Chains (kernel 2.2.x) or NetFilter (kernel 2.4.x when released) to watch and/or block ports, using tripwire to watch and/or booby-trap services, etc. Most of the rest of this book will be dedicated to software measures you can take to help secure things.

But make no mistake about it, the best protection for your system is vigilance on your part. This does not have to be a full-time proposition, just a few well-spent minutes a day. You'll learn more about how in subsequent chapters.

One thing you can look at, as mentioned earlier, is lsattr -v. This is not foolproof by any means. That is, if the inode version number on the file changed from 3302778664 to 1, you know beyond doubt the file changed. But if the version number did not change, you don't know that the file is the same or different. For that, you'll need something else.

The reason you can't tell if the file is the same or not lies in the way copy (cp) and move (mv) work. So take a quick look at the following if you are interested.

Linux's copy and move programs work differently, and even work differently depending on whether or not the two files are on the same partition. First, assuming the two different files are on the same partition:

◆ cp copies the data from one file's data block to the other file's data block and updates atime and mtime (access time and modify time).

◆ mv changes the directory pointer and points the filename from one inode to the other. Now the filename is pointing to a different inode. The atime and mtime are not updated.

Assuming they are on two different partitions:

◆ cp acts the same as above, no change.

◆ mv performs a copy of not only the data blocks, but also changes some inode information (but not all). The inode version number will not change, but the atime and mtime will. So in this case, the directory pointer doesn't change, the inode is reused, so the inode version number remains the same.

In only one of the four cases above (mv on the same partition) does the inode version number change.

Recovering from a breach

Once you detect or even suspect that someone has root access to your system, you have three choices. The first choice is to reinstall everything – back up and start from scratch, reformatting every partition. While certain, and the best (simplest, surest, most practical) method, it is not always the desired choice. A complete reinstall formatting all partitions will wipe away all traces of the breach. It will also wipe away all configuration files, data, etc. Sometimes, this just isn't an option.

 If you see a random log entry that looks like a garbled transmission, search the line for /bin/sh. Often it will be buried in the middle of the line surrounded by various control characters (normally appearing as an uppercase letter preceded by a carat (^). This is not random gibberish, but a deliberate buffer overflow attempt.

The second choice is to do nothing. This shouldn't be an option, and really isn't. If you have anything of any value on the system, you won't want any unknown persons doing what they want with it. If you don't have anything important and have good backups of all configuration and data files, then reinstalling the system is the best course.

The third choice, which is much more time-consuming, is to try to identify any and all changed files and replace them with known good files. Identifying how the intruder gained access is secondary to resecuring the system, although if the manner of entry cannot be determined, you may be in for a rerun. Copying all the system logs to another system or to tape may be the best course of action before doing anything else.

Configuring syslog and reading syslog files are covered in Chapters 22 and 23, respectively.

So what do you want to ensure is correct on your file system? This will be easiest if taken directory by directory. You can proceed first by ensuring you are not connected to the network. This can be as easy as just disconnecting your network connection. Now, you're ready to start.

First, you'll want to ensure that no changes have been made to any of your etc/ directories. You may have several of these. Often, programs installed from source will create configuration files in /usr/local/etc, var/etc, /usr/etc, and others. Your /opt subdirectories may also have etc/ directories in them. But your root level /etc directory is the most important.

The main /etc directory contains the passwd, shadow, group, and (possibly) gshadow files. You'll want to ensure that these have not been altered. It is nearly impossible (and actually futile) to try to determine if the shadow file has been copied off, so always assume that it has been and change the root password.

Changes to look for include any users other than root with UID of 0, null passwords for any account, locked accounts that are unlocked, users added to any of the system groups, etc. These checks may be performed by simple greps if the files are very large (as they would be on a college campus) or by hand for homes or small businesses.

The /etc subdir also contains pam.d, whose files for restricted services can be easily changed to allow entry via formerly closed avenues, or just bypass many checks. Chapter 1 discussed these files in detail. But remember that a number of these files point to other files in /etc that may have been changed as well.

The /etc directory also contains the rc.d subdir and the inittab. Since inittab and the rc.d subdirs are completely trusted, and everything in them is run by root, it is trivial to add a line that will put a root shell on any given port. Since the shell would be running as root, it does not need to be on a port below 1024.

The /etc/X11 subdir also contains a number of directories with files executed by root, and also makes a good stopping place for crackers, as does the /etc/cron.d directory. In fact, the /etc directory and its subdirectories are ideal places for crackers to insert one-liners to start services as root.

Other directories that you'll want to ensure were not altered include all the sbin/ and bin/ directories on your system. These hide in every major area, from the root directory (some of the most sensitive binaries are located here) to /usr, /usr/local, and even in subdirectories under /opt.

The most commonly altered binary on the system is /bin/login. Every system uses this binary as the gateway to the system. It is without doubt the most vulnerable binary. Don't even bother checking this one — just replace it. The package this service comes from is the util-linux-x.xx-x.i386.rpm. Always use the latest version for your system, and force it on. The kpackage RPM administration software allows you the option of forcing packages over installed packages. A good number of /bin and /usr/bin files will be replaced.

The next set of directories to be aware of changes in is the lib/ directories. The root lib includes a modules subdir with kernel modules inserted by root. These directories also contain all the shared code. If the login service was replaced, it may have come from one of three sources – built on your system against your libraries (so it will definitely work); built on a similar system using the same libraries you have, so again, it will work; or built against an arbitrary library with the library and binary installed on your system.

The final set of directories to check are the tmp/ directories. Here, you're checking not for changed files so much as for the existence of unknown files. If in doubt, remove it. This is a common location for "root kits" to be deposited just waiting for an opportunity to be used. Your tmp/ directories should probably have all files that have not been accessed during the previous week removed.

 The cleandir program will automate the task of cleaning the tmp directory for you and is included with Caldera OpenLinux 2.3.

You should not trust any database that can be written to on your system as an indication that things are OK. This includes the RPM database. Unless of course, you can compare the installed database against a known good database not acessible from the system.

A good routine check to run is shown in Listing 14-2.

Listing 14–2: A routine to check installed RPM packages

```
#!/bin/bash

PATH=/bin:/sbin:/usr/bin:/usr/sbin
export PATH
VFILE=/root/rpm.verify.`date +%d%m%y`

for i in `rpm -qa`
do
rpm -V $i > $VFILE
done
```

You can run a script like this from cron on a daily basis, then compare it to one you keep off-system by moving the daily to a diskette and comparing the archived one with the daily by using the diff utility. Differences will show which files may have changed.

A program called check-packages, which performs basic checks on installed packages, then checks those against a similar run from the previous day, is included with the dailyscript files.

Basically, the script loops through a list of every rpm file ever entered into the RPM database installed on your system, then performs a verify against it as shown in Listing 14-3.

Listing 14–3: An abbreviated rpm –V run on all installed packages

```
.M...UG.    /dev/vcsa1
.M....G.    /dev/vcsa2
....L...    /dev/video
S.5....T c /etc/printcap
.......T c /etc/sysconfig/daemons/bigfs
SM5....T c /usr/X11R6/lib/X11/app-defaults/Bitmap
missing     /usr/src/linux-2.2.10/vmlinux
```

The above lines read as shown in Listing 14-4 — letters designate the particular test failed, and dots indicate test passed.

Listing 14–4: Key to reading output from rpm –V

```
S       File size
M       Mode (includes permissions and file type)
5       MD5 sum
D       Device
L       Symlink
U       User
G       Group
T       Mtime
c       signifies configuration file
```

Note that only failures are output to the file. If all tests pass, no entry will appear. For example, if you verified the util-linux package and it verified correctly (all eight tests), you would not find it in the verify file.

Replacing any packages you did not change by using rpm's --force option is the best way to proceed.

You will also want to ensure that no user's home directory contains SUID or SGID root programs. Finding these was discussed in the first section of this book.

Preparing for the inevitable

The best way to be prepared for the day someone finally does get access to your system is simple, and you've heard it before: backups. This does not have to be a backup of the entire system. In fact, a backup of what you really need to recover to get back to where you are can be as little as the various etc/ directories and portions of the /var directory.

This might be understating the problem slightly if you don't have /home on a separate partition, or you are acting as a corporate FTP site. But apart from that, your backup needs might be fairly small. This could enhance your ability to recover quickly by just reinstalling and running your old configuration off of backup.

One of the most effective strategies — one that doesn't require a tape backup — is to identify those small areas you'll need to back up. For example, on many servers, a quick backup of /etc, /var/named (or /home/dns/ in its entirety if you've chroot jailed your DNS server), and /home/httpd, as well as a copy of the dump of any database, will probably be sufficient.

With the exception of the database, everything listed above is relatively static. Your Web server pages will change more than anything else. You could, however, go months and more without even looking at /etc or /var/named.

 Backups are key. Good ones can have you back up and running after a complete reinstall in minutes. If you cannot perform regular tape backups, back up important files to off-system media often. If you must use floppies, keep two copies around (in case one floppy has bad disk sectors).

So before you connect that Ethernet cable, take time to run the following:

```
cd / ; tar czvf etc.tar.gz /etc
tar czvf misc.tar.gz /var/named /home/httpd
```

and you will have saved a large portion of your initial configuration. Additionally, these files will each fit on a diskette. On many systems they'll both fit on one diskette. Copy these files off to two floppies, label them, and put them away.

Get in the habit of making regular backups of your important data file (this may include those files you save in your $HOME directory and any database files saved elsewhere on the system). "Regular" may be once a week, once a day, or even more frequently, depending on the amount of data you save to the system. You'll want to back up important system files as soon as they are changed. You'll want to keep several recent copies. If you do weekly backups, you'll want to keep at least the last month's (four weeks) worth of backups plus probably two backups from the first week of the month for two more months back. Old backups are better than none in many cases.

You're ready to go live. So plug in your Ethernet card and let the script kiddies come.

Summary

This chapter dealt with a number of miscellaneous issues. You learned that the ultimate objective of any script kiddie is to gain root access to your system. You also learned that system crackers can try to do this via a number of means, but most are through services offered. And because some services are so complex and powerful, they are almost impossible to secure.

For this reason, you learned some tricks like locking these services away in a chroot jail can often help. The example provided in this chapter used a built-in function in newer versions of DNS to allow just this. Other services, though, can be configured in a similar manner. But those that need to have this done are those that don't change ownership of the program to a non-privileged user. These programs are becoming fewer, since a number of advantages are gained by running a program, or at least the thread handling external connections, to a non-privileged user.

But if a cracker doesget through, you learned the best ways to approach the situation and how to use the tools provided with the system to recover. Starting with inode version numbers (chattr -v/lsattr -v) to rpm -V. You also learned which services you need to keep an eye on.

Finally, making recovery easier was the focus of the last section. Being prepared for a breach is one of the best ways to avoid one, since Murphy is always looking for an easy target.

Chapter 15

Using TCP Wrappers

THIS CHAPTER DEALS WITH TCP Wrappers, a program that will help you detect and deter intrusions and intrusion attempts. You'll look at TCP Wrappers; what it is, how it works, and how to configure this facility. Because of the nature of TCP Wrappers, you'll need to understand the /etc/inetd.conf file, what it contains, and its format. This chapter will address /etc/inetd.conf briefly, as well as /etc/hosts.allow and /etc/hosts.deny.

The TCP Wrappers program is a utility designed to help you detect and deter intrusions and intrusion attempts. TCP Wrappers normally works through inetd, but many server programs not started by inetd can be built with the TCP Wrappers library to include its functionality. To understand how to use TCP Wrappers to help stop intrusions, you'll learn how to configure the /etc/hosts.allow and /etc/hosts.deny files.

 For more information on inetd.conf, see Chapter 11.

What is TCP Wrappers?

A *wrapper* is something you put around something else to protect it or modify its environment. TCP Wrappers is a program that wraps around the tcp listener for a server to help protect the host from exploit via that server, or to record client access to a server. While not foolproof, TCP Wrappers provides a method to detect intrusion attempts and log the source of those attempts. You can then take steps to ensure the intrusion attempts don't become actual intrusions. But the program won't do it all for you, you need to use other programs, such as IP Chains or Netfilter to actively prevent future attacks.

IP Chains and netfilter are covered in Chapter 16.

In the case of TCP Wrappers, explaining what it isn't is easier than explaining what it is. TCP Wrappers isn't a program that you can run to monitor every server process. TCP Wrappers can only be effectively used by TCP-based servers started from inetd (the Internet superserver) or that have been compiled with the TCP Wrappers library. But not all TCP-based services can effectively use TCP Wrappers; the "r" commands, such as rlogin, rsh, rexec, are not good candidates for TCP Wrappers. And UDP-based services cannot use it at all.

No "silver bullet" exists for either internal or network security. Tools need to be used to complement one another. But nothing beats vigilance on your part.

How TCP Wrappers works

You can use TCP Wrappers in one of several different ways, depending on your particular situation. The first way is to replace the program binary with tcpd, the TCP Wrappers program. However, using tcpd as a replacement does not provide much flexibility and will result in any upgrade to the original package, wiping out the tcpd replacement. Given this lack of flexibility and the ease with which this method may be undone, it will not be discussed further.

The second method of employing TCP Wrappers is to have inetd call tcpd, instead of the original program, from the /etc/inetd.conf file. The tcpd program can then run, and exit or call the original program as you desire. This method of calling tcpd from /etc/inetd.conf is extremely flexible, and this chapter will explore this method of deployment. Your OpenLinux distribution and several others now come with tcpd already implemented, but you may want to make some changes based on this chapter.

The final method that may be used to employ TCP Wrappers is to have tcpd called from within the /etc/hosts.allow or /etc/hosts.deny files. This is a variation on calling it from inetd.conf. This chapter will not discuss this method, but the documentation that comes with the TCP Wrappers program explains it adequately.

The TCP Wrappers program, tcpd, is called in place of the actual service that it is to protect. There are two different ways to implement TCP Wrappers. The first is simply to replace the actual program with tcpd (the TCP Wrapper daemon). Since this is a rather limited usage, and the second method is more flexible, we'll be looking exclusively at the second implementation, which is to have inetd call tcpd for every invocation of a daemon. A variation on this method is to use tcpd within the /etc/hosts.allow file under certain circumstances.

Some of the functionalities of TCP Wrappers are based on options selected at the time of compilation. If you desire or require any of the functionalities not built in by default, you'll need to recompile tcpd, turning them on (or off). One of the default compile time functionalities is PARANOID. When compiled with -DPARANOID, TCP Wrappers will perform name-to-address lookups via DNS, and compare them to address-to-name lookups for the client requesting the connection. If this check fails, TCP Wrappers will assume the client is trying to fool (spoof) us as to his true identity and drop the connection. It is common for sites to recompile tcpd without this functionality.

The daemon provided in the Caldera OpenLinux distribution has been compiled without the PARANOID option. If you decide to recompile your OpenLinux binary with PARANOID, or the distribution you are using provides a binary built with PARANOID, you loose some flexibility. Because tcpd will immediately drop any connection whose forward name resolution does not match its reverse name resolution, nothing else will happen. This check is the first one to take place. So if you want to have tcpd run a finger on this host to find out more about it before connecting, you won't be able to.

Another reason not to include PARANOID is that many hosts connected to the Internet do not have DNS listings, so the reverse lookups will fail. They will also fail if the primary and secondary DNS servers happen to be off-line. So unless you have a compelling reason to include PARANOID, it's probably better not to use PARANOID and handle those suspect connections in another manner.

Another related functionality has to do with source-routing. To prevent address spoofing, TCP Wrappers can also be compiled to disallow host address spoofing by ignoring source routing information provided by the client. This is not effective for udp-based services, and depending on it to provide this functionality for udp will give only a false sense of security.

Source routing refers to the practice of providing the destination with the route to arrive back at the source, rather than letting the destination route the packets its own way. It is the equivalent of giving someone not only your address, but also a map telling him exactly how to get there. The route may not be correct, and if he follows it, he may find himself at a different address.

Another option you can use when you compile tcpd is to enable RFC 931 lookups. This RFC deals with the ident daemon. Compiling with this option will force tcpd to try to connect to the remote system's ident daemon. Since an ever-increasing number of clients on the Internet use Microsoft Windows, and Microsoft does not have an ident daemon, the attempt to contact the daemon will fail for those clients. While this will not terminate tcpd, it will cause an approximate 10-second delay for those clients (10 seconds is the default timeout for the ident client). Because Microsoft clients cannot request or answer ident lookups, many UNIX systems are also shutting this service down as superfluous. Additionally, this lookup is not effective for UDP-based services.

The OpenLinux version of tcpd does not use most of the compile-time options. While this is always subject to change, the package is compiled in a way that is deemed most useful to the most users – that is, without PARANOID, without RFC 931 (identd) lookups, and without ignoring source routing. If you want some of these features, other packages, such as netfilter, or the 2.2.x/2.4.x kernels have features to prevent IP spoofing and ignore source routing. If you still insist on having these features compiled into tcpd, you'll need to build tcpd yourself from source. Most other distributions are also built this way. If you have one of the RPM-using distributions, you can install the source rpm and inspect the <filename>.spec file. Debian has a similar tool to handle building that will provide you information about how it was configured for compiling. Please refer to a good administration book if you don't know how to inspect packages for your system.

See Chapter 16 for more information on netfilter.

The source code for tcpd is included on the CD-ROM that accompanies this book.

TCP Wrappers uses the syslog facility to log captured information pertaining to client:daemon connections. You'll look at the specifics of this configuration in the following sections.

Implementing TCP Wrappers

You can begin using the TCP Wrappers daemon by finding the line in /etc/inetd that looks like the following:

```
telnet  stream  tcp  nowait  root  /usr/sbin/in.telnetd  /usr/sbin/in.telnetd
```

and change it to look like this:

```
telnet  stream  tcp  nowait  root  /usr/sbin/tcpd  /usr/sbin/in.telnetd
```

Now, inetd will start tcpd, and when tcpd has logged the client:daemon request (and satisfied any preconditions), it will start the telnet daemon.

inetd will need to be signaled to re-read the /etc/inetd.conf file by sending a SIGHUP after each change.

Don't be surprised if the line in /etc/inetd.conf already has tcpd in it. Most distributions today are using TCP Wrappers by default. What they haven't done is perform specific configurations on it, which is what you'll learn about below.

If you make the change proposed above, with inetd calling tcpd instead of the telnet daemon, you'll have a log of all connection attempts to the telnet port. You can do this for every service started by inetd that you haven't commented out in the inetd.conf file, simply by using tcpd as the target and making the argument the service daemon as shown above. Just remember that tcpd cannot be reliably used with any service that uses UDP, or is one of the r services (rlogin, rsh, rexec).

However, if what you want to do is log all connection attempts, but either not provide the service at all or only provide the service to certain clients, you'll need to look at the /etc/hosts.allow and /etc/hosts.deny files. Whether connections are allowed or denied based on the contents of the hosts.allow and hosts.deny files, they will still be logged, so you will still know where connections and connection attempts came from – assuming you aren't using a binary compiled with PARANOID.

If you use IP Chains or netfilter to deny access to a port, as described in Chapter 16, then TCP Wrappers will not log a connection to that port because no connection will be permitted by the firewall rules. So if you want to booby-trap a port for TCP Wrappers to run a shell script on, or want to send a message back to the client, do not block that port with a firewall rule.

Originally, tcpd required both hosts.allow and hosts.deny for full functionality. And while this is available for those wishing to use it, you can now consolidate everything into /etc/hosts.allow and maintain only one file. This one-file-fits-all configuration is what you will look at later in this chapter, and you can enable it by ensuring that tcpd is compiled with the `PROCESS_OPTIONS` turned on (this is the default with OpenLinux and may be with other distributions as well). Some syntax, specifically in the shell commands used in the hosts.allow file with the binary compiled with `PROCESS_OPTIONS` and the binary without the `PROCESS_OPTIONS`, is different. So blindly combining the two files into one is not recommended and may produce undesired results.

As rules are being written, remember that the first match terminates the search. So subsequent rules will not be processed.

The format for the hosts.allow file is as follows:

```
daemon(s) : client(s) : option : option ...
```

Each line is a colon-separated list, as shown above, consisting of two or more columns. If you are using only the hosts.allow file (as will this text), the first options column will be mandatory, all other options columns are optional. The first column lists any daemon or daemons you want to protect. The second column lists clients you want to match. The third and subsequent columns will contain options that may be programs to run or actions to take. If any option uses colons within the option (as in a PATH statement), the colons that are not used as column separators must be protected by a backslash (\), called "escaping" the character. Also, every line must be terminated by a newline, including the last line in the file, or that line will not be executed.

The backslash is used whenever you have a character that will be interpreted by the shell or program as a special character, but that you want interpreted literally.

Using daemons and wildcards

The daemon(s) field is a list of daemons separated by white space and/or commas (either is acceptable). The daemon name should be the daemon as it is found on the system, i.e., in.telnetd in the case of an OpenLinux installation. In the case of multi-homed hosts, the form `daemon@host` is acceptable to differentiate one bound NIC from another. Wildcards are also acceptable. Valid wildcards include the following:

- `ALL`: universal match (all daemons/hosts)
- `LOCAL`: matches hosts whose names do not contain a dot, as in the hosts foo or baz
- `UNKNOWN`: matches any user whose name is unknown, or any host whose name or address are unknown
- `KNOWN`: matches any known user, and any host whose name and address are both known
- PARANOID: matches any host whose name does not match its address

Note that `KNOWN` and `UNKNOWN` are subject to the vagaries of DNS. When DNS is unavailable, these wildcards may not match properly. Likewise, with PARANOID, if DNS is not available, the hostname will not match an address, and the connection will be refused.

If DNS is not available and you are using `UNKNOWN`, you will get a match on a host when you probably shouldn't. This could affect subsequent rules, which now won't be processed because the first match terminated the search. So be careful with your rules so that you don't get an inadvertent match before you want to. See tcpdchk and tcpdmatch below.

Clients, patterns, and hostnames

The client(s) is a list of hostname(s), host IP address(es), patterns (see next paragraph), or wildcards to be matched.

Patterns may take one of several forms: leading or trailing dot.

If you have the following hosts table in your system (foo):

```
192.168.0.1  foo.void.org  foo
192.168.0.2  bar.void.org  bar
192.168.0.3  baz.void.org  baz
```

you can specify as a hostname .void.org, and you would match foo, bar, or baz at .void.org. If you omit the leading ".", then only the (non-existent) host void.org would be matched. Likewise, you can specify 192.168.0. (note the trailing ".") as a host and you would match all hosts that have an address beginning with 192.168.0.

The same wildcards available for the daemon(s) column are also available for the client(s) column.

Forms and operators

If you want to match a range of addresses, you can use a network/netmask form, such as 192.168.0.0/255.255.255.128, which will match 192.168.0.0 through 192.168.0.127. To match a single host, you can use the same notation: 192.168.0.64/255.255.255.255, which will match only 192.168.0.64.

The final pattern match possible is of the form "@" and the netgroup name (valid for clients only). Note that this form is available only if you are running NIS. Further, the netgroup name is case sensitive.

 A netgroup is a feature of NIS, which is why it is only available if you are using NIS. A netgroup accomplishes a similar function to a UNIX group, but for the NIS domain.

One operator is possible for use in either daemon or client lists, the operator EXCEPT. Caution should be exercised if EXCEPT is to be nested. An argument in the form 'a EXCEPT b EXCEPT c' would translate as (a EXCEPT (b EXCEPT c)). So you might want to polish up on your Boolean arithmetic before you start nesting exceptions, or use parenthesis to force the correct order of interpretation.

Two basic options you will want to use are ALLOW and DENY. You'll look at more advanced options later in this chapter.

Rules

You now have enough information to create some basic rules:

```
ALL : LOCAL, .void.org EXCEPT david@bar.void.org : ALLOW
ALL EXCEPT in.telnetd : david@bar.void.org : ALLOW
in.ftpd : ALL : ALLOW
ALL : ALL : DENY
```

Let's take the rules one by one from the top, since this is how TCP Wrappers will work. The first rule will match ALL daemons – it doesn't matter which daemon it is. So any port inetd is listening on that calls tcpd, as in the in.telnetd example above, will try to match the rules in the order they appear. Since ALL matches anything, the first part of this rule will always match. But the client(s) portion of the rule, which is looking for any LOCAL address, or any host from void.org (except david connecting from host bar at void.org) will only match a few addresses. Those matching client addresses will be allowed because the option is ALLOW (except david from host bar at void.org, who will drop down to the next rule because he doesn't match).

 The above paragraph discussed only those daemons started via tcpd from /etc/inetd.conf. However, other daemons that are compiled with libwrap, the TCP Wrappers library, will also go through this list of rules just as if they were called via tcpd from inetd.

If the first rule matched, access was allowed and the search stopped, and so no subsequent rules were processed. If the rule didn't match (the client wasn't LOCAL or didn't belong to the domain void.org or was that nefarious individual, david, trying to connect from host bar at void.org) then the next rule is processed. The second rule matches any daemon except the telnet daemon. But this time, the client list is very small, just our nefarious friend. As long as he's connecting to anything except telnet, he'll be ALLOWed in. Otherwise, he'll drop down to the next rule.

The third rule applies only to the FTP daemon. If the FTP daemon matches, then the client column will match the world. So this rule will ALLOW everyone to connect to your FTP site.

The final rule is a catch-all. It will match all daemons, all clients, and DENY them access. This rule should only be reached by david from host bar at void.org trying to telnet in, or anyone outside the LOCAL domain or void.org trying to get in via any daemon except FTP.

Now let's look at some of the interesting things you can do.

Additional options with any of these rules could include shell commands, network options, lookup option, and miscellaneous options. Two commands allow you to run shell commands as options: spawn and twist.

The spawn command lets you run a shell command as one of your options. The spawn command will not interfere with client/server communications because all stdin, stdout, and stderr are directed to /dev/null. A common usage for this is described in the man pages as:

```
spawn (/path/to/safe_finger -l @%h | /usr/bin/mail root) &
```

The above command mails root the results of a safe_finger on a connecting system (character expansion will be explained later). The above can be used with DENY as an option to booby-trap services not offered to outsiders. Be careful not to use this on the finger daemon, you may finger a host that fingers you, that you finger back, that ... ad infinitem (or until one of you runs out of resources).

Do not accept the information returned from the finger as authoritative. Remember that someone trying to access services on your system may be doing so from a compromised system or spoofing her source address.

In the example above, you may want to add a rule 3 that goes something like the following:

```
in.telnetd : david@bar.void.org : spawn (/usr/sbin/safe_finger -l @%h \
      | /usr/bin/mail root) & : DENY
```

to let root know when david@bar.void.org has been attempting to use telnet again. Add this just after the second line in your hosts.allow file.

Note that long lines like this may be broken over two lines by making the last character a "\" as in the example above. This is a line continuation character.

A second way to invoke a shell command is to use twist. The difference between spawn and twist is that spawn sends all communications to /dev/null, whereas twist sends all communications back to the client. This can be used to substitute a different command for the usual one:

```
in.ftpd : ... : twist /bin/echo 608 Message to client
```

twist must be the last option on the line. The above line would send a "608 Message to client" to any client matching the in.ftpd rule rather than invoking the ftp daemon.

Other options include: keepalive, linger, rfc931, banner, nice, setenv, umask, and user. These are used as shown in the following list.

- ◆ keepalive (no arguments): The server will periodically send a keepalive packet to the client. If the client does not respond, the server will terminate. Useful for users who turn off their machines while still connected to the server.

- ◆ linger <number of seconds>: Length of time the kernel is to continue to try to send undelivered data to the client after a connection is closed.

- ◆ rfc931 [timeout in seconds]: Perform RFC 931 username lookups. Valid only for TCP. If the client is not running IDENT or a similar RFC 931 service (such as many PCs), noticeable connection delays could result. Timeout is optional, if not specified, compile-time default is used.

- ◆ banners </some/path>: Look in /some/path/ for a file with the same name as the daemon process (e.g., in.telnetd for the telnet service), and copy its contents to the client. It uses character expansion within the file as explained below. Banners work only with TCP connections.

- `nice` [*number*]: Change the nice value from its default of 10.

- `setenv` `<name value>`: Used to set environment variables for those daemons that don't reset their environment on startup. The "value" is subject to character expansion.

- `umask` `< octal >`: Like the shell umask variable.

- `user` `<user[.group]>`: Sets the daemon's user and optionally the group.

Character expansion

The following list details character expansions available for use.

- `%a (%A)`: The client (server) host address.

- `%c`: Will return client information depending on what's available. May be a user@host or IP address, or just an IP address.

- `%d`: The daemon process name (e.g., in.telnetd)

- `%h (%H)`: Client (server) hostname or IP address.

- `%n (%N)`: Client (server) hostname or "unknown" or "paranoid" if not available.

- `%p`: Deamon process ID.

- `%s`: Server information: daemon@host or IP address, or just a daemon name, depending on available information.

- `%u`: Username (or unknown)

- `%%`: Expands to single "%".

Miscellaneous concerns

TCP Wrappers, despite its flexibility, and its utility for maintaining a connection log, is not without its shortcomings. First, TCP Wrappers will not work properly with UDP — if it did, I suspect the author would have called the program IP Wrappers or TCP/UDP Wrappers. Part of the problem with UDP is a result of the fact that it is called with wait in inetd. Daemons called with wait will not immediately leave the wait queue after receiving UDP packets. So while the first host to communicate with the service may be recorded, if a second client begins communications with the service before it leaves the wait queue, the second client will not be recorded. Additionally, RPC-based services, those in the /etc/services file marked as rpc/tcp, won't work properly either.

TCP Wrappers should not be used with the Apache Web Server. Apache has the TCP Wrappers functionality built into it. Use of tcpd in this case is redundant. The Apache configuration is similar to tcpd's and so should be understandable to anyone already familiar with tcpd.

tcpdchk

The tcpdchk utility allows you to check for syntax errors in your hosts.allow file. Several options are available including -d, which tells tcpdchk to use the hosts.allow file (and hosts.deny file if used) found in the current directory rather than in /etc. Obviously, this option if of little value if your current directory is /etc. But this option does allow you to create and test new rules before implementing them.

By using the -v option, you can see every line that tcpdchk is reading and how it will operate. See Listing 15-1 for a sample output. This output uses the basic rules from above with enhancements from the text.

Listing 15–1: Sample tcpdchk test output

```
# tcpdchk _v
Using network configuration file: /etc/inetd.conf

>> Rule /etc/hosts.allow line 1:
daemons:  ALL
clients:  .void.org EXCEPT david@bar.void.org
option:   ALLOW
access:   granted
>> Rule /etc/hosts.allow line 2:
daemons:  ALL EXCEPT in.telnetd
clients:  david@bar.void.org
option:   ALLOW
access:   granted
>> Rule /etc/hosts.allow line 4:
daemons:  in.telnetd
clients:  david@bar.void.org
option:   spawn (/usr/sbin/safe_finger _l @client_hostname |
/usr/bin/mail root) &
option:   DENY
access:   denied
>> Rule /etc/hosts.allow line 5:
daemons:  in.ftpd
clients:  ALL
option:   ALLOW
access:   granted
>> Rule /etc/hosts.allow line 6:
daemons:  ALL
```

```
clients:   ALL
option:    DENY
access:    denied
```

If tcpdchk is having trouble finding your /etc/inetd.conf file, the `-i path/to/inetd.conf` option can be used.

If tcpdchk is having trouble finding your /etc/inetd.conf file, the `-i path/to/inetd.conf` option can be used. It can also be used to specify a test inetd.conf configuration before implementing it.

Finally, the `-a` checks for any allows that aren't explicitly declared – that is, what daemons can be started by a client as a result of omitting a statement to specifically allow them.

tcpdmatch

The tcpdmatch utility allows you to test specific examples against your configuration files. Again, tcpdmatch allows you to test against a hosts.allow file in your current directory by specifying the `-d` option. It also recognizes the `-i /path/to/inetd.conf` if tcpdmatch has trouble finding it.

The syntax for tcpdmatch is as follows:

```
tcpdmatch daemon[@server] [user@]client.
```

The server option is for multi-homed hosts, and the user is for specific users at a client. Some examples are shown in Listing 15-2.

Listing 15-2: Example outputs from tcpdmatch

```
# tcpdmatch in.telnetd bar
warning: bar: hostname alias
warning: (official name: bar.void.org)
client:    hostname bar.void.org
client:    address  192.168.0.2
server:    process  in.telnetd
matched:   /etc/hosts.allow line 1
option:    ALLOW
access:    granted
# tcpdmatch in.telnetd david@bar
warning: bar: hostname alias
warning: (official name: bar.void.org)
client:    hostname bar.void.org
client:    address  192.168.0.2
client:    username david
server:    process  in.telnetd
matched:   /etc/hosts.allow line 4
```

```
option:   spawn (/usr/sbin/safe_finger _l @bar.void.org |
/usr/bin/mail root) &
option:   DENY
access:   denied

# tcpdmatch in.ftpd locutus2.calderasystems.com
client:   hostname locutus2.calderasystems.com
client:   address  207.179.39.2
server:   process  in.ftpd
matched:  /etc/hosts.allow line 5
option:   ALLOW
access:   granted

# tcpdmatch in.telnetd locutus2.calderasystems.com
client:   hostname locutus2.calderasystems.com
client:   address  207.179.39.2
server:   process  in.telnetd
matched:  /etc/hosts.allow line 6
option:   DENY
access:   denied
```

Summary

In this chapter you learned what TCP Wrappers is and how to implement it. You learned about the flexibility you have in its implementation, and that some of this flexibility is based on compile-time options. You also learned which options are compiled into the OpenLinux version of tcpd. You learned how to booby-trap services in inetd.conf, and even how to send messages back to the client.

You also learned how to test your rules before implementing them using the tcpdchk and tcpdmatch utilities included with tcpd.

Part III

Firewalls and special-purpose software

Chapter 16

Using packet filter firewalls

THIS CHAPTER WILL DISCUSS a little about firewalls in Linux — what they are, how they work, and how to begin building one. While this chapter will not make anyone an expert on firewalls, it will introduce the concepts and go into some detail about implementing a packet filter firewall with ipchains. The next chapter covers a proxy firewall using Squid.

The term firewall comes from the firewall used in cars (and other motorized vehicles) to protect the passengers from a fire in the engine compartment. A firewall on a network protects users and data on the local network from attacks coming from the Internet (or extranet). It can also be used to prevent users on the local network from connecting to "prohibited" sites, and compartmentalize the internal network.

Some people learn too late that a generic firewall will not protect against insiders. However, internal firewalls can be used to isolate departments so that damage is not widespread, e.g., protect accounting from engineering from sales, each of which likely has few business browsing files belonging to the other.

Introduction to firewalls

Basically, two kinds of firewalls are available for Linux. Each of these two basic types has two subtypes. The two basic types are packet filters and proxy firewalls. The packet filter firewalls can be of the forwarding type, where decisions are made to forward packets or not, and masquerading firewalls, which rewrite the source and destination addresses. Proxy firewalls can be of the standard (sometimes known as opaque) type, where a client connects to a special port and is redirected to go out through another port, or a transparent proxy, where the client doesn't use a special port, but the firewall software forwards the packets through transparently.

This chapter will deal principally with packet filtering firewalls. The next chapter will deal with proxying firewalls – specifically, using Squid – and the following chapter will deal with IP Masquerading, often called Network Address Translation.

Packet filters

Packet filtering firewalls work on the principle that the information needed to make a decision about what to do with a packet is contained in the header. The header contains information regarding the source and destination addresses, TTL (time to live), protocol, and much more. It also contains a header checksum to tell if the header has been corrupted, and the size of the payload. In all, some 13 separate fields of information are contained in an IP header, some fields containing multiple pieces of information.

For complete details on packet filters, refer to RFC 791.

IP does not check the payload other than to tell if the payload is the correct size. The transport control protocol (TCP) is responsible for ensuring the integrity of the data payload.

OpenLinux uses ipchains to provide packet filtering. If you plan to implement a packet filtering firewall, you must make some decisions about the type of packets to address specifically, and what to do with those packets when they are encountered.

The ipchains software permits a number of different criteria to be applied to packets. The criteria can be applied to incoming packets, outgoing packets, or packets that will pass through the firewall (forwarded packets). These decisions can be based on where the packets came from by address, where they are going to by address, or where they are going to by port. Different rules can be applied depending on whether these are tcp packets, udp packets, or icmp packets. Finally, for any packets not specifically addressed, the default policy determines the fate of the packets.

Any router, gateway, or host that transports a networking packet from one network to another rewrites the header. But this rewriting doesn't alter the source or destination addresses. It alters only the TTL and checksum, and on occasion, the total length and fragment offset (among others) if the packet needs to be fragmented to continue on. When header rewriting is discussed in this text, it refers to address rewriting.

The OSI (Open Source Interconnect) model is one of the popular (if not completely accurate, but a good theoretical paradigm nevertheless) models used to explain how packets move from the Application layer to the Physical layer. The seven layers are used to explain where certain software works. For the purposes of this text, it is important only to note that the level where each works is different and is one of the distinguishing characteristics between proxies and packet filters. But this difference is important. Proxies are more overhead-intensive; they can inspect entire packets more thoroughly (that is, they do a stateful inspection). They also tend to be a little more difficult to set up initially.

 The term stateful inspection refers to proxy software's examination of the entire packet in context, or its state, whereas packet filters only examine the IP header. This more detailed inspection is also more resource intensive.

Which to use?

Packet filtering firewalls and proxying firewalls perform similar functions, they just do so in different ways. They act as shields to protect trusted network segments from untrusted ones. In this regard, each works equally well. Both require monitoring and occasional reconfiguring. Both, if misconfigured, will provide only a false sense of security. Both, when implemented in a methodical, well-thought-out manner, will provide a modicum of security. Both are equally vulnerable to a determined, knowledgeable attacker.

If you remember that the only secure system is the one that is not assembled and powered on (and not of much use either), you'll have a more realistic perspective of what firewalls can buy you: time to react to an attack. It remains your responsibility to reconfigure the firewall to protect against this attack. Let me emphasize that: A firewall buys you time to react to an attack.

Basically, the decision to use packet filtering or proxying comes down to an individual choice and may be based on prior experience with firewall software. If you are implementing a firewall and have worked with proxies before and are comfortable with them, by all means continue. The use of one doesn't preclude use of the other. Some proxies that are designed to work specifically with Web (http) traffic can complement a packet filter nicely. For example, the use of Squid to block particular Web sites or advertising banners is often easier than writing packet filtering rules to deny or reject the banner sites. Conversely, ipchains rules can be created solely for the purpose of logging traffic, and used in conjunction with a proxy to track specific kinds of traffic. So the best option may be to mix and match depending on your overall objectives.

From a security standpoint, therefore, neither is better. The one place ipchains may tip the balance is in situations where you'll want to rewrite the Type of Service (TOS) field to optimize traffic flow. For example, if you have several systems that use the firewall and several folks are using it at the same time, you can use the TOS field as a queueing flag to give priority to HTTP packets at the expense of FTP packets, since someone is probably waiting impatiently for a Web page to download, but is more tolerant of the amount of time it will take to receive an FTP download.

TIP You can use ipchains to modify the TOS field to specify one of minimum delay, maximum reliability, maximum throughput, or minimum cost.

Physical configurations

In any discussion of physical configurations, you need to look at both the hardware and the software as they apply to the firewall. Remember that one of the reasons the firewall exists is to protect the trusted network from the untrusted network, so this host must necessarily be both the funnel for network traffic between the two networks (making it a possible choke point), and the focus for those looking to penetrate your security. If they want to come in, they've got to pass through here first.

The firewall host

You'll need to consider the type of host you are going to install. You can install a firewall that has only one interface and uses that interface for both trusted and untrusted connections. But you'll want to consider if this is wise considering the cost of a second interface versus the weakened security posture this configuration entails. Better is a host with two interfaces, one that completely isolates one network from the other. With this configuration, bypassing the firewall becomes more difficult.

NOTE A host that isolates an untrusted network from a trusted network by using two interfaces, one for each network, is called a bastion host, a bastion being a strong defense or bulwark. Bastions were once used to protect castle walls, as bastion hosts are used to protect networks.

The question of how powerful a system should be depends on many factors. If you are going to use the firewall to connect two 10MB Ethernet cards and use packet filtering and no proxies, an 80486-33 processor with 16MB RAM will be sufficient for low to moderate traffic loads. However, if you plan to use 100MHz (or faster) Ethernet cards in a high-traffic route, this CPU will not be able to keep up with the demand, and you'll experience significant packet loss.

The firewall kernel

This section deals with Linux kernel configuration. Because three options are available for kernel configuration purposes (make xconfig, make menuconfig, make config), and because the only similarity in option names between the three is the configuration (.config) file parameter (listed under help), the common name and the configuration parameter are shown in each case.

In building a firewall, you'll need to reconfigure the kernel. Several parameters must be set in the kernel to permit packet filtering. Some of these are subjective and will be based on your hardware, one must be turned off, and others are required. For more information on building a custom kernel, see the documentation from your distribution. The first parameter is in the Code maturity level options:

```
CONFIG_EXPERIMENTAL=y
```

The use of so-called experimental drivers within the kernel is not necessarily a bad thing and may be unavoidable for certain hardware or options. So enabling this will be a judgment call. It does mean the drivers haven't received the level of testing other kernel options have, and so could introduce instability or security risks. That said, don't shy away from using them when you need to. Those drivers and networking code that are experimental will be clearly marked as such, and you don't need to enable them. But unless you turn experimental code on, the experimental modules won't even show up.

The next section of interest is the "Loadable module support." It is no longer necessary that you consider compiling the kernel only as a monolithic kernel rather than a *modular* kernel (for more information on building a custom kernel, refer to your distribution's technical reference documentation). In previous kernel versions (2.0.*x* and below), the recommendation was to avoid building modular kernels in a firewall. But with the advent of kmod, a kernel module loader, modular kernels are much safer than in the past. This is because kmod is a kernel routine rather than a user-level process like kerneld. Since some options you'll need aren't available without module support, say yes to Enable loadable modules support. Also add the Kernel module loader, so modules will install as needed (when able).

```
CONFIG_MODULES=y                    recommended
CONFIG_KMOD=y                       recommended
```

The General setup section includes one absolutely vital option that is easily overlooked (though fortunately set to yes by default): Sysctl support. This creates the /proc/sys tree as discussed in Chapter 6 and is needed to enable the support required for firewalls.

```
CONFIG_SYSCTL=y                     required
```

In other sections, give careful thought to those parameters installed. You need to support your hardware (disk drives), the file system, Ethernet drivers, other communications drivers (modems, ISDN devices, and protocols such as PPP), and ELF formats. But sound and other unnecessary parameters should be disabled.

If yours is a home network or part of a small, low-profile business with low bandwidth, you may not need or want to go to the extremes detailed in this chapter. Only you can perform a proper risk assessment for your situation.

Assuming you've properly configured the other sections of the kernel configuration for your system, turn your attention to the "Networking options" and the text below. Although not the last section in the kernel configuration, it is certainly the most important for this chapter.

Networking options

The Linux 2.2.*x* kernel adds significant complexity to the networking options section compared with the 2.0.*x* kernels. The additional options can be daunting, and the help is not always helpful. This section will discuss the options available as of the 2.2.13 kernel; future kernels may add more options. Some of the options will be required, others recommended, and still others are, well, optional.

Items marked as not recommended may weaken your firewall. If you know you won't use it, don't install it.

The options below marked "no" will appear in your .config file as #<*option name*> is not set.

These are the kernel parameters:

◆ The first parameter is the packet socket and is required by a number of programs, including tcpdump. The tcpdump program, or any program calling it, will put your Ethernet card in promiscuous mode, and so should be avoided. If you think you'll need this (and you may), compile as a module. This particular module is not loaded automatically. If you get a setsocket error from any program, load this module to see if it helps.

```
CONFIG_PACKET=m                    not recommended except as a
module
```

◆ The Kernel/User netlink socket requires devices with major number 36 to communicate with. If this option is chosen, you should also choose "Routing messages" and "IP: firewall packet netlink device". Without these other two options, this option is irrelevant.

```
CONFIG_NETLINK=y                recommended
```

◆ The Routing messages option requires /dev/route created with major 36, minor 0 so you can read routing information. Writing to this device has no effect, but a user-level program can read routing-related information from it if you want.

```
CONFIG_RTNETLINK=y              optional, but recommended
```

◆ The netlink device emulation is only for backward compatability, and will be removed in the future.

```
CONFIG_NETLINK_DEV=y            required
```

If you intend to run a packet filter firewall, do IP masquerading, or port forwarding, you must say yes to this option. If you will not be running ipchains or ipmasqadm, but only running a proxy firewall (or this is to be a normal host) say no to this option.

```
CONFIG_FIREWALL=y/n             required for ipchains use,
otherwise not recommended
```

◆ The Socket Filtering option is used by user space programs to put filters on sockets. It is not required by ipchains.

```
CONFIG_FILTER=n                 not recommended
```

◆ The UNIX domain sockets option installs code to permit use of sockets in Linux. Without this code, syslogging will not work. This option must be installed, but may be installed as a module. This option should only be turned off in embedded systems, and not always then.

```
CONFIG_UNIX=y                   required
```

◆ The TCP/IP networking option is another non-option. If you will use TCP/IP to talk to any other TCP/IP connected host, including localhost, X, or certain other programs, this option is required.

```
CONFIG_INET=y                   required
```

◆ IP multicasting is a way for a host to communicate with several hosts at one time. It is used for some audio/video programs. This is likely of more use to hosts than a firewall.

```
CONFIG_IP_MULTICAST=y           optional
```

◆ The IP advanced router option only turns on or off several options below it; it does not affect the kernel. If you want to use type of service values (explained below), you'll need to enable this option in order to enable TOS below.

```
CONFIG_IP_ADVANCED_ROUTER=y    optional
```

◆ The IP policy routing allows for alternate routing for packets. That is, they will be routed based not only on their destination, but on other values as well. If you want to take advantage of TOS routing, you must say yes here.

```
CONFIG_IP_MULTIPLE_TABLES=y    optional
```

◆ The IP equal cost multipath option allows a deterministic approach to routing if multiple paths to reach a particular destination are available. Few sites will need this.

```
CONFIG_IP_ROUTE_MULTIPATH=n    optional
```

◆ The IP use TOS value as routing key permits you to prioritize the IP queue when multiple packets are waiting to go. You determine which are most important to go immediately and which can wait by setting the Type of Service bit to varying values.

```
CONFIG_IP_ROUTE_TOS=y          optional
```

◆ IP verbose route monitoring is an option that, when enabled, makes the kernel "chattier" when it sees packets out of the ordinary. These log entries can help you detect attacks on your system. Not required, but a very good idea. Just say yes here.

```
CONFIG_IP_ROUTE_VERBOSE=y      recommended
```

◆ The IP large routing tables option is principally for routers with several interfaces. If each interface is connected to a large network, the kernel routing tables may grow quite large. Probably not needed at most sites.

```
CONFIG_IP_ROUTE_LARGE_TABLES=n    optional
```

◆ IP fast network address translation is network address translation for routers where an actual firewall isn't required. If you're going to use NAT software other than ipchains, you'll want to select this option.

```
CONFIG_IP_ROUTE_NAT=n          optional
```

◆ The IP kernel level autoconfiguration option is principally for diskless hosts that load their root file system from another host. A firewall should never get its configuration from another system, but should always be completely self-contained. The following two parameters depend on this one.

```
CONFIG_IP_PNP=n                not recommended
CONFIG_IP_PNP_BOOTP=n          not recommended
CONFIG_IP_PNP_RARP=n           not recommended
```

♦ The IP firewalling option is required if you're going to use ipchains to create a packet filter firewall or an IP masquerading firewall. This option is not required to use squid or any other proxy firewall.

```
CONFIG_IP_FIREWALL=y          required
```

♦ The IP firewall packet netlink device option allows you to create a device that ipchains can write packets to. This device can then be read from by a user-space program and actions taken based on the contents of the packets. You'll need to create the device and find (or write) the user-space program.

```
CONFIG_IP_FIREWALL_NETLINK=y   optional
```

♦ The IP use FWMARK value as routing key option allows you to use a mark placed by ipchains for routing purposes.

```
CONFIG_IP_ROUTE_FWMARK=y       optional
```

♦ The IP transparent proxy support option is required for ipchains REDIRECT targets and for transparent proxies. Otherwise, it is not needed. If in doubt, include.

```
CONFIG_IP_TRANSPARENT_PROXY=y     optional/required
```

♦ The IP masquerading option is required for masquerading firewalls.

```
CONFIG_IP_MASQUERADE=y         optional/required
```

♦ The IP ICMP masquerading option is required only if you chose CONFIG_IP_MASQUERADE above and wish to masquerade outgoing ICMP. Without this, ping will not work. Also, Microsoft's tracert (which uses ICMP rather than UDP) will not work.

```
CONFIG_IP_MASQUERADE_ICMP=y    optional/recommended
```

♦ The IP masquerading special modules support option does nothing in itself except enable the selection of the next three options, the use of which requires the ipmasqadm utility.

```
CONFIG_IP_MASQUERADE_MOD=y     optional/required
```

♦ The IP autofw masq support option allows some protocols that would have trouble getting through a firewall to pass.

```
CONFIG_IP_MASQUERADE_IPAUTOFW=y    optional
```

♦ The IP ipportfw masq support option allows port forwarding of connections arriving on a selected port to be redirected to any host and port available. Requires ipmasqadm.

```
CONFIG_IP_MASQUERADE_IPPORTFW=y     optional
```

◆ The IP ip fwmard masq-forwarding support option lets you take advantage of the mark option of ipchains for redirecting packets.

```
CONFIG_IP_MASQUERADE_MFW=y    optional
```

◆ The IP optimize as router not host option attempts to remove an operation that performs a copy and checksum that is meant to verify the integrity of data packets. This is not recommended on a host that is meant to receive packets for end use, but a system that acts only as a router can gain a speed benefit from using this option.

```
CONFIG_IP_ROUTER=n            optional
```

◆ The IP tunneling option permits you to perform IP in IP encapsulation. This is good for laptops that might move from subnet to subnet and for which you need to maintain a static IP.

```
CONFIG_NET_IPIP=n             optional
```

◆ If you are connected to a CISCO router, the IP GRE tunnels over IP option will allow your gateway to exchange routing information with the CISCO router.

```
CONFIG_NET_IPGRE=n            optional
```

◆ The IP broadcast GRE over IP allows routing broadcasts to CISCO routers to construct a WAN on the Internet. Requires `CONFIG_NET_IPGRE` above.

```
CONFIG_NET_IPGRE_BROADCAST=n  optional
```

◆ The IP mutlticast routing option is only required if your system will route multicast packets. Requires `CONFIG_IP_MULTICAST` above.

```
CONFIG_IP_MROUTE=y            optional
```

◆ Multicast routing comes in three "flavors": dense mode, which is turned on by default, sparse move version one, and sparse mode version 2. Version 1 is more heavily used than version 2, so unless you have another system running it you won't need version 2. You may or may not want sparse mode version 1. The IP PIM-SM version 1 support option provides the most common sparse mode support, and IP PIM-SM version 2 support option the least common.

```
CONFIG_IP_PIMSM_V1=y          optional
CONFIG_IP_PIMSM_V2=n          optional
```

◆ The IP aliasing support option is required only if you need to use IP aliasing on one or more Ethernet cards to multi-home your system. This option is no longer available as a module. Some NICs will go into promiscuous mode if aliasing is used. You should have only one IP per card on a firewall.

```
CONFIG_IP_ALIAS=n             not recommended
```

◆ If you are directly connected to more than 256 hosts and have a low memory system (less than 16MB RAM), choosing the IP ARP daemon support option and running arpd will help. Otherwise, you'll want to say no here.

```
CONFIG_ARPD=n                    optional
```

◆ You might want to choose IP TCP SYN cookie support if your system is prone to SYN Denial of Service attacks. Choosing this option does not, however, enable this support by default; you must deliberately enable it. With TCP SYN cookies enabled, your system will suffer a slight performance hit. To enable, you must do the following: echo 1 > /proc/sys/net/ipv4/tcp_syncookies.

```
CONFIG_SYN_COOKIES=y             recommended
```

◆ The IP Reverse ARP option along with rarpd is designed to allow a system to respond to arp configuration requests. Your firewall should not do this.

```
CONFIG_INET_RARP=n               not recommended
```

◆ The IP Allow large windows option has nothing at all to do with a graphical user interface. The "window" referred to is a buffer with a static size. By choosing this option, you increase the static size. If you have very long slow links (like a satellite link) and more than 16MB of memory, you'll want to choose this.

```
CONFIG_SKB_LARGE=y               optional
```

◆ Unless you just want to experiment with IPv6, you won't want The IPv6 protocol option. IPv6 is not compatible with the IPv4 support in ipchains, and could bypass your firewall rules.

```
CONFIG_IPV6=n                    optional
```

◆ The next three options — IPv6 enable EUI-64 token format, IPv6 disable provider based addresses, and IPv6 routing messages via old netlink — will depend on your system and your connection to the experimental IPv6 network. These rely on CONFIG_IPV6 above.

```
CONFIG_IPV6_EUI64=n              optional
CONFIG_IPV6_NO_PB=n              optional
CONFIG_IPV6_NETLINK=n            optional
```

◆ The next four options enable your system to work with non-IP protocols, IPX, SPX, and AppleTalk. You should not select any of The IPX protocol, IPX Full internal IPX network, IPX SPX networking, or Appletalk DDP options.

```
CONFIG_IPX=n                     not recommended
CONFIG_IPX_INTERN=n              not recommended
CONFIG_SPX=n                     not recommended
CONFIG_ATALK=n                   not recommended
```

The ipchains software works only with IP, and the inclusion of non-IP protocols introduces a way to bypass your firewall.

Very few sites will need any of the three X25 or LLC protocol support options. If you do, ensure that you know how they will interact with your
chosen firewall software.

◆ The CCITT X.25 Packet Layer and LAPB Data Link Driver options are the
first two of three options concerning X25 on Linux and should not be
used on a firewall.

```
CONFIG_X25=n                    not recommended
CONFIG_LAPB=n                   not recommended
```

◆ The Bridging option is used to combine Ethernet segments into one
network.

```
CONFIG_BRIDGE=n                 optional
```

◆ The 802.2 LLC option is the final X.25 protocol support option.

```
CONFIG_LLC=n                    not recommended
```

◆ If you absolutely must have support for Acorn computers Econet, ensure
that you choose the AUN over UDP (which piggybacks on IP). The Acorn
Econet/AUN protocols, AUN over UDP, and Native Econet options configure Econet networking. The first is required for AUN, the second is the
only option you should choose on a firewall, and you should not choose
the third.

```
CONFIG_ECONET=n                 optional
CONFIG_ECONET_AUNUDP=n          optional
CONFIG_ECONET_NATIVE=n          not recommended
```

◆ The WAN router option can be used if needed for IP circuits. You should
avoid other non-IP protocols as they can bypass your firewall software.

```
CONFIG_WAN_ROUTER=n             optional
```

◆ The Fast switching option uses software to "short-circuit" between the
hardware layers of Ethernet cards and will bypass the rules of ipchains.
Do not use this option on a firewall.

```
CONFIG_NET_FASTROUTE=n          DO NOT USE
```

◆ Some Ethernet cards have a "throttle" to slow down traffic to a manage-
able speed for your system. If your card supports this, you may use
the Forwarding between high-speed interfaces option to slow down
traffic flow.

```
CONFIG_NET_HW_FLOWCONTROL=n    optional
```

◆ For those systems without supported Ethernet cards, but that need network traffic slowed down for the system, the CPU is too slow to handle
full bandwidth option is an alternative to the previous option.

```
CONFIG_CPU_IS_SLOW=n           optional
```

◆ Some 16 queueing options depend on the QoS and/or fair queueing option, but are omitted for brevity. If you truly need (or just want) to use
these, feel free to configure them.

```
CONFIG_NET_SCHED=n             optional
```

◆ If you have configured the FreeS/WAN software for your system (recommended), you'll have several more options in this section. The first is the
IP Security Protocol (FreeS/WAN IPSEC) option.

```
CONFIG_IPSEC=m                 recommended
```

◆ With only two exceptions and two options, you should select yes for all
IPSEC modules. The exceptions are noted.

```
CONFIG_IPSEC_IPIP=y            recommended
CONFIG_IPSEC_PFKEYv2=y         recommended
```

◆ The IPSEC Enable Insecure algorithms option operates the tunnel without
encryption. This, and the NULL pseudo-encryption option below, should
never be turned on.

```
CONFIG_IPSEC_INSECURE=n        not recommended
```

◆ Some hosts behind the firewall may be confused by receiving ICMP Path
MTU messages. If this is the case, turn this option off. This will reduce
connection speed, but improve reliability for those hosts. If you are running all Linux hosts, this should not pose a problem.

```
CONFIG_IPSEC_ICMP=y               optional
CONFIG_IPSEC_AH=y                 recommended
CONFIG_IPSEC_AUTH_HMAC_MD5=y      recommended
CONFIG_IPSEC_AUTH_HMAC_SHA1=y     recommended
CONFIG_IPSEC_ESP=y                recommended
CONFIG_IPSEC_ENC_3DES=y           recommended
```

- If you are offered the NULL pseudo-encryption algorithm option, do not choose it, or your connections will not be secure.

  ```
  CONFIG_IPSEC_ENC_NULL=n          not recommended
  ```

- The IPSEC Debugging Option is to aid you in troubleshooting by increasing IPSEC verbosity. This option is recommended, though not required.

  ```
  DEBUG_IPSEC=y                    optional
  ```

Software considerations

After the kernel is built, you can look over the system for software that isn't required for operation. Extraneous software should be removed. The use of the X Window software is discouraged, since this binds to ports 6000 through 6010, as well as UDP port 177 if you also use xdm. This does not mean you can't retain the X software on the system, merely that you shouldn't run the X server. If you feel that you need the X server, consider using ipchains to deny input on the untrusted network side. This includes nfs and other services that are not used or needed. If an intruder breaches the firewall, it doesn't make sense to provide tools to use or services to activate.

You probably will want software like ipmasqadm to help manage the ipchains rules. This program is not included on the standard OpenLinux CD, but is worth installing if you have many rules to track or want to do port forwarding. The Secure Shell (ssh) program is also a good idea from a security perspective. Running TCP Wrappers on ports that are not forwarded and not used (normal services should not run on a firewall) as well as tripwire to watch files is also a good idea. Another good program to add to your toolkit is a Perl program called courtney. This program (among others, such as perro) watches for port scans. The only service you should run on a firewall is sshd for secure remote administration.

Other considerations

A firewall should not be considered a normal network host or treated like one. Your firewall should not allow normal users to log in or share files or directories on the network. The use of good passwords for the accounts on the firewall, along with the use of shadow passwords, should go without saying. What may need to be said is that the firewall should not have the same password as any other host on your net. The fact that the firewall is broken because the attacker was able to break the password should not automatically provide access to other hosts on the internal network. Don't make further access easy.

This host should also be physically separated from the rest of the hosts and in a secure area where unauthorized users cannot gain physical access to it. Any machine a knowledgeable person has access to can be "broken," often in minutes. The case should be locked, and access to the system setup password protected. The system should be set to boot only from the hard drive.

A simple packet filtering firewall

In the next few sections you'll step through building a very simple firewall with ipchains. This firewall should not be considered adequate for use as is — you'll need to determine if this is what you need. Hopefully, you'll get a good idea about how to plan and implement a firewall, to include how to write ipchains rules correctly from the text below. In the real world, it's just not this easy; this is only a chapter, although the subject deserves a book.

To start off, you'll need to know something about the network you're connecting from, and the network you're connecting to. The following assumptions will be valid for the rest of this section:

```
Internal (trusted) Network: 209.191.169.128/25
External (untrusted) Network: 209.191.169.0/25
Bastion host: foo, with foo1/foo2 interfaces,
209.191.169.1/209.191.169.129
```

Planning

You can start from one of two general policies. The overall policy can be either "permit everything that is not specifically denied" or "deny everything that is not specifically permitted." The former is certainly the easier to configure initially, but the latter will be the more normal policy on a non-masquerading firewall. On a masquerading firewall (see Chapter 18), it makes little difference, since you can't just "pass through" the firewall by specifying an internal address from the outside. For now, you'll work with a non-masquerading firewall and a policy of deny.

The network is set up internally as trusted, and no services will be run from inside for now. All services the company wants to provide to the Internet will reside on the untrusted network: anonymous ftp, http, etc. The untrusted portion of the company's network is often referred to as the "DMZ" — the demilitarized zone. This is because it is like the front lines in a battle. If the bad guys are going to show their faces, this will be where they will try to penetrate. Keeping your servers that offer public access on the DMZ means you have more systems to monitor for intrusions, but on the other hand, you're not bringing these intruders inside your trusted network as you would do if you used port forwarding through your firewall.

Since this network is considered low-risk, the decision has been made to run mail on the firewall, with a pop server that will allow users to get mail whether they are at the office or home (imap will not be run for security reasons). The smtp and popd services will be moved inside via port forwarding later. Once they are moved inside (see "Port forwarding" in Chapter 18) the rules will remain the same, since accepting locally or for port forwarding is essentially the same. DNS will be run from inside, but will only service the internal network. Primary and secondary DNS will be provided externally by the Internet provider.

Internal clients should be allowed to use standard services on the Internet, except nntp. The next paragraph summarizes the policy you're going to implement:

```
Summary:
Default policy: prohibit
Anon FTP: external (deny incoming in to the firewall)
http: external (deny incoming in to the firewall)
ssh will be used: turn off telnet
smtp: firewall (future: port forward to internal machine)
popd: firewall (future: port forward to internal machine)
DNS: internal (no external access)
also stop incoming pings
```

ipchains in general

In order to understand how to proceed with ipchains, you need to understand how ipchains works. The next few sections will walk you through some of the finer points. Most ipchains text makes the assumption that all packets run through the "chains," the list of rules. But, in fact, ipchains will see a packet only if that packet is the first or only packet. Subsequent packet fragments do not traverse the chains. The reason for this is simple — a host cannot reassemble the fragments into a packet until it has the first packet. Deny this packet, and the others will time out and be dropped. By default, when you choose IP firewalling as an option, the Linux kernel will automatically defragment incoming packets. So the end result is that all packets (after defragmentation) do end up traversing all chains. This minor point is important only if a pre-2.2.13 (but post 2.2.10) kernel is used, since those two kernels dropped the IP_ALWAYS_DEFRAG option but didn't properly insert the defrag code.

 When you think "chain," think of a logically grouped list of rules. Each rule in a chain is a test to apply against the IP header for a match.

The chains contain rules numbered from one. As you will see, some rules can be referred to either by rule specification or rule number.

A rule specification is the set of conditions the packet must meet, i.e., the test. The same basic rule can exist in multiple chains, so the chain argument is required.

There are seven variations on the ipchains command line. The first six will contain a command as the first argument. All six variations accept options as a final argument.

The commands are as follows (all commands are preceded by a hyphen):

◆ A: append; this takes as mandatory arguments a chain name and a rule specification

◆ D: delete; this takes as mandatory arguments a chain name and a rule specification

◆ C: test (check) (-s, -d, -p, and -i are required); this takes as mandatory arguments a chain name and a rule specification

◆ I: insert (an extension of append, but is placed ahead of the rule referenced)

◆ R: replace (an Insert and Delete); this takes as mandatory arguments a chain name, a rule number, and a rule specification.

◆ D: delete; this takes as mandatory arguments a chain name and rule number (this is a variation on the delete command above where the rule number is known)

◆ L: list (show rules)

◆ F: flush (delete all rules)

◆ Z: zero (zero counters)

◆ N: new (create a user-defined chain); this requires a chain name but otherwise works on all chains

◆ X:- delete a user-defined chain; this requires a chain name, and the chain must be empty, but otherwise works on all chains

◆ P: policy; this takes as mandatory arguments a chain and a target

◆ M : masquerade

The -M option requires the following mandatory arguments:

- L: list

- S: set tcp tcpfin udp

◆ h: help this option lists the usage argument. (It can take the argument icmp to provide a list of ICMP code and type names it knows that can be used as arguments.)

The masquerade command, as opposed to the MASQ target, requires either L or S. The S command requires three arguments, the tcp (tcp session), tcpfin (tcp session after receiving a FIN packet), and udp timeout values in seconds.

The seventh variation on the ipchains command line is help, which takes no commands, and only accepts one option, and optionally one argument.

ipchains options

A number of options are available for ipchains. These include some options to save mistyping a second rule when it is the same as the first but in the opposite direction, as well as a way to reverse the meaning of a parameter. Where address masks are specified, the mask may be of the /N or N.N.N.N notation. Addresses may also be hostnames. Ports may be either numbers or service names.

◆ The -b option allows you to specify one rule with source and destination address, but have ipchains also build a rule with the addresses reversed.

◆ The ! can be used with a number of options to reverse the meaning.

The options include the following:

■ -p proto: protocol. Can accept ! as in -p ! icmp — to match all but icmp messages, or can accept all to match all protocols.

■ -s address: source address. Can optionally take !, a netmask, or a port. Note, an address of 0/0 matches all addresses and is the default if -s is not specified. For ICMP, instead of a port (since ICMP doesn't use them) you can follow -s with either an ICMP name (see Table 30-1) as listed by ipchains -h icmp or type number. If you use a name, you cannot also use -d code.

■ -d address: destination address. Same criteria as for -s. If you use -s and specify an ICMP type number, you can use -d and specify the code.

■ -i name: interface name. Can accept !. Also accepts "+" suffix on the interface name to signify all interfaces of that type, i.e., ppp+ is all ppp interfaces (ppp0–pppN).

■ -j target: target for rule (user-defined chain name or special value) if it matches. If special value is REDIRECT, port can be included.

■ -m mark: number to mark on matching packets.

■ -n: numeric output of addresses and ports. By default, ipchains will try to resolve them.

■ -: Log matching packets. These will be logged by the kernel.

■ -o: output matches to netdev, the userspace device.

■ -t and xor: masks for TOS field. Used to manipulate the TOS field. (See Table 30-2).

■ -v: verbose mode. Will output the interface address, rule options (if any), TOS masks, and packet and byte counters.

■ -x: expand numbers. When packet and byte counters are displayed, do not use the abbreviations K, M, or G, but display all zeroes.

- ■ -f : second and further fragments. Can be preceded by not.

- ■ -y: Matches tcp packets that have the SYN bit set. May be preceded by !.

The following are valid ICMP types and codes (indented under the main type):

- ◆ echo-reply (pong)
- ◆ destination-unreachable
  - ■ network-unreachable
  - ■ host-unreachable
  - ■ protocol-unreachable
  - ■ port-unreachable
  - ■ fragmentation-needed and DF set
  - ■ source-route-failed
  - ■ network-unknown
  - ■ host-unknown
  - ■ network-prohibited
  - ■ host-prohibited
  - ■ TOS-network-unreachable
  - ■ TOS-host-unreachable
  - ■ communication-prohibited
  - ■ host-precedence-violation
  - ■ precedence-cutoff
- ◆ source-quench
- ◆ redirect
  - ■ network-redirect
  - ■ host-redirect
  - ■ TOS-network-redirect
  - ■ TOS-host-redirect
- ◆ echo-request (ping)
- ◆ router-advertisement
- ◆ router-solicitation

- ◆ time-exceeded (ttl-exceeded)
  - ■ ttl-zero-during-transit
  - ■ ttl-zero-during-reassembly
- ◆ parameter-problem
  - ■ ip-header-bad
  - ■ required-option-missing
- ◆ timestamp-request
- ◆ timestamp-reply
- ◆ address-mask-request
- ◆ address-mask-reply

The following table shows values for use if you want to implement routing priorities based on the Type of Service (TOS).

TOS Name	Value	Example Uses
Minimum Delay	0x01 0x10	ftp, telnet, ssh
Maximum Throughput	0x01 0x08	ftp-data
Maximum Reliability	0x01 0x04	snmp, DNS
Minimum Cost	0x01 0x02	nntp, e-mail

The TOS is usable only if you compiled support into the kernel (CONFIG_IP_ROUTE_TOS).

The `-o` option requires kernel support (`CONFIG_IP_FIREWALL_NETLINK`) and a device with major 36 and minor 3.

Built-in chains

The three built-in chains in ipchains are input, forward, and output. Other user-defined chains may be created and destroyed, but these three cannot be destroyed and must always contain at least one rule (the default policy rule). By default, these rules are all policy DENY.

As packets are received, they traverse these chains, rule by rule, in the following order: input, forward, output. They will continue in the chain until a match is encountered. When a match is encountered, the chain is interrupted until the target is evaluated. If no target exists, the chain will continue with the next rule.

A rule does not have to have a target. Perhaps you want to know how many packets match a certain rule. As a rule is matched, the rule counter is incremented. Combined with the counter for the chain, you can see how many of the packets that traversed the chain matched any particular rule.

If a target exists, ipchains evaluates the target. The target can either be a user-defined chain name or a special value. If it is a user-defined chain name, ipchains will immediately transfer to that chain and begin traversing it. If no matches are found in the user-defined chain, ipchains will return to the chain that sent it, and continue with the next rule in the chain.

Think of user-defined chains as subroutines, and the targets sending them as GOSUBS.

If a target exists and it is not a user-defined chain name, then it must be one of the special values:

- ACCEPT: Accept this packet and jump to the next chain

- DENY: Drop the packet on the floor and exit all chains

- REJECT: Drop packet and exit all chains (same as DENY), but generate an ICMP destination not reachable response

- MASQ: Masquerade the packet _ forward and user-defined chains only

- REDIRECT: Redirect the packet locally and jump to the next chain. Input and user-defined chains only

- RETURN: Jump immediately to the end of the chain and continue

User-defined chains

User-defined chains provide a way to group rules logically. These chains are called from built-in chains as targets. At any point in the chain, you may call a user-defined chain. When a user-defined chain terminates with no matches, it returns to the calling chain, the next argument in the chain.

When creating user-defined chains, note that names may be up to eight characters long. Names should be lowercase, since uppercase is not used, but reserved for future use. A name cannot be one of the built-in names or special values.

How ipchains works

When ipchains looks at an IP header, the following occurs in this order:

1. perform checksum: Packet accepted and passed or denied and dropped.

2. perform sanity check: Looks for malformed packets and drops them.

3. traverse input chain: If not DENY or REJECT, continue to next step.

4. demasquerade: Responses to masqueraded hosts have addresses rewritten – otherwise skip.

5. route: Send packet to "local process" or forward chain.

6. traverse local process: Interface changed to "lo" and if destined for a local process, traverse the output and input chains, otherwise traverse the output chain only where the local process handles it.

7. route locally: If the packet went through the local process, but did not originate locally – that is, if it came from a remote host but was processed locally (above) for forwarding (proxy processing, port forward, etc.) and the final destination is remote, send to forward chain, otherwise (local) send to output chain (where if not DENY or REJECT) is passed to the localhost.

8. traverse forward chain: Chain for all packets using this host as a gateway to another remote host.

9. traverse output chain: For all packets leaving this host.

The "traverse local process" above is confusing. But if you think of HOST and LOCALHOST as two different hosts, things make more sense. To go from HOST to LOCALHOST you must traverse all the rules (except forward) leaving HOST and entering LOCALHOST, then going the other way for processes destined for remote hosts.

Simple firewall policies

Now you're ready to get down to specifying what you want to filter. Following are a few things to keep in mind. While you are making changes to rules, you can change /proc/sys/net/ipv4/ip_forward from 1 to 0 to "turn off" forwarding. This will prevent things from slipping through while you're making changes. This is also the first place to look if nothing is passing through your firewall when you expect it to.

If you change all the built-in chain policies to DENY or REJECT, be sure you do not specify rules that require lookups. Use IP addresses, not hostnames.

Keep in mind also that rules are matched in order. The first rule to match with a special value will terminate that chain (except as explained above). So be careful which rules come first. A rule that looks like: `ipchains -I input 1 -j REJECT` (insert as the first rule REJECT) may not behave the way you expect it to. Because this rule has no -s, it will apply to all addresses. Furthermore, because it has no -i, it applies to all interfaces, and finally, with no -p, it applies to all protocols. Essentially, this rule will reject everything – even messages from localhost, which now can't talk to local processes. Probably not what you want.

So to start, always keep your policies simple and build on them from there after testing at each point.

What to filter and where

Sometimes you need to think about not only what you want to filter, but where. Suppose you don't want to answer ping packets for any host. You can handle this two ways, but only one makes sense. The first way is to deny or reject echo-requests as follows:

```
ipchains -A input -s echo-request -j DENY
```

The second way is to deny or reject the echo-reponse before it goes out:

```
ipchains -A output -s echo-reponse -j DENY
```

While both methods will work, they have very different effects. You probably want to use the first method. Normally, your first reponse will be correct. But be aware that both will prevent the sender from receiving a reply. If the ping packet happens to be a big ping and is being sent to a vulnerable host inside your network, the first method will work. The second method will not. On the other hand, the first rule will stop pings to localhost. If you specify the interface, and drop only pings coming from the Internet, then you will be able to ping your firewall from the internal network (for connectivity testing) or from the localhost.

What not to filter

Some administrators believe that ICMP packets are not that important. They equate ICMP with ping. Unfortunately, a number of other important network messages use ICMP. The destination-not-reachable messages travel this way, so you won't receive them. While TCP will normally time out, these ICMP messages should still be passed. Your OpenLinux system, for example, uses ICMP messages to set the MTU (maximum transmission unit). For Ethernet, this is normally 1500 for maximum throughput. Fragmenting causes more delays than dropping the MTU. So Linux sets the DF (don't fragment) bit. If a host or router needs to fragment the packets, it can't because the DF bit is set, so it drops the packet and sends an ICMP message. Linux drops the MTU and tries again until it can pass packets. If you don't accept ICMP messages, your connections with some hosts may be excruciatingly slow.

Most administrators are also aware that DNS uses UDP, and they want to block TCP on port 53 (the DNS port). But when DNS needs to do a zone transfer or other large data transfer, it switches to TCP.

The bottom line is that if you experience network problems after implementing certain rules, back the rules out until you stop experiencing the problem, and then reimplement them one at a time with logging turned on until you can isolate the problem.

Implementing the policies

Now all that's left is to implement the policies. Let's declare a few variables, since doing so will reduce errors. Follow these steps:

1. Use the following names, which are similar to the ones in the previous summary:

```
foolint=209.191.169.1/25      # this is eth0
foo2ext=209.191.169.129/25    # this is eth1
```

2. Stop pings that come from outside:

```
ipchains -A input -s echo-request -i eth1 -j DENY
```

3. Now pass all traffic from inside out (except nntp):

```
ipchains -A input -s foolint ! 119 -d 0/0 -i eth0 -j ACCEPT
```

4. Block those pesky services that are a common security problem or you just don't want, such as telnet, FTP, http, and imap:

```
ipchains -A input -p tcp -i eth1 -s 0/0 -d foolint 23 -j DENY
ipchains -A input -p tcp -i eth1 -s 0/0 -d foolint telnet -j DENY
ipchains -A input -p tcp -i eth1 -s 0/0 -d foolint 80 -j DENY
ipchains -A input -p tcp -i eth1 -s 0/0 -d foolint imap -j DENY
```

In the previous step, you really don't need to specify eth1, because if it came from eth0, you've already accepted it above, and you won't get the chance to deny it.

5. Make sure you accept DNS (on foolint only), ssh, and returns on most upper ports (and on both networks) as well as smtp and pop-3:

```
ipchains -A input -p all -s 0/0 -d foolint domain -j ACCEPT
ipchains -A input -p tcp -s 0/0 -d fooall 22 -j ACCEPT
ipchains -A input -p tcp -s 0/0 -d fooall 1024:5999 -j ACCEPT
ipchains -A input -p tcp -s 0/0 -d fooall 6010: -j ACCEPT
ipchains -A input -p tcp -s 0/0 -d fooall 25 -j ACCEPT
ipchains -A input -p tcp -s 0/0 -d fooall pop-3 -j ACCEPT
```

6. Verify that localhost packets are OK:

```
ipchains -A input -i lo -j ACCEPT
```

7. Block the rest:

```
ipchains -P input DENY
```

8. You want to forward both ways — the input rules are taking care of most of the work:

```
ipchains -P forward ACCEPT
```

9. Make some optimizations:

Minimum delay for Web, telnet, and ssh traffic:

```
ipchains -A output -p tcp -d 0/0 80 -t 0x01 0x10
ipchains -A output -p tcp -d 0/0 telnet -t 0x01 0x10
ipchains -A output -p tcp -d 0/0 22 -t 0x01 0x10
```

Maximum throughput for ftp-data:

```
ipchains -A output -p tcp -d 0/0 ftp-data 0x01 0x08
```

Maximum reliability for smtp:

```
ipchains -A output -p tcp -d 0/0 smtp 0x01 0x04
```

Minimum cost for pop-3:

```
ipchains -A output -p tcp -d 0/0 pop-3 0x01 0x02
```

To finish up (if we got this far, let's just let it go), enter the rule:

```
ipchains -P output ACCEPT
```

There's just one more rule. You can also stop IP spoofing (someone from the outside pretending to be you). No one should connect to the external interface claiming to be from the inside (or from the localhost). This rule will allow you to log these attempts and REJECT them:

```
ipchains -I input 1 -i eth1 -s foolint -l -j REJECT
ipchains -I input 1 -i eth1 -s 127.0.0.1 -l -j REJECT
```

 You can also stop spoofing by using via the /proc/sys/net/ipv4/conf/*/rp_filter and putting a "1" into this file. However, this option will prevent the proper operation of the FreeS/WAN IPSEC module, which makes the ipchains rule the better choice.

Testing the policies

The easiest way to test the policies is to make up a few cases you do and don't want to get through and use the ipchains -C check option. You'll probably want to use the -v option to get a verbose listing of the check. This will tell you if the packet is passed. Remember that the -C option requires -s with address and port, -d with address and port, -p, and -i in addition to the chain name.

Often, enabling logging for some rules will help. This practice should be used judiciously or you will have very large logs, very quickly. One rule at a time is a good idea.

Monitoring

Remember to look through the logs from time to time, particularly if you put in rules designed to detect attacks. And just in case someone does break in, you might want to have a trusted internal host doing your syslogging for you.

Using and checking tcpd, tripwire, courtney, and all the other tools don't do any good if you don't keep an eye on them. The first thing an attacker will do is look for these things. Time is what your firewall is buying you. But time works for the attacker and against you. The best time to catch an attack is before the penetration occurs, when your network is being probed. To enter, an attacker must find your weaknesses. So you will have warning. It might not be much, though.

Port forwarding

Port forwarding is redirecting of a connection from one host to another. Port forwarding is what proxy firewalls do well. If you connect from host foo to host bar on port 80, and that port is redirected to host baz on port 80 by software, then host foo will think it's connected to host bar on port 80 while actually accessing host baz on port 80. Host baz will see a connection from host foo. This can work in either direction, permitting inside clients out, and outside clients in — but in a controlled environment.

The ipchains software does not do port forwarding. While one of the ipchains targets is REDIRECT, this target is for local redirection, not redirection to another host. If you use ipchains and want to do port forwarding, you'll need to use the ip-portfw module and ipmasqadm. The ipmasqadm program is a useful wrapper to ip-portfw. Outside connections coming in may require redirection, particularly if the internal (trusted) network is being masqueraded.

For more detailed information refer to Chapter 18, "Securing Samba — IP masquerading and port forwarding."

Once you have your rules the way you want them, two utilities, ipchains-save and ipchains-restore, exist to do exactly what they say: save rule sets in memory to a file and restore them from a file. By calling ipchains-save, you can see on the screen the chains currently in use, and if they are to your liking, run the command again redirecting to a file, which can then be used to ipchains-restore to restore the same rules. You might want to do this each time, before you make changes, to make it simple to get back to where you were. You can also copy the saved file and make additions, deletions, and corrections, and use it to restore the new rules quickly.

The Linux 2.4.x kernels and netfilter

This section will look briefly at the changes expected in the 2.4.*x* series kernel based on the state of the 2.3.*x* experimental kernel as of this writing. While further changes to the netfilter code are expected, the kernel configuration of the 2.3.*x* series should not change significantly.

Configuration changes from the 2.2.x kernels

The following are new or changed kernel configurations from those noted above. The configurations not changed will not be discussed again; see above for those not listed here.

◆ The first new option is Packet socket: This option is mmapped IO, and is optional.

```
CONFIG_PACKET_MMAP=y          optional
```

◆ The Network packet filtering option is the same as the Network firewalls option in 2.2.*x* and must be chosen for a firewall. The Network packet filtering debugging option may be useful if netfilter encounters problems. This latter option may go away in the future.

```
CONFIG_NETFILTER=y            required
CONFIG_NETFILTER_DEBUG=y      recommended
```

◆ The Kernel httpd acceleration option provides a kernel process http daemon. This is a service that should not be run on a firewall.

```
CONFIG_KHTTPD=n               not recommended
```

◆ The Asynchronous Transfer Mode (ATM) option provides ATM support for the kernel and enables four other more specific options.

```
CONFIG_ATM=y                    optional
```

◆ The classical IP over ATM option does just what it says, allowing IPv4 to route over ATM.

```
CONFIG_ATM_CLIP=y               optional
```

◆ The Do NOT send ICMP if no neighbor option attempts to circumvent problems with "disappearing" neighbors by discarding those ICMP packets rather than reporting continuously.

```
CONFIG_ATM_CLIP_NO_ICMP=y       optional
```

◆ The LAN Emulation (LANE) support option provides a bridge for LAN protocols over ATM. This bridge is protocol non-specific, and could cause non-IP packets to bypass your firewall rules.

```
CONFIG_ATM_LANE=n               not recommended
```

◆ The Multi-Protocol Over ATM (MPOA) support option is also protocol non-specific and could cause non-IP packets to bypass your firewall.

```
CONFIG_ATM_MPOA=n               not recommended
```

◆ The DECnet Support option is another non-IP protocol. It should not be chosen.

```
CONFIG_DECNET=n                 not recommended
```

New netfilter modules

Because netfilter is partially a kernel space program that interacts more closely with the kernel than the older user space ipchains tool, the code should work faster. Since netfilter hasn't yet been integrated into the kernel proper, it is only available as kernel modules. The logic has also been reworked so that packets do not go through all three chains. If a packet is destined for a local process, it passes through the input chain. If a packet is destined for, or coming from, a host behind the firewall, it traverses the forward chain, and if the packet is leaving a local process for a remote system it traverses the output chain. This should also speed things up considerably.

The (relatively) large number of modules provides for a high degree of configurability. Yet more modules will be added as they are finished.

As of this writing, the following netfilter modules are available:

◆ forward-fragment.o: Permits operation on fragments (-f option)

◆ ip_conntrack.o: Permits TCP/IP connection tracking, for following TCP connections

- ◆ `ip_conntrack_ftp.o`: Allows FTP over IP connection tracking, to permit active FTP sessions

- ◆ `ip_defrag.o`: Forces defragmentation

- ◆ `ip_nat.o`: Enables masquerading; primary masquerading (network address translation) module

- ◆ `ip_nat_ftp.o`: Allows active FTP with masquerading

- ◆ `ip_nat_map_masquerade.o`: Maps masqueraded addresses behind the firewall to those on the Internet

- ◆ `ip_nat_map_redirect.o`: Allows redirection

- ◆ `ip_nat_map_static.o`: Performs static mapping (static routing)

- ◆ `ipt_LOG.o`: Enables netfilter to use logging

- ◆ `ipt_QUEUE.o`: Enables iptables to pass packets to user space

- ◆ `ipt_REJECT.o`: Enables rejecting of packets

- ◆ `ipt_icmp.o`: Permits netfilter to work with ICMP

- ◆ `ipt_limit.o`: Permits rules to specify limits, principally used for logging

- ◆ `ipt_mac.o`: Allows matching of MAC addresses in rules

- ◆ `ipt_multiport.o`: Permits programs that use multiple UDP ports to operate correctly (e.g., RealPlayer)

- ◆ `ipt_state.o`: Allows connection state matching (-m state)

- ◆ `ipt_tcp.o`: Permits netfilter to work with TCP

- ◆ `ipt_udp.o`: Permits netfilter to work with UDP

- ◆ `ipt_unclean.o`: Performs some basic sanity checks on packets (-m unclean)

- ◆ `iptables.o`: Enables iptables to function; the core iptables module

- ◆ `netfilter_dev.o`: Permits use of the netlink device (major 36 minor 3)

The following modules are for backward compatibility. Only one of iptables, ipchains, or ipfwadm is possible at one time. Each precludes use of the others, and the below preclude use of any of the above.

- ◆ `ip_fw_compat.o`: Used for general compatibility with ipchains/ipfwadm

- ◆ `ip_fw_compat_masq.o`: Used for masquerading compatibility with ipchains/ipfwadm

- ◆ `ip_fw_compat_redir.o`: Used for redirection compatibility with ipchains/ipfwadm

- ◆ `ipchains.o`: Required to allow use of ipchains (and precludes use of iptables)

- ◆ `ipchains_core.o`: Required core module, goes with `ipchains.o`

- ◆ `ipfwadm.o`: Required to allow use of ipfwadm (and precludes use of iptables)

- ◆ `ipfwadm_core.o`: Required core module, goes with `ipfwadm.o`

The system was designed to be easily extensible by adding new modules. In fact, one module, `ip_nat_map_null.o`, doesn't yet exist, but is planned for future releases (and may be in the latest release).

Some basic netfilter rules

Under ipchains, the default policy was DENY on the three built-in chains. Under netfilter, this has changed. The DENY policy no longer exists. The targets are now ACCEPT, REJECT, QUEUE, RETURN, LOG, or DROP. If you create a user-defined chain it may also be a target. Both ACCEPT and DROP are built-in; REJECT, LOG, and QUEUE are loaded as modules before use. The RETURN target is used to terminate a chain. As already explained, the chain traversal also works differently, the INPUT and OUTPUT chains are for local processes. By default, they are ACCEPT. The FORWARD chain is for packets "just passing through" and the default FORWARD chain is DROP. If you want the default FORWARD policy to be ACCEPT when iptables starts up, load the iptables module with the option `forward=1`. To make the FORWARD chain REJECT, you'll have to change it after startup with a rule (you may also have to manually load the `ipt_REJECT.o` module). Understanding that chain traversal is different, one thing you'll need to do is have input rules for both the INPUT and FORWARD chains, since packets to be forwarded won't traverse the INPUT chain first. This also allows you the flexibility to DROP almost all packets bound for or originating in the localhost without affecting those packets just passing through.

Assume for a moment you have a network at home with two hosts, one of which dials in to the Internet. Assume also (for simplicity's sake) that both systems have live IPs and neither will be offering services to the Internet. To get these two systems up on the Internet with the least amount of problems, the next few lines will perform the job nicely. (Assume the command `depmod -a` has already been run.)

1. Load the ipt_state and iptables modules.

   ```
   modprobe ipt_state
   ```

2. Load the ip_conntrack module and allow you to use active FTP.

   ```
   modprobe ip_conntrack_ftp
   ```

3. Create default policy of DROP for all incoming packets.

   ```
   iptables -P INPUT DROP
   ```

4. Reinforce the default forward policy, just in case it changes in the future.

```
iptables -P FORWARD DROP
```

5. Create a user-defined chain so you don't have to duplicate rules over both INPUT and FORWARD since they'll be the same in this case.

```
iptables -N pass
```

6. Jump from INPUT to user-defined chain pass.

```
iptables -A INPUT -j pass
```

7. Jump from FORWARD to user-defined chain pass.

```
iptables -A FORWARD -j pass
```

8. Accept all incoming packets that are related to an established connection.

```
iptables -A pass -m state --state ESTABLISHED,RELATED -j
ACCEPT
```

9. Accept new connections from anywhere except any dialup line.

```
iptables -A pass -m state --state NEW -i ! ppp+ -j ACCEPT
```

A similar rule would be:

```
iptables -A pass -p tcp --syn -i ! ppp+ -j ACCEPT
```

Both versions of the last rule apply only to TCP, since UDP doesn't establish a connection.

10. Drop incoming ping packets.

```
iptables -A pass -p icmp --icmp-type echo-reply -j DROP
```

If you've worked with ipchains at all, the syntax above should be vaguely familiar to you. But a number of new options are now also available.

Given the current state of netfilter development, the text below will provide you with some differences (mostly additions to netfilter) between ipchains and netfilter. Several features lack implementation (such as the -C or check option), limiting the usability by inexperienced administrators. The netfilter author is also working on iptables-save and iptables-restore utilities à la ipchains. Those differences previously mentioned will not be covered again here.

- ◆ The -i flag in ipchains may now be either a -i if it applies to the INPUT or input side of the FORWARD chains, or -o if it applies to the OUTPUT or output side of the FORWARD chains. Using -i with OUTPUT or -o with INPUT is not permitted.

- ◆ If specifying ports, you must use the protocol (-p) flag and the notation --sport for source port or --dport for destination port.

◆ A `--tcp-flags` option (which must be preceded by the protocol flag) allows you to test the state of TCP flags (SYN, ACK, RST, FIN, URG, PSH, ALL, NONE) for set flags and act on that setting. Netfilter allows a shorthand way to invoke some rules. For example, part of your rule could look like this:

```
--tcp-flags SYN,RST,ACK SYN
```

The above examines the SYN, RST, and ACK flags looking to match packets with only the SYN bit set and the RST and ACK flags turned off. You can match exactly the same thing with this snippet:

```
-m state --state NEW
```

◆ A new option to match certain conditions, such as state (one of NEW, ESTABLISHED, RELATED, or INVALID), mac address (a colon separated grouping of six hexadecimal numbers), limit (principally for logging), each of which take one or more additional arguments.

◆ Removal of MASQ and REDIRECT from iptables. These now exist in ipnatctl (see Chapter 18).

Summary

In this chapter, you learned what a firewall is, the different kinds of firewalls available for Linux, and how they work. You also learned how ipchains works and how to set it up. Then you looked at some things you could do with ipchains via some of the rules. You also looked at the future of packet filter firewalls in Linux coming in the 2.4.*x* kernels and learned about some of the powerful and flexible rules possible once the code is complete.

Chapter 17

Implementing a proxying firewall with Squid

IN THIS CHAPTER

◆ Understanding proxy servers

◆ Configuring Squid

◆ Configuring clients

THIS CHAPTER WILL DEAL with setting up a proxy service. This service implements a basic type of firewall that may be used in conjunction with an IP packet filter, IP masquerading (aka Network Address Translation, NAT), or alone. By combining proxying with an IP packet filter, although it is not necessary except under certain circumstances, you can have the best of both worlds.

By far, the most popular proxy available for Linux systems is Squid. This particular proxy is both powerful and flexible. But as you've already learned, power and flexibility often come with a price. That price usually comes in the form of vulnerabilities. Fortunately, unless squid is binding a port below 1024, it does not need to run as root. By default, Squid will bind port 3128 and run as nobody. So this is one less network daemon you'll need to worry about.

Before you get started installing and working with squid, you should understand what it is and how it works. Squid can do a number of things for you. It can work as a normal proxy. That is, it can accept a connection on a non-privileged port and redirect the query to go out on privileged port. This is primarily what firewall proxies do. A firewall protects the internal trusted network from the external, untrusted network. It does this by blocking traffic between the two, while still allowing them to connect. Normally, then, anyone wishing to pass from the internal to external or vice versa has to actually log in to the firewall. By making the firewall the only point of access, you can very carefully control entry and exit.

You know that ports below 1024 must be bound by root, and that any vulnerability in the programs run as root could provide unintended root access to a system. To prevent this, most firewalls will not bind any ports below 1024, only those above. Now the program can run as a non-privileged user and not endanger the firewall because of an exploit. The problem becomes this: How do you move connections through the firewall without giving everyone who needs to surf the Web an account? Besides the fact that it's a bad idea to give anyone but the firewall administrator access, it's downright inconvenient to have to log in to the firewall, especially when the browser, etc., are all on the individual's workstation. Enter proxies. Most proxies are transparent. That is, they don't require you to provide them a username and password, they do the work without you having to do anything unusual other than initially configure your browser to interact with the proxy port rather than the actual port.

So by default, squid binds an upper port (3128). Now, any connection received by squid on port 3128 is redirected to out on port 80. Now, all lower ports can be blocked from incoming traffic (making the firewall fairly secure).

But to say squid just performs redirection is to vastly understate what this program is capable of. Squid can perform so many functions and has so many capabilities that the abbreviated FAQ runs to in excess of 100 printed pages.

One of the benefits of proxy software is that it is capable of inspecting much more than just the packet header. Otherwise, it would be nothing more than the packet filter software you learned about in the previous chapter. But squid performs inspections of the packet payload, that is, the TCP (or UDP) portion of the packet that's traversing the firewall. Based on the information in both the packet header (the IP portion of the packet) and the packet payload (the TCP portion), it can determine exactly where this packet is going and what it's asking for and take action based on all of the information the packet has to offer. Now you come to one of squid's strengths 3/4 the fact that it can cache incoming Web pages and offer them to subsequent surfers (thereby saving bandwidth). So squid is also a caching proxy. It caches (for a time) the results of a query for subsequent queries.

But caching software comes with a price. That price is a requirement for memory. If you want to run squid, you'll need to have sufficient memory for its cache. You will want as much (preferably all) of squid's cache held in RAM memory. Once squid runs out of RAM, it will begin to use swap. While reading from swap is faster than reading from a slow (relatively speaking) network link, you will notice a significant slowdown in operations, and a lot of disk thrashing. An old 486 with only 16MB (or even 32MB) of RAM will not be sufficient. If this is the only system you can spare for use as your firewall, then packet filtering only (as with ipchains) is your best bet.

Another area in which squid excels is in its use of access control lists (ACLs) and access rights lists (ARLs). Access control lists and access rights lists reduce potential abuse of Internet connections by preventing certain connections altogether. These lists are for those users who want to ensure that their systems cannot access potentially offensive or inappropriate sites for viewing by their children or employees. Lists of inappropriate (principally pornographic) sites have been compiled and are available for use. One such site is Hong Kong Linux Center (http://www.hklc.com/), which has a downloadable list. Another is Pedro Lineu Orso's List (http://www.ineparnet.com/orso/), which allows you to use the list directly by pointing to it in the Squid configuration file (details are listed on the site).

ACLs and ARLs, however, while very flexible, are also not easily configured. How the two interact must be understood. You'll look briefly at ACLs and ARLs, and see how they work together later in the chapter.

Finally, squid, when run as the user root, can bind the normal httpd port (80) and act to redirect queries and accelerate access to a local site. This particular use of squid can allow a company to build an isolated system for incoming httpd requests that can then be redirected to pages spread across multiple hosts to both accelerate access to the page (via squids cache) as well as to load balance between systems so as not to overload any particular system.

The above usages only scratch the surface of squid's capabilities and possible uses. This rest of this chapter introduces some fairly simple, fairly common configurations and problems with those configurations.

Default configuration

Custom compiles and installs of squid are beyond the scope of this book. If you want to learn more about these and other aspects of squid, you should read the user's manual, the FAQ, and other documentation offered by the squid developers. These are available from `http://www.squid-cache.org/DOC/`.

Listing 17-1 shows a stripped-down version of the very long (64k+), and fairly well annotated squid.conf configuration file (found in /etc/squid/). This listing omits all the explanations.

Listing 17-1: Abbreviated /etc/squid/squid.conf file

```
# NETWORK OPTIONS
#http_port 3128
#icp_port 3130
#htcp_port 4827
#mcast_groups 239.128.16.128
#tcp_incoming_address 0.0.0.0
#tcp_outgoing_address 0.0.0.0
#udp_incoming_address 0.0.0.0
#udp_outgoing_address 0.0.0.0
# OPTIONS WHICH AFFECT THE NEIGHBOR SELECTION ALGORITHM
#cache_peer hostname type 3128 3130
#icp_query_timeout 0
#mcast_icp_query_timeout 2000
#dead_peer_timeout 10 seconds
#hierarchy_stoplist cgi-bin ?
#acl QUERY urlpath_regex cgi-bin \?
#no_cache deny QUERY
# OPTIONS WHICH AFFECT THE CACHE SIZE
#cache_mem  8 MB
#cache_swap_low  90
#cache_swap_high 95
#maximum_object_size 4096 KB
```

```
#ipcache_size 1024
#ipcache_low  90
#ipcache_high 95
#fqdncache_size 1024
# LOGFILE PATHNAMES AND CACHE DIRECTORIES
#cache_dir /var/log/squid/cache 100 16 256
#cache_access_log /var/log/squid/logs/access.log
#cache_log /var/log/squid/logs/cache.log
#cache_store_log /var/log/squid/logs/store.log
#cache_swap_log
#emulate_httpd_log off
#mime_table /etc/squid/mime.conf
#log_mime_hdrs off
#useragent_log none
#pid_filename /var/run/squid.pid
#debug_options ALL,1
#log_fqdn off
#client_netmask 255.255.255.255
# OPTIONS FOR EXTERNAL SUPPORT PROGRAMS
#ftp_user Squid@
#ftp_list_width 32
#cache_dns_program /usr/bin/dnsserver
#dns_children 5
#dns_defnames off
#dns_nameservers none
#unlinkd_program /usr/bin/unlinkd
#pinger_program /usr/bin/pinger
#redirect_program none
#redirect_children 5
#redirect_rewrites_host_header on
#authenticate_program none
#authenticate_children 5
#authenticate_ttl 3600
# OPTIONS FOR TUNING THE CACHE
#wais_relay_host localhost
#wais_relay_port 8000
#request_size 100 KB
#refresh_pattern            ^ftp:        1440    20%    10080
#refresh_pattern            ^gopher:     1440    0%     1440
#refresh_pattern        .            0    20%    4320
#reference_age 1 month
#quick_abort_min 16 KB
#quick_abort_max 16 KB
#quick_abort_pct 95
#negative_ttl 5 minutes
```

```
#positive_dns_ttl 6 hours
#negative_dns_ttl 5 minutes
#range_offset_limit 0 KB
# TIMEOUTS
#connect_timeout 120 seconds
#siteselect_timeout 4 seconds
#read_timeout 15 minutes
#request_timeout 30 seconds
#client_lifetime 1 day
#half_closed_clients on
#pconn_timeout 120 seconds
#ident_timeout 10 seconds
#shutdown_lifetime 30 seconds
# ACCESS CONTROLS
acl all src 0.0.0.0/0.0.0.0
acl manager proto cache_object
acl localhost src 127.0.0.1/255.255.255.255
acl SSL_ports port 443 563
acl Safe_ports port 80 21 443 563 70 210 1025-65535
acl CONNECT method CONNECT
#Default configuration:
http_access allow manager localhost
http_access deny manager
http_access deny !Safe_ports
http_access deny CONNECT !SSL_ports
http_access deny all
icp_access allow all
miss_access allow all
#proxy_auth_realm Squid proxy-caching web server
#ident_lookup_access deny all
# ADMINISTRATIVE PARAMETERS
#cache_mgr webmaster
#cache_effective_user nobody
#cache_effective_group nogroup
#visible_hostname www-cache.foo.org
#unique_hostname www-cache1.foo.org
# OPTIONS FOR THE CACHE REGISTRATION SERVICE
#announce_period 1 day
#announce_host tracker.ircache.net
#announce_port 3131
# HTTPD-ACCELERATOR OPTIONS
#httpd_accel_host hostname
#httpd_accel_port port
#httpd_accel_with_proxy off
#httpd_accel_uses_host_header off
```

Continued

```
# MISCELLANEOUS
#dns_testnames netscape.com internic.net nlanr.net microsoft.com
#logfile_rotate 10
#append_domain .yourdomain.com
#tcp_recv_bufsize 0 bytes
#err_html_text
#memory_pools on
#forwarded_for on
#log_icp_queries on
#icp_hit_stale off
#minimum_direct_hops 4
#cachemgr_passwd secret shutdown
#cachemgr_passwd lesssssssecret info stats/objects
#cachemgr_passwd disable all
#store_avg_object_size 13 KB
#store_objects_per_bucket 50
#client_db on
#netdb_low 900
#netdb_high 1000
#netdb_ping_period 5 minutes
#query_icmp off
#test_reachability off
#buffered_logs off
#reload_into_ims off
#anonymize_headers
#fake_user_agent none
#minimum_retry_timeout 5 seconds
#maximum_single_addr_tries 3
#snmp_port 3401
#forward_snmpd_port 0
#Example:
#snmp_access allow public localhost
#snmp_access deny all
#snmp_incoming_address 0.0.0.0
#snmp_outgoing_address 0.0.0.0
# DELAY POOL PARAMETERS (all require DELAY_POOLS compilation option)
#delay_pools 0
#delay_pools 2      # 2 delay pools
#delay_class 1 2    # pool 1 is a class 2 pool
#delay_class 2 3    # pool 2 is a class 3 pool
#delay_access 1 allow some_big_clients
#delay_access 1 deny all
#delay_access 2 allow lotsa_little_clients
#delay_access 2 deny all
#delay_parameters pool aggregate
```

```
#delay_parameters pool aggregate individual
#delay_parameters pool aggregate network individual
#delay_parameters 1 -1/-1 8000/8000
#delay_parameters 2 32000/32000 8000/8000 600/64000
#delay_initial_bucket_level 50
#incoming_icp_average 6
#incoming_http_average 4
#min_icp_poll_cnt 8
#min_http_poll_cnt 8
#uri_whitespace deny
#acl buggy_server url_regex ^http://....
#broken_posts allow buggy_server
#prefer_direct on
#strip_query_terms on
```

Before we get into the nitty-gritty of the configuration file, you'll find that some configuration options will require that squid be compiled with those options enabled. So just because it's listed in the configuration file doesn't mean it's available. If you're not sure, you can enable it, restart squid, and test.

Network options

The squid.conf file is broken down into logical groupings. The first section is the Network Options section. In this section are all variables relating to networking, starting with the ports squid will listen on. By default, squid listens only on port 3128, but can listen on a number of ports simultaneously. They may either be a space-separated list in the configuration file or via a command line option. If listed on the command line, the configuration file list will be ignored. The port 80 should only be used as an accelerator for incoming requests to an httpd server, not as a transparent proxy for clients accessing the Internet. Used in this manner, squid could go into a cache lookup loop.

You'll see the terms ICP and HTCP used in the documents without much explanation. The ICP protocol is the Internet Cache Protocol designed to be used by all caching proxies. The protocol allows them to exchange cache information. The HTCP, the hypertext cache protocol, is used to actually exchange documents found via ICP. ICP uses UDP and HTCP uses TCP. If you have a parent and/or sibling caches listed, when squid receives a request for a document, it tries to find out if the document is cached by itself or, via ICP, by any of its neighbor caches. If it does not have it cached locally, but an ICP hit comes back faster than a ping to the actual site, then squid will request a cached copy rather than going to the site. By using rough measures of distance to actual Web sites versus a cache, it determines the fastest method to get the document. (Yes, you may participate in other's caches if you request permission – the FAQ will help). Most individuals and small businesses won't want to do this, at least not initially.

Distance on the Internet is measured in hops first, and for sites with the same number of hops, the round trip time. Squid, though, strictly uses round trip time, since what is important to someone using the Web is the time it takes to retrieve a page.

Also contained within the Network Options section are options for using multicast. If you are not familiar with multicast, or have a narrow bandwidth connection to the Internet, you won't want to use this option. Likewise, specifying fixed ports for use with HTTP and ICP is not necessary except under limited circumstances.

 Multicast is a fancy word for broadcast. In order to take advantage of multicast, you must have compiled your kernel with multicast support and have a client that understands how to use it. Additionally, all the routers leading to the Internet from your client must understand multicast. But if multicast is available to you, it provides a way for one client (in this case Squid) to get information from multiple servers simultaneously. Squid will try to use multicast to talk to other squid caches.

Neighbor selection algorithm options

If you do start using remote caches, you'll want to look into these options, but for a default configuration, they should be left commented out.

CACHE SIZE OPTIONS

As installed, squid does have some default cache size options. The biggest note for this section is that specifying the cache size does not limit the cache. The cache can grow beyond the specified memory size (and the amount of memory squid is using will be several times larger even than the cache size) if it thinks it needs to, although it will shrink back down as soon as it can.

The default cache is 8MB. This means that squid may use in excess of 32MB. Think of the squid cache_mem variable as the amount of cache squid will use for "hot" (meaning very popular) sites. But Squid will use more RAM than this depending on demand: you will find it to be a very RAM-hungry program. The more RAM Squid can use, the better and faster it will run. However, the amount of RAM usage will also depend on the amount of Internet access squid must deal with. For the home user, these limits will not be exceeded (in general). But for a business with hundreds of users accessing a smaller system via squid at any given time, the cache can easily grow too large. Depending on what you are running on your system, up to one-third can be specified as the cache_mem argument, but this will be determined by how much memory your system uses for other things. Rather than dedicating this much memory just to squid, especially for a system used as other than just an Internet gateway or squid host, before you start squid for the first time run the program `free` and look at the second line marked "-/+ buffers/cache:". This line contains two numbers, used and free. Your best bet is to either use the default 8MB or use one-third of the second number (rounding up to the nearest whole MB). What you're likely to find is that a system with 64MB will give an approximate suggested 12MB cache_mem using this method.

The Cache Size Options section also includes swap usage. Given squid's penchant for memory usage, you can be certain that it will resort to swapping at some time during use. Several settings exist, but the defaults will work for most lightweight users. For heavier usage, pay attention to the high and low water marks, as even a one-percent difference can mean 25+ MB of swap.

LOGFILE PATHNAMES AND CACHE DIRECTORIES OPTIONS
A few of the most important items you'll need to pay attention to in this section aren't listed in the configuration file. But note the default log and cache directories in the file. You must ensure that the user that squid will run as (squid or other non-privileged user) can write to these directories. This can be easily overlooked if squid is not run as root (and it shouldn't be unless you need to bind a port below 1024).

You also want to ensure that you have sufficient disk capacity for the logs and caches that squid will create. The cache should be on a partition sufficiently large to handle two to three times the cache size noted during normal operation. You'll want to keep an eye on disk space usage when squid is put to work initially.

EXTERNAL SUPPORT PROGRAMS OPTIONS
In this section, you may want to specify an ftp user. While most Internet sites do not care how you log in when you access the server anonymously, some check for valid e-mail addresses. Besides, common courtesy and netiquette suggest that this is proper. Note that this will be an issue only if you use squid for ftp connections via clients that use proxies. Not all ftp clients do.

This section also handles that number of dnsserver processes that start, as well as options to handle other external programs. On a small system, you might want to reduce the number of dnsserver children started. The default is five and is more than sufficient for home systems. If you are concerned that the number is too high, you can reduce it for a home system, but for a business where a number of employees are browsing the Internet at any given time, this may not be enough.

Tuning the cache options

These options deal with cache issues regarding individual cache size on disk as well as time-to-live (TTL) for DNS lookups and pages. These are fine-tuning options with reasonable values set for home users and small businesses. Larger organizations will want to tune these after they have time to evaluate cache usage.

TIMEOUT OPTIONS

The timeout options section is used to change values from predetermined defaults. The squid defaults correspond to basic TCP/IP defaults for most connection states. These timeouts also affect UNIX socket connections to squid itself. It should be fairly unusual to need to change these timeouts, and there are some values that you shouldn't change unless you understand how they may impact TCP and socket connections between clients and servers.

ACCESS CONTROLS OPTIONS

The access control options are at the heart of squid. Without the use of access controls, you have a wide-open system (although there are built-in defaults). You will want to look at and modify this section if no other.

Access controls, as mentioned previously, come in two flavors and are combined to permit or deny access to squid or to certain resources or URLs. The first part of the access control system is the Access Control List or ACL. This line consists of the declaration "acl" followed by a unique name (no two acls can have the same name), one of a list of specifications, then finally one or more arguments to that specification. The arguments to the specification are OR'd together, and if they are IPs, should contain a netmask to specify the range of IPs. Hostnames are permitted in the argument (if they are specified, the host is assumed to be just that host by that name and no other name), but this should be used with caution, since the host you wish to deny can often be accessed with another name or by IP number.

Once the acl itself is constructed, the acl name will be used in subsequent access rights lists to see if the resources specified by the acl are permitted access rights. The access rights lists are groups of rights to certain protocols. The protocol is followed by either allow or deny and an AND'd list of ACLs. That is, ALL conditions must be met for the rights list to be used.

For each protocol, once a rights list matches the conditions of a particular connection, squid stops looking and takes the action specified (ALLOW or DENY). If no rights lists match a connection, it looks at the last rule's action (ALLOW or DENY) and does the opposite. So make sure the last rule is either a global match for anything not already matched, or the last rule is the opposite of what you want to be the default policy.

Starting with an overly simple set of rules, examine Listing 17-2. This set of access controls and rights is the most simple possible. It permits everything.

Listing 17-2: Permitting world access

```
acl all src 0.0.0.0/0.0.0.0
http_access allow  all
icp_access  allow  all
```

The first line identifies every IP address possible. The second line permits http protocol access through squid for all of these addresses. The third line permits those addresses to also address the squid cache. The above is almost certainly not what you want; everyone in the world would be able to use your squid cache. There are programs designed to find proxy servers that are "promiscuous," that is, that allow anyone to connect to them. Once identified, they can be subverted and used for purposes beyond proxying. These purposes include scanning and attacking other systems. So Listing 17-3, a slightly more realistic basic configuration, expands on the above.

Listing 17-3: An expanded basic configuration

```
acl all src 0.0.0.0/0.0.0.0
acl manager proto cache_object
acl allowed_hosts src 192.168.0.0/255.255.0.0 127.0.0.1/255.0.0.0
http_access allow allowed_hosts
http_access deny all
icp_access   allow  allowed_hosts
icp_access deny all
```

The first line of Listing 17-3 is the same as in Listing 17-2. The second line refers to the protocol that accesses the squid cache. The third line references hosts we want to allow access to, and includes the 192.168 network (although it could just as easily be 192.168.0 or any other legitimate network), plus localhost. While most examples will show localhost to be 127.0.0.1 and that IP only, any 127 IP is a legal value for localhost. Using other than the first address is reserved for special uses, but is certainly legal, just not necessarily prudent.

The two http_access lines first permit "allowed_hosts" as defined in the acl lines (the 192.168 network plus the localhost) to go out, and the deny line blocks all others (so no one outside can use your squid server as a proxy). The two icp_access lines do the same thing for your squid cache. So if you're going to act as a parent or sibling cache for someone else, you'll be adding another acl and ip_access line (or at least expanding the definition of allowed_hosts).

It is a simple thing then to see what the default configuration that comes with squid will do — and gives some good examples of squid's flexibility. Listing 17-4 is an extract from the default squid configuration file in Listing 17-1.

Listing 17-4: Extract of access controls from default squid configuration file

```
acl all src 0.0.0.0/0.0.0.0
acl manager proto cache_object
acl localhost src 127.0.0.1/255.255.255.255
acl SSL_ports port 443 563
acl Safe_ports port 80 21 443 563 70 210 1025-65535
acl CONNECT method CONNECT
http_access allow manager localhost
http_access deny manager
http_access deny !Safe_ports
http_access deny CONNECT !SSL_ports
```

```
http_access deny all
icp_access allow all
miss_access allow all
```

The first line of Listing 17-3 is the same as in Listing 17-2. The second line refers to the protocol that accesses the squid cache. The third line refers to hosts we want to allow access to, and includes the 192.168 network (although it could just as easily be 192.168.0 or any other legitimate network), plus localhost. While most examples will show localhost to be 127.0.0.1 and only 127.0.0.1, any 127 IP is a legal value for localhost. Using other than the first address is reserved for special uses, but is certainly legal, just not necessarily prudent.

The first http_access line allows only connections from localhost. That is, this server isn't going to allow any neighbors to access it (a good rule for a home or small business with only one squid server). The second http_access line denies everyone not already permitted (localhost). The next http_access line denies the use of any ports that are NOT Safe_ports as defined in the acl's above. So squid could not connect to telnet (23), sendmail (25), etc. Squid will also deny new connections (incoming) to other than SSL ports, so you can't take advantage by running any kind of server to accept connections from the Internet unless they're SSL connections. The last http_access line denies everything else. The icp_access line allows anyone to access the squid cache on this host (probably a bad idea), and the final line allows neighbors (other squid hosts) to use you as a parent or sibling.

A parent is defined as a neighbor that, if it doesn't have a particular document cached, will retrieve that document. A sibling will not retrieve a document, only return a miss. Consider this for those you allow to access you as a neighbor. Not many resources are expended on returning a cached document, but significant resources (proportionally) are expended to retrieve a document.

Administrative parameters options

This section contains some basic parameters you'll want to set up before starting squid, such as the cache effective user (especially if started as root) and the e-mail address of the party responsible for the squid site. Some more advanced parameters are also included in this grouping.

Cache registration service options

This section deals with options to help cache hierarchy administrators maintain cache hierarchies as changes occur.

HTTPD-accelerator options

Some options for configuration when squid is used as only HTTPD an accelerator or as both cache and HTTPD accelerator. An HTTPD accelerator is a cache that helps your Web server. You use Squid to cache documents from the Internet to get faster access to them on subsequent requests. An HTTPD accelerator points at your Web server so that clients on the Internet get faster access to your Web server because pages are cached and sent out from the cache.

Miscellaneous options

A large number of miscellaneous options, principally dealing with logs, memory pools, snmp, etc., are available. Most of these options will not be of interest to the majority of casual Squid users. One exception might be the use of squid on a port forwarded (to an inside server) firewall, where squid should not handle the query for the inside systems, and that is the `never_direct` option. This option works much like the Access Control Options.

Delay pool options

The final section deals with a number of options for delay pools that are available only if compiled with this option available. Delay pools are a fairly advanced option, and it is left to the reader to determine if they are worth implementing or not.

A basic config file

Now that that we've looked at many of the available options, Listing 17-5 provides a basic squid configuration file (squid.conf) to work from as a better starting point for expansion than any of those provided with the squid distribution or documentation.

Listing 17-5: Basic squid.conf file

```
acl all src 0.0.0.0/0.0.0.0
acl manager proto cache_object
acl allowed_hosts src 192.168.0.0/255.255.0.0 127.0.0.1/255.0.0.0
acl SSL_ports port 443 563
acl Safe_ports port 80 21 443 563 70 210 1025-65535
acl CONNECT method CONNECT
http_access allow allowed_hosts
http_access deny manager
http_access allow manager localhost
http_access deny !Safe_ports
http_access deny CONNECT !SSL_ports
http_access deny all
icp_access  allow  allowed_hosts
icp_access deny all
miss_access deny all
cache_mgr david@localhost
cache_effective_user nobody
cache_effective_group nobody
```

Starting squid for the first time

Once you have a basic squid conf file and you're ready to start squid for the first time, you'll have to allow squid to initialize some configurations for itself. Just execute `squid -z`. This will tell squid to prepare some directories and set up cache directories, etc. Then squid may be started normally, either from a command line or via an init script.

Squid command line options

A number of command line options are available for squid and are especially useful for testing and debugging. Use of options overrides the pertinent part of the options found in squid.conf. These options are subject to change (principally though the addition of new options) with new releases.

- `-a port`: Specify HTTP port number (default: 3128)
- `-d level`: Write debugging to stderr also
- `-f file`: Use given config-file instead of /etc/squid/squid.conf
- `-h`: Print help message
- `-k reconfigure|rotate|shutdown|interrupt|kill|debug| check|parse`: Parse configuration file, then send signal to running copy (except -k parse) and exit
- `-s`: Enable logging to syslog
- `-u port`: Specify ICP port number (default: 3130), disable with 0
- `-v`: Print version
- `-z`: Create swap directories
- `-C`: Do not catch fatal signals
- `-D`: Disable initial DNS tests
- `-F`: Foreground fast store rebuild
- `-N`: No daemon mode
- `-R`: Do not set REUSEADDR on port
- `-V`: Virtual host httpd-accelerator
- `-X`: Force full debugging
- `-Y`: Return only UDP_HIT or UDP_MISS_NOFETCH during fast reload

The -d argument for debugging takes a debugging level. The debugging level can be set from 1 to 9, 1 being least verbose, 9 being most verbose.

Debugging

Many configuration options can cause problems for squid, especially in combination. While squid may still run, it may not perform as anticipated. Properly configuring squid for optimum performance will take some time and a willingness to understand how squid works. For this, sufficient documentation exists (the FAQ and user's manual referred to earlier in the chapter) to allow you to work through any special configurations for yourself.

One of the most baffling problems you may confront is a configuration (such as in Listing 17-5) that is known to work, but that causes your compilation of squid to spit out numerous error messages all pointing to acl's as a problem (despite their correctness) just before the program segfaults. The most perplexing part of this will be numerous pointers to rules beyond the actual configuration file (e.g., a reference to an incorrect syntax for the acl on line 58 when the configuration file is only 40 lines long). If you experience this, recompile with fewer options and reinstall. That should fix the problem.

Client-side considerations

Once you have properly configured and started squid, you'll need to configure your clients to use it. If your firewall is forwarding normal connections (that is, if, without configuring your Web browser to use squid, you can reach Internet sites), you might want to block that route to prevent bypassing squid, either accidentally or intentionally for all squid protocols (http, ftp, gopher, wais). This also applies to SSL.

Then, change your client software to point to the proxy port. In Netscape Communicator, you can do this via the pull-down menus in Edit/Preferences. Under the Advanced section is Proxies. By selecting Manual proxy configuration and selecting View..., you can fill in the FTP, Gopher, HTTP, and WAIS proxies with the squid host and port number. Don't forget to indicate which if any hosts should not use the proxy.

Extending Squid

The squid software enjoys sufficient popularity that there are many programs designed to help you use it. This list of software changes from time to time, mostly with new additions, but also with upgrades to existing programs. These programs can help you with nearly every aspect of squid's operation, from reading log files to providing port redirection, etc. A list of current add-ons to Squid is available on the Squid Web site: http://www.squid-cache.org/.

Summary

This chapter provided a very brief introduction to squid, the most popular caching proxy server software for Linux. You learned some of the basics of squid operation and control. You learned about the configuration file and looked at access control lists as well as other configuration options. You also learned how to set up the client side and what advantages running Squid can provide.

Chapter 18

Securing Samba – IP masquerading and port forwarding

IN THIS CHAPTER

- ◆ Understanding basic network designs
- ◆ IP masquerading: what, why, and how
- ◆ Understanding port forwarding
- ◆ What's coming in Linux kernel 2.4.*x*

IN ANY SITUATION WHERE you find you want to connect more than one computer to the Internet (be it simultaneously or not), you find yourself in the unenviable position of designing a network. I say unenviable, because most folks who end up doing it either have never done it before, and so have no idea what they want to do or the options available to them, or they are trying to work through a number of conflicting, sometimes diametrically opposing issues, to arrive at a *modus vivendi* that will be flexible and not compromise security.

For the home user connecting to the Internet who has no domain-name issues or need to provide services to others, the solution is fast and simple: Run a basic masquerading server and be done with it. Almost any old system can serve well as a masquerade host. If you are using dial-up with an ISDN or analog modem, an old 386-20 with 16MB RAM and a lean kernel (no X server) will be more than adequate. If you have a faster link, up to 10MBps Ethernet speeds, a 486-33 with 16–32MB RAM and a custom-built kernel (again, no X server) will suffice.

If you are strapped, have no old system collecting dust in the closet, or just want to use a better system to connect to the Internet, then your workstation will be fine. But since it will likely run more services and other packages than a dedicated dial-up system, you'll want to be careful what services you bind and make accessible to outside users. This system is the one that will protect the rest of your systems from the script kiddies. As little as possible should be running on this system (preferably no services at all) in order to provide maximum protection.

The contents of Chapter 16, "Using IP packet filter firewalls," are applicable here and should be used in conjunction with the information presented in this chapter.

As a dial-up user, you are probably assigned one single legitimate IP. You may have a static IP assigned, but more than likely it is a dynamic IP assigned to you from a pool each time you access the Internet. It makes no difference. The principles are exactly the same. The hows and whys of IP masquerading will be covered later in this chapter. For the moment, let's focus on the design of your network.

Starting with simple and moving toward more complex, a simple home or small business with no domain name won't need much in the way of network design. Figure 18-1 shows a simple bastion host that will also provide IP masquerading. The NIC (eth0) on the Internet connected box (HostA) connects to a hub, to which all other systems connect. The other systems list the address on eth0 (192.168.0.1) as their gateway. HostA, if it has a static IP, will list the ISP's gateway system as its gateway. If HostA gets a dynamic address, then HostA's configuration files will contain options `ipdefault` and `defaultroute` that will set up routing dynamically through ppp0 when the connection is made.

The interface naming convention in Linux is as follows:

ethernet: eth

token ring: tr

point-to-point (analog modem): ppp

isdn point-to-point: ippp

The first occurrence of an interface is numbered 0, and each successive interface is numbered sequentially. So if you have two Ethernet interfaces, they will be eth0 and eth1. If you have one Ethernet and one ppp interface, they will be eth0 and ppp0. Use this information to substitute the names for your interfaces to match the diagrams and discussion in this text.

Internal hosts will only need to have the Linux box's eth0 IP listed as their gateway.

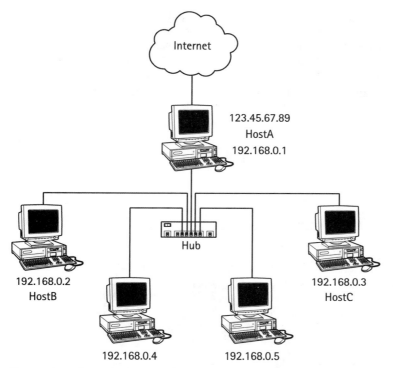

Figure 18–1: A very basic network

If you move up to a larger network connection to the Internet, perhaps with your own domain name or offering your own services, you change certain aspects of your relationship with the Internet. Normally, for larger businesses, more than one IP is available. Most ISPs offer subnets of eight IPs. This will give you five usable IP addresses for systems you may want to use to offer services, etc. How did I arrive at five usable IPs? Remember your basic networking. Assume you've been given the subnet 123.45.67.80/29 (netmask 255.255.255.248). In other words, you have from 123.45.67.80 to 123.45.67.87. The address ending 80 is your network address; no host may use it. The address ending 87 is your broadcast address. Again, no host may use that IP. That leaves six IPs. You will need one address for your network side of your ISP's router. So you will have five usable IPs.

One IP will go to your firewall/IP masquerade host. This system will offer no services. This leaves just enough systems to offer basic services: a Web (http) server, an anonymous FTP server, a mail server, and a DNS server. You can cut costs by using only one server and making it multi-purpose, but that means if one vulnerable service is compromised, all services are compromised. The tradeoff is price versus risk. If you can afford having all services down for several days while you restore everything, then the services you're offering probably aren't worth the cost of your persistent connection. Examining Figure 18-2, you have an FTP server (HostFTP) that can act as a secondary DNS if you wish. But considering the size of your subnet, you'll probably want to ask your ISP to provide secondary DNS services for you. That way, if your router goes down, the rest of the world will still get DNS resolution on you until you come back up (or the secondary DNS times out). The same applies to your sendmail (HostMTA) node. It's best to have your ISP provide backup mail service that can receive mail until your network or MTA server (HostMTA) is back up again.

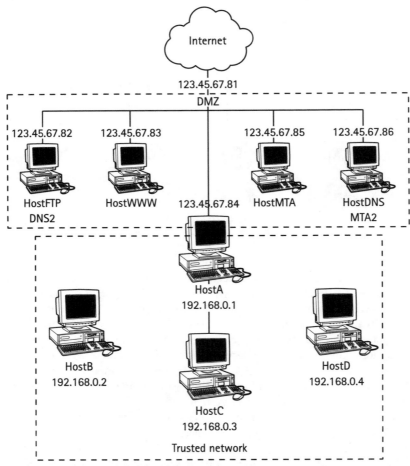

Figure 18-2: A small company network with public services on the DMZ

The system HostWWW is your Web server. Many Web servers are underutilized systems unless you're also running database applications, etc. But given some CGI-type exploits, it's better to keep this system separate. Finally, you have your primary DNS server (HostDNS). The nice thing about having a system like this is that it can hold copies of configuration files, data files, and binaries to nearly instantly come up as any other system. A backup like this is always good to have in case one of your other systems goes down. In the case of the HostMTA outage, if HostDNS is listed as a backup MX address, then you need do nothing (except work on restoring HostMTA to service). For any other host (except your firewall), just IP alias eth0 as eth0:1 with the address of the box that is down (HostFTP or HostWWW), fire up the service, and you can continue business as normal until the downed system is back on line.

Networks such as those discussed in this text can be divided into three parts. The first part is the Internet itself, which begins on the far side of the ISP's router (this may in fact be your router, but for the purposes of the discussion in this book, consider it your ISPs). You have no control over any aspect of the Internet. Once you reach your side of the router, you've reached your DMZ. The term was borrowed from the military. This "demilitarized zone," while consisting of resources you control, is the barrier between you and the savagery of the Internet. You have only limited control here; anyone may enter, although when you identify abusers, you can drop their connections or deny them access based on their source address. The DMZ stops at your firewall (or so you hope). The internal network is considered the "trusted" network. This term is used loosely, as many companies and institutions may have very untrusted trusted networks. This has more to do with the number and type of user on those trusted network segments than the fact that the firewall isn't doing its job. You have full control over who is permitted onto this portion of the network and where they can go and what they can do, at least in theory (as long as your firewall is doing its job).

Each Internet-connected system on your DMZ should be as self-sufficient as possible. That is, none should be using NFS. Logins by ordinary users should not be permitted; this gives you a stable, controlled environment, and in the event of a system compromise, you don't to worry about sensitive user's data. Every system should have its own set of passwords. That way, if one system's root password is compromised, the rest of the systems aren't automatically compromised. This is the same reason for not using NFS or sharing resources in any way. Finally, the firewall host, besides not running any services, should not be listed in any DNS server. That makes this system less of a target. While crackers will guess you have a system there, and can send a TCP "ping" to it, or otherwise detect its presence, drawing attention to it by having it listed in a DNS server is probably not what you want to do. Note that while one or two paranoid FTP servers on the Internet will not provide services to systems they cannot perform a reverse lookup on, this is the exception rather than the rule.

The final network configuration you'll look at in this chapter is a little more complex. In this setup, the DMZ partially moves behind the firewall. Figure 18-3 shows how this works. The firewall, when it receives a request on any of ports 21 (FTP), 25 (MTA), 53 (DNS), or 80 (HTTP), rewrites the packet headers and forwards the packets to the appropriate server. The danger with this setup is that you've brought onto your trusted network any script kiddies who can exploit vulnerabilities within any service inside your firewall. The good part is that this precludes certain attack profiles. For example, if an exploit on the Web server uses CGI to spawn a login as root on another port, that port will not be available, so the exploit will fail. But an attacker who manages to gain control through the forwarded port has access to your internal network. For that reason (as well as others), you'll want your workstations and file/print servers on one subnet, and your Internet servers on another. There's no sense in making things too easy. That subnetting also maintains a separation of services. Details on this setup will be discussed below. The same precautions apply to Internet servers inside the firewall as outside: isolated, with individual root accounts and passwords, no user logins, and no resource sharing; though this last item becomes less problematic in this configuration.

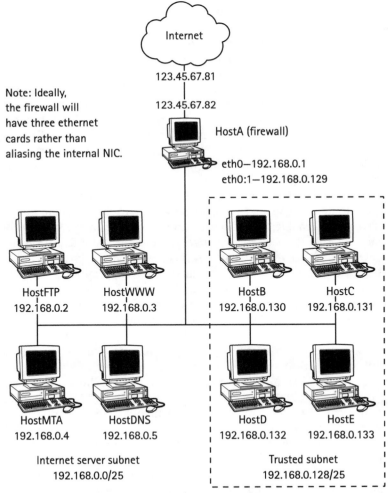

Figure 18-3: A small company network with Internet services behind the firewall

Other considerations

When you begin to use masquerading, some things will work differently, and some things may not work at all. For example, while you will be able to surf the Web and get to systems on the outside of your firewall from the inside, Web surfers outside cannot "see" past the firewall.

Normally, when IP masquerading is used, it is to permit IPs in the private address range that cannot otherwise route on the Internet to reach sites via the Internet. But IP masquerading is not restricted to the private address ranges. You can masquerade routable IPs, but the concept was principally designed to expand the usable address space.

What's more, until you've properly configured everything, clients inside trying to use a standard FTP client (not using FTP from within Netscape) will find they can't download files. This is a result of the way active FTP works. When you use FTP, you use port 21 to contact the FTP server. The server answers back on the upper port randomly chosen during initial connection negotiation. You'll be able to log in, and even change directories. But when you try to list a directory's contents or get a file you already know is there, you'll receive an error message. This is because by default, the FTP server opens a second channel — a data channel — on port 20 and tries to contact the client in order to pass data to it. (By the way, this is the reason an FTP server can be told to transfer a file to a third party — the original connection is not used, a second connection is set up, and this connection can be redirected to any other system the FTP server can access unless the FTP server, like the one in OpenLinux, doesn't permit it.)

Masquerading and proxying are two separate concepts. You may use either separately or both in combination.

For more details on proxying, see Chapter 17, "Implementing a proxying firewall with Squid."

The problem with the FTP server contacting the original client is illustrated in Figure 18-4. The client contacts the server on port 21. The client, HostB (with IP of 192.168.0.2), connects to the FTP server on the Internet. But to do so, HostB must go through the gateway, HostA, at 192.168.0.1. When HostA receives the packets destined for the FTP server, HostA masquerades those packets as coming from HostA's Internet interface, 123.45.67.89. The FTP server sees a connection coming to it from 123.45.67.89 on port 21. So when the time comes to open a data channel, the server tries to contact the client at 123.45.67.89 on port 20. But HostA, the system that corresponds to 123.45.67.89, is not listening on port 20, so drops the connection. The client, masqueraded behind 123.45.67.89, is listening on port 20 for a connection that will never arrive. This is because HostA does not know that HostB is waiting for a connection.

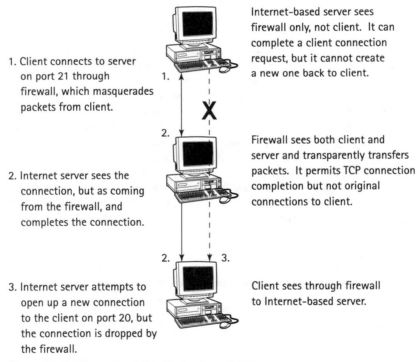

1. Client connects to server on port 21 through firewall, which masquerades packets from client.

Internet-based server sees firewall only, not client. It can complete a client connection request, but it cannot create a new one back to client.

2. Internet server sees the connection, but as coming from the firewall, and completes the connection.

Firewall sees both client and server and transparently transfers packets. It permits TCP connection completion but not original connections to client.

3. Internet server attempts to open up a new connection to the client on port 20, but the connection is dropped by the firewall.

Client sees through firewall to Internet-based server.

Figure 18–4: Why active FTP behind a firewall fails

Fortunately, the Linux kernel developers are well aware of the problem. Basically, you have two solutions available. The first solution is to use passive FTP. Netscape Navigator uses this type of a connection, which is why Netscape can download a file when normal FTP cannot. In passive FTP, the server does not try to contact the client via a separate data channel, but waits patiently for the client to open the connection on the original command channel (port 21). The second solution, which is more elegant and permits the use of active FTP through the fire-wall, is to ensure that your kernel build includes the IP masquerade modules listed under Networking Options. Listings 18-1 and 18-2 show the kernel configuration specifications and a list of modules built from this list.

For more detail on building a Linux kernel with support for ipchains, see Chapter 16.

Listing 18-1: Kernel configuration for IP masquerading modules

```
CONFIG_IP_MASQUERADE_ICMP=y
CONFIG_IP_MASQUERADE_MOD=y
CONFIG_IP_MASQUERADE_IPAUTOFW=m
CONFIG_IP_MASQUERADE_IPPORTFW=m
CONFIG_IP_MASQUERADE_MFW=m
```

Listing 18-1 shows the contents of /usr/src/linux/.config file after configuring for masquerading. The first line adds code to the masquerade portion of the kernel to allow ICMP to pass. By default, the kernel passes only TCP and UDP. Since you know that ICMP is its own protocol and not carried by IP, this line permits ICMP headers to be recognized and passed. Without this, pings and traceroutes performed from Microsoft systems will not work (all systems except Microsoft use UDP for traceroute, so this is not needed if you want only traceroute from other than Microsoft systems to pass).

The second line builds a number of modules. Listing 18-2 shows these modules, plus the modules that correspond to the final three lines in Listing 18-1. Those three lines result in ip_masq_autofw.o (for protocols not otherwise identified), ip_masq_portfw.o (for port forwarding to work), and ip_masq_mfw.o (for ipchains mark forwarding to work). The last one is incorrectly referred to in the kernel help file as ip_masq_markfw.

These modules will not load automagically as many others will. If you intend to use the functions they permit, you'll need to load them at boot time or manually. On an OpenLinux system, this means adding them to the /etc/modules/default file (minus the ".o" portion of the name) to configure them for use during bootup. You'll also need to ensure that port 20 isn't blocked. Then, if the ip_masq_ftp module is loaded, your masquerading firewall will be able to recognize active FTP and will pass the connection back to the client. As you can see, there are similar modules to pass CUSeeMe, IRC, QUAKE, RealAUDIO, ViDeO LIVE, and special user protocols through. The kernel recognizes the server/client connection based on IP address, ports, and sequence numbers. The modules will not load automatically, but may be loaded during system boot. Each distribution has a slightly different file and file lo-cation to load modules at boot time. With Debian, this is a file called /etc/modules with a list of modules to load. With the Caldera 2.3 distribution, module names can be added to the file /etc/modules/default. If you want these modules loaded, you can add them to the files mentioned above (for other distributions, check your documentation) or load them manually before they are needed:

```
modprobe <module_name>
```

When they are called from the command line or added to the files mentioned above, omit the .o suffix on the module name.

Listing 18-2: Masquerade modules

```
ip_masq_autofw.o
ip_masq_cuseeme.o
ip_masq_ftp.o
ip_masq_irc.o
ip_masq_mfw.o
ip_masq_portfw.o
ip_masq_quake.o
ip_masq_raudio.o
ip_masq_user.o
ip_masq_vdolive.o
```

The new Linux 2.4.x kernel (not released as of this writing) will not need these modules. The new netfilter software for firewalls is, unlike the ipchains of the 2.2.x kernels, not a user space program. This should also make the software faster.

IP masquerading

If there are so many problems with IP masquerading (also commonly referred to as Network Address Translation – NAT), why use it? A number of good reasons exist, not the least of which is increased security.

Under the present networking standard that uses the IP protcol, in a very few years you'll see the complete exhaustion of available legitimate Internet-routable IP addresses. As explained previously, the network address space consists of a finite number of hosts. The total address space is easily computed. As a binary number of 32 decimals, that is just slightly over 4 billion unique numbers. But practically, fewer than half are usable. The number grew considerably in 1993 after the arbitrary classful A, B, and C addressing was declared obsolete and replaced with classless addressing. Classless Inter-Domain Routing permits network administrators to make better use of the addresses they have. But it's not enough. This is also why

ISPs or anyone else who holds address blocks wants justification (and often increased monthly rates) for companies or individuals demanding more IP addresses.

By making use of freely usable IP addresses that will not route on the Internet, you can have as many IPs as you could use. All you need to do is choose among those specially designated private addresses.

Specifically, RFC 1918 allocates three large address blocks for private use. The first is the entire 10.0/8 address block, specifically 10.0.0.0 through 10.255.255.255, corresponding to one entire former Class A address block. The second block corresponds to 16 Class B address blocks at 172.16.0.0 through 172.31.255.255. The last block corresponds to 256 Class C address blocks at 192.168.0.0 through 192.168. 255.255. Because these addresses will not route on the Internet (Internet routers are programmed to drop these packets), you may use them as you see fit without fear of interfering with anyone else.

The advantages of IP masquerading are that, once you set them up, you never need to worry about changing the IP on your machines again. If you change ISPs, you'll need to change the addresses on the external DMZ and make any DNS changes that are applicable (master and secondary DNS server with the InterNIC and changes within your DNS files). But your internal network will remain undisturbed. The second advantage is that, unless you've set up port forwarding, no one can enter your internal network from the outside without coming through the firewall first. That means that one host becomes the focus of your security efforts rather than your efforts being diffused among every system you have.

The Linux 2.2.*x* kernel makes IP masquerading simple. Once you've chosen your subnet, only three quick lines and you'll be up and running. Assuming you've chosen the subnet 192.168.0.0/24, and you're connected directly to the Internet, the three lines in Listing 18-3 are all you need. You will want to ensure any IP masquerading modules are loaded first.

Listing 18-3: IP Chains rules to masquerade a 192.168.0.0/24 network

```
ipchains -P forward -j DENY
ipchains -A forward -b -s 192.168.0.0/24 -d 0/0 -j MASQ
echo 1 > /proc/sys/net/ipv4/ip_forward
```

The listing is self-explanatory if you've read the preceding chapter. For those of you who haven't, the first line sets the firewall policy: DENY. You can change this to ACCEPT if you choose, since most packets will never see the default policy. Once a matching rule has been found, that chain terminates, and all packets should fit the rule on the second line. This rule does all the work. It takes anything coming from the 192.168.0.0 subnet and forwards it to the Internet. The -A appends this rule (the default policy is always the last rule) to any other rules (none at this point) in the forward chain. The -s specifies the source of the packets and the -d specifies the destination. But this rule must apply in both directions, so you can either write a corresponding rule that swaps the -s and -d arguments or just use -b, which means both ways. Any packets that match this rule are masqueraded and sent on their way (the -j option, meaning "jump" to this objective). With this rule, you're masquerading in both directions. The final line turns on IP forwarding. By default, IP forwarding is turned off in the Linux kernel. The "file" /proc/sys/net/ipv4/ip_forward has a 0, meaning no forwarding, and by changing this to a 1, you've enabled IP forwarding. You enable IP forwarding with the following command:

```
echo 1 > /proc/sys/net/ipv4/ip_forward
```

Port forwarding

An alternative to setting up systems exposed to various types of attack on your DMZ is to move them inside your trusted network. Port forwarding provides a way for you to transparently transport a connection to your firewall on a designated port to an internal system on the same or a different port. And different ports on your firewall can be forwarded to different hosts on your inside network.

Moving services to your inside (trusted) network has both advantages and a disadvantage. The disadvantage is that if a cracker does manage to compromise one of the systems your firewall is port forwarding to, then she now has access to your internal network. But going through a firewall makes this slightly more difficult than attacking a host on the DMZ. The advantages are numerous. You do get increased security because a cracker will have to work through the forwarded ports. If different ports forward to different machines, the cracker will not know that and will not be able to take advantage of using one port to gain access to another port (assuming the firewall does not forward these two ports to the same host). And if your ISP only provides you with one permanent IP address rather than a block, port forwarding allows you to use internal multiple hosts to provide services to the Internet rather than having to run vulnerable services on your firewall (a bad idea at best).

Port forwarding under OpenLinux is also an exercise in simplicity, but unfortunately, the Caldera distribution that comes with this book does not come with the tools to set up forwarding out of the box. You must find and install the ipmasqadm package first. But once installed, port forwarding is no more difficult than masquerading.

 The CD-ROM provided with this book contains a directory col/security/ with the ipmasqadm RPM.

You don't need to have masquerading set up in order to use port forwarding — assuming, that is, that the address you're forwarding to is a legitimate address and your gateway box is acting only as a router and not doing IP masquerading.

You'll need to ensure that the `ip_masq_portfw` module is loaded, either at bootup (by listing the module in /etc/modules/default) or manually via modprobe. This module will not load automatically just because you call ipmasqadm.

Once you're sure you're ready to begin port forwarding, implement any ipchains rules you want, and then any masquerading rules. Finally, apply the port forward rules. Listing 18-4 shows the correct syntax. Then, make sure you've turned on IP forwarding in the kernel.

 TIP If you've loaded the necessary modules, but your firewall is not forwarding packets, the most common cause is that /proc/sys/net/ipv4/ip_forward still contains a 0 disabling forward. Always check this first.

Listing 18-4: IP port forward example rules

```
ipchains -P forward -j ACCEPT
ipchains -A forward -b -s 0/0 -d 192.168.0.0/24 -j MASQ
ipmasqadm portfw -a -P tcp -L 123.45.67.89 80 -R 192.168.0.2 80
ipmasqadm portfw -a -P udp -L 123.45.67.89 53 -R 192.168.0.3 53
ipmasqadm portfw -a -P tcp -L 123.45.67.89 53 -F 192.168.0.3 53
echo 1 > /proc/sys/net/ipv4/ip_forward
```

The first line in Listing 18-4 sets the default forward chain rule to ACCEPT. The second line sets up IP masquerading (needed since we're using a private IP network, but otherwise not needed). If you don't need the second rule because you're using live, routable IPs behind the firewall, you'll need the first rule (forward ACCEPT). Alternately, you can use a DENY policy, but you'll then need to append rules to AC-CEPT from all ports that are forwarded.

The next three lines show the ipmasqadm rules. Examine the two commands that forward DNS service. Note that one line for each of TCP and UDP is listed. DNS is one protocol that will use both UDP and TCP, so make sure you've listed all the protocols that will be used. If you don't have connectivity to the Internet (and therefore can't resolve domain names during bootup), you might want to append "-n", which specifies use numbers, as the final argument. Finally, you need to turn on IP forwarding in the kernel.

The ipmasqadm command has five options and six possible arguments. The initial options will be one of the following: a (add), d (delete), f (flush), l (list), n (numeric). The f option takes no arguments. The l may only take -n as an argument. The -n is optional with all but the -f option.

The -a and -d options are all followed by -P <protocol>, then the -L and the local IP address and port where traffic is expected to arrive, and the -R remote IP address and port where this traffic is to be redirected. If you want to add several different servers (for load-balancing purposes), you can specify several rules to take (for example) traffic to port 80 and send it to different servers. You'd use -p #

(that's a lowercase "p" followed by a number). This provides a primitive form of preference control where after # number of connections, the next forward rule for that local IP:port is used.

Linux kernel 2.4.x

For the new Linux 2.4.*x* series kernels, IP masquerading and port forwarding has been rewritten into netfilter. The new netfilter package is modular and breaks out the firewall code from the IP masquerading and port forwarding code. Fortunately, though, all netfilter rules will be seen via the iptables -L command, the forwarding and masquerading rules as well as the firewall rules. This tool is called ipnatctl. All forms of NAT will be performed via this tool, and it will require loading separate NAT modules.

The changes come as a result of confusion with ipchains and its inability to do port forwarding to remote systems (although there is a redirect object for forwarding ports within a system). The new ipnatctl takes care of all of this.

First, you must ensure that the modules you'll need are loaded. This will be handled automatically once depmod -a is run after the modules are built and installed. As of this writing, the automatic module loading wasn't working completely, but with any luck it will be by the time the 2.4.x kernel is released. The netfilter modules haven't yet been integrated into the kernel, so these two separate steps, build and install netfilter, and run depmod, are still required. This is expected to change in the future.

If you find you need to load the modules manually, run depmod -a and then use modprobe to handle dependencies for you. The modules you'll want to load include: `ip_nat_map_masquerade`, `ip_nat_ftp` (to handle FTP connections), `ip_state`, `ip_defrag`, and `ip_conntrack_ftp`. Other modules will also be loaded with these.

The format of the new ipnatctl is not so different from the old ipchains. If you run ipnatctl with no arguments, it will give you a very brief usage statement, as it will with an incorrect argument. With ipnatctl you can insert (-I) or delete (-D) any rule(s) you wish. You may also flush (-F) or list (-L) all rules. All options can take the numeric (-n) argument, which tells ipnatctl not to resolve individual IP or service names.

After telling ipnatcl what you want to do (insert or delete), you'll need to specify one of a number of parameters. The rule you're going to use for masquerading looks like the following:

```
ipnatctl -I -o eth0 -b source -m masquerade
```

The `-o` is the output interface and is whatever interface packets will leave on that you want the rule to apply to. This is tied to the next option, which is

-b source. The -b, meaning binding, will have one of two arguments — source or destination. The binding specifies whether you want the address rewritten as the packet leaves or arrives. The source argument tells the ip_nat module to rewrite the address as it leaves the host, and destination dictates rewriting the address as it arrives. Since with the above rule you want to masquerade outgoing packets, you'll want to do it as the packet leaves. The -o (output interface) <device> and -b source are complementary: You must specify -b source with -o, just as you must specify -b destination with the -i (input interface) <device>. The final argument is the specific mapping (-m), in this case masquerade. In all, four arguments are available for the -m option: masquerade, redirect, null, and static. At this juncture, only masquerade, redirect, and static are available, but null should follow before integration into the kernel. This particular syntax is greatly simplified from the ipchains masquerading syntax.

The other syntax available is for port forwarding. To implement port forwarding with ipnatctl, you'll use arguments more like ipchains than the NAT syntax above. Specifically, if you want to forward all incoming connections on port 80 to another system on port 8080, the following rule will work:

```
ipnatctl -I -p tcp -s 0/0 --sport 80 -d 192.168.0.5 --dport 8080 -b
dest
```

In this example, you're looking for any connections coming from the Internet (0/0) on source port 80. These packets will be rewritten to go to 192.168.0.5 on port 8080. The source and destination are used here instead of the input interface or output interface. Because you are using the extended specifications --sport and --dport, you must specify the protocol (-p) option. So if you're port forwarding DNS, you'll need two rules, one for tcp and the other for udp. Again, the b option is required, and since you're rewriting as the packets arrive, you're going to specify -b destination.

You can rewrite the port forward rule above this way:

```
ipnatctl -I -p tcp -i eth0 --sport 80 -d 192.168.0.5 --dport 8080 -b
dest -m redirect
```

The -i eth0 and -s 0/0 are identical. Additionally, you're specifying redirect. This makes specific use of the ip_nat_map_redirect module.

The masquerade rule above does not need a reverse rule (as needed with ipchains) to allow return packets. The ip_conntrack (IP connection tracking) module handles this detail. If anything, the upcoming netfilter rules for IP masquerading (NAT) and port forwarding should simplify administration.

Once you have the three rules above listed entered, running ipnatctl -L should result in output such as that in Listing 18-5.

Listing 18-5: Sample output from ipnatctl –L

```
masquerade [SRC] 0.0.0.0/0->0.0.0.0/0 tap0TO:
generic [DST] 0.0.0.0/32->192.168.0.5/32 proto=6 srcpt=80 dstpt=8080
TO:
redirect [DST] 0.0.0.0/0->192.168.0.5/32 eth0proto=6 srcpt=80
dstpt=8080 TO:
```

Notice the difference between the second and third rules as entered above. In the second rule, you're port forwarding to 192.168.0.5 port 8080 whatever arrives from 0/0 on port 80. In the third, you're redirecting to 192.168.0.5 port 8080 whatever arrives on eth0 port 80. They have the same effect, but the third rule is more intuitive when viewed as listed.

Summary

In this chapter you learned about some basic network design considerations. The first was a simple, at-home network for personal or small business use. The second took a more conventional approach to basic network design by putting Internet servers on the DMZ outside the firewall. The final basic design brought all Internet servers inside the firewall via port forwarding.

Then you learned about IP masquerading, why you'd want to use it, and how. Following this, you learned how to use IP port forwarding to allow Internet surfers to reach servers located behind your firewall, and the advantages and disadvantages of doing so.

Finally, you learned what's in the code for the 2.4.x kernels to prepare you for the changes.

Chapter 19

Assessing Samba security

IN THIS CHAPTER

- ◆ Setting up swat
- ◆ Running swat from inetd
- ◆ Running swat from a Web server
- ◆ Networking Samba
- ◆ Understanding Samba shares
- ◆ Understanding Samba security concerns

MOST NETWORK ENVIRONMENTS TODAY are a mix of network operating systems. Most small to medium-size businesses will have the ubiquitous Microsoft NT server, Microsoft Windows desktops, and possibly other server or network operating systems, such as Banyan VINES, Novell Netware, or any of several brands of UNIX systems. Linux programmers have had to overcome many obstacles in order to interact with these systems. Microsoft eschews the NFS (network file system) common to all UNIX systems (which Linux supports natively) in favor of NetBEUI, an extension of NetBIOS, which is based IBM's LanManager protocol. User demand for Internet access, however, forced Microsoft to allow the NetBIOS protocol to work over TCP/IP.

Samba

Frustrated with their inability to easily network with Microsoft systems, a group of Linux users set out to design a program to allow Linux to network on Microsoft's terms. The Linux programmers, led by Andrew Tridgell from Australia, worked to reverse-engineer the NetBEUI protocol and the contents of the server message blocks to allow Linux to mimic a Microsoft system. From these efforts emerged Samba.

Samba is a set of programs that will allow UNIX and UNIX-like operating systems (including Linux) to communicate with Microsoft hosts. Microsoft often refers to the NetBEUI protocol as CIFS, the Common Internet File System. The term is a misnomer, because NetBEUI is only common to Microsoft systems. The protocol is a broadcast protocol that has each system announce itself as it enters or leaves the network and periodically while connected.

Throughout the text, three terms will appear: NT hosts (any of NT Workstation, stand-alone or member server, or Primary or Backup Domain Controller — PDC or BDC respectively) running the NT OS, Win9x hosts, and Microsoft hosts. The first two references (NT or Win9x hosts) are specific to the OS running on the host, and the third (Microsoft hosts) refers to either. The distinction is required because of the way each participates in the networked environment. (For more information, see the "Understanding Microsoft network environments" section below.)

The Samba suite of programs consists of several different programs, two designed to mimic Microsoft hosts on the network, one to assist you in configuring Samba, and one to test your Samba configuration and other utilities. Some of these programs include:

◆ smbd: the Samba daemon that provides SMB services to clients

◆ nmbd: the NetBIOS Name server daemon that provides NetBIOS over IP naming services to clients, to allow the UNIX host to appear in the "Network Neighborhood"

◆ smbclient: a client utility to allow ftp-like access to SMB resources on the network

◆ swat: Samba Web administration tool. This tool configures the smb.conf file

◆ testparm: a sanity checking tool for the smb.conf configuration file

You'll look at some of these programs in this chapter. But the focal point will be swat, since proper swat configuration is not obvious, and improper setup can result in anything from an inability to run swat to a server that isn't secure because anyone on the network can run swat and overwrite the smb.conf file.

You must protect your smb.conf file (and by extension your swat binary). This file defines what access is permitted to those using the Samba services to access your OpenLinux host. Since smbd runs as root, an improperly configured smb.conf can give any user coming in root privileges. The smbd program will override all security settings and permissions the user would have as a standard UNIX user.

Understanding the Samba Web administration tool

When Samba 2.0 was released, a new Samba Web Administration Tool (SWAT) was released along with it. SWAT was an answer to many administrators' request for a configuration tool – made necessary by the sheer number of smb.conf configuration options. Samba documentation was overwhelming, both in volume and complexity. SWAT is intended to reduce the complexity and provide context sensitive help. While the help file is still difficult to understand for newcomers, overall, SWAT is an immense help just in organizing all the configuration variables.

Getting ready to run swat

If installed via RPM or during the initial installation, Caldera offers SWAT as a separate package. Note that the Red Hat distribution does not offer a separate package; SWAT is installed along with the main Samba RPM. Each distribution appears to be handling SWAT installation slightly differently, so you'll need to look at your distribution to see where it varies from this text.

When installed via RPM, Caldera (and probably most other distributions) include swat in the /etc/inetd.conf file. Caldera follows the Samba team's recommendation of using port 901 for swat. So if port 901 is bound by inetd, swat is probably set up in this manner.

STARTING SWAT FROM INETD

If you are installing Samba by downloading, compiling, and installing the latest version and want to run swat from inetd, you'll need to configure several things. While these were taken care of automatically during installation of the Samba RPM, the process is explained here for troubleshooting purposes. The first of step involves /etc/services and /etc/inetd.conf files. As root, you'll need to add the following line to /etc/services:

```
swat 901/tcp
```

This line assigns port 901 as a tcp connection to the program swat.

Then, according to the Samba documentation, you'll need to add the following to inetd.conf:

```
swat stream tcp nowait.400 root /path/to/swat swat
```

The above line tells inetd, the Internet metadaemon, to spawn swat as a tcp stream as the user root. The Samba documentation also suggests the "nowait.400". This permits swat to be spawned up to 400 times per minute. Without this option, the default is 40 – very likely sufficient. You don't need to append anything to the nowait parameter, but feel free to append any number you feel is appropriate.

If you want to have tcpd, the TCP Wrappers program, spawn swat as discussed in Chapter 15, you'll want your entry to look like the following:

```
swat stream tcp nowait root /usr/sbin/tcpd /path/to/swat
```

Feel free to add a .100 or any number of your choosing as the maximum number of instances of swat that may be spawned during a given 60-second period.

 The "/path/to/swat" should have the correct value substituted in the examples above. On a default OpenLinux install, this binary is located in /usr/sbin, though it may be located in /usr/bin or elsewhere depending on your distribution and method of installation. Use the "locate" command to find swat.

The Samba utilities are "pam aware." They make use of the password authentication modules found in /etc/pam.d as discussed in Chapter 1. The particular file you need to verify is "samba." This file will contain several lines as follows:

```
auth        required    /lib/security/pam_pwdb.so shadow nullok
account     required    /lib/security/pam_pwdb.so
```

If any of the above lines say pam_deny.so, you'll be unable to start swat. Other combinations are possible, but the above is the default as installed by Caldera. Other distributions may use something different. Feel free to add or stack modules as discussed in Chapter 1.

By default, Caldera also includes a line in the hosts.deny file that looks like the following:

```
swat: ALL EXCEPT 127.0.0.1
```

This line prevents anyone from administering Samba remotely. You may want to change the 127.0.0.1 to LOCAL if you trust that your local network is secure, because with the default installation, you will pass the username and password in the clear when you log in.

You are now ready to access swat. Start up your Web browser and enter http://localhost:901/ in the location bar and hit Enter. You should be prompted for a username and password. If you are, log in with username root, and root's password.

You can use any valid hostname belonging to your host instead of "localhost," including the IP 127.0.0.1. If you want to be able to administer Samba remotely, you'll probably may want to use a secure Web server (with SSL) to encrypt all sessions.

Setting up a secure Apache server is discussed in Chapter 20.

If you enter any other valid username/password pair at the prompt, you'll get the swat screens, but some of the options will not be available. The "commit changes" button will not appear, as only root can make changes to smb.conf (assuming smb.conf has the proper file permissions), and the ability to start and stop the smbd and nmbd daemons will not be available.

If, when swat is started, a smb.conf file does not exist, swat will open with some default values.

If you have a hand-configured smb.conf that you want to preserve, make a copy of it, or don't use swat. The swat program will read what it can (comments will not be preserved) and will rewrite the file in its own format. Includes and copy statements will be lost.

STARTING SWAT FROM APACHE

Configuring swat to run from the Apache Web server is a little more involved and requires more attention to detail, or you'll compromise the security of your system. With that in mind, if you're already running Apache and feel comfortable configuring it, then the following steps will help guide you through.

First, create a directory called swat below your Apache document root. If this system is to be administered remotely, consider using your secure document root. Copy the contents of the samba/swat directory to the Apache documentroot/swat directory. The subdirectories to be copied are help, images, and include. Copy the binary "swat" to your cgi-bin directory.

In the swat directory below Apache's document root, create a file called .htaccess. In this file put the following:

```
AuthName "swat restricted"
AuthType Basic
AuthUserFile /etc/swat.users
require valid-user
```

Next, you'll want to create the authorized user file. You'll do that with the following command:

```
htpasswd -c /etc/swat.users root
```

You'll be prompted for a password. The file will be created with a user root and a hashed password inside.

 You will want to ensure that only root can write to this file. Also, passwords that are used in this file should be strong passwords to prevent your system from being compromised.

Finally, in your Apache access.conf file, find the line that begins "Allow-Override" and ensure that is set to AuthConfig. Then just SIGHUP your server. (For Apache 3.1.*x*, you should use the "apachectl" command with the argument restart.)

Now you should be able to access swat with your Web browser by pointing it to `http://localhost/swat/cgi-bin/swat`.

 Regardless of which of the two foregoing methods you choose, be aware that the passwords are being sent over the network in the clear unless you have set up your Apache server with SSL and have swat in the SSL document root.

Using swat

Once you start using swat, you can quickly become spoiled. Nearly anything you can do from a command line to configure smb.conf, including reloading nmbd and smbd, and getting the status of Samba, can be done from this tool. (See Figure 19-1.) You can also access all the man pages for Samba, which will open in a separate browser window.

When you start swat for the first time, you'll be prompted for a username/password pair. Use root unless you want to view only the smb.conf file, since only root should be able to change it. Swat will open on its "Home Page" as shown in Figure 19-1. As can be seen, this is principally a documentation page. The various links point to man pages, but don't actually run any of the programs. Across the top of the page, you'll have various icons that will take you to pages dedicated to the indicated purpose, Home (the page you started on), Global configuration, User shares, Printer configuration, Status, View configuration, and Password.

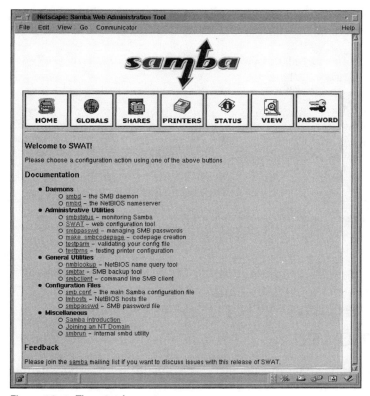

Figure 19-1: The swat home page

 If you use Netscape to access swat, unless you close your Web browser and reopen it, you will not be prompted for a username and password again; the browser remembers (caches) it for this session. This is normal behavior. Once you exit your Web browser, you will once again be prompted for a password when you enter.

When you start Samba, if you have no smb.conf file, Samba will start with all defaults. If you look at the View page, you will see exactly what will be written. This file is written each time you press "Commit Changes" or "Create Share" or "Create Printer." If you leave a page (Globals, Shares, or Printers) without committing the changes, they will be lost. A default smb.conf file, with no changes, will look like the following:

```
# Samba config file created using SWAT
# from localhost (127.0.0.1)
# Date: 1999/01/09 13:06:14
# Global parameters
```

As changes from the default are made and committed, the file will be written. You'll still need to send a SIGHUP to the smbd and nmbd daemons for the changes to take effect.

 Currently, swat does not create a backup file when it starts, so it is wise to have a copy of your current smb.conf file before starting swat.

Understanding Microsoft network environments

With Microsoft networking, you will normally have one of two network environments. While you can have both, this is rare. The first environment is the NT Domain, in which you'll have one NT Server acting as a Primary Domain Controller (PDC), and, often, one or more NT Servers acting as Backup Domain Controllers (BDC). Other NT Servers and NT Workstations may be on the network, usually as member servers. A PDC and BDCs act in a manner similar to a Network Information Server (NIS) master and slaves, granting users network permissions within the NT Domain.

 An NT Domain bears no relation whatsoever to the IP address domain normally referred to when networking IP is discussed. This text will make use of the term "NT Domain" to describe the Microsoft idea of a domain, and just "domain" to describe IP networking.

The second type of network is a peer network. On this type of network, no PDC exists. All machines are stand-alone. While they can share information amongst themselves, directory and file sharing is performed on a share, with access granted by each machine individually.

NT Server as PDC on a local network

When running Samba on a network with a PDC, you'll want to pay attention to certain settings. Within an NT Domain, hosts have a "pecking order." Microsoft hosts all have hard-coded values for their OS levels and positions. These define the way a Microsoft host acts as it enters and leaves the NT Domain.

When a new host that uses SMB enters a network, it looks at the other hosts on the network. If no other system "outranks" it, it triggers a "browser war." That is, it challenges the other systems present on the network regarding which host is to be the browse master on the network. The same also happens when a host that acted as the browse master leaves the network. But because a Samba host isn't a Microsoft host, it doesn't have a hard-coded value. Samba's OS value can be raised or lowered as part of the Global configuration. Its ability to initiate a browser war can also be turned on and off.

 A Samba server can be set up to outrank any machine on the network and win (hands down) all browser wars. However, this may be a very bad idea, particularly in an NT Domain. While a Samba server is capable of wresting control of the domain away from the PDC, this is can cause all manner of erratic browsing behavior among Microsoft hosts.

Entering an NT Domain

One feature introduced in the Samba 2.0.*x* version is the ability for it to enter an NT Domain. The procedure is simple.

First, create an entry on the PDC in the Server Manager with the NetBIOS name of the Samba server. This name does not have to correspond to the DNS hostname of the Samba server, but will usually be easier if it does. Enter this host as a stand-alone server or workstation.

The rest of the steps will be performed from the Samba server. Note that for the purpose of this text, NTDomain will be the NT Domain name, PDC is the NetBIOS name of the PDC, and BDC is the NetBIOS name of the Backup Domain Controller(s).

Stop all Samba daemons and make the following entries in your smb.conf file (if you use swat, you must choose the Advanced View at the top of the Global page):

```
Security = Domain
Workgroup = NTDomain
Password Server = PDC BDC(s)
encrypt passwords = yes
```

You may also want to set the WINS server. This particular variable requires either the IP address or DNS name (not the NetBIOS name) of the WINS server.

Then run the following command:

```
smbpasswd -j NTDomain -r PDC
```

If successful, the message `Joined domain NTDomain` will appear. This creates a file in the samba private directory with a suffix of .mac for Machine.

More setup needs to be done to this host, but it will be visible in the "Network Neighborhood," and shares made available on the host.

While you are doing this, you'll want to be fairly certain that no one is running a sniffer of any kind on the network. The reason for this is that the one time NT passes cleartext is during the initial key exchange process. The private key is sent in the clear over the wire. Anyone who has this private key can enter the domain as the server you just set up.

One final step remains for users to be able to log in to the Samba server, and that is to create a samba password. This is done with the smbpasswd program, by passing the arguments "-a" to add a user, and the username of the user to create. You'll then be prompted for a password. This addition will fail if the user does not exist as a valid Linux user on the system.

 To reduce administrative burdens, you can have new users dynamically created as they attempt to access shares on the Samba server by adding the following to the Global parameter 'add user script': /usr/sbin/useradd %u.

Shares still remain to be created, but the above will prepare a Samba server for use in an NT domain.

 Another administrative timesaver comes in the form of a the "UNIX password sync" parameter on the Global page, "Advanced View." Setting this to true updates the UNIX password each time the NT password is changed.

Networking with the PDC on a distant subnet

On some occasions, you will find that your Samba server is connected to a subnet with no PDC or BDC on the local subnet. That is, traffic on the local network must pass through a gateway to reach the PDC or a BDC. If this is true, the Samba server is on a "broadcast isolated" network. The NetBIOS protocol is a broadcast protocol – that is, the local network browse master periodically sends broadcast traffic to all hosts on the local net to update its browse lists, and as hosts enter the network they broadcast their presence. But NetBIOS won't pass through a gateway: Broadcasts are isolated to the local network. So hosts on a broadcast isolated network will have names of the local machines, but not the names of machines on other subnets.

Enter local browse masters. These hosts act as browse masters for the local subnet, and also know the location of the domain master browser – normally the PDC. In order to allow the Samba server to act as a local browse master, you need to set the "local master" and "preferred master" settings to true. The Samba server will also need to know the IP address (or DNS name) of the WINS server. Upon restarting the nmbd daemon, the Samba server will force a browser election (browser war). Set this parameter to 65 to win all elections. By default, the OS level is 0, but all the parameters discussed in this paragraph are available on the Global page "Basic View." You may also want to set the wins support parameter to yes if no other WINS server exists on the local subnet.

The WINS support should never be set to yes on a subnet with a Microsoft WINS server. This Samba server should be the only WINS server on the subnet, or erratic browsing behavior will result.

Peer networking with Microsoft hosts (NT and/or Windows 9x)

This configuration is the default for Samba. If no changes are made, only shares need be added, and Samba can be used as is – although from this starting point, it is almost certain some changes will be made. For example, Win NT 4 with Service Pack 3 or 4, and Win 95 with the OSR2 updates or Win 98, will require the use of encrypted passwords. Some common changes of interest will be discussed below.

All that is required from here is to set up shares and printers. You may also tell Samba to act as a WINS server for the Windows 9x machines and NT workstations and stand-alone servers.

Using Linux as a PDC substitute

The Samba team has been working to implement Samba as an NT PDC replacement. As of this writing, the code is still experimental, but is included.

This setup should not be used in a production environment yet, since some users report that the Samba code has corrupted the SAM databases (the databases used by NT that permit logins and grant permissions). This should be considered alpha code.

However, with the assumption that these bugs will be fixed, here is a short recipe for creating a Samba PDC and how to have hosts enter its domain. This recipe is subject to change. The Samba documentation that comes with the package should be considered authoritative.

1. Make the following changes in the Global section of swat (some of these parameters may be found on the Advanced View page):

```
workgroup = SAMBA (substitute a name of your choice for your
domain)
encrypted passwords = yes
domain logon = yes
domain master = yes
preferred master = yes
security = user (if using another smb server, this may be
changed to "server", but then you'll also need to fill in the
"password server =" value with an IP address or DNS name)
```

2. Additionally, you may want to add the following:

```
wins support = yes
logon script = %U.bat
```

3. In order to use the logon scripts, you'll also need to create a share to keep the netlogon scripts, as follows:

```
[netlogon]
path = /path/to/netlogon
writeable = no
guest = no
```

The above can be added easily in swat in the Shares section.

4. Then you'll need to create machine entries in the Samba server. This is equivalent to creating entries in the Server Manager for Domains:

```
smbpasswd -m NetBIOSname
```

(This is the NetBIOS name of the machine(s) that will enter the SAMBA domain.) You will be prompted for a passwd. Use the password machine.

5. You'll also need to create (if you haven't already) some logins with smb-passwd as previously discussed.

6. Now restart (SIGHUP) smbd.

7. On the Microsoft host, go to Start → Control Panel → Networking and change the domain to SAMBA (substitute the name from workgroup =, above). Do not select "Create an Account." When you select OK, you should see the message "Welcome to the SAMBA Domain."

8. Reboot.

On NT Workstations, it should be less than 20 seconds from the time you hit Ctrl+Alt+Del to the time when you receive the login box (or something is probably wrong). You should see three text boxes labeled Name, Password, and Domain.

Sharing directories

Sharing directories is a fairly straightforward affair with Samba. The swat utility makes setting up shares no more difficult than selecting a name for the share and reviewing some of the parameters, such as the path. Most selections don't require any extraordinary measures: If you want a particular option, it's just a matter of selecting it. However, one or two parameters can cause problems. These will be noted below. In addition, one share name, Homes, has a special significance for Samba and will also be explained. The Share section is broken down by functional areas that correspond to sections below.

Base options

After naming a share, select "Create" and swat will write default values for that share to smb.conf. For all except the special Homes share, the path defaults to /tmp, and the comment is blank. These may be changed as desired.

Shares define an area below that a user cannot leave unless wide links is yes (default). Within that share, the user has whatever privileges Samba is told to grant. These privileges may exceed what the user has when logging in as a Linux user.

Security options

The security section deals with permissions users will have to read, write, and create files, etc. Guest permissions and the identity of the "guest" are configured here. If "guest only" is chosen, then all users will be forced to be the guest account user when accessing this share.

This is also the place to allow or deny host access to the share. This option works in a fashion similar to the /etc/hosts.allow and /etc/hosts.deny files.

The revalidate option will force users to log in to the share each time they access it.

The most confusing parameters in this section deal with "create mask," which is a synonym for "create mode." The value to insert here is the value you would use in a chmod command.

Logging options

The logging options serve several purposes. In addition to logging access to the share, it also enables or disables the ability to see, via smbstatus, if anyone is accessing the share. This parameter should be left as yes.

Tuning options

The default max connections 0 means unlimited connections. The number is enforced via locks.

The two sync variables that default to "no" require some explanation. Many Windows applications, including the Windows 98 Explorer, confuse flushing a buffer with doing a sync to disk. Under Linux, a sync to disk normally suspends the client process until the buffers are written to stable storage. Having a large number of Windows applications allowed to do syncs to disk when they mean to flush a buffer can seriously degrade performance, hence the "no" default for "strict sync."

The "sync always" option has to do with whether a sync to disk call will return before the write has finished. The Samba server will then follow the clients lead for syncs. If this is set to yes, then "strict sync" must be yes or sync always will be ignored.

Again, be careful with these parameters, since performance will suffer considerably if they are set to yes and large numbers of clients are performing file writes.

Filename handling

The file handling defaults should suffice for most environments with NT 4 and Win 95 or later. Environments that still have DOS or Windows 3.*x* may have to look into various of the filename handling routines to ensure that clients can read and access files properly.

This section also deals with how to map differences between the Microsoft OS files, (such as hidden and system files), and UNIX files (dot files). Since a one-to-one correlation does not exist, administrators can choose how different types of files should be handled.

Browse options

The only browse option is whether a share is browseable or not. Windows NT has a default method for hiding shares. Any sharename that ends with "$" is hidden and does not show up in a browse list. With Samba, you can hide any share just by setting the browseable option to no. This does not prevent access; it only prevents the share from displaying in the "Network Neighborhood" window. The share can still be accessed by sharename.

Locking options

The parameters in this section by default will protect shares that are set to read-write. The parameters are also set to the enable fast operations where they don't interfere with actual locking (blocking locks). But for some shares that are read-only, you can affect tremendous performance increases by setting "fake oplocks" to yes.

 Before changing locking options on shares or files, be sure you understand what the implications are. Setting "fake oplocks" to yes on read-write shares can cause file corruption with several clients writing to the file at the same time.

Some parameters can be changed depending on the network. For example, on a reliable network, leaving oplocks (opportunistic locks) set to yes will increase speed. However, on an unreliable network, you'll want to forgo the speed so that files aren't locked by clients that become disconnected.

Miscellaneous options

The miscellaneous section contains a host of options that impact various areas or don't clearly belong to any of the preceding areas. Options here range from share availability to whether or not to follow symlinks.

Among the options that bear consideration is the "wide links" option. This option controls whether areas outside the share can be accessed. If wide links is yes (default), then a symlink to another part of the system outside the share will be followed. The follow symlinks option, which defaults to yes, determines whether symlinks can be followed or not. When these two options are considered in combination, you have three possible scenarios:

◆ With follow symlinks set to no, symlinks will not be followed regardless of the wide links option setting.

◆ With follow symlinks yes and wide links no, users can follow symlinks, but will be confined to the share; symlinks with targets outside the share will not be followed.

◆ With follow symlinks yes and wide links yes, users will not be confined to the share. If the user can create or modify a link, she can go anywhere on the system.

Setting wide links to no will cause directory browsing to slow down substantially, since Samba will always check the target to see if it falls inside or outside the share.

The other parameters of interest are the four "exec" options. These options will execute programs either as the user logs in or out, and either as the user or as root. Consideration should be given regarding the security risk or necessity of running a program either as the user or root. For example, the mount (and umount) command may need to be run as root unless you have an entry in the /etc/fstab file for that mount permitting the user to perform the action.

Homes share

The Homes share is a special share. When implemented, each user accessing the Samba box has his username compared to /etc/passwd for his home directory. That user's Linux home directory will be made available as a share, but other users' home directories will not appear. This can provide users a directory "safe" from the prying eyes of other Samba users. It may be prudent to give users a subdirectory to use to avoid naming convention problems between Linux and Microsoft clients. This is one share that does not default to /tmp, but will automatically default to the user's home directory.

Restricting access to services

The large number of options available in Samba provide great flexibility over user privileges on the Linux system. Samba can take advantage of UNIX NIS groups (if NIS is implemented). Some of the ways Samba allows you to control user privileges are:

◆ By forcing users logging into a share to become a particular user (guest, nobody, root, samba, or any other Linux user)

◆ By forcing users logging into a share to use a specified group

◆ By specifying which users by username can and cannot access the share

◆ By specifying a list of users with admin privileges on the share

◆ By specifying a list of users who can read and write on the share

◆ By specifying a list of users who can only read files on the share

◆ By specifying which users can print

The above options are available from the Advanced View of each Share's configuration page under Security Options.

By making use of these advanced security options, you can maintain very tight control over users' connections to any given share. Also available on the Global page is an option to set a "root directory" to something other than the default of "/".

If you set the root directory, you'll need to ensure that everything required to run the Samba server, plus binaries and all libraries used by users, is copied below this new root directory. This option creates a change root jail for Samba, and as such, is subject to all the constraints and "gotchas" of implementing a change root jail as described in Chapter 12.

Basically, Samba will allow you to create a chroot jail just as you did for the DNS server in Chapter 12. The same principles apply here, but more libraries are likely to be necessary. Creating a Samba chroot jail is slightly more complex only because it entails copying more libraries, devices, configuration files, and binaries down under the chroot jail.

One of the benefits of doing this, however, is that everything, including /etc/passwd (etc.), will be copied down here and can then be modified from the original with different passwords. That way, should the chroot jail be compromised, the Linux system will not also be compromised.

Details on setting this up vary with the Samba setup and binaries to be made available to users. But a basic guideline would be as follows:

```
/etc: all configuration files for Samba as well as most of the pam.d/
subdirectory and those /etc files pointed to by the pam.d file. All login files
(passwd, group, shadow). Configuration files for logins, and modified
syslog.conf file with syslog including an append (-a) to read this syslog file.
/home: home directories if used by users (Homes share created)
/dev: any devices to be made available to users, and the appropriate <samba
root>/etc/fstab entries to allow users to mount them.
/lib: libraries needed for binaries plus the security subdir for pam.
/bin and /sbin: all Samba related binaries, plus binaries for any other required
programs, such as mount if users can mount CDs or floppies, etc.
/var: a log, and run directory (perhaps others)
/tmp: a temp directory with appropriate privileges (chmod 1777)
```

Again, more can be required depending on the setup.

Variables available to Samba

If you've followed along in swat and looked at any of the default entries on the Advanced View pages, you've see use of variables, in the form %X, where X is one of many upper- or lowercase letters. These variables may be used to extend the flexibility of Samba. The following is a list of the variables and a short explanation of each.

- ◆ %S = the name of the current service, if any

- ◆ %P = the root directory of the current service, if any

- ◆ %u = user name of the current service, if any

- ◆ %g = primary group name of %u

- ◆ %U = session username (the username that the client requested, not necessarily the same as the one received)

- ◆ %G = primary group name of %U

- ◆ %H = the home directory of the user (%u)

- ◆ %v = the Samba version

- ◆ %h = the Internet hostname (DNS) that Samba is running on

- ◆ %m = the NetBIOS name of the client machine

- ◆ %L = the NetBIOS name of the server. This allows you to change your config based on what the client calls you. Your server can have a "dual personality."

- ◆ %M = the Internet name (DNS) of the client machine

- ◆ %N = the name of your NIS home directory server. This is obtained from your NIS auto.map entry. (Without NIS, will be the same as @L.)

- ◆ %p = the path of the service's home directory, obtained from your NIS auto.map entry. The NIS auto.map entry is split up as "%N:%p".

- ◆ %R = the selected protocol level after protocol negotiation. It can be either CORE, COREPLUS, LANMAN1, LANMAN2 or NT1.

- ◆ %d = the process ID of the current server process

- ◆ %a = the architecture of the remote machine. Only some are recognized, and those may not be completely reliable. It currently recognizes Samba, WfWg, WinNT and Win95. Anything else will be "UNKNOWN".

- ◆ %I = the IP address of the client machine

- ◆ %T = the current date and time

Global configuration page

Listing 19-1 is a list of all the Global configurations and their defaults. The most commonly changed variables are on the Basic View page, but many more that are often needed are hidden. The list can be overwhelming, especially when you take into account that the printers section has over 25 values, and that shares has more than twice that many. In total, over 190 configurable parameters exist. Some settings are mutually exclusive of others. Some modify or depend on others.

 Global configurations apply to all shares, including special shares, unless overridden within the share listing.

Listing 19-1: Comprehensive global variables listing with defaults as created by swat

```
workgroup = WORKGROUP
netbios name =
netbios aliases =
server string = Samba 2.0.0beta5
interfaces =
bind interfaces only = No
security = USER
encrypt passwords = No
update encrypted = No
use rhosts = No
map to guest = Never
null passwords = No
password server =
smb passwd file = /usr/local/samba/private/smbpasswd
hosts equiv =
root directory = /
passwd program = /bin/passwd
passwd chat = *old*password* %o\n *new*password* %n\n *new*password*
%n\n *changed*
passwd chat debug = No
username map =
password level = 0
username level = 0
unix password sync = No
log level = 1
syslog = 1
syslog only = No
log file =
```

```
max log size = 5000
timestamp logs = Yes
protocol = NT1
read bmpx = Yes
read raw = Yes
write raw = Yes
nt smb support = Yes
nt pipe support = Yes
announce version = 4.2
announce as = NT
max mux = 50
max xmit = 65535
name resolve order = lmhosts host wins bcast
max packet = 65535
max ttl = 259200
max wins ttl = 518400
min wins ttl = 21600
time server = No
change notify timeout = 60
deadtime = 0
getwd cache = Yes
keepalive = 300
lpq cache time = 10
max disk size = 0
max open files = 10000
read prediction = No
read size = 16384
shared mem size = 1048576
socket options =
stat cache size = 50
load printers = Yes
printcap name = /etc/printcap
printer driver file = /usr/local/samba/lib/printers.def
strip dot = No
character set =
mangled stack = 50
coding system =
client code page = 850
stat cache = Yes
domain groups =
domain admin group =
domain guest group =
domain admin users =
domain guest users =
machine password timeout = 604800
```

```
add user script =
delete user script =
logon script =
logon path = \\%N\%U\profile
logon drive =
logon home = \\%N\%U
domain logons = No
os level = 0
lm announce = Auto
lm interval = 60
preferred master = No
local master = Yes
domain master = No
browse list = Yes
dns proxy = Yes
wins proxy = No
wins server =
wins support = No
kernel oplocks = Yes
ole locking compatibility = Yes
smbrun = /usr/local/samba/bin/smbrun
config file =
preload =
lock dir = /usr/local/samba/var/locks
default service =
message command =
dfree command =
valid chars =
remote announce =
remote browse sync =
socket address = 0.0.0.0
homedir map =
time offset = 0
unix realname = No
NIS homedir = No
panic action =
comment =
path =
alternate permissions = No
revalidate = No
username =
guest account = nobody
invalid users =
valid users =
admin users =
```

```
read list =
write list =
force user =
force group =
read only = Yes
create mask = 0744
force create mode = 00
directory mask = 0755
force directory mode = 00
guest only = No
guest ok = No
only user = No
hosts allow =
hosts deny =
status = Yes
max connections = 0
min print space = 0
strict sync = No
sync always = No
print ok = No
postscript = No
printing = bsd
print command = lpr -r -P%p %s
lpq command = lpq -P%p
lprm command = lprm -P%p %j
lppause command =
lpresume command =
queuepause command =
queueresume command =
printer name =
printer driver = NULL
printer driver location =
default case = lower
case sensitive = No
preserve case = Yes
short preserve case = Yes
mangle case = No
mangling char = ~
hide dot files = Yes
delete veto files = No
veto files =
hide files =
veto oplock files =
map system = No
map hidden = No
```

```
map archive = Yes
mangled names = Yes
mangled map =
browseable = Yes
blocking locks = Yes
fake oplocks = No
locking = Yes
oplocks = Yes
strict locking = No
share modes = Yes
copy =
include =
exec =
postexec =
root preexec =
root postexec =
available = Yes
volume =
fstype = NTFS
set directory = No
wide links = Yes
follow symlinks = Yes
dont descend =
magic script =
magic output =
delete readonly = No
dos filetimes = No
dos filetime resolution = No
fake directory create times = No
```

Security concerns with local use of Samba

The information presented in this chapter should make you aware of Samba's over-all potential to cause problems on a local Microsoft subnet by interfering with nor-mal operation between Microsoft hosts. This will principally affect browsing on the Windows side, where groups of computers may suddenly disappear. The suspect in this case is the Samba server's forcing and then winning a browser election when it should not, or acting as a browse master or WINS server when an NT server should act in that role.

   If the browsing problem is isolated to the Samba server, it may be a matter of permissions or non-use of encrypted passwords, or of not knowing the IP of the WINS server. In Windows, only small subnets will get away without using a WINS server, but without one, Samba may have a difficult time seeing all the Microsoft hosts. Larger networks must use them, particularly in broadcast isolated subnet configurations. Wherever possible, NT servers should be used on isolated subnets as secondary WINS servers, although this is not necessary, and a Samba server can do just as well.

The large number of often confusing and poorly explained options can lead to the misconfiguration of the system. This large number of options adds to the overall flexibility of the Samba server, but poses problems for inexperienced administrators. The defaults for the most part are considered "safe" — that is, they are meant to not cause interference, yet still allow a Samba host to join a Microsoft network, be it a peer network or NT Domain. But joining the NT Domain can be dangerous. Once part of an NT Domain, the Samba server can wrest control of the network away from the PDC, so the Samba server that is part of the NT Domain needs to be protected especially well.

Because of the security measures inherent within an NT Domain, a Samba server joining an NT Domain is less apt to cause security problems, even though it can cause browsing problems. But on a Win9x–only peer network, Samba can subvert security by passing itself off as an NT Server.

Another area you'll want to consider within a Microsoft network is whether to run TCP/IP as the only protocol, or both TCP/IP and NetBEUI. Running both protocols is not required. If you run TCP/IP, then NetBEUI should be shut off.

The use of protocols other than IP on the network increase the amount of traffic. NetBEUI, as a broadcast protocol, will use both protocols if available, particularly for broadcasts or if searching for a host it believes may still be on the network. Restricting the network protocol to TCP/IP, then, does two things: reduces traffic by reducing broadcast activity to one protocol, and allows you to contain NetBEUI over IP behind the firewall.

The second area of concern comes with the level of access that Samba can potentially provide to users of the Samba server. Configuring users with share admin privileges or privileges that would otherwise go beyond those they would have as ordinary Linux users may not be advisable, especially if that would allow them to alter the system. On a larger network with various departments and many different users, setting up a chroot jail for Samba is a sensible way to allow select individuals more privileges than would be wise with a standard setup. A nontrivial undertaking, changing the Samba root can allow you to provide this access while ensuring the integrity of the underlying Linux system.

Security concerns with network use of Samba over Internet-connected subnets

One of the biggest security problems comes not with Samba's being used between Internet-connected subnets, but the belief that the Microsoft-provided VPN (virtual private networking) options are both virtual and secure. Recent studies indicate that while virtual, a Microsoft VPN is anything but private. Although Microsoft hosts encrypt passwords, the basic information passing between subnets is anything but secure. While cryptographically challenged crackers might not be able to enter your subnet pretending to be one of your other systems, they will be able to read the contents of the packets passing between the subnets. If you pass sensitive data, it can be easily picked up and read by others. So the way to create a truly private VPN using the Microsoft hosts is to follow the steps outlined in Chapter 21, and set up an encrypted VPN between Linux gateways through which information is exchanged. To ensure that the packets do not bypass the tunnel, only use IP on the two subnets.

When setting up the two subnets, remember that a local browse master must be present for systems to be aware of hosts on the other subnet. If you are dealing with three subnets with local browse masters that update the master, be aware that local systems can take up to 45 minutes to add or remove a host the enters or leaves the network on the other subnet. Before blaming a Samba server for not showing all hosts in the NT Domain, make sure the remote system has been up (or down) for the better part of an hour (45 minutes plus).

Summary

In this chapter you learned about Samba and swat. You learned about security concerns related to the use of swat and how to protect the swat binary by restricting use to the localhost (via tcpd or ipchains) or how to safely administer Samba remotely by using Apache with SSL.

You also looked at Samba and the NetBIOS protocol and security concerns with Samba because of its invocation as root (and its ability to give users up to and including root powers). You also learned how Samba can wreak havoc on local Microsoft networks by causing erratic browsing with improper settings. You also learned the dangers of Samba networking between subnets (particularly over the Internet).

Chapter 20

Installing and running a secure Apache Web server

IN THIS CHAPTER

◆ Building Apache with SSL and PHP3

◆ Configuring Apache

◆ Using .htaccess files with AuthConfig

◆ Using khttpd

THE APACHE WEB SERVER is the most popular Web server on the Internet today by a very large margin. This is not an accident, but a result of the fact that Apache is one of the most powerful and configurable Web servers available. By now you know that power, configurability, and flexibility almost always have a price when it comes to security. Apache is no exception. But as you'll see, Apache has ways to restrict user privileges and contain them. And just as with other powerful, highly configurable programs, you can configure security right out of the system.

Building Apache

The Apache Web server installed on your system is a fine tool as it is. But it lacks a number of important features that no distributor of Linux includes (though that may change at any time). Current distributions provide a very basic implementation. If you are not using Apache for anything other than simple flat Web pages and a few CGI programs, this is probably acceptable. But if you need security for any reason, or you need to work with databases, etc., you'll quickly find you need to compile Apache for yourself.

Compiling a program like Apache is a fairly straightforward process. But when you start adding things like encryption packages or other third-party packages, things quickly become more complicated (but definitely not impossible).

Before you start to compile any program, you should ensure that you have the appropriate libraries and programs installed. You will need several -devel RPMs, including the glibc-devel, libpam-devel, and possibly the XFree -devel libs. You'll also need gcc, the gcc-related libs (libstdc++) and devel packages, as well as the as86 package. Others may also be needed and can be identified by a particular error message. The devel packages are only needed for compiling and can be removed later if desired. The Perl packages are also highly recommended.

This text will assume you want to install Apache with SSL (secure sockets layer) and PHP, two very popular packages. The SSL package described in this text will be the mod_ssl package (although this is not the only SSL package available for Apache). The mod_ssl package will permit you to make secure, encrypted connections from your Web client (encryption at 40 bits or 128 bits will depend on the client). The PHP package will be compiled with MySQL, and so will require the MySQL and MySQL-devel packages installed. If you are not interested in database connectivity, you can skip all references to PHP. Likewise, if you want to install PHP for a different database (msql or Postgres), merely substitute those for the MySQL reference. Again, you'll need the appropriate -devel packages installed.

The RSA libraries contain a security vulnerability that can compromise your server. Check to see if you are still required to use this library, because the patent is up for renewal during the year 2000. If you still need to use this library, contact RSA regarding a patched version.

Getting the packages

You can obtain the latest copies of all packages from the following locations. Versions of packages are noted; more current ones may also be used.

Apache-1.3.9 (apache_1.3.9.tar.gz): `ftp://ftp.apache.org/apache/dist/`

PHP-3.0.13 (php-3.0.12.tar.gz): `ftp://ftp.php.net/pub/distributions/php-3.0.12.tar.gz`

mod_ssl-2.4.9 (mod_ssl-2.4.8-1.3.9.tar.gz): `ftp://ftp.modssl.org/source/`

OpenSSL-0.9.4 (openssl-0.9.4.tar.gz): `ftp://ftp.openssl.org/source/`

RSAref-2.0 (rsaref20.tar.Z): `ftp://utopia.hacktic.nl/pub/replay/pub/crypto/LIBS/rsa/`

This package is no longer available for download from RSA.

MM-1.0.12 (mm-1.0.12.tar.gz): `http://www.engelschall.com/sw/mm/`

A word about encryption and U.S. export controls

The information in this sidebar should not be construed as legal advice, but is based on discussions with encryption export analysts working for the U.S. Department of Commerce. Seek legal counsel if you plan to engage in encryption-related activities outside your own home.

You will notice that none of the encryption-related packages discussed in this chapter are included on the enclosed CD. This is the result of U.S. export law. Encryption technology, as important as it is today for individuals as well as businesses, is considered a munition and has very strict export controls. Encryption technology can be imported, but cannot be either exported or re-exported. So while you'll have to download all the files from foreign countries like Finland, etc., once you have introduced them into the United States, you cannot re-export them. This regulation goes so far as to prohibit a U.S. citizen from doing so much as traveling to a foreign country, downloading the code from Finland and compiling it for someone in that country. Despite the fact this technology is available anywhere in the world, if you are a U.S. citizen, you could face stiff penalties for exporting "cryptographic technology" by compiling this cryptographic software for a Japanese company in Japan (substitute any country in the world for Japan in the above sentence). Caution: This could include compiling the software for a Japanese company located in the United States as well — the regulation is very open to this interpretation as well. This means you are walking a fine line by doing something as simple and innocuous as telneting into a server in a foreign country and downloading and installing SSH or software to complete an encrypted tunnel. This regulation has made the United States the world follower in cryptography. It is unlikely the United States will ever be able to take the lead here again.

Cryptography regulations are changing all the time, so check with the export control folks at the Commerce Department if you have questions.

If you are a U.S. citizen, you may want to (you'll have to if you will be using the SSL package commercially) include the RSA package. RSA claims patent on some algorithms used in most cryptographic packages. Although these algorithms have been independently developed and are freely available outside the United States, within the United States you are cautioned that you could be in violation of U.S. patent law for not including the package. Every other country in the world has refused to enforce this patent. Include the package or not if you feel strongly one way or another. The text will describe it for those who need to include it.

The 1.3.9 portion of mod_ssl-2.4.8-1.3.9.tar.gz must match the version number of Apache. So if Apache goes to 1.3.10 and you download that version, you'll need a mod_ssl-x.x.x-1.3.10.tar.gz to match (get the latest one).

Preinstall preparation

Before you begin, you should prepare a place to open and compile all packages. While this text will not describe installation on the system per se, some of these packages can be installed on the system for use in building other packages. If you've already built and installed some of these packages, you can set some environment or configuration variables to handle using them. Those will be noted in the text. For simplicity, the text will assume that you've put all these packages in one common directory and will be building and installing from there.

Create a directory ($HOME/src/ will be assumed in this text) somewhere where you have sufficient space (150+ MB) to hold all the packages and change to that directory with all the packages present. Packages can be opened individually in this directory by issuing the command: tar xzvf *filename*, except for rsaref20.tar.Z. With rsaref, first create a directory called rsaref-2.0 and cd into it. Then issue the command tar xzvf ../rsaref20.tar.Z. This will open the rsaref package in this directory.

Once all the packages have been opened, ensure you still have sufficient space (100+ MB) for building the packages.

Building the packages

The first step is to configure Apache. This must be accomplished in order for some other packages (primarily PHP) to build properly. The best way to start is to use the same configuration options that Caldera uses for its Apache RPM. That way, if you've installed the Apache RPM, this can be installed on top and will overwrite the RPM files. Listing 20-1 was taken from the apache.spec file.

Listing 20-1: Configuration from the apache.spec file

```
./configure \
 --prefix=/etc/httpd \
 --disable-rule=WANTHSREGEX \
 --sysconfdir=/etc/httpd/conf \
 --datadir=/home/httpd \
 --bindir=/usr/bin \
 --sbindir=/usr/sbin \
 --libexecdir=/usr/libexec/apache \
 --includedir=/usr/include/apache \
 --logfiledir=/var/log/httpd \
 --localstatedir=/var \
 --runtimedir=/var/run \
 --proxycachedir=/var/cache/httpd \
 --mandir=/usr/man \
 --enable-module=most \
 --enable-shared=max
```

For now, put the contents of Listing 20-1 in a file (apache.conf) in the apache_1.3.9 directory, chmod 755 apache.conf, and execute it (./apache.conf). You can make modifications later. Most of the configuration options above change the default installation locations for binaries. Three actually change the build process, and one (`--disable-rule=WANTHSREGEX`) is required or the build will fail. You'll revisit this file and add to it later.

Before continuing, if you have any other modules (such as `mod_dav`, the author revisioning module) that you want to install, this would be a good time to install them. If the module installation wants to perform a build of Apache, decline that option.

This second step is optional, but recommended if you want to include support for database access. If you do, and haven't installed the MySQL RPMs, you'll need to do that first. If you want to use a different database, consult the ./configure --help and substitute your database for mysql below. Alternately, you can go through "setup." Listing 20-2 shows an acceptable base configuration for PHP. A number of options can be changed, either on the command line or in the php.ini file. You may want to remove imap support if you haven't loaded the imap-devel RPM.

Listing 20-2: Configuration for PHP

```
./configure \
  --with-apache=../apache_1.3.9 \
  --with-mysql=/usr \
  --with-imap \
  --enable-sysvshm=yes \
  --enable-sysvsem=yes \
  --with-config-file-path=/etc \
  --enable-debug=no \
  --enable-track-vars=yes \
```

You can copy the above to a file in the php-3.0.12 directory, make it executable (chmod 755) and run it. Then just run: `make && make install` to build and install the php module in the apache source tree. You'll configure Apache to build with PHP later.

The command used above to build PHP (make && make install) is really two separate commands. The && is used to sequentially execute the two commands, but only if the first one terminates successfully. Alternately, you could separate make and make install with a semicolon (;). This would sequentially execute both commands regardless of whether the first one failed or not. The text uses && so that execution will stop where the make failed. That way, you have a clue on the screen as to why the make failed.

The next step is required only if you're going to run the server using SSL on the Internet as part of a business in the United States. Otherwise, this step may be skipped. The following assumes you untarred the rsaref libraries as noted above. First, cd into the rsaref-2.0 directory. Then `cp -rp install/unix linux`. This step copies the unix directory in the install directory as a directory called linux. Then just cd into inux and run make. When that finishes, you'll have a file called rsaref.a. You'll want to `cp rsaref.a librsaref.a`, since builds may look for librsaref.a instead of rsaref.a.

The fourth step, unlike the second and third, is not optional. This step builds the openssl libraries required by mod_ssl. Change directory to the openssl directory. Here, you'll see two configuration files. You may use either (both do the same thing) but the Configure file requires one additional argument (linux-elf). Beyond that, they will both take the same arguments. If you want, you may install openssl on your system. The default directory where openssl will install (if you don't change it during configuration) is /usr/local/ssl/. This is where software looking for the openssl files will look by default, so if you change this and install it elsewhere, you'll need to make those changes when compiling with openssl in the future.

As before, this text will provide a suggested build configuration. Feel free to change it. If you live in Europe, you may need to include `no-idea` to exclude building the idea ciphers. Likewise, -fPIC is optional as is the rsaref line for those who don't want to include it. A suggested configuration line at this point then is:

```
./config -L$(pwd)/../rsaref-2.0/linux/ rsaref -fPIC
```

which will take care of properly configuring an OpenLinux system for building with RSAref.

 The `-fPIC` option is required if you are building shared libraries. Shared libraries (as opposed to static libraries) create smaller binaries and are generally preferred except in special situations (such as at boot time, when a library might not be available). Static libraries end in .a, and shared libraries carry .so at or near the end of their name.

When the configuration finishes, type `make && make test`. This will build and test the openssl distribution. If you want to install the distribution on your system, become root (su) and issue the `make install` directive. If you have RSAref installed on your system, export the environment variable RSAREF_BASE=/path/to/rsaref/ instead of using the -L option above.

The fifth step, building and installing the MM (memory module) library, is also optional. This library permits Apache to use available RAM, rather than disk as cache, which provides an obvious speed advantage. You might want to consider using this module if yours is a medium- to high-traffic site. The more traffic you get, the more advantage using this module will give you, but even small sites can benefit at little if any risk to security. To build the MM library, cd to the mm directory. If you want to install MM on your system (recommended), just execute:

```
./configure && make
```

which will automatically configure and build the MM libraries. After that, you can become root and issue a `make install`. This will configure and install the libraries to your system as if you passed configure the `--prefix=/usr/local`. That is, all files will be installed in /usr/local/lib, /usr/local/bin, /usr/local/include, etc. If you'd rather install in /usr/lib, /usr/bin, etc., you need to issue the above configure command with `--prefix=/usr`.

Once you've installed the library, ensure /etc/ld.so.conf includes a line to the library (/usr/local/lib by default) and, as root, run `ldconfig`. This will allow the system to recognize the MM shared libs. If you don't want to install MM on your system, but want Apache to take advantage of MM, configure MM with `--disable-shared` so Apache isn't looking for the shared libraries.

The sixth (and penultimate) step is not optional. Here you will build the SSL module. This is the easiest step since it requires only one command, configure, and one or three arguments, --with-apache=../apache_1.3.9, --with-crt=/path/to/your/server.crt, and --with-key=/path/to/your/server.key. The first argument is mandatory, and last two are used if you already have a valid server certificate (see below). This text will assume you do not have a server certificate. In this case, the command line will appear as:

```
./configure --with-apache=../apache_1.3.9
```

and when that finishes, you're done with this step. You can ignore the text regarding how to build Apache, because there's more involved now.

The seventh and final step is doing the final configuration on Apache, and then building and installing it. The next section will deal with the httpd configuration and startup. Change directories to the apache_1.3.9 directory to get started.

Remember your apache.conf file? Now is the time to add to it. Before you do, you might want to note what modules are currently enabled and disabled (optional). You can review this by running `./configure --help`. You'll be enabling the SSL module, but make note of any other module you want to enable or disable. Regardless of whichever other modules you want to modify, the lines in Listing 20-3 must be added. Don't forget to append a "\" to the last line of text (enable-shared=max) in the file before adding the rest of the options.

Listing 20-3: Minimum additions to Listing 20-1, apache.conf

```
--enable-module=so \
 --enable-module=ssl \
 --activate-module=src/modules/php3/libphp3.a
```

Some other useful modules to enable include the so module and info module. If you plan to chase the mod_ssl upgrades and don't want to rebuild everything, consider also including `--enable-shared=ssl`. This will build the SSL module as a shared library that can be upgraded by itself. You may add other configurations as well, but note that including suexec could compromise security.

Before you execute apache.conf, you need to set some environment variables. If you set them, and what you set them to depends on what you did above. The three variables are SSL_BASE, RSA_BASE, and EAPI_MM. The SSL_BASE variable is mandatory and must be set to the location of the ssl installation. If you did not install openssl on your system, but only built it for use by Apache, then you'll declare something like: SSL_BASE=../openssl-0.9.4, otherwise, use SSL_BASE=SYSTEM or the specific path to the installation (SSL_BASE=/usr/local/ssl). The RSA_BASE can also take SYSTEM, but will usually need to be specified as RSA_BASE=../rsaref-2.0/linux if you need to declare it at all. The EAPI_MM variable will also be either SYSTEM or ../mm-1.0.12 or will not be used, depending on whether or not you even built it. Once they are declared, don't forget to export any declared variables. Run the configure script and fix any errors (they should only be path errors to RSAref, SSL, or MM). Run `make`.

The build should go uneventfully. However, the Apache configuration script has a fatal bug associated with egcs used by Caldera. If the build stops with an error referencing "-rpath", you'll need to make changes in the Makefiles in a few subdirectories. If the build completes successfully, skip the next paragraph.

To repair the broken Makefiles, you'll need to cd src/modules then into each of standard, proxy, extra, and ssl and change the following two lines in the Makefile in each directory (the second line is only partial):

```
LDFLAGS_SHLIB= -rpath /usr/local/lib -rpath /usr/lib/mysql -shared
LIBS1= -Wl,-rpath,/usr/local/lib -Wl,-rpath,/usr/lib/mysql
```

to:

```
LDFLAGS_SHLIB= -L/usr/local/lib -L/usr/local/lib/mysql -shared
LIBS1= -Wl,-L/usr/local/lib -Wl,-L/usr/lib/mysql
```

The `-rpath` (plus the space or comma) is to be replaced by `-L` with no space between the L and the path. Once these four occurrences of rpath in each of the four Makefiles are changed, the build should continue without a hitch. Do not alter any of the paths. Your paths may be different from those shown. Only adjust the rpath option.

Assuming you don't have your own certificate, just type `make certificate` and follow the prompts. Mostly, you can take the defaults, but fill in the certificate information with your own information when prompted. The last question will ask you if you want to encrypt the server key with a pass phrase. If you do encrypt the server key, you'll be prompted for this key every time the Apache server is started in SSL mode. If you want unattended restarts, you won't want to do this. But weigh the risks carefully. Using a PEM pass phrase will increase your security posture, but will also mean entering that phrase with each SSL server startup.

 Server security certificates are documents that can be bought from places like Verisign or Thawte Consulting. If you don't want to buy one, you can create your own. The idea behind a commercial certificate is that an independent third party is verifying that you are who you say you are. You don't get this with a certificate you create on your own, but you do get the encryption. Encryption goes hand-in-hand with the certificate. No certificate, no encryption. If you're not going to offer anything to the public that requires secure services that anyone can trust (such as for financial transactions), then you can probably do just as well creating your own certificate per the instructions in this text.

Finally, become root and issue the `make install` directive to install your new SSL-enabled Apache Web server. The make will tell you that you can start Apache with the apachectl command and either start for a normal Web server, or startssl to start both the normal and SSL-enabled server. But you'll need to configure a few things first.

Configuring Apache

Once upon a time, Apache had four configuration files: httpd.conf, access.conf, srm.conf, and mime.types. For convenience sake, the access.conf and srm.conf have been merged into httpd.conf, but can be used separately if desired. Change directories to /etc/httpd/conf, and you should see these files plus magic and several ssl.* directories. The recommended method is to use only httpd.conf, and this text will assume you are doing this.

The httpd.conf file provided by default is quite large, but is mainly explanations and examples. These explanations, however, are not detailed. I will not attempt to add detail to them in this section. Apache provides on-line documentation (at http://www.apache.org/) for those who require more detailed explanation. Here, security-related settings will be are explained in-depth.

The default httpd.conf file comes with some very sane settings with security in mind. If you make no changes, you will be able to start and run the Apache Web server in normal mode only. If you do start your Web server without making any changes to your httpd.conf (assuming it's using the httpd.conf file installed above and not an already existing httpd.conf), and attempt to access it via your Web browser by pointing your browser at http://localhost/, you'll be disappointed. This is because the port your Web browser is looking at by default is not the one Apache binds by default, so you do have some changes to make.

Starting at the top of the httpd.conf file, most defaults will be appropriate. Looking down to the "MaxClients" and "MaxRequestsPerChild" entries, the first will limit the number of clients permitted to connect at any given time. You can adjust this number (150 by default) up or down to suit the amount of memory you have. If you don't know what you need, leave this and keep an eye on the load/amount of free RAM when clients are connected until you have a feel for system loading. The important one here is the MaxRequestsPerChild. This defaults to 0, which means that a client can spawn an infinite number of child requests. This is probably not a good idea as it leaves you open to Denial of Service attacks. Limiting the number to 25 is usually more than adequate.

Skipping down below the modules lists, one default is the "Port." This number defaults to 8080 and is the reason why, when you start Apache, your Web browser fails to connect. If you wish to use the "standard" port for offering Web services, you'll need to change this to 80. Remember that this requires Apache to be run as root. If you want to run the server as a user other than root, you'll need to choose a port above 1024. If you're running the Apache server behind a firewall, you can easily run with this configuration by redirecting connections on the firewall from 80 to 8080 and 443 to 8443, permitting you to run Apache as a non-privileged user and increasing security.

The Linux 2.4.*x* kernel adds a new dimension to security for Web servers that will be discussed below, but for now, either use port 80, or you'll need to connect to `http://localhost:8080/`.

A little farther down in the file is a section that starts <IfDefine SSL>, ends </IfDefine>, and contains two "Listen" statements. These define the ports Apache will listen to if started with the `startssl` argument. This is independent of the "Port" argument above, which is used if Apache is started with just the "start" argument. Again, the default unsecure port is 8080 instead of 80, and the default secure port is 8443 instead of the standard 443. Change these if you want to bind the standard ports. Otherwise, client connections must specify the port. The standard port connection is as noted above.

To connect to the secure port, you'll need to specify `https://localhost:8443/`. Note the use of the "s" on https. The client must (at least in the case of Netscape) know it is being directed to a secure port or the connection will fail since the plaintext and secure protocols are different (i.e., one is encrypted, and the other is not).

The next configuration lines of interest define the User and Group for the Web server to run client requests as. These will default to the user and group nobody (the group may be different on other distributions). The effect of these two statements is that, if the Web server is started as root (so that it can bind ports 80 and 443), the child processes that actually service the clients are spawned as the user nobody. If you review a process listing (ps aux) of the httpd processes, you'll note that one is running as root, and (by default 5) others are running as nobody. The child processes are the ones servicing clients. This limits the damage these processes can do as long as other permissions don't add to their power (more on this below). So if a client needs to have permission to write to a directory, that directory will need to be writable by nobody. This permission should be given as either owner or group rather than world. Any directory writable by nobody should have other restrictions as well (discussed below). If you desire, you can create another user for the clients to run as and use that instead (www is often a good choice). But for most applications, user and group nobody will suffice.

If Apache is started as a non-privileged user, the User and Group declarations will be ignored, and all processes will run as the user that started Apache. In this case, Apache will not be able to bind ports below 1024.

The next declaration of security import is the DocumentRoot declaration. This will default to "/home/httpd/htdocs" if you compiled Apache per the configuration above. This declares the "chroot jail" Apache will restrict clients to (given no Alias declarations further down). Ordinarily, this is where you'll want clients to start. This directory should contain a file "index.html", which will be accessed as the default root document. Apache provides one as a starting point.

Below the DocumentRoot declaration will be one or more <Directory> statements (each one containing declarations specific to that directory and those below it and ending with a </Directory> statement). The first Directory grouping should list "/" as its argument. This means that it applies to the previously defined DocumentRoot. Subsequent <Directory> statements will start from this DocumentRoot. Within the Directory statement will be declarations that apply to that and subsequent directory levels unless overridden with further Directory statements. This top-level directory statement will contain, by default, two declarations – "Options None" and "AllowOverride None". This severely restricts what a client may do. For security reasons, this should not be changed at this level. Listing 20-4 details statements and declarations that may be used within Directory statements and options available to those declarations. All arguments to declarations are a space separated list (except for the Order declaration).

Listing 20-4: <Directory> statement statements and declarations

```
Options
     None, Indexes, Includes, IncludesNoExec, FollowSymLinks,
SymLinksIfOwnerMatch, ExecCGI, Multiviews, All.
AllowOverride
     None, FileInfo, AuthConfig, Limit, All
Order
     One of allow,deny or deny,allow
Allow
     All or specific hosts, domains, networks, IPs
Deny
     same as for Allow
<Limit> (terminated with </Limit> and must be contained completely
within a <Directory> statement)
Limit arguments include: GET, POST, OPTIONS, PROPFIND, PUT, DELETE,
PATCH, PROPPATCH, MKCOL, COPY, MOVE, LOCK, UNLOCK with declarations:
Order, Allow, Deny as defined above.
```

◆ The None argument to any declaration prohibits any changes to
   that declaration.

◆ The All argument is the same as listing every argument available
   for that declaration. However, the MultiViews argument must also
   be provided with All if it is wanted, since it is not included in the
   All argument to Options.

◆ The Indexes argument allows a client to view the contents of a directory
   if a DirectoryIndex document (as defined in httpd.conf) does not exist.
   (See the <Files> statement below to restrict viewing of one or more files).

◆ The Includes argument allows a file to include other files, even those outside
   the DocumentRoot or aliased directory. This can allow an execution of a file
   embedded in an include. This option is extremely dangerous and should be
   used with caution.

◆ IncludeNoExec allows a way to permit includes without allowing those
   includes to be executed. This provides a safer alternative to Includes.

◆ FollowSymLinks is an argument equally dangerous to Includes and permits
   clients to follow links outside the directory tree.

◆ The SymLinksIfOwnerMatch is a much safer way to permit following
   of symlinks. Since little outside non-privileged directories are owned
   by non-privileged users, this permits users flexibility (particularly
   within the user directories) without compromising security the way
   the FollowSymLinks argument can.

◆ The ExecCGI is another very dangerous option that permits execution of files. If these are SUID files, they will be run as the file owner. Caution should be exercised in the selection of the directory files that can be run ExecCGI.

◆ MultiViews is an argument that allows the server to negotiate content with a client if a requested file doesn't exist. This particular option opens a potential security hole as large as the Grand Canyon, since the client and server will negotiate the file to be returned. You have no control over this process except to restrict which files that directory contains.

 Exercise care with the Options `Includes`, `FollowSymLinks`, `ExecCGI`, and `MultiViews`. Substitute the safer `IncludesNoExec` and `SymLinks IfOwnerMatch` where possible, and avoid `MultiViews`.

◆ The AllowOverride declaration also contains some potential problems and must be used with care.

◆ The Options argument allows specific options declared for this directory to be changed within an .htaccess file. If you don't want certain options used, then AllowOverride Options or All should not be specified.

◆ The FileInfo argument permits changes to the file type as declared (or not) in the httpd.conf file. It also allows changes to icons used to portray certain file types.

◆ The AuthConfig argument is used to permit access controls to be used on the subdirectory to permit authentication before entry. This will be discussed in more detail below.

◆ The Limit argument allows limit restrictions (discussed below) to be changed within .htaccess.

 AllowOverride can both tighten and loosen existing controls on a directory. Specific arguments, particularly All, Options, or Limit, should be used with care.

◆ The Order directive is self-explanatory.

◆ The Allow and Deny directives, accessed per the Order directive, can be used to restrict, by any number of methods, where clients may access the system from. But Apache may see a redirection from proxying software as if all clients were coming from the proxy (depending on the proxy used). So under a limited set of circumstances, these directives may not perform as anticipated. Ensure that your proxy transparently passes the client connection through.

♦ The <Limit> statement provides flexibility within a directory to permit certain actions while denying others. The arguments are a space-separated list within the Limit statements brackets. Specific declarations to Order, Allow from, and/or Deny from are contained between the extents of the Limit (terminated by </Limit>). Specific arguments (methods) to Limit include:

- GET – Download a file (via http or ftp)

- POST – Put information into a form

- PUT – Upload a file via ftp

- DELETE – Self-explanatory

- CONNECT – Any connection

- OPTIONS – Restrict permitted options

- TRACE – Enable a trace

- PROPFIND – Get a document's properties

- PATCH – Change (patch) a file

- PROPPATCH – Change (patch) a document's properties

- COPY – Self-explanatory

- MOVE – Self-explanatory

- LOCK – Prevent other processes from accessing a file

- UNLOCK – Remove a file lock

Directory statements below the DocumentRoot Directory statement will be assumed to be part of the DocumentRoot (that is, the subdirectory listed will be assumed to start at DocumentRoot) or will have one of three declarations prior to that Directory statement. The declaration may be one of the following, each of which takes two arguments – the directory access argument, which is what the client will use as part of the URL, and the actual directory location, which is where Apache will redirect the client to. The directory access argument is usually in the form /cgi-bin/ and the actual directory location is a full system path to the directory in the form /home/httpd/cgi-bin/

♦ Alias – allows redirection to a particular location

♦ ScriptAlias – same as alias, but the directory is assumed to have ExecCGI permissions (although that must be specifically declared in a <Directory> statement)

♦ UserDir – the user's home directory, usually accessed by /~username/

Another useful statement that is similar to the <Directory> statement is the <Files> statement. The <Files> statement also contains a space-separated list within the brackets surrounding the word Files (terminated by </Files>). By default, the httpd.conf will contain two entries, ~ and "^\.ht". The first entry refers to all files containing a tilde. This entry is usually used by programs that create backup files, and it is unlikely you'll want clients accessing these old files. The second entry is a regular expression (regex) the denoted any file whose first three characters are ".ht". The first symbol, the carat (^), means the first character, and the second symbol, the backslash (\) is an escape that tells the system not to interpret the following character. This is needed because the character following the escape, the ".", stands for "any character" in a regex (much like a "?" on a bash command line). In this case, you want specifically a "." and not "any character". Within the statement, you can use Order with Allow and/or Deny declarations to control access to these files.

One declaration used within the htpd.conf file, and normally preceding a <Files> statement, is AccessFileName declaring .htaccess, containing access modifications (if modifications are permitted) within that directory. If you change this filename, be sure to change the <Files> statement that refers to it or anyone will be able to read this file (and if permitted to write to the directory, change or replace the file).

Another declaration important for those directories not permitted to view the directory directly is the DirectoryIndex declaration. This space-separated list specifies the files to be searched for (in order) and presented to any client that provides a URL terminating in a directory name only. If none of these files are present, then the directory listing (if permitted) will be provided, and if a directory listing is not permitted, an error message. If you are using PHP3, your DirectoryIndex line may look like the following:

```
DirectoryIndex index.html index.php3 index.phtml
```

Additionally, one line you might want to uncomment (for PHP3) and expand on as shown is:

```
AddType application/x-httpd-php3 .php3 .phtml
```

This will permit use of PHP3 files carrying either a php3 or phtml extension.

The following three directives allow CGI and/or server-parsed html to be run by the server. The CGI directive permits cgi scripts to be run outside of scriptalias directories. This directive is not needed for CGI scripts within directories declared via scriptalias.

```
#AddHandler cgi-script .cgi
```

```
#AddType text/html .shtml
#AddHandler server-parsed .shtml
```

The second two directives combined declare shtml and direct the server to parse (and execute) server-parsed html files. These files add flexibility, but at some risk to security. Both the CGI and shtml directives reduce the level of security and are often used by attackers to gain access to the system. For a few sites, they are indispensable, but if not needed should not be used.

There is one final statement you might want to add to protect your system from an unintentional misconfiguration:

```
<Directory />
 Order deny,allow
 Deny from all
 </Directory>
```

What this will do is prevent anyone from being able to peruse your entire file system, whether accidentally or deliberately. But see the cautions in the "Additional security notes" section below.

You might also want to disable root's userdirectory with this simple directive:

```
UserDir disabled root
```

The SSL entries

When you build a server with mod_ssl, Apache adds a section at the end of the httpd.conf file that deals strictly with SSL.

Before you begin to use your SSL-enabled server, you *must* configure this section.

A number of the defaults should be left as is. You've already had the chance to adjust the port SSL listens on. But the first part you must change is listed under the <VirtualHost> statement. The VirtualHost statement includes the term _default_, which means the following entries will be used unless another VirtualHost entry exists for the SSL server and the client accesses that virtual server by name. You'll also want to adjust the port number to correspond to any change you made above.

For this host, the General setup will look exactly like the normal http side. That is, the secure DocumentRoot points to the same location as the non-secure side.

Having the secure DocumentRoot point to the same directory as the non-secure DocumentRoot is a uniformly bad idea. The secure DocumentRoot and the non-secure DocumentRoot should never coincide nor share any common subdirectories. These two directories trees should be completely separate, or the whole purpose of having a secure server is defeated.

You have several choices for separating the two trees. The first is to use /home/httpd/htdocs strictly for the unsecure side and create a parallel structure by another name, perhaps "secure". So you would create the directory "secure" in httpd, and use /home/httpd/secure as your secure location. Another option is to create two subdirectories below htdocs, nonsecure and secure, or public and private, and make the appropriate changes above for the normal Web server and also in the SSL section.

You will also want to create separate cgi-bin directories for each. While this is not mandatory, if your unsecure side uses many CGI scripts, you might not want those scripts run as part of the secure Web server.

The ServerName can remain the same, since the secure side will be accessed by the client as https, while the non-secure side will be accessed by simply http.

It might be less confusing to have separate error and transfer logs for the secure side and the nonsecure side, but this is also purely a matter of preference.

Many of the options discussed above can be applied to the secure side of the server as well. The use of these options is left as an exercise for the reader.

 If you are running both a non-secure and secure server on the same system, and one side is compromised, the other side is equally affected. Exercise care in choosing non-secure-side CGI scripts and options.

A number of advanced options are available for Apache, but will not be covered in this text. These include directives to restrict the ciphers used (such as idea) and the level of encryption to require from the clients (e.g., forbidding 40-bit cyphers), etc. For more information, refer to the Apache on-line text.

Starting and accessing Apache for the first time

Once you've made the minimum changes above and populated your secure server tree with at least an index.html you're ready to start serving documents. And if the secure index.html is different from the index.html used on the non-secure side, any problem will be immediately obvious.

First, start Apache using just the non-secure server. You can do this with the command apachectl start. Then open your Web browser and try to access http://localhost/ to see if the Web server is running. If you've chosen a port other than the default of 80 (such as 8080), you'll need to specify the port number on the command line, as in http://localhost:8080/. If the correct index page shows up, you know that half of the server is working correctly. If this doesn't work correctly, check the log files to see what went wrong. If it does work correctly, stop the Web server with apachectl stop.

Now start the Apache Web server with SSL by using apachectl startssl. You will be asked for a passphrase if you specified it while creating the server certificate. Once Apache is started, access the non-secure Web page as you did in the paragraph above just to ensure it is working. Then point your browser to https://localhost/. Note the "s" on the http. If you've used a port other than 443 (such as 8443), you'll need to specify it the same as above with https://localhost:8443/. The first thing that will happen if all is working correctly is that you will receive a New Site Certificate dialog box. You'll receive this box because your browser doesn't recognize the signing certificate authority. Go ahead through the dialog boxes, read and make any selections asked for (such as length of time to accept the certificate) and accept the certificate. If you created the certificate for your actual hostname, you will receive a dialog box telling you that the site (localhost) doesn't match the site name in the certificate. This is normal. If you access your server with the same hostname you used to create the server certificate (`make certificate` earlier in this chapter) you won't receive this warning box. Ensure that the server is accessing the correct DocumentRoot. If all is well, you're ready to start using your secure Web server.

Using .htaccess files

The .htaccess file can contain a number of different options and have many purposes. The first purpose is to restrict access within a directory. That is, if you want to require only folks with valid usernames and passwords to access a particular directory, you can do this via an .htaccess file.

First, edit your /etc/httpd/conf/httpd.conf file and insert a <Directory> statement with an "AllowOverride Authconfig" declaration. This will permit you to configure specific authorizations for that directory. Remember to issue an `apachectl restart` to tell Apache to reread the configuration file.

Then, create your .htaccess file. When you create an .htaccess file, you'll want four lines in the file (see Listing 20-5). The first line should contain AuthName and a name. The name isn't important, but should be meaningful to what you're protecting. The AuthType will always be Basic. The AuthUserFile should point to the file you want to use for validation. You will create the user validation file with `htpasswd`. The final line will be `require valid-user`.

Listing 20-5: An .htaccess file

```
AuthName "foo"
AuthType Basic
AuthUserFile /path/to/.htpasswd
require valid-user
```

The .htaccess file can also be used to expand or change any directives in the /etc/httpd/conf/httpd.conf file for that directory. For this use, you need to an 'AllowOverride Options' declaration within a <Directory> statement for that directory. The format for the .htaccess file is exactly the same as used in the http.conf file, and nearly anything used with the httpd.conf file can be used in the .htaccess file.

Additional security notes

Not discussed above, because it was not part of the default httpd.conf file, are several statements related to the Directory and Files statements. These additional statements include DirectoryMatch, FilesMatch, Location, and LocationMatch. These statements are syntactically the same as the Directory and Files statements, but the "Match" statements refer specifically to regex arguments. These arguments are necessarily different from non-regex arguments. This advanced configuration information is explained in the documentation.

 The term regex is short for regular expression. A regular expression in Linux describes a pattern of characters, but without necessarily stating those characters explicitly. You use glob symbols (* and ?) to represent unknown multiple or single characters with commands like ls. With regex, this syntax changes slightly, but you can still specify single and multiple unknown characters as well as patterns that begin or end a line, and more. For a detailed explanation of regular expressions and how to use them, see any book on sed, awk, or Perl programming. Regular expressions are very powerful and very flexible, but can be difficult for novices to grasp.

Also explained is the Location and LocationMatch, which refer to URLs rather than directories or files. What must be kept in mind is the order in which these are processed. Any reference to a Directory is processed first. If a subsequent Files statement contains contradictory declarations, it will override the Directory directives. This configuration makes a good deal of sense, since a file is more specific than an entire directory. Likewise, a Location statement with conflicting directives will override both Directory and File statement declarations. However, this isn't intuitively obvious, since a URL location is a virtual concept, as compared to the more concrete directory/file relationship, and doesn't share an analogy. The Location statement provides much flexibility, but adds complexity and makes it easy to inadvertently override a Directory or File configuration. Exercise caution with Location statements.

Notes about suEXEC

The suEXEC program is a wrapper that allows for program execution as a user other than the user running the Web server. Under normal operations, all programs run as the user the Web server is running as, 3/4 (in the case of the configuration used earlier in this chapter) as the user nobody. Under certain conditions, this may not be acceptable. For example, if users have individual databases that you (or they) don't want just anyone writing to, you might want to compile the suEXEC program in and include the userdir configuration. This feature should be considered where .htaccess files are considered inappropriate or unworkable.

Properly setting up suEXEC will initially take some time. This does need to be configured and compiled in. Some of the additional configuration directives include:

```
--enable-suexec
--suexec-caller=UID
--suexec-docroot=DIR
--suexec-logfile=FILE
--suexec-userdir=DIR
--suexec-uidmin=UID
--suexec-gidmin=GID
--suexec-safepath=PATH
```

There are some drawbacks to this configuration option. It does, however, allow great flexibility in specifying, via VirtualHosts statements, the user a particular program should run as. Unfortunately, compiling in the suEXEC option and using it with VirtualHosts does impose some limitations on the location of the VirtualHosts directories — they must all be located below the main DocumentRoot. This may not always be desirable.

The biggest danger inherent in using suEXEC is specifying an unsafe (untrusted) PATH for binary locations. Any binary would run as the specified user, which may be fine from a system standpoint, but could be disastrous for the user, particularly if that binary is a malicious Trojan.

Linux 2.4.x and khttpd

Coming in the Linux 2.4.x kernel (still under development as of this writing) is a kernel-level http daemon (khttpd). This daemon is not designed to replace the Apache Web server, but enhance it. The idea behind the daemon is that most Web pages are static, and that these are good candidates for a small, fast, secure, kernel-level daemon to hand to clients. The khttpd would listen on port 80 (a privileged port anyway) for requests. Requests for simple, static pages would be handled by khttpd. Any document khttpd couldn't handle, such as any complex document or a document with PHP3, etc., would be handed off to another http daemon like Apache listening on port 8080. Apache, then, would handle these more complex requests. The redirection would be from khttpd on port 80 to localhost on port 8080 (or any other configured port).

The kernel http daemon can be configured as a module or built into the kernel, and easily configured in /etc/rc.d/rc.local at startup or afterwards. If configured as a module, the khttpd directory will not exist in the /proc tree until the module is loaded. Then a directory, /proc/sys/net/khttpd, comes into existence. Within this directory are the following files:

```
clientport
documentroot
dynamic
logging
maxconnect
perm_forbid
perm_required
serverport
sloppymime
start
stop
threads
unload
```

Each of the above files can be configured to your specific setup. The first file contains the clientport, the port khttpd goes to (as a client) when a request goes beyond a simple "copy to network" operation. By default, this port is 80 where the Apache Web server will be listening. This means that by default, khttpd is configured as a helper rather than as the main http daemon. Change this to 8080 (or any other unused port), and have Apache listen on that port to make khttpd the primary Web server and Apache the helper. Also make the changes as recommended in the serverport file (below).

The second file contains the location of the DocumentRoot, which is configured by default as /var/www, so would need to be changed as follows: echo "/home/httpd/htdocs" > /proc/sys/net/httpd/documentroot.

The third file is not as intuitive as the first two. The dynamic file holds the dynamic strings khttpd will look for. By default this file contains "Dynamic strings are : -cgi-bin- -..- - -". You would probably want to add php3 (echo php3 > /proc/sys/net/khttpd/dynamic) if using PHP.

The fourth file, logging, specifies whether logging via syslog should occur and will contain either a 0 or 1 – by default the answer is 0. The fifth parameter limits maximum simultaneous connections, and by default is 1000 (which should be sufficient for even the largest sites, but sites with low bandwidth may want to reduce this to 100 or less).

The perm_forbid has a very sane value by default of 16969. This number is used as a mask to determine if a file has any of the characteristics contained in the mask. These characteristics include (reading the numbers from left to right) being a FIFO (a named pipe, indicated by the first 1), either of SUID or SGID (a 4 or 2 respectively which equals 6), all of read, write, execute (7) or write-only (2) for the owner, which combines to a mask of 9, both read (4) and write (2) permissions for the group, which combines to a mask of 6, or a mask for the world bit the same as for the user mask. If you change this value, ensure that you understand how this works. Another sane value would be 16999. Bad values for this mask could compromise your system.

The perm_required works much like perm_forbid, but this time it is looking for read-only for the file for world access. If the file is not world readable, it will not be served.

The serverport file contains the port number khttpd will listen on for incoming requests. Again, by default, khttpd is set is set up as a helper rather than the main server, and contains a value of 8080. If you want to make khttpd the primary server and Apache the helper, make the appropriate change here and in Apache's httpd.conf file. If you make Apache the helper (recommended), change Apache's BindAddress declaration from * to 127.0.0.1. Apache will then only accept requests from khttpd.

The sloppymime file will contain either a 1 or 0. If this value is set to 1, any unknown mime types are set to text/html and handled by khttpd. When set to 0 (the default), any unknown mime types are passed to the user-space Web server (Apache).

The next two files, start and stop, are both 0 by default. When a 1 is entered into start, stop is automatically set to 0, and khttpd begins servicing requests. When stop is set to 1, start is automatically set to 0, and khttpd stops handling requests.

The threads file contains a 2 by default. This specifies the number of server-threads that may run per CPU. Unless you have a large site (so large that all the active files will not fit in RAM), this number should be set to 1.

The final file, unload, prepares the khttpd module for unloading. Before unloading the module, you should first echo a 1 to stop (which will put a 0 in start and prevent more khttpd threads from starting). Currently running threads will continue, and you need to wait for them to terminate or send them a SIGHUP (kill -HUP `pidof khttpd`). Then prepare the khttpd module for unloading by echoing a 1 to unload. It is now safe to `rmmod khttpd`. Reloading the module will write a 0 to unload.

Summary

In this chapter you learned how to configure and compile Apache-1.3.9 with SSL and PHP3. You also learned how to configure Apache, and about a few of the dangerous (with regards to security) configurations. To recap, dangerous configurations to avoid include:

- Allowing plain-text and SSL DocumentRoot locations to coincide.

- Using IncludesNOEXEC vice Include where Includes are necessary.

- Using SymLinksIfOwnerMatch vice FollowSymLinks where necessary.

- Omitting the use of safe CGI directories via ScriptAlias.

- Using <Location> statements that override <Directory> or <File> configurations.

- Not avoiding use of the ExecCGI directive.

- Using an Alias directive that exposes your system root.

- Omitting use of "AllowOverride AuthConfig" and .htaccess files to better secure sensitive areas on your Web server.

- Not disabling root's userdir.

- Not adding a Directory statement to deny everyone access to "/".

You also learned about the coming kernel http daemon that will debut in the Linux 2.4.*x* kernel.

Chapter 21

Using Secure Shell and VPNs

ONE OF THE BIGGEST security problems facing users and administrators today is having a secure way to communicate with home- or business-based systems from a remote location. Accessing these systems isn't a big problem. Every Linux system comes with a telnet client and server. But this means that the username and password are sent over the wire in plaintext. While this may not be a big problem over a dedicated dialup line, as soon as the connection reaches beyond the server terminating the dialup access, anyone with tcpdump or another sniffer program can read the username and password.

To compound this problem, many travelers use a nationwide ISP to gain access via a local call to be able to pick up e-mail. If they use that same connection to gain access back to home or their place of business, the connection could travel over several networks, allowing anyone connected to those networks to capture those packets as they pass by. The packet headers will tell them the packet destination and contain the username and password. Even baby wannabe crackers can enter a system armed with this information. This is one reason that by default, root cannot log in remotely to an OpenLinux system. The flaw with this security model is that is doesn't prevent someone from logging in as himself and then using `su` to become root, doing essentially the same thing.

But if access to a system is accomplished via an encrypted connection that cannot be easily broken, it becomes nearly impossible for anyone to sniff a username and password pair from your packets. It now requires much more sophistication for crackers to insert themselves between you and your servers — to perform what's known as "a man in the middle" attack. This particular attack is very difficult to pull off, and as long as a large number of vulnerable systems remain on the Internet for the taking, the man in the middle attack will likely remain the domain of a few knowledgeable, determined, and properly positioned individuals.

There are a number of tools and programs that enable Linux to achieve secure connections to systems. You looked at one such system in the previous chapter, using SSL with Apache. While this may seem limiting, users can run secure Web servers on unprivileged ports with .htaccess controls in order to view and download (via http, not ftp) documents from their own directories.

But to accomplish much more, basically what could be accomplished via a telnet session (which is actually almost anything you can do from the console), you need the equivalent of a telnet session. In the following sections, you'll look at two alternative ways to do this. The first is to use a program called Secure Shell, and the second is to create a true, virtual private network using FreeS/WAN.

As mentioned in the previous chapter, the CD-ROM does not contain any of these software products, in order that the author and publishers can remain in compliance with cryptographic export controls. That said, any system administrator who needs to work as root over an untrusted network and does not use these tools can expect to see his systems broken into regularly. The programs are available from `ftp://ftp.cs.hut.fi/pub/ssh/ssh-1.2.27.tar.gz` and `ftp://ftp.xs4all.nl/pub/crypto/freeswan/freeswan-1.1.tar.gz`.

Secure Shell

Currently, Secure Shell (SSH) comes in two flavors, a version 1 and a version 2. Both are maintained by their authors. The difference between them is in the capabilities (version 2, as you've probably guessed, has a few extra "goodies") and in the license. Basically, for noncommercial use, SSH version 1 is free for the using. But version 2 requires almost anyone using it to purchase a license. This text, therefore, will deal with version 1, specifically, ssh-1.2.27.

Building and installing SSH

After downloading SSH, decide where you want to build it (the location of the file doesn't matter, your $HOME directory is fine). Then open it using the following command:

```
tar xzvf ssh-1.2.27.tar.gz
```

This will create a directory ssh-1.2.27 that you need to cd into to continue.

For those not yet familiar with building software packages, the SSH package uses new GNU autoconf files. These files are a simple alternative to hacking the Makefile directly and make creating different configurations simple, as well as performing some sanity checks. The GNU autoconf system isn't foolproof, and some packages will fail to properly find software installed on a system. In this case, the ssh-1.2.27 autoconf file works flawlessly with OpenLinux.

First, issue the command ./configure --help. This will provide a (long) list of options available to you to build the package in many different configurations. This text will touch on only a few. The defaults are generally good, but you may need to make some changes for your situation. Near the top are the directory prefixes for installation. They default to /usr/local, which should probably be left unless you want to use /opt instead. Below that are host types that are not needed if you are building on the system the software is to be installed on. The last section is features and packages, which you'll want to scrutinize the first time through. Here, important configuration options include:

◆ `--with-x`: if you want to include the X11 developmental libraries (a good idea)

◆ `--without-idea`: if you are in Europe and cannot use the IDEA encryption routines

◆ `--without-rsh`: if you want to prohibit SSH from falling back to the unsecure rsh if it cannot find the ssh server (another good idea)

◆ `--with-secureid=/path/to/secureid`: if your system makes use of the Security Dynamics SecurID card

◆ `--with-kerberos5`: if you use Kerberos 5 (Kerberos 4 is not supported)

◆ `--with-libwrap`: if you want to use TCP wrappers (/etc/hosts.allow)

◆ `--with-socks --with-socks4 --with-socks5`: if you want SOCKS firewall support

◆ `--with-rsaref`: if you want/need to comply with the RSA patent (US)

You can select from a long list of other options if desired. Pick those options you are sure you want to enable/disable. I recommend you create a small executable script like the one in Listing 21-1.

Listing 21-1: A possible configuration for SSH

```
./configure --with-x \
            --without-rsh \
            --with-rsaref
```

If you need/want to use RSAref, you'll need to follow the instructions in this paragraph. While the configuration help suggests you can tell SSH where to find the RSAref libraries, that portion of the script is broken. From the directory where you ran ./configure --help, create the directory "rsaref2" (mkdir rsaref2). Do not change this name; it must appear exactly as is. Then cd into rsaref2 and execute `tar xzvf /path/to/rsaref20.tar.Z`. Now just cd back up to the configure directory and run your configure script, and continue.

After executing your configuration file, note and correct any deficiencies (will normally be missing libraries or incorrect paths). Once your configure script runs to completion, you can issue the `make` command. This command will take a while to finish, but when it does, `su` to root and issue a make install. This will install everything in preparation for running, including creating initial private system keys.

Once everything is installed, you need to ensure that the sshd binary is run during system startup. The simplest way to do this is with the following line:

```
echo "/usr/local/sbin/sshd" > /etc/rc.d/rc.local
```

By default, this will start the Secure Shell server daemon with a default RSA keysize of 768 bits. If you want to use a larger key (which will require more computational time and could slow connections, but provides for more security), add a `-b 1024` substituting any desired number of bits for 1024. Do not lower the 768-bit default, as today's technology can easily decrypt keys 512 and below, and even 768 is suspect. Given the time required to generate a key at each sshd startup, running from inetd is not recommended. To start sshd without rebooting, issue the sshd command from the command line for sshd to start.

 While not required, it is a good idea to ensure that /etc/services lists port 22 as ssh:

```
ssh             22/tcp
ssh             22/udp
```

During install, SSH will have created several files in /etc:

- ◆ sshd_config: the default SSH server daemon configuration

- ◆ ssh_config: the SSH default configuration file

- ◆ ssh_host_key: the host's private key, which should be rw root only, no other accesses allowed

- ◆ ssh_host_key.pub: the host's public key

- ◆ ssh_random_seed: created during each sshd startup (rw root only, no other accesses allowed)

- ◆ sshd_config: the default SSH server daemon configuration

The `ssh_host_key` will have been created by the install as a 768-bit key. If you wish to increase the size of this key, say to 1024 bits, you'll need to issue the command `ssh-keygen -b 1024`. When the key is generated, save it as /etc/ssh_host_key. This will create new `ssh_host_key` and `ssh_host_key.pub` files. When asked for a passphrase, *do not enter one.* If you enter a passphrase here, the sshd program will wait for startup until you've entered a passphrase. This is not conducive to an unattended sshd startup.

Once you have performed all the above steps on each system you want to install SSH to and restarted sshd, collect all the /etc/ssh_host_key.pub files (optional) and copy the contents into one large file to be saved to each host as /etc/ssh_known_hosts (chmod 644). This will help prevent IP spoofing and provide increased security. You are now finished with all root tasks.

 If any of your system's root account is compromised, you cannot trust the SSH keys and should replace all of them to ensure that another system hasn't stolen your identity.

Using SSH

As a user, you can now begin communicating securely with any host running sshd on which you have an account. You connect the same way as with telnet, but SSH will pass your username to the remote system. You will be asked for the password corresponding to that user. If the username you wish to use on the remote system is different from the username you are logged in as on the local system, use the `-l` option to specify a different username. SSH, unlike telnet, does not carry any restriction about logging in as root. This is because once the TCP connection is established, the first thing SSH does is exchange public keys and create an encrypted tunnel. Everything, including the user to log in as, is encrypted.

When you first start SSH, it will create a directory, .ssh, in which you will have a randcom_seed each time an active session is open. If you did not perform the optional step above of creating an /etc/know_hosts file, or connected to a system not listed in the /etc/known_hosts file, you will also have a know_hosts file here. (You will first be told no know_hosts entry exists and asked if you wish to continue — say yes.) The SSH program will automatically copy the remote system's `ssh_host_key.pub` to this file, which will be compared each time a connection is made. If the key in the known_hosts file doesn't match the one tendered by the remote host, you will be warned that the keys don't exist, that someone could be performing a man in the middle attack (SSH is very paranoid about this), and ask you if you wish to continue anyway. To stop the warning, delete the offending key from the known_hosts file (assuming it really has changed). You will get the "no known_hosts entry" at the next connection and a question whether you want to connect anyway which, if accepted, will copy the remote key over.

To make things easier, each user who communicates regularly via SSH can set up her own identity file. Suppose user sally regularly logs in to several different systems, all with different usernames and passwords. While generally the different usernames don't pose a problem and can easily be designated with the `-l` option, a large number of different and difficult passwords can slow down logins. In this case, sally will want to create her own identity file. By issuing the `ssh-keygen` command (`-b` optional), she can create an identity and identity.pub files in $HOME/.ssh. She will also be asked for a passphrase when the identity file is ready to be written. The generated identity.pub file's contents should be copied to the remote system's $HOEM/.ssh/authorized_keys file (it will need to be created). Now, when sally logs in to the remote system, she will be asked for the passphrase for the identity file, not the password for the user on the remote system. So only one password now needs to be remembered for all the different remote systems and users where this authorized_keys file contains sally's identity.pub file.

As regards the passphrase, sally actually has two options: type in a passphrase or leave the field empty. The security implications here are important. The $HOME/.ssh/identity file will be read-write owner (sally) only. If sally's account is compromised, her identity can be stolen and used if no passphrase has been supplied, and she will need to generate new identity files and make appropriate changes on all the remote systems. While the no passphrase option would permit unattended logins (because no password would be requested for access to the remote system) it does increase the exposure to the remote systems. So sally could run unattended scripts or log in to remote systems without being asked for any password. Convenient, but it exposes remote systems to a local system exploit for that user.

 If the above scenario (a user needing to log in to multiple remote systems) is the case, note that a graphical tool, sshbuddy, is available to speed logins by saving the remote server name and corresponding username, and can be accessed with two mouse clicks.

SSH and SSHD configuration

SSH comes with two default configuration programs, one for the client (ssh_config) and one for the server (sshd_config). When either program starts, it first reads any configuration from the command line, then from an individual user's .ssh files, then from the system configuration files. Once an option is set, subsequent usages of the same option are ignored.

The /etc/ssh_config file, shown in Listing 21-2, contains the defaults the system will use if no options are overridden elsewhere.

Listing 21-2: /etc/ssh_config extract showing default options

```
#    Host *
#        ForwardAgent yes
#        ForwardX11 yes
```

```
#    RhostsAuthentication yes
#    RhostsRSAAuthentication yes
#    RSAAuthentication yes
#    TISAuthentication no
#    PasswordAuthentication yes
#    FallBackToRsh yes
#    UseRsh no
#    BatchMode no
#    StrictHostKeyChecking no
#    IdentityFile ~/.ssh/identity
#    Port 22
#    Cipher idea
#    EscapeChar ~
```

Despite the fact that all configurations are commented out, this is still what SSH will use if the configuration is not modified here or elsewhere. Modifications can be host-specific. If host-specific modifications are desired, they should be added in a Host section before the "all other" Host section.

A few options deserve some notes. The `ForwardX11` option allows transparent and automatic forwarding of the X11 display back to the local host. In effect, this is the same as running `xhost +remotehost` on the localhost, then on the remote host setting the DISPLAY environment variable to the localhost (export DISPLAY= CLIENTHOST:0.0). Use of this depends on SSH's finding the xauth program on the remote host (this may be a problem on some non-Linux systems). If X11 forwarding is requested, but SSH is unable to comply, you will receive a message indicating as much. If available, X11 connections will come back through the encrypted tunnel. So if you `ssh foo`, then run xterm from foo, you will receive an xterm on your local system (assuming you are logged in to an X session). The host foo does not need to be running X, only to have the client programs available. Note that over a slow connection (analog modem), this option may not be desirable.

Note also that by default, SSH will use IDEA as the cipher. If you wish to use triple DES, uncomment the Cipher line and change idea to 3des or start ssh with the option `-c 3des.`.

The SSH server daemon default configuration file is shown in Listing 21-3.

Listing 21-3: The default /etc/sshd_config file

```
Port 22
ListenAddress 0.0.0.0
HostKey /etc/ssh_host_key
RandomSeed /etc/ssh_random_seed
ServerKeyBits 768
LoginGraceTime 600
KeyRegenerationInterval 3600
PermitRootLogin yes
IgnoreRhosts no
```

```
StrictModes yes
QuietMode no
X11Forwarding yes
X11DisplayOffset 10
FascistLogging no
PrintMotd yes
KeepAlive yes
SyslogFacility DAEMON
RhostsAuthentication no
RhostsRSAAuthentication yes
RSAAuthentication yes
PasswordAuthentication yes
PermitEmptyPasswords yes
UseLogin no
# CheckMail no
# PidFile /u/zappa/.ssh/pid
# AllowHosts *.our.com friend.other.com
# DenyHosts lowsecurity.theirs.com *.evil.org evil.org
# Umask 022
# SilentDeny yes
```

First, notice that this server configuration file does not have lines commented out (except for a few example lines at the bottom). This is because the server requires these values for operation — it does not have compiled-in defaults for these values. Most may easily be changed. Some will affect the way users interact with the system or with what they receive. These values may be changed to conform to local system policies. The range of effects of changes is great, and will not be covered in detail here, since few directly affect security except the "RHosts" options above. Disable these if you don't want to allow users .rhosts files to permit logins à la rsh. Permitting the use of rhosts files is generally a bad idea. The use of identity and authorized_keys files makes for improved security.

FreeS/WAN

The FreeS/WAN package is a little different from the SSH package. This package is designed to provide an encrypted tunnel between any two networks separated by an untrusted network (usually the Internet). While secure operations with SSH are limited to those things that can be done via telnet (except with the version 2 package), FreeS/WAN permits all traffic between the two WAN segments to be encrypted.

Building and installing FreeS/WAN

In order to install FreeS/WAN, you must compile it into the kernel. First, obtain a pristine kernel source. Do not use the kernel source that comes with the OpenLinux package: The source Caldera supplies (including the one with this book) is modified and will not build outside the RPM environment. While this may be fixed in more recent releases, you'll experience less problems with pristine sources You can get pristine sources from `http://www.us.kernel.org` or a mirror site. Create a directory (mkdir linux-2.2.14) and make sure the link "linux" points to that directory. Untar the kernel source, enter the directory, build and install a kernel tailored to your system. Once you're sure this kernel works (builds, installs, boots), return to /usr/src.

If you have trouble booting the new kernel, ensure that your /etc/lilo.conf is correct and run lilo again. Make sure lilo was able to see your new kernel.

This time, untar the FreeS/WAN package from here (/usr/src). Then cd into freeswan-1.1. Now issue one of the following commands:

```
make menugo (corresponds to make menuconfig)
make xgo (corresponds to make xconfig)
make ogo (corresponds to make config)
make oldgo (corresponds to make oldconfig)
```

This will patch the kernel source and begin the kernel make. Select the Networking Options items you want to set (do not unset Kernel/User netlink socket). Selecting IP: optimize as router not host will make the system slightly faster if it is a router only. If this system acts as a workstation, do not select this option, since it could introduce some packet errors.

You may also select the IP: advanced router options and select those you want. If you do, you will have to turn off rp_filter during bootup by putting the following line in /etc/rc.d/rc.local:

```
echo "0" > /proc/sys/net/ipv4/conf/all/rp_filter
```

Down at the bottom of the Networking options section you should see some new choices. The first is IP Security Protocol (FreeS/WAN IPSEC). This may be built into the kernel or enabled as a module. By enabling this, a number of other options below it will be available. The defaults are reasonable. If you understand the implications, turn on or off whatever options you feel you will need in this section. Under no circumstances should you turn on IPSEC: Enable Insecure algorithms. Turning this on defeats the purpose of having an encrypted link.

When you are finished, Exit and save the new kernel configuration. You must save the new kernel configuration whether you made any changes or not or the FreeS/WAN patches will not be compiled.

When you save and exit, the kernel build will start automatically. This does not perform all necessary steps. When the kernel build finishes, you will need to cd ../linux, run `make modules_install`, then move the kernel, run lilo to recognize the new kernel, and finally, reboot into the new kernel.

The kernel build process also installed a number of utilities and man (manual) pages.

Configuring FreeS/WAN

This configuration will address a very basic setup — two systems that need to talk to each other securely on the same wire — and expand from there. At each step, you should test to make sure the new configuration is working properly.

Once you've rebooted, you probably received several console messages about ipsec during system initialization. Ignore these until you've configured ipsec. The first thing you'll want to do is turn ipsec off on your systems until you are ready to connect them.

This text will use for the first part of this configuration two systems, HostA with IP 192.168.0.1 and HostB with IP 192.168.0.2. They are on the same wire. The test connection will be called "HostA2HostB" (hey, I could have been real original and called it foo-test). They will each use their eth0 Ethernet connection.

On HostA, move the default /etc/ipsec file (which has some rather bland name values) out of the way and use the following:

```
config setup
    interfaces="ipsec0=eth0"
    #(later you can change the above to interfaces="ipsec0=eth0
ipsec1=ppp0"
    klipsdebug=all #(or none if you like)
    plutodebug=all #(again, none if you like)
conn HostA2HostB
    HostA=192.168.0.1
    HostB=192.168.0.2
    keyingtries=0 # this is actually a very large number
```

Pay close attention to indentation. This is required in most ipsec files. Copy this file to HostB. Then, edit ipsec.secrets as follows:

```
192.168.0.1 192.168.0.2 "256 random bits from 'ipsec ranbits >
tmpfile`"
```

 The ipsec.secrets file must be closely guarded — owned by root and readable only by root. Anyone who gets this key can break into your secure tunnel and read all your encrypted messages.

You can use the `ipsec ranbits` command to generate random bits for the ipsec.secrets file. Both systems (192.168.0.1 and 192.168.0.2) listed on the line (more systems may be added) must have identical copies of the ipsec.secrets file (at least the random bits portion). Make sure the 256 bits are enclosed in double quotes.

Once both systems have copies of the two files (with correct permissions on the /etc/ipsec.secrets file), use modprobe to insert the ipsec module (if you built ipsec as a module) and execute /etc/rc.d/init.d/ipsec start on each system.

You can verify that ipsec is running by looking at several things. First, looking at ifconfig will show a new interface, ipsec0 and its relevant parameters. You will also have new entries in your routing table corresponding to ipsec0. Finally, the ipsec utility itself will show you some of these same things via `ipsec look` and `ipsec tncfg`.

Expanding the network

If you look at the default ipsec.conf file, you'll notice that it has a few more variables, like a "nexthop" variable. In our configuration file, this would be HostAnexthop and HostBnexthop. If the two systems to pass encrypted information between each other are physically separated by several hops on the Internet (or any other network) — that is, they don't share the same gateway address — then the "nexthop" needs to contain the gateway address each machine has. If you're using PPP, you'll have a local and remote address for the point-to-point connection. The local address is used as HostA (use a better hostname than this, OK?) and the remote address constitutes the HostAnexthop. Your HostB (or as in the default ipsec.conf file rightnexthop) contains the other hosts next hop IP. And of course, each system's IP must be listed in the ipsec.secrets file.

Up to this point, you've been constructing a tunnel strictly between two systems. This has necessarily been very restrictive, but also very easy. In order to expand this tunnel to include systems behind it, you need to know a few things and add a few more variables.

The first additional piece of information you'll need is the network mask of the subnet behind the gateway, which is then added as HostAsubnet= and is a network/bitmask address, as in 192.168.0.0/24. This says that HostA is acting as the gateway for (and should be listed as the gateway by) all the systems with IPs in the 192.168.0 range.

When you add the "subnet" variable, the gateway system is excluded. That is, traffic originating in the gateway system or terminating on the gateway system does not go through the tunnel. You must set up a separate tunnel omitting the "subnet" variable or specifying 192.168.0.1/32.

The other thing you must know is whether or not the gateway acts as a firewall (masquerading host or not). If yes, you must have a "firewall" variable and make it yes: HostAfirewall=yes.

Expanding beyond two networks

Expanding beyond two subnets (connecting three or more subnets) is an exercise in expanding the ipsec.conf file and ipsec.secrets file. The most difficult part is ensuring that if you have 50 non-routable subnets (those using 192.168.x.x Ips), the IPs are unique among the subnets. The second hardest part is thinking up gateway naming pairs so these virtual connections make sense at first glance.

For example, say you want to connect three subnets. The three gateways are called moe, larry, and curly. Host moe will have an ipsec.conf file with two "conn" sections that may look like Listing 21-4.

Listing 21-4: ipsec.conf file extract without config setup portion

```
conn moe-larry
     moe=192.168.0.1
     moenexthop=Internetgatewaymaewest
     moesubnet=192.168.0.0/24 #remember, moe is not secure to larry
     moefirewall=yes
     larry=192.168.1.1
     larrysubnet=192.168.1.0/24
     larrynexthop=Internetgatewaymaeeast
     larryfirewall=yes
     keyingtries=0

conn moe-curly
     moe=192.168.0.1
     moenexthop=Internetgatewaymaewest
     moesubnet=192.168.0.0/24 #remember, moe is not secure to larry
     moefirewall=yes
     curly=192.168.2.1
     curlysubnet=192.168.2.0/24
     curlynexthop=Internetgatewaymaesouth
     curlyfirewall=yes
     keyingtries=0
```

Host larry would have an exact copy of the conn moe-larry above, and host curly would have a copy of the conn moe-curly section. Likewise, larry and curly would each have a "conn larry-curly" section in their ipsec.conf files.

The ipsec.secrets file would also carry two another set of secrets. moe would share a secret each with larry and curly, but wouldn't need a copy of the secret shared between larry and curly (although it wouldn't hurt to have it there, it just wouldn't be used). The same goes for the connection information between the other two servers in the ipsec.conf file.

And of course, if you wanted secure traffic to originate on one of the gateways (moe) and terminate on another gateway (larry), you'd need yet another connection specification, like moe-larry-gates that would set up a simple (second) tunnel with the moesubnet and larrysubnet omitted or specific to that host (192.168.0.1/32 and 192.168.1.1/32).

OpenSSH

As of this writing, the OpenSSH package is under development, the developer's intention being that OpenSSH will replace the original SSH package. The OpenSSH package's license will be more open, and development will continue (while ssh-1.2.27 is being maintained, all development is going into the 2.0.x package which license is basically commercial).

The OpenSSH project's goals include providing secure ftp and rcp capabilities as well as the normal SSH functionalities. The developers are removing all cryptographic code with possible patent problems (IDEA, the RSA routines) but retaining strong cryptography.

Summary

In this chapter you learned how to configure, build, and install SSH, a strong encryption package for remote administration and work. You learned how to configure it, and how to use it to seamlessly connect to other systems.

Then you learned how to compile the FreeS/WAN package into your kernel, and configure it to provide a secure WAN connection, or simply a secure connection between two systems.

Part IV

Security auditing

Chapter 22

Configuring syslog

IN THIS CHAPTER

◆ Understanding the syslog and klog daemons

◆ Configuring syslog.conf

◆ Understanding facilities and priorities

◆ Finding available facilities and priorities

◆ Configuring syslogd

◆ Understanding syslogd options

◆ Specifying options during bootup

THE SYSTEM LOGGER, syslog, will give you many clues about your system. All restricted services have a means to communicate with the syslog. But system logging seems lost on many system administrators. Often, they know it's there, but not how it works or how to configure it for their particular situation.

This chapter will show you what syslog is, what it does, how it works, and how you can put it to use for yourself. Your system comes with a default configuration, but because changing it seems like a black art to many, they ignore all the things syslog can do for them. This chapter will change all that.

Under Linux, two different loggers are started, the system logger and the kernel logger. Under default conditions, the kernel logger sends all messages to the system logger, where they merge with system log messages. The kernel logger, klogd, can be told to pass all kernel messages to a file other than syslog if so desired, but you have to tell it at startup. Just change the /etc/sysconfig/daemons/syslog file from:

```
OPTIONS_KLOGD="-k /boot/System.map-`uname -r`"
```

to

```
OPTIONS_KLOGD="-k /boot/System.map-`uname -r` -f /var/log/kmesg"
```

the -f and /path/to/filename option specify where to log messages.

> **TIP** Explore the files in /etc/sysconfig/daemons/ because all daemons launched at boot time are configured in this subdirectory.

The reason the kernel messages are normally passed to syslog and not to a file is that klogd has no facility for remote syslogging. When a number of static systems are set up in one location, it is often easier to designate one system as the central system logger than to have to process system logs on several systems. You'll look more at this capability below.

Basic syslog configuration

In order to understand what gets logged, when, and to where, you need to understand a few basic concepts about system logging. System logging can be broken down into three parts: a facility, a priority, and a logging location.

The syslog facility is the specific facility that a restricted service will write to. The facilities have specific definitions that can be found in /usr/include/sys/syslog.h. Portions of that file are shown in Listing 22-1.

Listing 22-1: Extract from /usr/include/sys/syslog.h showing syslog facilities

```
/* facility codes */
#define LOG_KERN (0<<3) /* kernel messages */
#define LOG_USER (1<<3) /* random user-level messages */
#define LOG_MAIL (2<<3) /* mail system */
#define LOG_DAEMON (3<<3) /* system daemons */
#define LOG_AUTH (4<<3) /* security/authorization messages */
#define LOG_SYSLOG (5<<3) /* messages generated internally by
syslogd */
#define LOG_LPR (6<<3) /* line printer subsystem */
#define LOG_NEWS (7<<3) /* network news subsystem */
#define LOG_UUCP (8<<3) /* UUCP subsystem */
#define LOG_CRON (9<<3) /* clock daemon */
#define LOG_AUTHPRIV (10<<3) /* security/authorization messages
(private) */
#define LOG_FTP (11<<3) /* ftp daemon */
 /* other codes through 15 reserved for system use */
#define LOG_LOCAL0 (16<<3) /* reserved for local use */
#define LOG_LOCAL1 (17<<3) /* reserved for local use */
#define LOG_LOCAL2 (18<<3) /* reserved for local use */
#define LOG_LOCAL3 (19<<3) /* reserved for local use */
#define LOG_LOCAL4 (20<<3) /* reserved for local use */
```

```
#define LOG_LOCAL5 (21<<3) /* reserved for local use */
#define LOG_LOCAL6 (22<<3) /* reserved for local use */
#define LOG_LOCAL7 (23<<3) /* reserved for local use */
#define LOG_NFACILITIES 24 /* current number of facilities */
#define LOG_FACMASK 0x03f8 /* mask to extract facility part */
 /* facility of pri */
#define LOG_FAC(p) (((p) & LOG_FACMASK) > 3)
#ifdef SYSLOG_NAMES
CODE facilitynames[] =
 {
 { "auth", LOG_AUTH },
 { "authpriv", LOG_AUTHPRIV },
 { "cron", LOG_CRON },
 { "daemon", LOG_DAEMON },
 { "ftp", LOG_FTP },
 { "kern", LOG_KERN },
 { "lpr", LOG_LPR },
 { "mail", LOG_MAIL },
 { "mark", INTERNAL_MARK }, /* INTERNAL */
 { "news", LOG_NEWS },
 { "security", LOG_AUTH }, /* DEPRECATED */
 { "syslog", LOG_SYSLOG },
 { "user", LOG_USER },
 { "uucp", LOG_UUCP },
 { "local0", LOG_LOCAL0 },
 { "local1", LOG_LOCAL1 },
 { "local2", LOG_LOCAL2 },
 { "local3", LOG_LOCAL3 },
 { "local4", LOG_LOCAL4 },
 { "local5", LOG_LOCAL5 },
 { "local6", LOG_LOCAL6 },
 { "local7", LOG_LOCAL7 },
 { NULL, -1 }
 };
#endif
```

The information in this file is included in every service that the developer feels should make use of the system log. As a basic guideline, all restricted services and all network services will have logging available. The upper portion, starting with #define statements, shows each of the facilities by code. These codes are translated farther down in the section on facilitynames. These facilitynames are the names that you will use to configure the syslog daemon. All you need to know is which log facility any particular service will use.

Examining the list of log facility names, many are self-explanatory or are explained in the facilitycodes as remarks. The ones that are not explained are the lo-

cal[1-7] facilitynames, which are for use by those services that don't have designated facilitynames. For example, while telnet doesn't show up, it will use the auth
and authpriv facilities because anyone telneting to the system will be authorized (or
not) based on a username/password pair login.

On the other hand, the program pppd, which runs as root (so it can alter routing
tables, read privileged files, etc.), doesn't have a specific facilityname identified with
it. So it logs messages to daemon, and if it is compiled with "debug", logs debug messages to local2. The OpenLinux version of pppd is compiled with debug by default.
But debug messages will not be written to local2 by default. You must turn this on
explicitly by putting kdebug 1 in your /etc/ppp/options file, or in the command string
that calls pppd.

If a program that uses system logging does not have a specific facility identified
with it, the developer can choose one. In some cases, this can be changed when the
program is compiled.

The second part of any system logging convention is the priority. This is the priority of the particular message to be logged or dropped. Not all possible messages for
every facility are logged. Priorities are also found in /usr/include/sys/syslog.h as
shown in Listing 22-2.

Listing 22-2: Extract of /usr/include/sys/syslog.h showing priorities

```
/* priorities (these are ordered)
 */
#define LOG_EMERG 0 /* system is unusable */
#define LOG_ALERT 1 /* action must be taken immediately */
#define LOG_CRIT 2 /* critical conditions */
#define LOG_ERR 3 /* error conditions */
#define LOG_WARNING 4 /* warning conditions */
#define LOG_NOTICE 5 /* normal but significant condition */
#define LOG_INFO 6 /* informational */
#define LOG_DEBUG 7 /* debug-level messages */

#define LOG_PRIMASK 0x07 /*mask to extract priority part(internal)*/
 /* extract priority */
#define LOG_PRI(p) ((p) & LOG_PRIMASK)
#define LOG_MAKEPRI(fac, pri) (((fac) << 3) | (pri))
#ifdef SYSLOG_NAMES
#define INTERNAL_NOPRI 0x10 /* the "no priority" priority */
 /* mark "facility" */
#define INTERNAL_MARK LOG_MAKEPRI(LOG_NFACILITIES, 0)
typedef struct _code {
 char *c_name;
 int c_val;
} CODE;

CODE prioritynames[] =
 {
```

```
 { "alert", LOG_ALERT },
 { "crit", LOG_CRIT },
 { "debug", LOG_DEBUG },
 { "emerg", LOG_EMERG },
 { "err", LOG_ERR },
 { "error", LOG_ERR }, /* DEPRECATED */
 { "info", LOG_INFO },
 { "none", INTERNAL_NOPRI }, /* INTERNAL */
 { "notice", LOG_NOTICE },
 { "panic", LOG_EMERG }, /* DEPRECATED */
 { "warn", LOG_WARNING }, /* DEPRECATED */
 { "warning", LOG_WARNING },
 { NULL, -1 }
 };
#endif
```

Based on the priority codes and their corresponding prioritynames, you now know that eight different priorities are available for services to report back on the state of the service. These codes are listed in order of priority in Listing 22-2.

OpenLinux comes with a standard syslog configuration file, /etc/syslog.conf. This configuration file contains most commonly configured services and points them to files down in /var/log. The standard configuration file is shown in Listing 22-3.

Listing 22-3: Default OpenLinux /etc/syslog.conf file

```
# Log all kernel messages to the console.
# Logging much else clutters up the screen.
kern.*          /dev/console
# Log everything (except mail and news) of level info or higher.
# Hmm--also don't log private authentication messages here!
*.info;news,mail,authpriv,auth.none -/var/log/messages
# Log debugging too
*.debug;news,mail,authpriv,auth.none -/var/log/debug
# The authpriv file has restricted access.
authpriv.*;auth.* /var/log/secure
# true, 'auth' in the two previous rules is deprecated,
# but nonetheless still in use...
# Log all the mail messages in one place.
mail.* /var/log/mail
# As long as innd insists on blocking /var/log/news
# (instead of using /var/log/news.d) we fall back to ...
#news.* /var/log/news.all
# Save uucp and news errors of level err and higher
# in a special file.
#uucp,news.err /var/log/spooler
# Everybody gets emergency messages, plus log them on
```

```
# another machine.
*.emerg *
#*.emerg @loghost
```

Lines beginning with "#" are comments and are ignored by syslogd. The comments are meant to help explain what is being logged where.

The syntax of the syslog.conf file is as follows:

```
facility.priority                        /path/to/logfile
```

A facility corresponds to the facilities discussed previously. The two parts are separated by a period. The priority listed is the minimum priority to be logged. That priority and any higher priorities will be logged unless further specified. The full path to the log file is then specified, and all messages for the designated facility at the designated priority or higher will be sent to that file.

The above example is the simplest case but does not suffice for all situations. While you could list each facility and priority one to a line, it is often easier to combine lines that will log to the same file. So decide which is less — the facilities you want to log or the facilities you don't want to log. The shorter list could be used, and the list separated by commas.

Successive definitions on a line rewrite preceding ones, either adding to or subtracting from previous declarations. This makes explicit exclusions possible. That, combined with the "*" for either facility or priority designating everything, makes possible short, succinct rules.

For example, if you want to log just lpr, news, and mail to one log (/var/log/lnm) with all messages of info or higher, you could use a line like the following:

```
lpr,news,mail.info                       /var/log/lnm
```

This is the same as writing:

```
lpr.info;news.info;mail.info             /var/log/mail
```

The two separators are the comma and the semicolon. The comma separates successive facilities entries. If priorities are included in a comma-separated list, all but the last priority is ignored. The semicolon separates full facility.priority pairs.

On the other hand, if you want to log all messages except cron and news messages to /var/log/messages, rather than list every facility except cron and news, you can use an exclusion:

```
*.*;news,cron,authpriv.none                    /var/log/messages
```

The first part, *.*, says log everything. But because specific listings later in the line rewrite the earlier ones, the "news,cron,authpriv.none" rewrites the news, cron, and authpriv facilities part. The special priority "none" tells syslogd that no priorities are of interest. So you've rewritten the line from log everything to log everything except news, cron, and authpriv messages.

 The authpriv facility is very sensitive. This facility should be written only to a secure (read-write root only) file because it may contain passwords.

Two additional signs may be used with priorities. These two are the = and ! signs meaning only and not exclusively, respectively. For example, if you wanted all facilities, but only debug priority logged to the file /var/log/debug, the following would work:

```
*.=debug                        /var/log/messages
```

If you also wanted info priorities logged, you could alter the above as follows:

```
*.!notice                       /var/log/debug
```

Progressing further, if you wanted all messages except info written to /var/log/noinfo, you could use the following:

```
*.!=info                        /var/log/noinfo
```

In this example, you've used both the ! and = to exclude only info priority messages. However, when you use both symbols, you must do so as shown in the example, the ! (not) first.

Up to now, you've specifically indicated a file for messages to go to. By default, syslogd issues a "sync" command after every write to flush the buffers and ensure that the entry is written to the file. This may help in the event that the system crashes. If the file isn't sync'd immediately, you could lose some valuable information about what was happening just prior to the crash.

But beware. If you have messages sent to a central logging server, having every message received immediately sync'd to disk will cause the system to do more writing and slow down other processes. So non-critical logs should be explicitly told not to sync. You can do this by prefixing the log file name with "-". The example from the Caldera-supplied default syslog.conf is:

```
*.debug;news,mail,authpriv,auth.none -/var/log/debug
```

In the above line, the debug log is not sync'd after every message.

The other specification that can be used as the target for all logging messages is @hostname, substituting your central logging server for hostname. This will send all messages you want logged out to the loghost on udp port 514.

The loghost must be set up to accept these messages, or they will be dropped.

Once the central logging server receives the messages, they will be handled by syslogd per the /etc/syslog.conf on that system. Messages without a destination (no facility.priority declaration or that facility.priority excluded) will be dropped.

While you can do a simple:

```
*.*               @central-log-host
```

and let the central logger determine whether to log or drop the message, doing so will create additional traffic on your network.

A central logging host should block unauthorized clients from sending syslog messages. Further, the logs should be maintained on a non-root file system. This will preclude a denial of service attack aimed at filling the logfile and stopping the log server.

One final destination specification is available: a user list. This can be a comma-separated list of users to send messages to. This is normally done only for emergency priority messages. A user who is not logged in will not get the message. Use "*" to designate all. This uses the wall command to broadcast to every logged-in user on the local network. Since emergency messages are reserved for systems about to panic, they are rare, and you will want to get the message no matter who you're logged in as.

syslogd

Setting up the syslog.conf file is only half of the equation. Some options can be activated only on the syslogd startup command line. You did this earlier during the creation of a chroot DNS server by specifying the -a and the path to the additional log file to watch. But this was only one of the options.

The default configuration file for syslogd is /etc/syslog.conf. This can be overridden by use of the -f switch and a full path and filename of the alternate configuration file.

In order to allow syslogd to act as a central logging server, it must be able to receive messages from clients. To turn on receiving of messages, you need to specify the -r option. Note that, since syslog listens on UDP port 514 for syslog messages, syslog must be run as root, since only root can bind ports below 1024. Also, syslog will not forward any messages received from a client. That is, if the /etc/syslog.conf file for the host receiving messages from another client lists yet another host as the target for a particular facility, those messages received from the remote client(s) will not be sent on — that is, unless the -h option is specified.

With the -h option, messages can be relayed from a client to a server, then on to another server. Under normal circumstances, you wouldn't want to do this. But if you have systems outside a firewall, the central logging server is inside the firewall, and you aren't forwarding UDP port 514 on the firewall to the central server, the firewall can act as a relay. This is not an ideal situation, but will work.

If you do choose to use a central server, your systems will be logged with their fully qualified domain name. This could lead to some very long log lines. The way around this is to specify the -l option. This option uses a colon-separated list of hosts whose hostname listed in the syslog is only to be the hostname. Alternately, you can use the -s option to specify a comma-separated list of domains whose domain name should be dropped from the log.

These two options are not the same, despite their similarity. The -l will log only the hosts short name. The -s will drop the domain name. Assume the following address: roadrunner.marketing.acme.com. If you specify -l and your host roadrunner, you'll only see the name roadrunner in the log as only the originating host. If you specify -s acme.com, only the acme.com will be stripped off, and the logs will have the host roadrunner.marketing. This can be handy if you have subdomains and hostnames duplicated in the different subdomains.

Another handy option is the -p option. With this option, you can easily change the socket (name or location) that syslogd is using to write through. The purpose of this would not be to enhance security. The default is /dev/log. Little reason exists to hide this pipe; it is easily visible to anyone who can run netstat on the host as shown in the abbreviated Listing 22-4.

Listing 22-4: Abbreviated listing of netstat -a output showing syslog pipe

```
Active UNIX domain sockets (servers and established)
Proto RefCnt Flags Type State I-Node Path
unix 0 [ ACC ] STREAM LISTENING 12556 /dev/log
unix 1 [ ] STREAM CONNECTED 12560 /dev/log
```

And while anyone can read from or write to this socket, there's little reason to do so. What intruders will want to do is remove entries from the logs. So logs should be writable only by root (or the user syslog is running as).

 For security purposes, syslogd may be run as a non-privileged user, but will not be able to be used as a central logging facility. This is because only root can bind UDP port 514.

Other options are available for syslogd, but only one final option will be discussed here. The -m option can be used to set marks in the log files. While "mark" is available as a facility, it is not a standard facility, and it exists only to put time ticks in the logs. This particular "feature" seems to annoy a lot of folks. But those marks, or the absence of them, can suggest that the logs have been tampered with. The default interval is 20 minutes. The -m switch (which takes the time interval in minutes as an argument) can alter the time between ticks. If a time interval of 0 is designated, marks will cease to be sent to the log files.

What are you looking for?

Of course, once you have system logging set up, what is it you want to see? Or better yet, what can you obtain from system logging that you'll want to have set up? Mostly, you'll be interested from a security point of view about activities of users on your system or connections to your system from the outside.

While system logging provides ample information about what any particular service is doing, often providing debugging information for errant processes, etc., this is the realm of system administration and won't be addressed here. Often these messages are quite detailed regarding a problem.

From a security standpoint, you'll want to know if local users are using the su command or a login prompt to gain root access. This will usually show up best if someone logs in as a user, then performs an su to root. One of the most used methods for gaining root access by local users is social engineering. The infamous cracker Kevin Mitnick used this method to gain access to systems he was not authorized to enter. Restricting root logins to local terminals, denying root access via telnet will help. This is the default configuration in OpenLinux.

For external connections, you'll want to know if anyone is probing (scanning) your system for open ports. In order to attempt to root your system, a cracker must first know what's available to make an attempt against. So you'll see a number of different ports connected to from outside. Some time later, you may or may notice a connect that is just trying to get a status from the server, not actually use it. The cracker wants to narrow down the tools by finding out which server you're running, and which version. Armed with this information and a quick search for vulnerabilities, the cracker will begin the attempt. This may show up as a connection with syslog showing invalid data from a client. This invalid data is probably a buffer overflow attempt. The syslog'd string may look like garbage, but will contain a full legitimate path to an executable.

Network scanning is the subject of Chapter 25, "Using network monitoring tools."

If you're lucky, one of two things has occurred: The program core dumped and exited, or the program trapped the bad data, rejected and logged it, and continued. If you're not so lucky, the program just spawned a root shell as it exited (probably ungracefully), leaving the attacker sitting with a root prompt from your system on his terminal. Sounds too easy? That's why large portions of the Internet have turned into such a zoo.

You'll read more about reading log files in Chapter 23, "Reading var/log/ files."

Summary

In this chapter you learned how to set up system logging. You learned the syntax for the /etc/syslog.conf file. You learned about legal values for the facility and priority and where they came from. You learned how to read and write logging specifications. You also learned how to designate the various targets for log messages.

Then you learned how to turn on certain options at the syslogd command line and where to put those options to start up each time the system boots. You learned about setting up a central system logger and syslog vulnerabilities from Denial of Service attacks.

Chapter 23

Reading var/log/ files

IN THIS CHAPTER

◆ Understanding log file types and locations

◆ Understanding log file permissions

◆ Understanding how system logging works

◆ Using dmesg

◆ Reading non-ASCII logs

IN THE PRECEDING CHAPTER, you learned how to manage syslog and tailor it so that you could log those things you wanted to log. This chapter will look at some of those log files, plus a few other log files on the system.

Most log files are created as simple ASCII text files. You can read them with any text editor or just cat them to the console or xterminal. But as you begin to examine them, you'll begin to see many routine messages that can be ignored. They are there if you need them, but to read through them on a routine basis wouldn't accomplish much beyond establishing what is normal and what is abnormal.

You do need to discover your system's baseline information — that is, the kind of messages you normally have — so that you'll notice anything out of the ordinary. Of course, since you're talking about hundreds or thousands (perhaps more) of entries per day, you're better off using a script to cull the routine entries (once you learn what they are) and show you just the "anomalies."

If you see anomalous activity, such as an entry containing:

`H^N^L^K^^N^H^V^L^^?^?^?/bin/sh^^?^?^?^?^?^?^?^?^?^?^?^?`

an attempt (perhaps successful, perhaps not) has been made on your system. Begin an assessment immediately; there's nothing random about "/bin/sh".

/var/log files

The subdirectory /var/log, as you learned in the previous chapter, is the default location for system logging files. Most log files are created by syslog if they don't exist. A couple of log files (not created by syslog) must be created manually (these will be discussed later).

Just because log files are created, if not already present, does not mean they were created properly. Study your /var/log directory. You want to think about what goes into each log and whether or not you want to allow anyone else to be able to view those files.

If the log files have incorrect permissions on them, performing a simple chmod to change the mode will suffice. Some log files may be of use to "power users" or advanced users who compile and run their own programs that may output debugging or other results to syslog. They would want to be able to see certain files. This determination must be made on a site-by-site, system-by-system basis. Most likely, if you are large enough to want to use a central logging server, this server will be restricted and not permit casual logins.

Certain log files should never be readable by the public. Any file containing authpriv.* messages could contain passwords. A sample line containing a password in the "secure" log file will appear as in Listing 23-1.

Listing 23-1: A /var/log/secure log file extract

```
Oct 3 16:22:54 volcan login[1549]: FAILED LOGIN 1 FROM (null) FOR
mypassword, User not known to the underlying authentication module
```

What the above message is telling me is that someone called 'mypassword' tried to log in but was denied because he doesn't exist. A user just goofed and put in his password instead of his username. This actually occurs frequently with folks used to Windows, which has the last user logged in listed by default. These are the remnants of the "one host, one user" mentality that plagues all Windows systems, and conditions those users to having to enter only a password as if the system should know who they are. So the user login failed to log in on the first try. The very next entry shows that root successfully logged in. So the log shows a legitimate password (mypassword), and the next line shows who logged in, and someone examining this file doesn't need to guess whose password he has.

 If you use any log rotation software, ensure that the software creates a replacement file with the correct permissions for that log.

The various files and directories in /var/log, which should be reserved exclusively for use by log files, should look something like Listing 23-2.

Listing 23-2: Listing of the /var/log directory

```
drwxr-xr-x 2 root root 1024 Oct 27 00:00 atsar
drwxr-x--- 2 root root 1024 Oct 25 12:42 httpd
-rw-r--r-- 1 root root 1702 Aug 5 09:06 kdm
-rw-r--r-- 1 root root 146876 Oct 27 06:50 lastlog
-rw------- 1 root root 180264 Oct 27 09:34 mail
-rw------- 1 root root 323304 Oct 25 11:58 mail.0.gz
drwxr-xr-x 2 majordom majordom 1024 Jul 27 19:55 majordomo
-rw------- 1 root root 1425209 Oct 27 09:39 messages
-rw------- 1 root root 1667546 Oct 25 12:05 messages.0.gz
drwxr-xr-x 3 news news 1024 Aug 5 08:52 news.d
drwxr-xr-x 2 root root 1024 Jul 28 00:00 samba.d
-rw------- 1 root root 331161 Oct 27 09:38 secure
-rw------- 1 root root 0 Aug 5 09:04 spooler
drwxr-x--- 2 root root 1024 Jul 14 20:08 squid
drwxr-xr-x 2 uucp uucp 1024 Jul 27 20:53 uucp
-rw-rw-r-- 1 root utmp 1276032 Oct 27 09:37 wtmp
-rw-r--r-- 1 root root 4193 Oct 25 11:16 xdm-errors
-rw------- 1 root root 52626 Oct 27 08:57 xferlog
```

Note that some of the files are world readable. On this system, these files were deemed necessary for some users to be able to read, and in any case, contained nothing sensitive. Some files, principally those in subdirectories, are created by programs other than syslog. In some cases, they belong to other users. Generally, if a program is going to create a log file, this file must be owned by the user that program is running as. If the files and directories were owned by root, some programs, like uucp, majordomo, etc., couldn't write to the subdirectory or file without being world writable. Not a good idea.

How system logging works

When dealing with syslogd, you should understand what happens when syslogd starts. The syslog daemon, syslogd, is one of the first processes started early in the system startup process. This is done to allow syslog to begin logging all messages immediately.

The first thing syslog does is read the /etc/syslog.conf file (as described in the previous chapter). It creates a socket (by default /dev/log) to write through, and attaches that socket to all log files listed in /etc/syslog.conf (or other configuration file specified on the command line).

Once syslogd is ready to start writing, it reads the kernel ring buffer. This is how all those kernel messages you see during bootup about what the system is detecting get transferred into the system logs. Since syslogd hasn't started until after the kernel boots, the kernel must store kernel messages in a buffer. In fact, all kernel messages are so stored until the buffer is full. Then the oldest messages are over-written first.

You can start syslogd as a non-privileged user to avoid the problems that can arise if a vulnerability is found and exploited in syslogd. However, before you do, you must consider one thing: syslogd cannot bind the syslog port as a non-root user. This would not necessarily preclude the system from use as a central logging server, but you would need to have syslog bind a port above 1024 and have all UDP packets arriving on port 514 redirected to that higher port. You can do this by changing the /etc/services definition of syslog, then using a redirector (ipchains, etc.) to redirect UDP port 514 to the new syslog port. If syslogd is told to open the syslog port (via the -r option) and can't, it will exit with an error.

You must also ensure that all files in /var/log that are writable only by root are writable by the new syslogd user. The directory and files by default are configured for writing by root. You must change the ownership of the log files, or syslogd will not be able to write to the logs.

Once syslogd is up and running, the log files are always active. That is, they are always open. This can be easily seen by using `lsof` to show a list of all open files. Listing 23-3 has been grep'd for "log", and the results further refined to show only those entries of interest.

Listing 23-3: Extract of lsof output showing syslog and klog entries

```
COMMAND    PID    USER    FD     TYPE    DEVICE      SIZE      NODE   NAME
syslogd    1040   root    cwd    DIR     3,1         1024         2   /
syslogd    1040   root    rtd    DIR     3,1         1024         2   /
syslogd    1040   root    txt    REG     3,1        27772    184444
/usr/sbin/syslogd
syslogd    1040   root    0u     unix    0xc7feccc0   118     22643   /dev/log
syslogd    1040   root    1u     unix    0xc21d7000   118     22645
/home/dns/dev/log
syslogd    1040   root    2u     unix    0xc5166360   118     65006   /dev/log
syslogd    1040   root    4w     CHR     4,0          123       388   /dev/tty0
syslogd    1040   root    5w     REG     3,11      524040     75780
/var/log/messages
syslogd    1040   root    6u     unix    0xc2577960 52739        52   /dev/log
syslogd    1040   root    7u     unix    0xc68bb000   118     19313   /dev/log
syslogd    1040   root    8u     inet    612          UDP         *   :syslog
syslogd    1040   root    9u     unix    0xc21d7960    61         5   /dev/log
syslogd    1040   root    10u    unix    0xc214d680    65         1   /dev/log
syslogd    1040   root    11u    unix    0xc214dcc0    66         3   /dev/log
syslogd    1040   root    12u    unix    0xc2c7a680 56748        55
/home/dns/dev/log
syslogd    1040   root    13u    unix    0xc2577640    19        81   /dev/log
syslogd    1040   root    14w    REG     3,1       333293     75968
/var/log/secure
```

```
syslogd   1040   root   15w   REG     3,1   191389   75781
/var/log/mail
syslogd   1040   root   16w   REG     3,1        0   75970
/var/log/news.all
syslogd   1040   root   17w   REG     3,1        0   75971
/var/log/spooler
klogd     1043   root   cwd   DIR     3,1     1024        2   /
klogd     1043   root   rtd   DIR     3,1     1024        2   /
klogd     1043   root   txt   REG     3,1    19932   184443
/usr/sbin/klogd
klogd     1043   root   0r    REG     0,2        0        5   /proc/kmsg
klogd     1043   root   1u    unix  0xc21d76     40      614   socket
```

Examining the right-most column, you'll see that several processes are connecting through the /dev/log socket. The /home/dns/dev/log socket is the one you created in Chapter 14, and will not be explained further. The entry *:syslog shows syslogd binding the syslog port to receive messages from other servers. That can be easily seen in the UDP section of a `netstat -an` listing.

Each of the active log files is also obvious in the above listing. The log files messages, mail, news.all, secure, and spooler, all show up.

Since syslog maintains contact with these log files, they cannot be arbitrarily moved, renamed, or deleted. If an active log file is moved or renamed, the moved or renamed file will continue to receive messages. That is, if you move messages to messages.0 and then `touch messages`, the messages.0 file is the one that will continue to grow. You've literally connected a pipe from syslogd to the file messages at startup, and now that it's been renamed, the pipe is still connected to it. The file can be edited, but the pipe will remain connected until syslogd is restarted.

Reading log files

Most log files—all those written by syslogd—are easily read. The following line is typical of a syslog entry:

```
Oct 3 10:56:18 volcan sshd[5915]: log: Generating 768 bit RSA key.
```

The format will always be the same. The first column is the date and time the log entry occurred. The time is local server time. The next entry is the host making the log entry. This will often be the fully qualified domain name for external hosts on a central logging server, but that can be changed on the command line (see previous chapter). In this case, the local system name is volcan. The next column is the particular daemon that created the entry, here sshd, and the PID (process ID of the process). The PID isn't always included. Then comes the actual entry—that is, the message the daemon is sending. You can see that this message is a log message telling you that sshd (the Secure Shell Daemon), PID 5915, regenerated the 768-bit encryption key for connection purposes.

So root can easily read any syslogd-created log. No special programs are required. But some programs are available for use. The first of these is dmesg. The dmesg program, depite what some may think, doesn't read a log file at all. This particular utility reads the kernel's ring buffer. The ring buffer is just a buffer like any other except that it is deliberately designed to wrap around back onto itself, in a circle or ring.

The dmesg utility will return the last 8192 (not 8196 as the documentation suggests) bytes from the kernel ring buffer. This matches the size of the old 2.0.*x* kernel ring buffers. The size of the ring buffer was increased at some point prior to 2.2.13 to 16384 bytes. If you wish to see the entire buffer, you can specify the -s<number> option with dmesg:

```
dmesg -s16284
```

This will show you the entire ring buffer. If you believe you need a larger buffer, you can make the change in:

```
/usr/src/linux/kernel/printk.c to LOG_BUF_LEN. If you do increase
the size, you should make it an even mutltiple of 8192 bytes.
```

TIP Because dmesg reads the kernel ring buffer and not the /var/log/messages file, even if the system is booted with "init=/bin/sh", the kernel ring buffer messages are still available for hardware troubleshooting.

Two more options exist for use with dmesg; however, only one of these can be used at a time. Either may be used with the '-s', but not with each other. The two options are -c, which will clear the ring buffer, and -n<#>, which will tell syslogd the lowest messages to send to the console. If you want only panic messages to go to the console, specify -n 1. As the number increases, the allowed priority decreases, allowing more to be logged. For a sample of the kinds of messages you'll get from dmesg, see Listing 23-4.

Listing 23-4: Extract of dmesg output

```
ppp: channel ppp0 closing.
ppp0 released
ppp0: ccp closed
hdb: ATAPI 24X CD-ROM drive, 120kB Cache
Uniform CDROM driver Revision: 2.56
VFS: Disk change detected on device ide0(3,64)
ISO 9660 Extensions: Microsoft Joliet Level 3
```

```
ISOFS: changing to secondary root
Uniform CD-ROM driver unloaded
PPP: ppp line discipline successfully unregistered
CSLIP: code copyright 1989 Regents of the University of California
PPP: version 2.3.7 (demand dialling)
PPP line discipline registered.
registered device ppp0
```

None of these log messages contains the date, time, or system, just the log entry you see here. The rest is added by syslogd after the kernel messages are handed off.

utmp, wtmp, and lastlog

While the file created by syslogd and some other daemons that create their own logs (such as uucp, httpd, et. al) are easily readable ASCII files, some are not. Notably, three files, lastlog, utmp and wtmp, which maintain login information, are not.

Do not be surprised if you cannot find utmp or wtmp residing on your system. If these files are moved or removed (or just never created), record keeping is turned off. This is considered a feature for those who don't want those files. If you do want those files and they don't exist, you'll need to create them. A simple `touch *file-name*` in the correct directory will suffice. These files provide login information and are used by several programs. The correct directory for wmtp is /var/log, while the correct directory for utmp is /var/run.

 Nothing will be harmed if utmp or wtmp isn't created, but record accounting will be turned off. This may be desirable on a small system that is not generally accessible.

The utmp file contains information about current logins. The wtmp file contains historical login data. The lastlog file contains information about the last time a user successfully logged in and from where. These files are used by last, lastlog, uptime, utmpdump, w, and who. The files are in a binary format, so they cannot be read directly, although each can be read by one or more of the above programs. If you don't want users to be able to use who, for example, you can simply change the utmp mode so it is not world readable.

Although utmp and wtmp maintain login information, not all programs use them. Some programs, such as xdm (or kdm) cannot, or should not, create utmp records, although they will create wtmp records. This has to do with the way a user logs in when using xdm or kdm. None of the display manager programs has a controlling TTY, so the record isn't valid, and the login is not supposed to create a utmp record. This means that xdm and kdm act similarly to FTP, which writes only to wtmp.

 The controlling terminal is the terminal the process was started from, and where all its messages will be directed to (unless either standard output and standard error, or both, is specifically redirected).

Examining the output from several of the programs that use utmp and wtmp reveals the information about logins, reboots, etc. The first is heavily edited output in Listing 23-5 from `last`.

Listing 23-5: Output from last (edited for brevity)

```
david pts/2 volcan.pananix.c Thu Oct 28 08:50 - 08:54 (00:03)
david pts/1 volcan.pananix.c Thu Oct 28 07:52 still logged in
david pts/1 volcan.pananix.c Wed Oct 27 22:38 - 22:55 (00:17)
david pts/2 Wed Oct 27 20:49 - 08:50 (12:00)
root tty2 Wed Oct 27 20:48 - 21:12 (00:23)
david ftp volcan.pananix.c Wed Oct 27 19:15 - 19:16 (00:01)
reboot system boot 2.2.13 Sun Oct 24 08:46 (4+00:18)
root tty1 Sun Oct 24 08:31 - crash (00:14)
```

The above listing comes from the wtmp file. Reading across, you have user, controlling terminal (or ftp or system boot), host (if not localhost, or kernel version if system boot), date and time of login and logout (or GMT offset if system boot). One note: The last entry shows "crash" in the ending login column. This does not indicate that the system crashed; in fact this was a controlled shutdown. But the login session terminated because of a runlevel change, so the login session exited abnormally.

The output (truncated) from lastlog, shown in Listing 23-6, displays information from /var/log/lastlog and correlates that against /etc/passwd.

Listing 23-6: Truncated output from lastlog

```
Username Port From Latest
root tty2 Wed Oct 27 20:48:59 1999
bin **Never logged in**
daemon **Never logged in**
majordom **Never logged in**
postgres **Never logged in**
mysql **Never logged in**
silvia tty1 Sat Aug 7 22:55:54 1999
david pts/2 volcan.pananix.c Thu Oct 28 08:50:18 1999
dns **Never logged in**
```

The uptime program uses information from utmp to determine information about logins but uses /proc for process information. The uptime output appears as follows:

```
10:11am up 2 days, 19:29, 1 user, load average: 0.00, 0.01, 0.00
```

The only field that comes from utmp is the column containing number of users, in this case, 1.

The utmpdump program will read any file provided on the command line, but can only interpret the /var/run/utmp and /var/log/wtmp files, since they have similar formats. Truncated output from utmp is shown in Listing 23-7, and from wtmp in Listing 23-8.

Listing 23-7: Dump of utmp

```
Utmp dump of /var/run/utmp
[8] [00651] [bw ] [ ] [ ] [ ] [0.0.0.0 ] [Sun Oct 24 08:46:17 1999
EST]
[1] [20021] [~~ ] [runlevel] [~ ] [ ] [0.0.0.0 ] [Sun Oct 24
08:46:17 1999 EST]
[8] [00899] [15 ] [ ] [ ] [ ] [0.0.0.0 ] [Sun Oct 24 08:46:40 1999
EST]
[8] [09264] [P001] [ ] [pts/1 ] [ ] [0.0.0.0 ] [Wed Oct 27 22:55:41
1999 EST]
[7] [13696] [P001] [david ] [pts/1 ] [volcan.pananix.com] [0.0.0.0 ]
[Thu Oct 28 07:52:07 1999 EST]
```

Given that the dump of utmp should show only current login sessions, some very old entries remain. In fact, if you compare a dump of wtmp to utmp, it is obvious that there are several stale entries. They remain because the sessions terminated abnormally. Reading the table from left to right, you should see an id in the first column. This will be a single-digit number, and has little value. The second number is the PID of the process. If you searched this system for the listed PIDs, you would find only the last PID, 13696 active. The third column is one of ~~, bw, a number, or a letter and number. These correspond to a runlevel change or reboot, a bootwait process, and either a TTY number or PTY letter/number combination. The fourth column will be null, a user, reboot, or runlevel, depending on information available. The fifth column will contain a controlling TTY or PTY if known. The sixth column is the hostname of the remote host or blank if localhost. The seventh column should display the IP address of the remote system. And the last column is the date and time of the entry. Both utmp and wtmp tables show the same information.

Listing 23-8: Truncated output from wtmp

```
Utmp dump of /var/log/wtmp
[2] [00000] [~~ ] [reboot ] [~ ] [2.2.12 ] [0.0.0.0
```

```
] [Fri Aug 27 20:40:16 1999 EST]
[8] [00631] [bw ] [ ] [ ] [ ] [0.0.0.0
] [Fri Aug 27 20:40:16 1999 EST]
[1] [20021] [~~ ] [runlevel] [~ ] [ ] [0.0.0.0
] [Fri Aug 27 20:40:16 1999 EST]
[5] [00879] [15 ] [ ] [ ] [ ] [0.0.0.0
] [Fri Aug 27 20:40:16 1999 EST]
[7] [02976] [/3 ] [silvia ] [pts/3 ] [ ] [0.0.0.0
] [Fri Aug 27 23:35:42 1999 EST]
[8] [02753] [1 ] [ ] [tty1 ] [ ] [0.0.0.0
] [Fri Aug 27 23:40:10 1999 EST]
[7] [13368] [ ] [david ] [ftpd13368 ] [volcan.pananix.com] [0.0.0.0
 ] [Thu Oct 07 08:09:30 1999 EST]
```

In Listing 23-7, the utmp table is in cronological order from top to bottom. The wtmp table in Listing 23-8 will be in cronological order, but reversed, entries nearer the bottom being older.

The final listing, Listing 23-9, showing output from w and who, are also combined listings that use data from utmp and /proc to display the provided information.

```
[root@chiriqui]# w
 10:35am up 2 days, 19:52, 1 user, load average: 0.00, 0.00, 0.00
USER TTY FROM LOGIN@ IDLE JCPU PCPU WHAT
david pts/1 volcan.pananix.c 7:52am 0.00s 0.25s 0.02s w

[root@chiriqui]# who
david pts/1 Oct 28 07:52 (volcan.pananix.com)
```

The w command provides slightly more information regarding the system and what users are doing than just who, but the output of who is easier to use as input to scripts. Both show the user david logged in on psuedo-terminal 1 since 7:52 a.m. on 28 Oct from the remote host volcan. The w command also provides information regarding how much processing david has done from that psuedo-terminal. If this user had other sessions opened that are now closed, the amount of resource usage for those would not be shown. The w command also shows the command process david is running, as well as information in the first line about system uptime.

All the above commands have various switches to change their behavior, and only the basic command was illustrated. Depending on what is logged, a lot of information regarding the health of the system can be derived. But one thing should become apparent: The logs cannot be completely trusted.

Those who gain root access to a system can, and likely will, alter logs to hide their presence and activities. Unless logs are written directly to printers or non-erasable media, they should be considered suspect.

Let me emphasize that point. Log files may not be complete or totally accurate. They may be altered or have information added or deleted. The information available also depends on what daemons are running, collecting information for logging in their own files or passing to syslog.

System logging on sensitive systems (such as firewalls) can and probably should be set up directly to a printer. In this case, you'll want to log judiciously to have enough information, without overtaxing the printer.

Summary

This chapter has provided information about the contents of some common log files found on your system. While not perfect, they can provide you information about system activity for anything from debugging purposes to user login and usage information. You should now have a better understanding of how these logs work, and how syslog itself works, as well as complementary programs. Shortcomings of the syslog system should also be clear.

Chapter 24

Using network security monitoring tools

IN THIS CHAPTER

◆ Securing your system

◆ Following initial system installation

◆ Recurring tasks

ONE OF THE MORE difficult and cumbersome tasks new administrators face, particularly if they've never used any form of UNIX before, is maintaining the system and its security. Often, the manner in which they go about maintaining system security is reminiscent of the blind men describing an elephant. Some learn that it's important to check the system logs daily, some learn that checking the intergrity of the system files is important, some know to look for rogue programs binding a port as root, and so on. But what is most important is putting it all together.

Some tasks need to be accomplished more often than others. On a small, single-user system, connected to the Internet only intermittently, with packet filter rules to block all privileged ports, and only one user, many tasks can be performed once a week, or even once a month. On the same system, connected to the Internet 24-7 with a large number of daily accesses and many users, these same tasks must be performed daily.

The bottom line is, it depends. The only person who can make decisions about how often tasks should be accomplished is the administrator. These decisions should involve sound reasoning on the administrator's part.

When the system is loaded

The best place to start is before connecting to a network. At this point, after that system is loaded, but before you've connected anywhere or permitted anyone to enter (either via a network or the console), you can be relatively certain that the system is intact and contains no Trojans, etc.

This assumes you trust your distribution. Companies like Caldera and Red Hat go to great lengths to see that everything is installed in a manner that is safe for that program. That is, when you install the netkit-telnet RPM, the server (telnet daemon) and client are installed with the safest configuration possible. The server is also enabled.

If you need the telnet client, but don't need the telnet server, then you'll want to disable the telnet server. But the file and directory permissions on the files and file ownerships will be correct.

First, take stock of your system. One program included with the "dailyscript" package is called check-packages, and is installed in /etc/cron.d/lib to be run daily when dailyscript is installed. If you install and run this package, you will get an error message on the first run because the database for comparisons does not yet exist. If you run it a second time, you should see no differences between the two runs (except you won't get the error message). Now, each time this script is run, the only thing you will be presented with is the changes. The script will take approximately 15 minutes to run on a fairly full Caldera install. If you don't want to install dailyscript, you can get the same thing out by running `rpm -qa` and saving the output to a file. Then use `rpm -Va` and save the output to a different file. Whenever you want to compare your system with the original, just repeat the procedure, and then compare the outputs of each command with the outputs of those commands you generated when the system was new. If all looks well, save the new outputs for comparison next time. That's basically all the check-packages script does. It just saves the files on the hard drive. You'll want to put them on a floppy, and lock the floppy away for safekeeping.

If you also save to a file the output of:

```
find / -perm +600 -print
```

You'll have a list of all SUID/SGID file (directories and executables). Performing this task occasionally and comparing it to the original will tell you if new SUID/SGID files show up.

A quick check of the /etc/passwd file for all users with UID or GID of 0 (only root and a few system accounts should have entries with UID or GID of 0):

```
grep ":0:" /etc/passwd
```

And a check to ensure that no account has a null password:

```
awk -F: ' { print $2 ":" $1 } ' /etc/shadow | grep "^:" - | sed
"s/://g" -
```

Once you go through /etc/inetd.conf and comment out all unneeded services and restart (or SIGHUP) inetd, then it's time to begin "hardening" your system. When you do go through /etc/inetd.conf, if you don't know what it is, comment it out. When you finish, if you have any more than ftp, pop3, and swat, you probably have too much.

Last but not least, edit /etc/aliases and make sure the entry near the bottom of the file is changed so that root's mail goes to a user. Don't forget to run `newaliases`.

Rebuild your kernel

The next step is to rebuild your kernel. The wisest choice is to connect to the Internet, download the latest pristine kernel source, and compile it. While there is likely nothing wrong with the Caldera-supplied kernel, it's probably not the latest, and can often be difficult to build because of modifications and patches added. If you have little or no experience, using a pristine source and following the instructions in any of the many administration books will have you running a new kernel, built for your system (and therefore faster and leaner) in no time. This will also prepare you to install the FreeS/WAN package, if you wish, as in Chapter 21. This applies to Red Hat, Mandrake, SuSE, and in fact, most distributions. While the various distributions understandably want to give you more for your money, the kernel package is the most important part of the system and should be treated as such. Get the latest pristine kernel so you know it's properly built for your system.

Once you've rebuilt and rebooted into your new kernel, ideally with support for ipchains, you can start blocking ports that localhost may be using, but that you have no need for outsiders to access. Alternately, this may include allowing internal systems to access some services as well, just not external services.

Install and configure ipchains

If you haven't installed ipchains, this is a good time to do so. Start by configuring ipchains to block (deny or reject) all (or most) incoming connections below port 1024. As you find it necessary, begin opening ports, one at a time, as they are needed. But make sure these ports are ones with relatively secure daemons. The telnet and imap daemons are two of the biggest headaches for administrators. And unless you feel confident of your abilities to spot an intruder, you probably won't want those ports open to the world. You can also configure your system to use tripwire as secondary protection.

For more information on ipchains, see Chapter 16.

Daily/weekly/monthly security tasks

In Chapters 22 and 23 you learned about syslog. Apart from the checks for SUID/SGID files, the integrity of the installed files (rpm -qa and rpm -Va), and a quick look for users with UID/GID 0, and null passwords, the log files will tell you what, if anything, has been taking place while the system has been on.

If you decide to use the dailyscript package (modified for OpenLinux), you will want to let this script run once per day. The script itself performs many sanity checks, mostly going over the log files, but also running the rpm scripts (checkpackage) and some maillog checks. The script will then mail root (you have aliased that account to yourself, haven't you?) the results of the day's run. You can follow the next few paragraphs in Listing 24-1.

If you run a program that periodically rotates your logs, make sure dailyscript runs and can finish before the log rotate program moves them.

First, dailyscript uses last (which reads wtmp) to check a list of who logged in. If wtmp does not exist, then this particular portion of the report will be blank. Various entries here may also be in error. For example, they may show "still logged in" when in fact that connection terminated abnormally. It may or may not show up as a remote connection when it was. What it will show is who logged in and the initial access time.

Second, dailyscript greps through /var/log/messages looking for anomalous messages — those that don't fit a general description (via a regex pattern). This shows you anything "strange" in /var/log/message. You may find the first few runs you need to narrrow this down. Most outgoing ppp and chat messages are not "anomalous." You can adjust what appears here by judiciously putting select words in /etc/dailscript.conf in the ALWAYS_IGNORE="variable". That variable needs to be a quoted, space-separated list of words (usually syslog facility names) to ignore. So if the ALWAYS_IGNORE variable contains "pppd chat" you won't see these often unnecessary messages (see Listing 24-1).

Listing 24-1: Abbreviated listing of /etc/dailyscript.conf

```
TMP2=/var/tmp
SERVICES="syslog named identd pam PAM_pwdb ftpd in.ftpd sshd kernel
talkd in.telnetd in.rlogind login xntpd CRON --"
SCRIPTDIR=/usr/local/sbin/dailyscript
SEDSCRIPT1=$SCRIPTDIR/sed-script-1
SEDSCRIPT2=$SCRIPTDIR/sed-script-2
MAILSTATS=$SCRIPTDIR/todays_stats
MAILLIST=$SCRIPTDIR/smtpstats
```

```
LOGFILES="/var/log/messages /var/log/secure"
ALWAYSIGNORE="chat pppd cardmgr Pluto"
INCOMINGDIRS="/home/ftp/pub/incoming"
PERMDIR=/var/local/dailyscript
MAILLOG=/var/log/mail
```

The /etc/dailyscript.conf file can be used to configure what you get and what you don't get. Obviously, anything not logged can't be shown (see below), but what is in the logs can be adjusted. The pertinent lines for performing any adjustments are the "LOGFILES" line, which tells dailyscript which files to read; ALWAYS_ IGNORE, which tells dailyscript which facilities not to report on; and MAILLOG, which tells dailyscript which file to use for the mail statistics.

The script's only shortcoming is that it was intended for use on each machine performing its own logging, not for a central logging server.

If you are running a central logging server, you may want to adjust dailyscript itself to work with each system's logs separately. As the script is currently, you'll get one report with the log entries jumbled together. The simplest way to fix this is to create a loop just after the current day's entries are pulled from the logs to loop through each system. That will at least provide separate reports for each system. Note that, since wtmp is not one of the logfiles with entries sent to a central logging server, you'll need to run the script in Listing 24-2 on each system to get the equivalent of the entire dailyscript report for each system.

Listing 24–2: Script to get the list of users who logged on

```
D=`date -d "1 day ago" +"%b %d" | sed 's/ 0/  /'`
mail you@your.org -s "People who logged on to `hostname`" <<EOF
$(last -ad | grep $D | grep -v ".* *ftp" | cut -c-22,34- )
.
EOF
```

To modify dailyscript to provide separate sections per system, do the following:

1. Just before the line "# Set up temporary directory" put the following two lines:

   ```
   for s in `echo $SYSTEMS`
   do
   ```

   and put a line at the end of the script:

   ```
   done
   ```

2. Then add this line to /etc/dailyscript.conf (substituting your system names for *system1* and *system2* respectively):

   ```
   SYSTEMS="system1 system2"
   ```

If you are running a full report on each system, or want to modify what you see from each system on a central logging server, the best way is to adjust what goes into the logs via /etc/syslog.conf on each system as described in Chapters 21 and 22. If you do make adjustments to the syslog facilities, don't forget to restart syslog.

 Often, after installing a log rotation utility, people will notice that suddenly no logs are being generated. This is because the logs were moved, and syslog was not restarted. An alternative to restarting syslog is to copy the log file, then cat /dev/null > logfile to zero it out.

After the general log entries, dailyscript goes through the PAM_pwdb entries, and those that correspond to logins are checked. These are read from /var/log/ secure. Here you can see who used the su facility. You'll also see root logins.

The named daemon will be checked next (assuming you run bind). If you don't run a name server on your host, this section will be blank.

FTP transfers, both in and out, if any, will be listed, followed by Identd lookups. The Identd section should be blank unless you're allowing identd to run from inetd. Unless you absolutely need this facility, you should turn it off. Why give crackers and script kiddies additional information about your system? If you do use it, consider limiting access to known and trusted sites.

The next section is a misnomer. While labeled "Kernel errors" in the listing, these are just kernel entries unless you've changed the syslog priority for what to log. Often, this section will be full of informational messages. Again, you can control this by changing /etc/syslog.conf.

Next, you'll see a report on programs run by cron. The code has been modified to exclude atrun (if you're using it — if you're running atd, you won't need or have these entries) and the daily, weekly, and monthly cronloops. Since these are trusted programs, you shouldn't be concerned unless they're just not running (and then you wouldn't be seeing this report daily anyway).

An important section comes next, a df output. Even conscientious administrators can forget to keep an eye on disk usage. So dailyscript does that for you.

NFS exports are next. While not critical, it is nice to see what's exported. This version of dailyscript doesn't include the output from `showmount`, but that could be easily incorporated, and may be in subsequent versions.

The next section includes statistics from your mail server. These statistics will provide you with information about your usage of mail. If you suddenly see a large number of messages relayed by a particular host, your system may have been exploited by a spammer. This report will provide all the information you need to close that hole.

After the mail statistics is a report generated by check-packages. It is included in the same mail, but isn't actually part of dailyscript. The check-package script runs by itself, but is included so you can see what an average day might look like (Listing 24-3).

Your run will probably be longer. Listing 24-3 was edited to save space. Changing /etc/syslog.conf or adding syslog facilities to /etc/dailyscript.conf's ALWAYS_IGNORE variable will help keep these reports a managable length.

Listing 24-3: Edited dailyscript mail message

```
*****************************************************************
General Daily Run -- chiriqui.pananix.com -- Dec  3
*****************************************************************
People who logged in:

david               22:38 - 11:51  (13:12)
david               20:48   still logged in
david               20:39 - 21:44  (01:05)
root                15:40 - 15:40  (00:00)
david               15:30 - 15:31  (00:00)     volcan.pananix.com
david               09:22 - 09:45  (00:22)     volcan.pananix.com
root                07:17 - 07:28  (00:11)
david               07:04 - 09:22  (02:18)


*****************************************************************


Checking System Log Files.....


################################################################
###  Unmatched entries in /var/log/messages!!!!!!!!!!   ###
################################################################


Dec  3 07:05:08 chiriqui modprobe: modprobe: Can't locate module
char-major-108
Dec  3 10:35:13 chiriqui ipsec_setup: Starting FreeS/WAN IPSEC
1.1...
Dec  3 10:35:13 chiriqui ipsec_setup: Loading KLIPS module:
Dec  3 10:35:18 chiriqui ipsec_setup: KLIPS debug `all'
Dec  3 10:35:18 chiriqui ipsec_setup: KLIPS ipsec0 on eth0
192.168.0.2/255.255.255.192 broadcast 192.168.0.255
Dec  3 10:35:18 chiriqui ipsec_setup: Disabling core dumps:
Dec  3 10:35:18 chiriqui ipsec_setup: Starting Pluto (debug `all'):
```

```
Dec  3 10:35:19 chiriqui ipsec_setup: Enabling Pluto negotiation:
Dec  3 10:35:19 chiriqui ipsec_setup: ...FreeS/WAN IPSEC started
Dec  3 15:40:37 chiriqui ipsec_setup: Stopping FreeS/WAN IPSEC...
Dec  3 15:40:37 chiriqui ipsec_setup: Shutting down Pluto:
Dec  3 15:40:38 chiriqui ipsec_setup: Misc cleanout:
Dec  3 15:40:38 chiriqui ipsec_setup: ...FreeS/WAN IPSEC stopped
Dec  3 07:07:35 chiriqui ipop3d[17166]: connect from 127.0.0.1
Dec  3 07:17:00 chiriqui  -- root[15087]: ROOT LOGIN ON tty1
Dec  3 07:18:32 chiriqui ipop3d[17406]: connect from 127.0.0.1
Dec  3 10:35:18 chiriqui Pluto[18142]: Starting Pluto (FreeS/WAN
Version 1.1)
Dec  3 10:35:18 chiriqui Pluto[18142]: | opening /dev/urandom
Dec  3 10:35:18 chiriqui Pluto[18142]: | inserting event
EVENT_REINIT_SECRET, timeout in 3600 seconds
Dec  3 10:35:18 chiriqui Pluto[18142]: | listening for Whack on
/var/run/pluto.ctl, file descriptor 5
Dec  3 10:35:18 chiriqui Pluto[18142]: | next event
EVENT_REINIT_SECRET in 3600 seconds
Dec  3 10:35:19 chiriqui Pluto[18142]: |
Dec  3 10:35:19 chiriqui Pluto[18142]: | *received whack message
Dec  3 10:35:19 chiriqui Pluto[18142]: listening for IKE messages
Dec  3 10:35:19 chiriqui Pluto[18142]: | IP interface lo 127.0.0.1
has no matching ipsec* interface -- ignored
Dec  3 10:35:19 chiriqui Pluto[18142]: adding interface ipsec0/eth0
192.168.0.2
Dec  3 10:35:19 chiriqui Pluto[18142]: loading secrets from
"/etc/ipsec.secrets"
Dec  3 10:35:19 chiriqui Pluto[18142]: | next event
EVENT_REINIT_SECRET in 3599 seconds
Dec  3 10:37:00 chiriqui ipop3d[18186]: connect from 127.0.0.1
Dec  3 11:35:18 chiriqui Pluto[18142]: |
Dec  3 11:35:18 chiriqui Pluto[18142]: | *time to handle event
Dec  3 11:35:18 chiriqui Pluto[18142]: | event EVENT_REINIT_SECRET
handled
Dec  3 11:35:18 chiriqui Pluto[18142]: | inserting event
EVENT_REINIT_SECRET, timeout in 3600 seconds
Dec  3 11:37:10 chiriqui ipop3d[18539]: connect from 127.0.0.1
Dec  3 15:40:30 chiriqui  -- root[17534]: ROOT LOGIN ON tty1
Dec  3 15:40:37 chiriqui Pluto[18142]: |
Dec  3 15:40:37 chiriqui Pluto[18142]: | *received whack message
Dec  3 15:40:37 chiriqui Pluto[18142]: shutting down
Dec  3 15:40:37 chiriqui Pluto[18142]: forgetting secrets
Dec  3 15:40:37 chiriqui Pluto[18142]: shutting down interface
ipsec0/eth0 192.168.0.2
Dec  3 20:40:02 chiriqui ipop3d[22133]: connect from 127.0.0.1
```

```
Dec  3 20:50:02 chiriqui ipop3d[22278]: connect from 127.0.0.1

#########################################################

PAM_pwdb Messages:
   Sucessful SU's:
      david -> root
      david -> root

   Successful logins:
      -> root

   Successful graphical logins:

   Authentication Failures:

   Sucessful Logins:
      root logged in 1 time(s)

Syslogd Restarted:      0 Time(s)...
Failed login(s) due to invalid username:

----- named ------

Named had      0 Malformed Response(s)...
Named had      0 Learned Response(s)...
Named loaded      0 zone(s)...
Other Named Errors:
   Dec  3 06:38:51 chiriqui named[1069]: ns_forw:
sendto([128.9.64.26].53): Network is unreachable
   Dec  3 06:38:51 chiriqui named[1069]: ns_forw:
sendto([152.158.36.48].53): Network is unreachable
   Dec  3 11:50:27 chiriqui named[1069]: Lame server on
'tipworld.com' (in 'tipworld.com'?):
[207.82.198.150].53 'NS2.EXODUS.NET'
   Dec  3 16:37:08 chiriqui named[1069]: ns_forw:
sendto([206.217.29.220].53): Network is unreachable
   Dec  3 18:37:08 chiriqui named[1069]: ns_forw:
sendto([206.217.29.220].53): Network is unreachable
   Dec  3 20:45:16 chiriqui named[1069]: ns_forw:
query(images.sourceforge.net) NS points to CNAME
(ns1.sourceforge.net:)
   Dec  3 20:50:47 chiriqui named[1069]: "SOURCEFORGE.NET IN NS"
points to a CNAME (ns1.sourceforge.net)
   Dec  3 20:51:25 chiriqui named[1069]: Lame server on
```

'www.elxsi.de' (in 'DE'?): [128.63.31.4].53 'ADMII.ARL.MIL'
   Dec 3 21:01:54 chiriqui named[1069]: Lame server on
'ns.Germany.EU.net' (in 'eu.NET'?):
[198.6.1.81].53 'AUTH01.NS.UU.net'

----- FTPD ------

FTP Users Logged in:
    david from volcan.pananix.com
          Deleted   0 file(s)....
          Transfered   5 file(s)....
             /root/openssl-0.9.4.tar.gz c
             /root/Net_SSLeay.pm-1.05.tar.gz c
             /etc/dhcpd.conf c

Identd Lookups:

            *********** Kernel Errors ***********

Dec 3 06:38:46 chiriqui kernel: PPP: ppp line discipline
successfully unregistered
Dec 3 07:05:08 chiriqui kernel: CSLIP: code copyright 1989 Regents
of the University of California
Dec 3 07:05:08 chiriqui kernel: PPP: version 2.3.7 (demand
dialling)
Dec 3 07:05:08 chiriqui kernel: PPP line discipline registered.
Dec 3 07:05:08 chiriqui kernel: registered device ppp0
Dec 3 09:05:21 chiriqui kernel: tty02 unloaded
Dec 3 09:05:22 chiriqui kernel: eth0: 3Com 3c589, io 0x300, irq 3,
auto xcvr, hw_addr 00:10:5A:8B:0C:FA
Dec 3 09:05:22 chiriqui kernel: 8K FIFO split 5:3 Rx:Tx
Dec 3 09:05:34 chiriqui kernel: PPP: ppp line discipline
successfully unregistered
Dec 3 10:35:18 chiriqui kernel: klips_debug:ipsec_init: ipsec
module loading. freeswan version: 1.1
Dec 3 10:35:18 chiriqui kernel: klips_debug:ipsec_init: ipsec_init
version: RCSID $Id: ipsec_init.c,v 1.34 1999/10/03 18:46:28 rgb Exp
$
Dec 3 10:35:18 chiriqui kernel: klips_debug:ipsec_init:
ipsec_tunnel version: RCSID $Id: ipsec_tunnel.c,v 1.82 1999/10/08
18:26:19 rgb Exp $
Dec 3 10:35:18 chiriqui kernel: klips_debug:ipsec_init:
ipsec_netlink version: RCSID $Id: ipsec_netlink.c,v 1.35 1999/10/08

18:37:34 rgb Exp $
Dec 3 10:35:18 chiriqui kernel: klips_debug: rj_init: version:
RCSID $Id: radij.c,v 1.21 1999/10/08 18:37:34 rgb Exp $
Dec 3 10:35:18 chiriqui kernel: FreeS/WAN: initialising PF_KEY
domain sockets.
Dec 3 10:35:18 chiriqui kernel: klips_debug:ipsec_tunnel_init:
initialisation of device: ipsec0
Dec 3 10:35:18 chiriqui kernel: klips_debug:ipsec_tunnel_init:
initialisation of device: ipsec1
Dec 3 10:35:18 chiriqui kernel: klips_debug:ipsec_tunnel_init:
initialisation of device: ipsec2
Dec 3 10:35:18 chiriqui kernel: klips_debug:ipsec_tunnel_init:
initialisation of device: ipsec3
Dec 3 10:35:18 chiriqui kernel: klips_debug:ipsec_tunnel_ioctl:
tncfg service call #35312
Dec 3 10:35:18 chiriqui kernel: klips_debug:ipsec_tunnel_attach:
physical device eth0 being attached has HW address:
0:10:5a:8b:0c:fa
Dec 3 10:35:18 chiriqui kernel: klips_debug:ipsec_tunnel:
ipsec_tunnel_neigh_setup_dev
Dec 3 10:35:18 chiriqui kernel: klips_debug:ipsec_tunnel_open: dev
= ipsec0, prv->dev = eth0
Dec 3 10:35:18 chiriqui kernel: ipsec_device_event: NETDEV_UP...
Dec 3 15:39:56 chiriqui kernel: ipsec_device_event: NETDEV_DOWN...
Dec 3 15:39:56 chiriqui kernel: ipsec_device_event: NETDEV_DOWN...
Dec 3 15:39:56 chiriqui kernel: klips_debug:ipsec_tunnel_detach:
physical device eth0 being detached from virtual device ipsec0
Dec 3 15:39:56 chiriqui kernel: ipsec_device_event:
NETDEV_UNREGISTER...
Dec 3 15:40:38 chiriqui kernel: klips_debug:ipsec_callback:
skb=0xc2387d20 skblen=48 em_magic=1400332654 em_type=8
Dec 3 15:40:38 chiriqui kernel: klips_debug:ipsec_callback: set
ipsec_debug level
Dec 3 15:40:38 chiriqui kernel: klips_debug:ipsec_callback: unset
Dec 3 15:40:38 chiriqui kernel: FreeS/WAN: shutting down PF_KEY
domain sockets.
Dec 3 15:40:38 chiriqui kernel: klips_debug:ipsec_cleanup: ipsec
module unloaded.
Dec 3 20:37:35 chiriqui kernel: tty02 at 0x03e8 (irq = 3) is a
16550A
Dec 3 20:39:07 chiriqui kernel: CSLIP: code copyright 1989 Regents
of the University of California
Dec 3 20:39:07 chiriqui kernel: PPP: version 2.3.7 (demand
dialling)
Dec 3 20:39:07 chiriqui kernel: PPP line discipline registered.

```
Dec  3 20:39:07 chiriqui kernel: registered device ppp0
Dec  3 21:45:00 chiriqui kernel: PPP: ppp line discipline
successfully unregistered
Dec  3 21:45:05 chiriqui kernel: tty02 unloaded


       ****************************************


*****************************************************************

All programs executed by cron (except atrun and cronloop):
06:38:46 (/usr/local/bin/webcal_remind.pl > /var/webcal/message.log
2>&1)  by root
06:38:46 (/usr/local/bin/atsa1)  by root

All Connections (/var/log/secure):
   Connections for in.ftpd:
      3 connections(s) by 192.168.0.1
   Connections for ipop3d:
     33 connections(s) by 127.0.0.1


File-systems...

Filesystem            1k-blocks     Used Available Use% Mounted on
/dev/hda1              4382509    3355428    800283  81% /
/dev/hda3              1462974    1179615    207759  85% /home

NFS Exports.....

/mnt/cdrom       (ro,no_root_squash)
/home            (rw,no_root_squash)
/usr             (ro,no_root_squash)
/tftpboot/volcan      (rw,no_root_squash)
/opt             (ro,no_root_squash)
/tmp             (rw,no_root_squash)

Mail Queue.....

Mail queue is empty

*****************************************************************
Syslog   Input:                    Output:           90th     Msgs
User Host
File      Msgs Kbytes AvgSz Rcips  Sent  Avg Delay  Percentile Dferd
Unkn Unkn
summary   4657  25050  5508  4626  4557 00:00:09.22 00:00:20.00    3
```

```
30     0

#################### Begin Mail Information ######################

Total messages   handled: 4624
Total recipients handled: 4668
Total bytes      handled: 25.65M


------------------------------------------------------------
Part I -- Mail relayed from:
------------------------------------------------------------

   4657 chiriqui.pananix.com


------------------------------------------------------------
Part II -- Mail sent from:
------------------------------------------------------------

   4657 chiriqui.pananix.com


------------------------------------------------------------
Part III -- Mail sent to:                 Avg delay   Max delay
------------------------------------------------------------

 4522  localhost                          8.95 secs   8.63 mins
   99  chiriqui.pananix.com               4.74 mins  41.53 mins
    1  lesbell.com.au                    56.00 secs  56.00 secs
    1  jordanheart.org                    3.60 mins   3.60 mins
    1  fftw.com                          11.10 mins  11.10 mins

#################### End Mail Information ######################

check-packages run on Fri Dec  3 06:39:18 EST 1999
Listing installed packages...
619 packages installed
changes from previous run...
---

---
Checking Packages...
changes from previous run...
---
1d0
< .....U..   /dev/console
---

runtime 848 seconds
```

Additional notes

You should never play games, particularly networked games, as root. Often, games push the limits of hardware. The coders are more interested in speed than security, and security checks (for overflow conditions) are often not trapped and dealt with.

Games are also less likely than servers to be fixed quickly if an exploit is noted. This is not meant to impugn any games programmers, but vulnerabilities in essential services will more often be noticed before a similar vulnerability in a game. Unfortunately, some game instructions state that certain functions (such as using XFree's DG extensions) require you to run the game as root. If your assessment is that this is not a problem (for example, you're not connected to a network or are not playing a networked game), then feel free, just understand the risk may still remain.

Once you've secured your system as well as you can, you probably won't be bothered by too many folks. There are easier targets out there now than you. And if you report scanning activity you see, depending on the service provider's acceptable use policies, the accounts scanning your system may be fined or terminated. If you get no satisfaction, you can just drop all packets coming from that block of addresses. If that doesn't discourage them, your service provider may be able to filter those addresses for you. Remember that his circuits are tied up as well if you're experiencing Denial of Service attacks. So it is often in a service provider's best interests to help you. When I have noted system scans against my own systems, I've usually noted that my service providers' systems are being scanned as well. When the service provider sees this, the accounts are terminated quickly in most cases. The individual account holder frequently consumes significant bandwidth while engaging in this dubious practice.

Summary

In this chapter you learned how to quickly set up your system and save a few files to disk for later comparison. You learned how to set up security checks via cron and have the results mailed to you. While much of this chapter should not have been new to you, the presentation was designed to show you how easily it can be done, so that you support doing security checks rather than avoiding them.

Chapter 25

Using network monitoring tools

IN THIS CHAPTER

- ◆ Using courtney
- ◆ Understanding how courtney works
- ◆ Understanding courtney's capabilities and vulnerabilities
- ◆ Using nmap
- ◆ Using xnmap, the graphical front end
- ◆ Understanding xnmap's capabilities and cautions

THIS CHAPTER WILL COVER two tools as examples of the kinds of things you need to do to keep your network secure. You will look first at software to detect network scans, the kind of activity that signals that someone is interested in you for other than your well-designed Web site. Then you will look at a tool crackers use to perform scans.

Protecting your network is more than just looking over the logs, ensuring the firewall is up and running, and blocking sites you don't want to let in. It's a mind-set. You have to put yourself in the place of someone who wants to get in. You must start to look for your own security vulnerabilities, assess those vulnerabilities, and decide if you need to close them or take other measures. But the only way to know they're there is to look for them.

 A number of good programs are available that will accomplish the same purpose. They include Port Sentry, Perro, Snort, IPPL, and IPLogger, to name a few. But remember, logging packets is only half the equation. The other half is checking the logs. These programs and more may be found at `http://freshmeat.net/`.

courtney

The courtney software package is a network monitor written in Perl by the University of California's Lawrence Livermore Laboratory for the U.S. Department of Energy in 1995. The courtney program was released just after the authors of SATAN decided to release their program to anyone for the downloading. SATAN, the Systems Administrator's Tool to Assess Networks, was the first port scanner released to the public.

Following the release of SATAN, numerous sites began experiencing a higher incidence of attack. Site administrators astute enough to watch logs for signs of scans began to notice a correlation between a scan and an intrusion attempt.

 Many administrators, including this author, consider a port scan an attack. The only reason to conduct a port scan is to probe for vulnerabilities, and the only reason to probe for vulnerabilities is to attempt a breach. Port scanning sites will get your address marked as one to be watched or blocked at the least, if you aren't disconnected by your ISP. Port scanning should be performed only with the permission of the administrator.

To run the courtney package, you will need to install both the libpcap library and tcpdump. The tcpdump program is available as part of the standard OpenLinux install, but libpcap is not. courtney runs tcpdump and filters the output via libpcap, scanning the stream for certain patterns. You'll look at exactly what courtney does below.

The tcpdump program, when executed, puts your Ethernet card in promiscuous mode. This mode can be both a blessing and a curse. The blessing is that it allows you to read all packets on the wire whether for your system or not. So if you have a Web server, anonymous ftp server, DNS server, and mail server outside your firewall, you could run courtney on any one of them (or another server altogether), and see attacks directed against any one of them.

On the down side, an Ethernet card in promiscuous mode doesn't ignore any packet on the wire. This is how sniffers work, so this software, since it's written in perl, can be easily subverted to watch for usernames and passwords. Remember from Chapter 12 how the ftp client preceded a username with USER and the password with PASS? Often it's as easy as just grabbing those packets and mailing them somewhere. Also, while Linux is not susceptible to a big ping attack (anymore), other platforms capable of running courtney are. One such platform actually only needs to see the last packet of a big ping in order to cause a kernel panic. So view all software that puts an Ethernet card into promiscuous mode with some modicum of distrust and only use such software on a "safe" system. A safe system is one that ordinary users don't (or shouldn't) log in on routinely. This prevents them from taking advantage of what this card sees. While your firewall should be a safe system, putting a firewall NIC into promiscuous mode is not recommended.

Once you get courtney running, look at the output from a process listing. What you'll see should be similar to Listing 25-1.

Listing 25-1: Process list extract (ps axww) showing courtney and tcpdump

```
2979 pts/1    S       0:00 perl /usr/sbin/courtney
2980 pts/1    S       0:03 tcpdump -1 ?    (icmp[0] == 8 ) or ?
(port sunrpc) or ?    ((port (1 or 10 or 100 or 1000 or 5000 or
10000 or 20000 or 30000) or ?    (port (6000 or 6001 or 6002 or
6010 or 6011 or 6012)) ) and ?    (tcp[13] & 18 == 2) )  or ?
(port (tcpmux or ??    echo or ??    discard or ??    systat or ??
daytime or ??    netstat or ??    chargen or ??    ftp or ??    telnet
or ??    smtp or ??    time or ??    whois or ??    domain or??    70 or
??    80 or ??    finger or ??    tftp or ??    login or ??    uucp or ??
printer or ??    shell or ??    exec or ??    name or ??    biff or ??
syslog or ??    talk) and ?    (tcp[13] & 18 == 2) ) ?
```

So what courtney is doing is filtering all the datastreams tcpdump sees against a list of common services. Those services are what is seen above. This aspect of courtney can be easily modified if necessary. Since the code is all in perl, modification is very simple. While the entire perl script is not long, in the interests of space, only those portions of interest will be shown. Listing 25-2 shows the part of courtney that can be modified if necessary.

Listing 25-2: Extract from courtney perl script showing services monitored

```
@assoc_list  = (  'sunrpc',   'icmp',    'ttime',   'telnet',   'smtp',
                  'ftp',      'whois',   'domain',  'gopher',   'www',
                  'finger',   'exec',    'login',   'shell',    'printer',
                  'uucp',     'tcpmux',  'echo',    'discard',  'systat',
                  'daytime', 'netstat', 'chargen', 'tftp',      'name',
                  'biff',     'syslog',  'talk',    'portscan', 'xwindows' );
```

If any of the above services are not listed in /etc/services, courtney will bail out with an error message. So if, for some reason, you've deleted a service from /etc/services, you'll either need to remove it from this associative array or substitute the port number for the service.

How courtney determines if a scan has occurred is to compare the source address for hosts connecting to different ports. So courtney creates a list of hosts that have tried to connect to ports. Too many connections to too many different ports, and courtney decides the system is under attack.

courtney uses two factors to determine what constitutes too many connections — number of ports connected from one host and number of ports connected over a time interval. Listing 25-3 details these two factors.

Listing 25-3: Thresholds for courtney's "under attack" decisions

```
$UPDATE_INTERVAL = 5;          # update host information every
                               # X minutes
$OLD_AGE = 7;                  # get rid of hosts that are
                               # older that X minutes.
$HIGH_THRESHOLD = 15;          # heavy  "SATAN" attack
$LOW_THRESHOLD  = 9;           # normal "SATAN" attack
```

By default, courtney looks for any host (source address) connecting to more than nine services within seven minutes, or more than 15 services within seven minutes, and labels those hosts as either executing a normal or heavy attack respectively.

On a Linux system, courtney will recognize three different types of scans. These are connect, SYN stealth, and FIN stealth probes. A number of different systems don't respond to these probes, or just don't see them (courtney will not register). This has to do with the way the arriving packets are treated by the kernel. On a Linux system running a 2.2.x kernel, the kernel becomes involved in all of them, so courtney will alarm on all of them. For explanations of these probes, see the nmap section.

Now that you know what courtney is looking for, you have an idea what it will not see — that is, what courtney's vulnerabilities are. The first vulnerability comes from the speed of the scan. If a scan takes place over hours, as some stealth scans can, older entries will have been flushed from the table and not trigger an alarm. By probing only six ports every 15 minutes, an attacker can easily and successfully avoid detection. This is also true for an attacker who is only interested in seeing if you have one vulnerability in particular. Only one port may be "scanned."

An attacker who has changed the source address (or is using an ftp proxy to scan you) can take advantage of another vulnerability. You will see a scan via courtney, but the information provided regarding the source of the attack will be incorrect. That is, you'll be looking left while the attack is coming from the right. More aptly, you'll block access from evil.net, where the scan appears to have originated, while the scan actually came from archevil.net.

Can any other of courtney's limitations be overcome? Yes. You are certainly free to modify any of the variables in the source. But before you do, you need to examine the consequences.

Start with the time variable. This is probably the most innocuous of the variables you can change. Normally, a fast scan will hit all the well-known services in just a few seconds. But you'll still probably not want to reduce the seven-minute limit. You may want to increase it, but be careful here — courtney is using memory to store arrays of source:port, destination:port, and time. This can quickly fill memory on a busy network, because courtney is watching all traffic, not just that destined for the localhost. If you are on a subnet where a lot of traffic passes, even though it is not destined for your subnet, courtney will still see and record it. You may see attacks from a host on one foreign subnet against another foreign subnet because the packets just happened to pass through your subnet (or be leaked onto your subnet by an upstream router). Setting it much higher probably won't net you much except the use of more memory.

Either or both of the threshold variables can be adjusted. You can lower the normal variable, but you might get a few false alarms. For instance, someone on the road might connect to a local ISP and then connect back home. She might upload or download a file or two via FTP, use POP to retreive mail, by default hit the Web server before surfing to another site, maybe even use telnet (or ssh) to enter the site. That's five legitimate services, possibly within five minutes. Of course, you could combine lowering these thresholds with removing some of the services from the @assoc_list array of services. If you want to watch only one or two ports that no one should be connecting to, you're better off using tripwire on those hosts. In fact, if you look closely at the @assoc_list, you may notice a few services missing, such as POP2, POP3, IMAP, and SSH. You may want to add these, especially since IMAP is such a tempting target for crackers. If you add SSH, you'll need to make sure you've also added it to your /etc/services file.

You may invoke courtney with any of several options. The most common option, and the way the init script is set up, is to mail a user (normally root) notices of attacks. The options include:

- `-i` *interface_name*: default Interface if blank
- `-d`: debug/verbose mode on
- `-l`: syslog Logging off (logs to user)
- `-s`: screen output on
- `-c`: display Connections
- `-m` *address*: mail alerts to address
- `-h`: help

The courtney program has proven very valuable as one more tool to aid systems administrators in detecting attacks. Specifically, courtney is able to detect port scans from nmap, NESSUS, SAINT, GtkPortScan or any of a number of other port scanners available on the Internet. Just remember that it can be fooled. Use it if you wish, but remember what it can and can't do for you.

nmap

As the first publicly released network scanner, SATAN was very popular and extremely effective in identifying open ports on networked systems. Today, SATAN has fallen out of favor for a number of reasons, not the least of which being that it doesn't compile easily on Linux systems, and binaries are hard to come by. So administrators, faced with a number of more recently developed choices, are using other tools. One of the most popular is nmap. Written by Fyodor (fyodor@dhp.com), nmap has more options for scanning and has a user mailing list for those with questions or needing help. The nmap site is http://www.insecure.org/nmap/.

This book does not judge the relative merits of nmap versus any of the other currently popular port scanners, which include SAINT (SATAN's replacement), NESSUS, GtkPortScanner, or any of a number of others, or endorse any one over the others. Most have similar features, and all perform the same basic function: scanning networked hosts for open ports. You'll be able to make a more informed choice if you try each one out. The nmap program is merely one of these and was chosen for its simplicity.

 The nmap program performs functions that can result in network degradation (denial of service) and crash-sensitive servers. This program should not be used indiscriminately.

The nmap program can be run by any user on the system. If you install nmap, but don't want just anyone running the program, you'll want to change the permissions to prevent access. Despite the fact that anyone can run the program, nmap has a number of options that are not available to anyone except root. This is because those options require that the user be capable of writing to a raw socket or of creating a custom packet. In general, the Linux kernel will not permit these requests by non-privileged users to perform these operations.

The nmap program comes with a graphical front end, xnmap (written by Fyodor), that can be invoked for those no familiar with the command line. One of the nice features of this graphical front end is that it shows you the nmap command line being used. Besides providing a graphical front end for nmap, the author made effective use of color as well as the textual output from the startup to indicate the users status: The dialog box backgrounds will by default be pink for the root user (with the text indicating all options are granted) or green for a non-privileged user (with the text indicating some options aren't available). Figure 25-1 shows the nmap front end.

The front end is divided into four parts: the hosts section, the scan options section, the general options section, and the output section. The Host(s) text box defaults to 127.0.0.1 (localhost). This text box can take a list of hosts by name, IP address, or a specified range of hosts by specifying a dotted decimal notation network number and subnet mask in the form 123.34.67.00/24. You may also substitute globs (*) for any number, as in 123.*.67.00/24. This does exactly what it appears, it scans all networks in the 123 net, but only the 67 subnet. You can also select a range by specifying the range, as in 1–33, and substituting that in the dotted decimal notation (123.1-33.67.00/24), or by specifying a comma-separated list of hosts (123.1,3,7,10.76.00/24). Note that depending on the shell you use, you may need to escape the glob. You may also specify a hostname and mask.

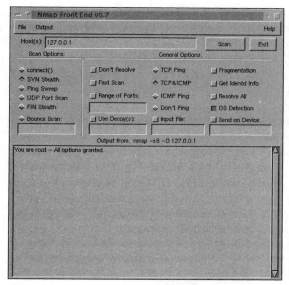

Figure 25-1: The nmap front end, xnmap

When you're satisfied with the selection in the hosts box, selecting Scan will put nmap to work. But beware, some scans may take a long time. If you want to cancel the scan, selecting the Scan button again will do so.

nmap scan options

Six of the nine possible scan types available to nmap are listed in the Scan Options section. One scan type must be selected. The connect() scan option is normal. This connects to a target host just as you would from a telnet client. Since these are connects, and only TCP creates a connection, this is a TCP scan. This scan will be picked up by even the most primitive of scan detection software.

The SYN stealth is a little different. Remember your TCP connection sequence: Client sends a packet to host:port with the SYN bit set; host replies with a packet with the SYN and ACK bit set; client responds, and the connection is complete. But in this case, instead of responding to the SYN-ACK, you send a RST, and the connection is immediately torn down. No connection, so no detection. Well, almost. courtney and Synlogger will pick these up.

The Ping Sweep does exactly what it says. It just sends out a ping looking for responses. If you've blocked pings with IPChains or NetFilter, the target will appear dead. This can pose a problem for other scans in that nmap sends a ping to see if it should bother flooding a host address with TCP connect requests. If the host doesn't respond to the ping, that host will be skipped. Later on, you'll see another option that you can use against hosts that drop pings.

The UDP port scan works a little differently. Instead of trying to create a TCP connection, it probes for open UDP ports by sending a zero-byte UDP packet. If a server is listening, the UDP packet will be received, and nothing further will happen. If a server is not listening, then the target host should send an RST (reset) packet (this packet signals the client to tear down the connection – I'm not listening).

A FIN scan is a specially built packet that is normally used by a client to signal the termination of a TCP connection. If you remember the netstat states, sending or receiving a FIN packet triggers a FIN_WAIT, either FIN_WAIT1 or FIN_WAIT2. But this packet is normally sent only at the end of a TCP connection to signal a shutdown of the connection. But what if there is no connection? If there's a server listening, then it will just drop the packet, assuming the packet was misdirected or otherwise in error. But a closed port (no server listening) will send an RST.

The final option under scan options is called a bounce scan. A bounce scan is designed to exploit a hole (a very large hole) in FTP servers that allow them to be used as proxies. So this "bounce" scan should probably be renamed an FTP proxy scan. Fortunately, the FTP server on your OpenLinux system rejects hijacking of privileged ports. But if you're curious, try a bounce scan against 127.0.0.1/24, and put an address such as 127.1.1.1 in the Bounce Scan text box.

Of the six scan options available under xnmap, only two, connect() and Ping Sweep, can be used by non-privileged users.

Three other scans options are available from the command line. Two are variations on the FIN scan. The first, the Christmas tree scan, sets two other bits, the URG and PUSH bits, along with the FIN bit. The second, the null scan, turns off all bits.

The final scan option is the RPC scan. This is a specialized scan that looks for open RPC ports. This particular scan should be used in conjunction with another scan option.

nmap general options

For the most part, the General Options are just that, options. With few exceptions, nmap will execute without choosing any General Options. They are there to modify nmap's behavior. The Don't Resolve option prevents DNS lookup on the scanned hosts. This can speed up scanning, if only a little.

The Fast Scan option uses the nmap-services file found in ../lib/nmap/nmap-services. This file lists some 1975 TCP and UDP ports (1022 TCP and 953 UDP). Scans are much faster than those covering 64k ports. The Range of Ports option is similar to the Fast Scan, and can cover more or less territory, but is completely configurable, so preferable to some folks.

The Use Decoy(s) option is the option that allows source rewriting. By using the Decoy option, the target will appear to be under attack from several hosts at once. A comma-delimited list of hosts, with ME nestled within the list, will put your host at that location. If ME is not used, nmap will choose a random location in the list.

All decoys should be operational on the network when used as such, or you may inadvertently cause a SYN DoS attack against your target.

Fortunately, if so constructed, your OpenLinux host will drop source-routed frames (aka spoofed packets).

The next column of options are all related (except the final option). Each option specifies the type of "ping" to send. ICMP packets are true ping packets, sending an ICMP echo request message and waiting for an ICMP echo reply from the target. You can also turn off ICMP pings or combine them with TCP "pings." A TCP ping takes advantage of hosts that respond correctly to connection requests to closed ports by sending an RST back. No response, open port or non-existent host. But receipt of an RST packet is the same as getting an echo reply back.

The final option in this column, Input File, allows you to use a file rather than a command line (or in the case of xnmap a text box) to list hosts. If you regularly scan your own network but want only selected systems, this is the option you'll want to use.

The final column of General Options on the nmap front end handles other common options. The first is Fragmentation. The Fragmentation option tells nmap to deliberately fragment the packet header in an attempt to slip the fragments through. Most firewall software will pass fragments unless told not to. The Linux kernel can be compiled with the option to not pass fragments (CONFIG_IP_ALWAYS_DEFRAG), and this should always be on any system used as firewall. Note that this option no longer appears in 2.4.x kernels; defragmenting is the built-in default.

The Get Identd Info option is used to trick hosts that run the identd service into displaying the username of the user running the service. This can confirm if a particular service is running as a non-privileged user, or root. Weren't you told to disable identd in /etc/inet/conf? This is the other reason to do so.

The Resolve All option is the opposite of Don't Resolve, but no longer exists in nmap, since that is the default behavior.

The OS Detection option tells nmap to attempt to identify the operating system of the target: It accomplishes this through TCP/IP fingerprinting. This fingerprinting is not 100 percent reliable. If you run this against your localhost as a class C block (127.0.0.1/24), you will receive several replies that nmap is unable to identify the host, or that it took two or three tries to do so.

The Send on Device option is for those with multiple NICs who want to specify which NIC the probe is coming from.

From a command line, a few other interesting options become available. The first of these options (not all options will be mentioned here) is the -S <IP address> option. This allows you to rewrite the source address to the IP given as an argument to the option. Unlike the decoy option, which makes it look like several hosts are scanning you, the -S option shows only one host scan. Unfortunately, it's the wrong host.

Another very interesting option is the -g <portnumber> option. Just as an IP address can be spoofed, this option sets the source port number. By spoofing the port number, you may get some firewalls to proxy you through.

The final option worth looking at is the -T or timing option. This option allows you to set one of six levels from 0 to 5 corresponding to Paranoid, Sneaky, Polite, Normal, Aggressive, and Insane. The paranoid timing is very slow and will obviate courtney detection. The Insane setting will get the attention of the network administrator of the target machine since the scan will be parallelized and pushed out as fast as possible, saturating the slowest network link between the source and the target.

nmap output

Just above the output window is the command line that will be executed when you select the Scan button. This makes learning the command line easier, but still no substitute for reading the man pages to understand the latest changes and how they will affect your scan. More important, you get an idea of what to try for scanning your own hosts, and can watch to see if courtney or other scan detection programs catch the scan or are fooled.

Listing 25-4 shows the return from a scan of the localhost with SYN Stealth scan of all ports (this comes back rather quickly on localhost, as opposed to a much longer response time even on a local Ethernet network).

Listing 25-4: An nmap run against localhost

```
Starting nmap V. 2.3BETA6 by Fyodor (fyodor@dhp.com,
www.insecure.org/nmap/)
Interesting ports on localhost (127.0.0.1):
Port     State       Protocol    Service
21       open        tcp         ftp
22       open        tcp         ssh
25       open        tcp         smtp
80       open        tcp         http
110      open        tcp         pop-3
111      open        tcp         sunrpc
901      open        tcp         unknown
3306     open        tcp         mysql
6000     open        tcp         X11

TCP Sequence Prediction: Class=random positive increments
                         Difficulty=599840 (Good luck!)
Remote operating system guess: Linux 2.1.122 - 2.2.12
Nmap run completed -- 1 IP address (1 host up) scanned in 1 second
```

The number of hosts you're scanning, the network bandwidth available, and whether you've selected Fast Scan or not will determine how long it takes for scan results to come back. In many cases, you may be better off scanning a larger network from a command line and shoving the scan into the background.

The output of nmap in Listing 25-4 compares favorably with those services offered on the target system. Note the TCP Sequence Prediction. This is a prediction of just how difficult it will be to perform a connection hijacking. The TCP Sequence

Prediction for Linux generally runs from between 500,000 to 2,500,000. The higher the sequence number, the larger the variance. Sun Solaris rates even higher. Lower numbers will have a much smaller variance. See Listing 25-5 for some sample TCP Prediction Sequences from the same Linux host.

Listing 25-5: TCP Prediction Sequence from localhost at 30-second intervals

```
TCP Sequence Prediction: Class=random positive increments
                         Difficulty=2177514 (Good luck!)
Remote operating system guess: Linux 2.1.122 - 2.2.12
TCP Sequence Prediction: Class=random positive increments
                         Difficulty=4453284 (Good luck!)
Remote operating system guess: Linux 2.1.122 - 2.2.12
TCP Sequence Prediction: Class=random positive increments
                         Difficulty=871237 (Good luck!)
Remote operating system guess: Linux 2.1.122 - 2.2.12
```

You may choose more options and in more and different combinations than available in xnmap from a command line as shown in Listing 25-6. And if you choose options that are incompatible or just don't make sense together, nmap will tell you, but attempt to complete the scan anyway (just don't expect too much).

Listing 25-6: nmap listing from a command line with an option mix unavailable from xnmap

```
[root@chiriqui /root]# nmap -sFUR localhost
Starting nmap V. 2.3BETA6 by Fyodor (fyodor@dhp.com,
www.insecure.org/nmap/)
Interesting ports on localhost (127.0.0.1):
Port    State     Protocol  Service (RPC)
21      open      tcp       ftp
22      open      tcp       ssh
25      open      tcp       smtp
67      open      udp       bootps
80      open      tcp       http
110     open      tcp       pop-3
111     open      udp       sunrpc
111     open      tcp       sunrpc
177     open      udp       xdmcp
514     open      udp       syslog
901     open      tcp       unknown
3306    open      tcp       mysql
6000    open      tcp       X11
Nmap run completed -- 1 IP address (1 host up) scanned in 3 seconds
```

Now, in Listing 25-6 are several ports not seen before — the UDP ports that you would have had to scan for separately. Listed numerically by port, all open ports are shown, both TCP and UDP. BTW, port 901 is swat (Samba Web Administration Tool). This same scan (full 64k TCP/UDP/RCP) on another host on the same Ethernet segment took 1586 seconds or over 26 minutes.

nmap versus netstat

You may wonder why use nmap when you have netstat. Using netstat -an will show you all open ports that the local host is binding as well as UNIX servers. But the real difference between the two is that by using nmap, particularly from an outside host, you will see what the wannabe crackers and script kiddies see. This may be significantly different from what you see on your system.

You will be able to see firsthand how effective your firewall rules are, whether you're properly blocking ICMP echo requests, open ports you thought you blocked, or ports you just missed. The nmap output is not as cluttered as the netstat output, so is easier to read.

By running nmap from localhost, from outside your network, and from inside, you can compare the results. You should run an nmap scan regularly, the frequency of your scans depending on your specific situation. The greater your vulnerability and the volume of incoming traffic, the more often you should scan your own network. This could be monthly, weekly, or more often. But again, be careful. Scanning slowly during off hours over several nights would be a better idea than one fast scan during the day. For example, nmap will automatically slow down as it senses a remote host throttle back on responses. This is normal and can be expected. Linux will only provide 80 ICMP port unreachable responses during a span of four minutes, then cut back. Sun Solaris will provide even less. Microsoft will never throttle back, but this means you run the risk of crashing the server, tying up the network (which will show up as excess collisions), or just tying up system resources to the point where users are furious.

Summary

This chapter presented opposites to show both the detection side of intrusion detection software, its capabilities and limitations, and the scanning side, to show the level of sophistication of such software and how it is being written to avoid scan detection.

First you looked at courtney and how it works. You looked at the variables in courtney and how they can be changed and the results of changing them. You looked at courtney's vulnerabilities and saw how easily its thresholds can be defeated once you know about them.

Then you looked at nmap, one of the most popular port scanners as of this writing. You saw how the default scans would be picked up by courtney. You also learned how options could be enabled, which would allow nmap to go undetected.

Chapter 26

Finding information to keep your system secure

IN THIS CHAPTER

◆ Finding security information

◆ "Official" security sites

◆ Sites of questionable purpose

THE INTERNET IS RIFE with information regarding security and security practices. With this book, I have attempted to provide a source of information for beginning and intermediate-level administrators. More in-depth information is available from specialized books that address just one of the many relevant topics. These books will often cover theory, operation, and practice in detail that can be overwhelming to all but a security guru. And even they may find the detail both tedious and daunting.

But one thing is certain—security doesn't end with this book. New exploits are found on a regular basis. You must keep up with these new trends. For example, during the writing of this book, I became aware of a new method to ping scan hosts that drop pings. Previously, scanning software would look for normally open ports to send SYN-ACK messages, hoping to get a RST in response indicating a host was listening. But this depended on the host listening. What if the host just dropped all packets (didn't offer any services, but instead dropped all ICMP echo-request packets and TCP packets that weren't return packets to outgoing connection requests), thus making it look as if it weren't online when it was? So some ingenious folks decided to try sending ICMP echo-reply packets to systems. While you may have ICMP echo-requests blocked (dropped), you probably aren't dropping echo-replies. If you did, you couldn't use that system to ping out on.

Actually, note that being able to "ping" is not such a big deal. You could always use traceroute, which uses UDP. Be aware, however, that Windows systems use ICMP instead of UDP for traceroute, so Windows systems could not go through that system for tracerouting. I wouldn't worry too much about someone knowing you have a system online, though. What matters is the vulnerability of services exposed to the Internet, and ICMP doesn't lend itself to breaking into a system.

Finding security information

You have a choice today in how you want to receive security information. There's certainly a lot of it out there. Sifting through it, or picking responsible sites, is often the hard part. Listed here are a few e-mail lists that can be very valuable. Later on, a number of other sites, both good and questionable in nature, often with mailing lists of their own, are also listed.

Depending on how much information you want, how often, and whether or not you care if you receive redundant information, you can subscribe to several. None of the information-only security lists are high-volume, and receiving information about a particular vulnerability twice is better than not getting it at all.

E-mail lists

The first mailing list you will probably want to subscribe to is a security list dealing with your particular distribution. In the case of the distribution provided with this book, Caldera Systems OpenLinux, a security mailing, the Caldera Security Advisory list, is available. You may choose to subscribe by going to the Caldera site (www.caldera.com). Caldera Systems will send e-mail when it is made aware of a security issue affecting any of its officially distributed programs. The advisory will include a link to the fixed RPMs (when available) or provide a work-around. This will not include programs provided by third parties, such as those found in the "contrib" directories. In lieu of subscribing, or if you just want to see previous advisories, they are available on the Caldera Systems site. Look at http://www.calderasystems.com/news/security/index.html for more information.

Another good list to subscribe to is the CERT Advisory list. CERT, the Computer Emergency Response Team, issues e-mail advisories to subscribers. These advisories are issued each time CERT finds a vulnerable application that could compromise a system. The advisory will generally explain the particular vulnerability in detail, provide a temporary workaround for those who need the service the vulnerable application provides, and a recommendation for a permanent solution. The advisory provides sufficient detail for you to determine if you are vulnerable and assess whether you are at risk. Not all vulnerabilities increase the risk for a site. While full of technical jargon, these advisories get straight to the point. If you aren't sure, follow the recommendations. More information can be found at http://www.cert.org/.

A number of general security-related newsletters are also available. One, called the SANS NewsBites, is a Weekly Security News Overview. This weekly e-mailing contains a potpourri of items from around the globe in issues related to computer security. You can subscribe by sending e-mail to autosans@sans.org with the subject Subscribe NewsBites.

Security-related Web sites

Security-related Web sites abound these days. Many are just a convenient repository for recent information, and contain pointers to other sites. Others have original content. Still other sites that are not particularly security-related will post security information their owners become aware of.

For example, both `http://slashdot.org` and `http://freshmeat.net` (the former a "geek" news site, the latter a site containing information about newly released software packages or software upgrades) will post information about vulnerabilities. Neither site posts detailed information, but each does post a link, usually to the specific CERT Advisory. Listing 26-1 shows the contents of a CERT advisory. Those of you who followed the instructions in Chapter 21 and included the RSAref library because you felt the need will be interested in this Advisory.

Summary of the CERT Advisory: The rsaref2 library contains a bug that can allow malicious code to be run from any service compiled with the rsaref2 library. The code will run as the user running the service (normally root). To eliminate the bug, you should apply a patch (listed in the Advisory message) to the rsaref library and recompile the library, and also recompile all applications using the rsaref2 library. The patch file may be obtained from `http://www.cert.org/advisories/CA-99-15/rsa-patch.txt`.

Listing 26-1: Sample CERT advisory

```
Subject: CERT Advisory CA-99.15 - Buffer Overflows in SSH Daemon and RSAREF2
Library
        Date: Mon, 13 Dec 1999 18:49:47 -0500
        From: CERT Advisory <cert-advisory@cert.org>
    Reply-To: cert-advisory-request@cert.org
 Organization: CERT(sm) Coordination Center - +1 412-268-7090
          To: cert-advisory@coal.cert.org
-----BEGIN PGP SIGNED MESSAGE-----
Hash: SHA1
CERT Advisory CA-99-15 Buffer Overflows in SSH Daemon and RSAREF2 Library
    Original release date: December 13, 1999
    Last revised: --
    Source: CERT/CC
       A complete revision history is at the end of this file.
    Systems Affected
      * Systems running some versions of sshd
      * Systems using products that use RSAREF2 (e.g., some SSL-enabled
        web servers)
I. Description
    Some versions of sshd are vulnerable to a buffer overflow that can
    allow an intruder to influence certain variables internal to the
    program. This vulnerability alone does not allow an intruder to
```

execute code.

However, a vulnerability in RSAREF2, which was discovered and
researched by Core SDI, can be used in conjunction with the
vulnerability in sshd to allow a remote intruder to execute arbitrary
code.

Additional information about the RSAREF2 vulnerability can be found at
http://www.core-sdi.com/advisories/buffer%20overflow%20ing.htm

The RSAREF2 library was developed from a different code base than
other implementations of the RSA algorithm, including those from RSA
Security Inc. The vulnerability described in this advisory is specific
to the RSAREF2 library and does not imply any weakness in other
implementations of the RSA algorithm or the algorithm itself.

Also, only versions of SSH compiled with RSAREF support, via the
--with-rsaref option, are vulnerable to these issues.

The use of the RSAREF2 library in other products may present
additional vulnerabilities. RSAREF2 may be used in products such as
SSL-enabled web servers, ssh clients, or other cryptographically
enhanced products. Appendix A of this advisory will be updated with
new information as it becomes available regarding problems in other
products that use the RSAREF2 library.

II. Impact

Using the two vulnerabilities in conjunction allows an intruder to
execute arbitrary code with the privileges of the process running
sshd, typically root.

We are investigating whether vulnerabilities in other products may
expose the vulnerability in RSAREF2, and will update this advisory as
appropriate.

See Appendices A and B for more information that may affect the impact
of this vulnerability.

III. Solution

Apply patch(es) from your product vendor

Apply patch(es) to the RSAREF2 library. RSA Security Inc. holds a
patent on the RSA algorithm and a copyright on the RSAREF2
implementation. We encourage you to consult your legal counsel
regarding the legality of any fixes you are considering before
implementing those fixes. Please see RSA's vendor statement in

Appendix A.

Exploiting the vulnerability in RSAREF2 requires an application program to call the RSAREF2 library with malicious input. For products that allow an intruder to influence the data provided to the RSAREF2 library, you may be able to protect against attacks by validating the data they provide to RSAREF2.

Appendix A contains information provided by vendors for this advisory. Appendix B contains information regarding test performed by the CERT Coordination Center and other people, and advice based on those tests. We will update the appendices as we receive or develop more information. If you do not see your vendor's name in Appendix A, the CERT/CC did not hear from that vendor. Please contact your vendor directly.

Use a non-vulnerable implementation of the RSA algorithm

Sites not restricted by patent law may choose to use a non-vulnerable implementation of RSA. Since RSA Security Inc. holds a patent on the RSA algorithm, this option may not be legally available to you. Please consult your legal counsel for guidance on this issue.

Appendix A. Vendor Information

Compaq Computer Corporation

(c) Copyright 1998, 1999 Compaq Computer Corporation. All rights reserved.

SOURCE:
        Compaq Computer Corporation
        Compaq Services
        Software Security Response Team USA

Compaq's Tru64 UNIX is not vulnerable. Compaq does not ship ssl

Covalent Technologies

Covalent Raven SSL module for Apache

The Raven SSL module is not vulnerable to this attack since the SSL library used does not use the RSAREF library.

Data Fellows Inc.

F-Secure SSH versions prior 1.3.7 are vulnerable but F-Secure SSH 2.x and above are not.

FreeBSD

FreeBSD 3.3R and prior releases contain packages with this problem. This problem was corrected December 2, 1999 in the ports tree. Packages built after this date with the rsaref updated should be unaffected by this vulnerabilities. Some or all of the following ports may be affected should be rebuilt:

p5-Penguin, p5-Penguin-Easy, jp-pgp, ja-w3m-ssl, ko-pgp, pgpsendmail, pine4-ssl, premail, ParMetis, SSLtelnet, mpich, pipsecd, tund, nntpcache, p5-Gateway, p5-News-Article, ru-pgp, bjorb, keynote, OpenSSH, openssl, p5-PGP, p5-PGP-Sign, pgp, slush, ssh, sslproxy, stunnel, apache+mod_ssl, apache+ssl, lynx-ssl, w3m-ssl, zope

Please see the FreeBSD Handbook for information on how to obtain a current copy of the ports tree and how to rebuild those ports which depend on rsaref.

Hewlett-Packard Company

HP does not supply SSH. HP has not conducted compatibility testing with version 1.2.27 of SSH, when compiled with the option --with-rsaref. Further, RSAREF2 has not been tested to date. As far as the investigation to date, HP appears to be not vulnerable.

IBM Corporation

IBM AIX does not currently ship the secure shell (ssh) nor do the base components of AIX ship or link with the RSAREF2 library.

IBM and AIX are registered trademarks of International Business Machines Corporation.

Microsoft

The Microsoft Security Response Team has investigated this issue, and no Microsoft products are affected by the vulnerability.

NetBSD

> NetBSD does not ship with ssh in either its US-only or International variants at this time, so no default installation of NetBSD is vulnerable.
>
> However, ssh is installed and widely used by many NetBSD installations, and is available from our software package tree in source form. The NetBSD ssh package can be compiled either with or without RSAREF2, settable by the administrator at compile time according to local copyright and license restrictions.
>
> Installations which used RSAREF2 in compiling ssh are vulnerable, and we recommend recompiling without RSAREF2 if their local legal situation permits.
>
> In addition, the following list of software packages in the NetBSD "packages" system are also dependent on the RSAREF2 library:
> * archivers/hpack
> * security/openssl
> * security/pgp2
> * security/pgp5
> * www/ap-ssl
>
> of those, the security/openssl package is itself a library, and the following packages depend on it:
> * net/ppp-mppe
> * net/speakfreely-crypto
> * www/ap-ssl
>
> We recommend recompiling and reinstalling these packages without RSAREF2, if your local legal situation permits.

Network Associates, Inc.

> After a technical review of the buffer overflow bug in RSAREF, we have determined at Network Associates that PGP is not affected by this bug, because of the careful way that PGP uses RSAREF.
>
> This applies to all versions of PGP ever released by MIT, which are the only versions of PGP that use RSAREF. All other versions of PGP, such as the commercial versions and the international versions, avoid the use of RSAREF entirely.
>
> Philip Zimmermann
> 10 December 1999

[CERT/CC Note: A PGP signed copy of this information and additional technical details are available as well.]

OpenSSL

OpenSSL with RSAREF is not vulnerable.

OpenBSD / OpenSSH

More information is available from:

http://www.openbsd.org/errata.html#sslUSA

RSA Security Inc.

RSA Security Inc. recommends that developers implement the proposed or similar patch to RSAREF version 2.0 or otherwise to ensure that the length in bits of the modulus supplied to RSAREF is less than or equal to MAX_RSA_MODULUS_BITS.

RSA Security Inc. is no longer distributing the RSAREF toolkit, which it offered through RSA Laboratories in the mid-1990s as a free, source implementation of modern cryptographic algorithms. Under the terms of the RSAREF license, changes to the RSAREF code other than porting or performance improvement require written consent. RSA Security hereby gives its consent to implement a patch to RSAREF to address this advisory.

This advisory only applies to RSAREF, not RSA Security's current toolkits and products, which were developed independently of RSAREF.

Although RSA Security is no longer distributing RSAREF, the toolkit is still available in a number of "freeware" products such as SSH under RSA Security's original RSAREF v2.0 software license ("license.txt", March 25, 1994), which is distributed along with those products. As a reminder, that license limits the use of RSAREF to noncommercial purposes. RSAREF, RSAREF applications, and services based on RSAREF applications may not be sold, licensed or otherwise transferred for value. (There is a minor exception for small "shareware" deployments as noted in the "info.txt" file, March 25, 1994.)

SSH Communications

The bug only affects ssh when it is compiled with RSAREF (i.e., only when --with-rsaref is explicitly supplied on the command line). Any

version compiled without --with-rsaref is not affected. The problem
should not affect users of the commercial versions (who are licensed
to use the built-in RSA) or users outside the United States (who are
presumably not using RSAREF and can use the built-in RSA without
needing a license). I.e., only those non-commercial users who actually
compile with a separately obtained RSAREF should be affected.

The bug is present in all versions of SSH1, up to and including
1.2.27. It will be fixed in ssh-1-2.28 (expected to go out in a few
days to fix this problem). It does not affect SSH2. (Please note that
ssh1 is no longer maintained, except for security fixes, due to
certain rather fundamental problems that have been fixed in ssh2.)

Any implementation compiled without an explicitly specified
--with-rsaref is not affected by this problem.

A patch provided by SSH Communications is available from the CERT/CC
web site. This version of the patch has been signed by the CERT/CC.

Stronghold

Stronghold does not use RSAREF and is unaffected.

Appendix B. CERT/CC and Other Third-Party Tests

RSAREF Patch from Core SDI and the CERT/CC

With the assistance of Core SDI, the CERT Coordination Center tested
sshd version 1.2.27 running on an Intel-based RedHat Linux system and
found that configuration to be vulnerable. Tests conducted by Core SDI
indicate that sshd 1.2.27 running on OpenBSD and FreeBSD on Intel is
also vulnerable, and it is likely that other configurations are
vulnerable as well.

CERT/CC has developed a patch for the RSAREF2 vulnerability based in
part on work done by Core SDI. This patch is available at

ftp://ftp.core-sdi.com/pub/patches/rsaref2.patch
        http://www.cert.org/advisories/CA-99-15/rsa-patch.txt

You can verify this patch with a detached PGP signature from the
CERT/CC.

We believe the patch originally provided by Core SDI in their advisory
may not be a complete fix to this particular problem. We have worked

with them to develop an updated patch and gratefully acknowledge their
contribution to the fix provided here. Neither the CERT/CC, the
Software Engineering Institute, nor Carnegie Mellon University
provides any warranties regarding this patch. Please see our
disclaimer at the end of this advisory.

Possible vulnerability of ssh clients

The possible vulnerability of ssh clients is of particular concern. As
we learn more regarding the vulnerability of ssh clients, we will
update this advisory. One possible way to attack an ssh client would
be to construct a malicious ssh server and lure or trick victims into
connecting to the server. The ssh client will warn users when it
connects to a site that presents a key that does not match one
previously associated with the server. The dialog may be similar to
the following:

```
% ssh badhost
@@@@@@@@@@@@@@@@@@@@@@@@@@@@@@@@@@@@@@@@@@@@@@@@@@@@@@@@@@@@@@@@@@
@       WARNING: HOST IDENTIFICATION HAS CHANGED!        @
@@@@@@@@@@@@@@@@@@@@@@@@@@@@@@@@@@@@@@@@@@@@@@@@@@@@@@@@@@@@@@@@@@
IT IS POSSIBLE THAT SOMEONE IS DOING SOMETHING NASTY!
Someone could be eavesdropping on you right now (man-in-the-middle attack)!
It is also possible that the host key has just been changed.
Please contact your system administrator.
Add correct host key in /etc/.ssh/known_hosts to get rid of this message.
Are you sure you want to continue connecting (yes/no)? no
%
```

If you see this warning, you should answer "no" to the prompt and
investigate why the key you received does not match the key you
expected.

The CERT Coordination Center would like to thank Alberto Solino
<Alberto_Solino@core-sdi.com> and Gerardo Richarte
<Gerardo_Richarte@core-sdi.com> of Core SDI S.A. Seguridad de la
informacion, Buenos Aires, Argentina (http://www.core-sdi.com), who
discovered the problem in RSAREF2 and provided valuable technical
assistance. We would also like to thank Andrew Cormack of JANET CERT,
who provided technical assistance; Theo de Raadt of the OpenBSD
project, who provided valuable feedback used in the construction of
this advisory; Burt Kaliski of RSA Security Inc.; and Tatu Ylonen of
SSH Communications Security.

```
This document is available from:
http://www.cert.org/advisories/CA-99-15-RSAREF2.html
```

```
CERT/CC Contact Information

    Email: cert@cert.org
           Phone: +1 412-268-7090 (24-hour hotline)
           Fax: +1 412-268-6989
           Postal address:
           CERT Coordination Center
           Software Engineering Institute
           Carnegie Mellon University
           Pittsburgh PA 15213-3890
           U.S.A.

    CERT personnel answer the hotline 08:00-20:00 EST(GMT-5) / EDT(GMT-4)
    Monday through Friday; they are on call for emergencies during other
    hours, on U.S. holidays, and on weekends.

Using encryption

    We strongly urge you to encrypt sensitive information sent by email.
    Our public PGP key is available from

    http://www.cert.org/CERT_PGP.key

    If you prefer to use DES, please call the CERT hotline for more
    information.

Getting security information

    CERT publications and other security information are available from
    our web site

    http://www.cert.org/

    To be added to our mailing list for advisories and bulletins, send
    email to cert-advisory-request@cert.org and include SUBSCRIBE
    your-email-address in the subject of your message.

    Copyright 1999 Carnegie Mellon University.
    Conditions for use, disclaimers, and sponsorship information can be
    found in
```

```
http://www.cert.org/legal_stuff.html

* "CERT" and "CERT Coordination Center" are registered in the U.S.
Patent and Trademark Office.
```

```
NO WARRANTY
Any material furnished by Carnegie Mellon University and the Software
Engineering Institute is furnished on an "as is" basis. Carnegie
Mellon University makes no warranties of any kind, either expressed or
implied as to any matter including, but not limited to, warranty of
fitness for a particular purpose or merchantability, exclusivity or
results obtained from use of the material. Carnegie Mellon University
does not make any warranty of any kind with respect to freedom from
patent, trademark, or copyright infringement.
```

```
Revision History
December 13, 1999:  Initial release

-----BEGIN PGP SIGNATURE-----
Version: PGP for Personal Privacy 5.0
Charset: noconv

iQA/AwUBOFV9alr9kb5qlZHQEQI7bACg1xlZVHntIvhRHjUlf8BaNVGJlbkAnA6Y
kOuU3ddTO9uguGEvOEuR9Rw3
=IqXt
-----END PGP SIGNATURE-----
```

If you actually read the advisory, you can see the level of detail. Fortunately, advisories are not propagated often, so joining this list should not tax your mail server.

The SecurityFocus Web site, `http://www.securityfocus.com`, also has good information on security. This is the old BugTraq site and is now more commercial. Much good information can still be had, although the site caters more to computer security professionals than to mere mortals. The site has several mailing lists for those with varying interests.

Another good, but purely informational, site is Lance Spitz's at `http://www.enteract.com/~lspitz/pubs.html`. The site does a good job of documenting many aspects of how a cracker works and countermeasures you can take. The information at the site is generally for more advanced users, but most anyone can learn something. The site has a number of papers that can be read online or downloaded in a tarball and read off-line.

A site hosted by Fyodor, the creator of the nmap network mapping tool (a scanner), `http://www.insecure.org/`, provides information about security vulnerabilities with a focus on the latest technology in network scanning. Here you can find out about some of the latest scanning techniques meant to bypass scan detectors, etc.

Sites of a questionable nature

A number of sites post more than just security announcements: They post code that will actually take advantage of known vulnerabilities. Many of the visitors to sites like these are there for one reason: to download new code for new exploits. These people usually do not know how the code works, or anything about the exploit itself, but they can run the script (hence the name script kiddies). More often than not, they are also juveniles with nothing better to do than display their anti-authoritarian attitude.

One of the oldest and best-known sites is `http://www.rootshell.com/`. This site contains news on exploits, archives of exploits that have taken place, and code to reproduce those exploits.

Another site is Cult of the Dead Cow, `http://www.cultdeadcow.com/`. Cult of the Dead Cow is more than just a hangout for script kiddies: The members of cDc are also authors of Back Orifice, the Windows remote control software.

Another site worthy of mention is the home page of *2600* magazine, which bills itself as "the hacker quarterly." The magazine and Web site use the term "hacker" very loosely. What they mean is cracker and script kiddie. The site can be found at `http://www.2600.com/`.

All these sites post notices on their sites stating they oppose the illegal use of their software or information. This is the publisher's "get out of jail free" card. Visit these sites if you like, but expect to be underwhelmed at their presentation. They appear targeted at undereducated 12-year-olds for the most part.

One last note

When you do look to download software from the Internet, you'll often see files containing PGP (Pretty Good Privacy) signatures to compare against the software on the site, same as the signature on the CERT Advisory in Listing 26-1. This is common for any software that provides a restricted service and CERT Advisories. You can trust that no one has tampered with the software on the site (an inadvisable practice), or you can check the software tarball against the signature for it. The signature will tell you the author's name (author of the tarball) as well as whether the software package is intact as far as the author is concerned. These signatures have found, in at least one instance, a modified tarball. Use them or not, they are available. They do require that you have PGP in your system.

Summary

Security is not something you'll learn once and use forever. Security requires you to continue to learn. The folks writing programs to probe and penetrate systems come up with more ingenious methods every day. Only by keeping abreast of new attacks and new vulnerabilities can you keep the savages at bay. But remember, too, that as long as your system is just a little more secure, just a little more difficult to break into than the next guy's (unless yours is truly a high-profile site), you should have not have too many problems with script kiddies. They're looking for easy pickings. More sites and information can be obtained by entering "Linux security" in any search engine.

Appendix A

Guide to network scanners and security utilities

THIS APPENDIX PROVIDES SOME pointers to network scanners and security utilities. This list should not be considered all-inclusive; new software is being developed, and old software is discontinued. This appendix should give you an idea of what is available. Two searchable sources that are extremely good are `http://www.linuxberg.com/` and `http://freshmeat.net/`. Both will provide you ways to look for all types of security and other tools.

Following is an alphabetical list of some of the security tools you can download and install. Included is the home page for the application, or, if no home page is available, a download location.

- ◆ AIDE: Free replacement for tripwire (`http://www.cs.tut.fi/~rammer/aide.html`)

- ◆ BASS: Bulk Auditing Security Scanners (download only: `http://www.securityfocus.com/data/tools/network/bass-1.0.7.tar.gz`)

- ◆ Bastille Linux: A hardening program for Red Hat Linux 6.0 (`http://bastille-linux.sourceforge.net/`)

- ◆ Check.pl: Filesystem permission auditing tool (`http://checkps.alcom.co.uk/`)

- ◆ firesoft: Tools for viewing ipchains firewall logs and snort logs (`http://www.unix.gr/`)

- ◆ Firewall Manager: Graphical interface for firewalls (`http://www.tectrip.net/arg/`)

- ◆ FreeS/WAN: A secure WAN patch for Linux 2.0 and 2.2 kernels (`http://www.xs4all.nl/~freeswan/`)

- ◆ Fwctl: High-level configuration tool for Linux 2.2 packet filters firewall (`http://indev.insu.com/Fwctl/`)

- ◆ gfcc: GTK+ firewall (ipchains) (`http://icarus.autostock.co.kr/`)

- ◆ gSentinel: GTK-based graphical frontend tool for Sentinel (`http://zurk.netpedia.net/zfile.html`)

- ◆ gShield: Godot's Modular Firewall (`http://muse.linuxgeek.org/`)

◆ HostSentry: Host-based login anomaly detection and response tool (`http://www.psionic.com/abacus/hostsentry/`)

◆ hping2: Network auditing and testing tool (`http://www.kyuzz.org/antirez/hping2.html`)

◆ ipchains: Linux packet filter control utility (for 2.2.*x* kernels) (`http://www.rustcorp.com/linux/ipchains/`)

◆ ipchains-firewall: Rules-based ipchains firewall and IP masquerade script suite (`http://ipchains.nerdherd.org/`)

◆ ipfa: IP firewall accounting (`http://www.soaring-bird.com.cn/oss_proj/ipfa/`)

◆ ISIC: Sends controlled, semi-random packets to test IP stacks and firewalls (`http://expert.cc.purdue.edu/~frantzen/`)

◆ John the Ripper: Password cracker to detect weak UNIX passwords (`http://www.openwall.com/john/`)

◆ Linux Intrusion Detection System: Linux Kernel-Based Intrusion Detect System (`http://www.soaring-bird.com.cn/oss_proj/lids/`)

◆ Logcheck: Helps spot problems and security violations in your logfiles (`http://www.psionic.com/`)

◆ maillog: Mails system logs an off-site address via a cron job (`http://old.dhs.org/`)

◆ Mason: An automated firewall builder for ipfwadm or ipchains firewalls (`http://www.pobox.com/~wstearns/mason/`)

◆ Nessus: An easy-to-use security auditing tool (`http://www.nessus.org/`)

◆ netfilter: IP packet filter software for Linux kernel 2.4.*x* (`http://www.samba.org/~netfilter/`)

◆ nmap: A network scanning and mapping tool (`http://www.insecure.org/nmap/`)

◆ nstreams: Network streams analyzer (`http://www.hsc.fr/cabinet/produits/ndex.html.en`)

◆ OpenSSH: Open source secure shell replacement (`http://www.openssh.com/`)

◆ Ping Sting: ICMP traffic identifier (`http://www.ksrt.org/psting/`)

◆ PMFirewall: An ipchains firewall and masquerading configuration utility (`http://www.pointman.org/`)

◆ PortSentry: Detects and responds to port scans against a target host in real time (`http://www.psionic.com/abacus/portsentry/`)

◆ PSPG: Pretty simple password generator (`http://members.xoom.com/miscreants/`)

◆ QIPchains: A shell script that helps you quickly add/remove Linux FW rules (`http://www.vano.odessa.net/software/`)

◆ redir: Redirects TCP ports to another IP address and port (`http://sammy.net/~sammy/hacks/`)

◆ S/key: One-time password system (download only: `ftp://thumper.bellcore.com/pub/nmh/`)

◆ SAINT: Security Administrator's Integrated Network Tool (`http://www.wwdsi.com/saint/`)

◆ samhain: File integrity verifier (`http://samhain.netpedia.net/`)

◆ SARA: SATAN/SAINT-like security auditing tool — takes advantage of nmap if present (`http://home.arc.com/sara/index.html`)

◆ secure delete: Secure deletion of files, secure overwriting of swap and unused diskspace (download only: `http://thc.pimmel.com/files/thc/secure_delete-2.1.tar.gz`)

◆ Secure Remote Password Protocol: Zero-knowledge password-based authentication and key exchange protocol (`http://srp.stanford.edu/srp/`)

◆ Secure Shell (ssh): Shell script for secure logins using encryption and dual authorization (download: `ftp://ftp.cs.hut.fi/pub/ssh/`; home page: `http://www.ssh.fi/`)

◆ Secure-Linux Patch: Linux kernel patch to block most stack overflow exploits (`http://www.openwall.com/linux/`)

◆ Sentinel: Fast system file scanner (`http://zurk.netpedia.net/zfile.html`)

◆ sifi: Stateful TCP/IP packet filter for Linux (`http://www.ifi.unizh.ch/ikm/SINUS/firewall/`)

◆ Slinux Kernel: Security Enhanced Linux Kernel (`http://www.slinux.cx/`)

◆ snort: A lightweight network intrusion detection system `http://www.clark.net/~roesch/security.html`

◆ sslwrap: A service that acts a SSL wrapper to existing servers such as POP3/IMAP daemons (`http://www.rickk.com/sslwrap/`)

◆ Sportal: A file watcher with a GTK frontend (`http://sportal.sourceforge.net/`)

◆ sXid: All-in-one suid/sgid monitoring script written in C (download only: `ftp://marcus.seva.net/pub/sxid/`)

- ◆ TARA (Tiger Analytical Research Assistant): Local Security checking scripts (`http://home.arc.com/tara/index.html`)

- ◆ The Phreak Firewall: Tool to set up your own firewall with IP masquerading (`http://bewoner.dma.be/Phreak/`)

- ◆ TheBox: Set of scripts for and installing managing IP Masq and Transparent caching (`http://yak.airwire.net/`)

- ◆ Triplight: Intrusion detection/integrity monitor, uses md5sum to verify a list of files (`http://linux.rice.edu/magic/triplight/`)

- ◆ Tripwire: Intrusion Detection System for Linux (`http://www.tripwiresecurity.com/`)

- ◆ Wipe: Secure deletion of files from magnetic media (`http://gsu.linux.org.tr/wipe/`)

- ◆ ya-wipe: Secure file wiper (`http://www.erols.com/thomassr/zero/download/wipe/`)

Appendix B

What's on the CD-ROM?

THE CD-ROM ACCOMPANYING this book contains the following:

◆ Complete Caldera System OpenLinux 2.3 distribution (binaries only). Install this distribution by inserting the CD in the CD-ROM drive while Windows is running. The CD will autorun, presenting a menu; just follow the instructions. Alternately, you may boot from the CD-ROM (if your BIOS permits) to start the install. Visit Caldera Systems' web site (www.calderasystems.com) for more information.

There are also three directories of interest:

◆ The ../col/contrib/RPMS directory, containing unsupported, unofficial RPMS

◆ The ../col/RFC directory, which contains 10 RFCs directly related to the material presented in this text

◆ The ../col/security/RPMS directory, which contains a number of items of interest, including:

- courtney-1.3: A Perl script to monitor overt scans

- dailyscript-3.9.2: Scripts to automate daily log tasks – looks for anomalies in logs (with modifications for Caldera OpenLinux)

- ipmasqadm-0.4.1: A program to provide port forwarding with ipchains

- libpcap-0.4: A library needed for various "sniffers"

- makepasswd-1.7: A program to create secure passwords

- mason-0.13.0.92: A script to help create ipchains and netfilter firewall packet filter rules

- mucreate-0.1: A script to help create multiple users with secure passwords

- nmap-2.3BETA10: A network scanner (currently one of the most popular)

- rfc-0.2: A Perl script to lookup RFCs

- squid-2.2Stable5: Caching proxy software (if an earlier version is included in contrib/, don't use it)

- sudo-1.6.1: A program to allow users to run programs as root without having to become the user root or even know root's password

- tknotepad-7.1: A tk script that mimics the Windows Notepad, to easily edit configuration files (bonus)

◆ Not in RPM format are two other programs that may be found below security directory in a subdirectory called tarballs:

  ■ nessus-0.99.1: Network scanning software

  ■ SAINT: Network scanning software and successor to SATAN

◆ These programs are tarred and compressed, but also include directories with precompiled binaries. To install and use nessus, enter each of the following directories in order and run `make install`:

  ■ nessus-libraries

  ■ libnasl

  ■ nessus-core

  ■ nessus-plugins

◆ After installing libnasl, but before running the program for the first time, run `ldconfig`.

◆ To use SAINT, you should copy the entire saint directory to a directory of your choice (/root would be a good location) and run it from there.

Index

Numerics

Continued

IDG Books Worldwide, Inc.
End-User License Agreement

4. <u>Restrictions on Use of Individual Programs</u>. You must follow the individual requirements and restrictions detailed for each individual program in Appendix B of this Book. These limitations are also contained in the individual license agreements recorded on the Software Media. These limitations may include a requirement that after using the program for a specified period of time, the user must pay a registration fee or discontinue use. By opening the Software packet(s), you will be agreeing to abide by the licenses and restrictions for these individual programs that are detailed in Appendix B and on the Software Media. None of the material on this Software Media or listed in this Book may ever be redistributed, in original or modified form, for commercial purposes.

5. <u>Limited Warranty</u>.

   (a) IDGB warrants that the Software and Software Media are free from defects in materials and workmanship under normal use for a period of sixty (60) days from the date of purchase of this Book. If IDGB receives notification within the warranty period of defects in materials or workmanship, IDGB will replace the defective Software Media.

   (b) IDGB AND THE AUTHOR OF THE BOOK DISCLAIM ALL OTHER WARRANTIES, EXPRESS OR IMPLIED, INCLUDING WITHOUT LIMITATION IMPLIED WARRANTIES OF MERCHANTABILITY AND FITNESS FOR A PARTICULAR PURPOSE, WITH RESPECT TO THE SOFTWARE, THE PROGRAMS, THE SOURCE CODE CONTAINED THEREIN, AND/OR THE TECHNIQUES DESCRIBED IN THIS BOOK. IDGB DOES NOT WARRANT THAT THE FUNCTIONS CONTAINED IN THE SOFTWARE WILL MEET YOUR REQUIREMENTS OR THAT THE OPERATION OF THE SOFTWARE WILL BE ERROR FREE.

   (c) This limited warranty gives you specific legal rights, and you may have other rights that vary from jurisdiction to jurisdiction.

6. <u>Remedies</u>.

   (a) IDGB's entire liability and your exclusive remedy for defects in materials and workmanship shall be limited to replacement of the Software Media, which may be returned to IDGB with a copy of your receipt at the following address: Software Media Fulfillment Department, Attn.: *Linux Security Toolkit*, IDG Books Worldwide, Inc., 10475 Crosspoint Blvd., Indianapolis, IN 46256, or call 1-800-762-2974. Please allow three to four weeks for delivery. This Limited Warranty is void if failure of the Software Media has resulted from accident, abuse, or misapplication. Any replacement Software Media will be warranted for the remainder of the original warranty period or thirty (30) days, whichever is longer.

(b) In no event shall IDGB or the author be liable for any damages whatsoever (including without limitation damages for loss of business profits, business interruption, loss of business information, or any other pecuniary loss) arising from the use of or inability to use the Book or the Software, even if IDGB has been advised of the possibility of such damages.

(c) Because some jurisdictions do not allow the exclusion or limitation of liability for consequential or incidental damages, the above limitation or exclusion may not apply to you.

7. <u>**U.S. Government Restricted Rights**</u>. Use, duplication, or disclosure of the Software by the U.S. Government is subject to restrictions stated in paragraph (c)(1)(ii) of the Rights in Technical Data and Computer Software clause of DFARS 252.227-7013, and in subparagraphs (a) through (d) of the Commercial Computer – Restricted Rights clause at FAR 52.227-19, and in similar clauses in the NASA FAR supplement, when applicable.

8. <u>General</u>. This Agreement constitutes the entire understanding of the parties and revokes and supersedes all prior agreements, oral or written, between them and may not be modified or amended except in a writing signed by both parties hereto that specifically refers to this Agreement. This Agreement shall take precedence over any other documents that may be in conflict herewith. If any one or more provisions contained in this Agreement are held by any court or tribunal to be invalid, illegal, or otherwise unenforceable, each and every other provision shall remain in full force and effect.

GNU General Public License

Version 2, June 1991
Copyright © 1989, 1991 Free Software Foundation, Inc.
59 Temple Place – Suite 330, Boston, MA 02111-1307, USA
Everyone is permitted to copy and distribute verbatim copies of this license document, but changing it is not allowed.

Preamble

The licenses for most software are designed to take away your freedom to share and change it. By contrast, the GNU General Public License is intended to guarantee your freedom to share and change free software – to make sure the software is free for all its users. This General Public License applies to most of the Free Software Foundation's software and to any other program whose authors commit to using it. (Some other Free Software Foundation software is covered by the GNU Library General Public License instead.) You can apply it to your programs, too.

When we speak of free software, we are referring to freedom, not price. Our General Public Licenses are designed to make sure that you have the freedom to distribute copies of free software (and charge for this service if you wish), that you receive source code or can get it if you want it, that you can change the software or use pieces of it in new free programs; and that you know you can do these things.

To protect your rights, we need to make restrictions that forbid anyone to deny you these rights or to ask you to surrender the rights. These restrictions translate to certain responsibilities for you if you distribute copies of the software, or if you modify it.

For example, if you distribute copies of such a program, whether gratis or for a fee, you must give the recipients all the rights that you have. You must make sure that they, too, receive or can get the source code. And you must show them these terms so they know their rights.

We protect your rights with two steps: (1) copyright the software, and (2) offer you this license which gives you legal permission to copy, distribute and/or modify the software.

Also, for each author's protection and ours, we want to make certain that everyone understands that there is no warranty for this free software. If the software is modified by someone else and passed on, we want its recipients to know that what they have is not the original, so that any problems introduced by others will not reflect on the original authors' reputations.

Finally, any free program is threatened constantly by software patents. We wish to avoid the danger that redistributors of a free program will individually obtain patent licenses, in effect making the program proprietary. To prevent this, we have made it clear that any patent must be licensed for everyone's free use or not licensed at all.

The precise terms and conditions for copying, distribution and modification follow.

Terms and Conditions for Copying, Distribution, and Modification

0. This License applies to any program or other work which contains a notice placed by the copyright holder saying it may be distributed under the terms of this General Public License. The "Program", below, refers to any such program or work, and a "work based on the Program" means either the Program or any derivative work under copyright law: that is to say, a work containing the Program or a portion of it, either verbatim or with modifications and/or translated into another language. (Hereinafter, translation is included without limitation in the term "modification".) Each licensee is addressed as "you".

   Activities other than copying, distribution and modification are not covered by this License; they are outside its scope. The act of running the Program is not restricted, and the output from the Program is covered only if its contents constitute a work based on the Program (independent of having been made by running the Program). Whether that is true depends on what the Program does.

1. You may copy and distribute verbatim copies of the Program's source code as you receive it, in any medium, provided that you conspicuously and appropriately publish on each copy an appropriate copyright notice and disclaimer of warranty; keep intact all the notices that refer to this License and to the absence of any warranty; and give any other recipients of the Program a copy of this License along with the Program.

   You may charge a fee for the physical act of transferring a copy, and you may at your option offer warranty protection in exchange for a fee.

2. You may modify your copy or copies of the Program or any portion of it, thus forming a work based on the Program, and copy and distribute such modifications or work under the terms of Section 1 above, provided that you also meet all of these conditions:

   a) You must cause the modified files to carry prominent notices stating that you changed the files and the date of any change.

   b) You must cause any work that you distribute or publish, that in whole or in part contains or is derived from the Program or any part thereof, to be licensed as a whole at no charge to all third parties under the terms of this License.

   c) If the modified program normally reads commands interactively when run, you must cause it, when started running for such interactive use in the most ordinary way, to print or display an announcement including an appropriate copyright notice and a notice that there is no warranty (or else, saying that you provide a warranty) and that users may redistribute the program under these conditions, and telling the user how to view a copy of this License. (Exception: if the Program itself is interactive but does not normally print such an announcement, your work based on the Program is not required to print an announcement.)

These requirements apply to the modified work as a whole. If identifiable sections of that work are not derived from the Program, and can be reasonably considered independent and separate works in themselves, then this License, and its terms, do not apply to those sections when you distribute them as separate works. But when you distribute the same sections as part of a whole which is a work based on the Program, the distribution of the whole must be on the terms of this License, whose permissions for other licensees extend to the entire whole, and thus to each and every part regardless of who wrote it.

Thus, it is not the intent of this section to claim rights or contest your rights to work written entirely by you; rather, the intent is to exercise the right to control the distribution of derivative or collective works based on the Program.

In addition, mere aggregation of another work not based on the Program with the Program (or with a work based on the Program) on a volume of a storage or distribution medium does not bring the other work under the scope of this License.

3. You may copy and distribute the Program (or a work based on it, under Section 2) in object code or executable form under the terms of Sections 1 and 2 above provided that you also do one of the following:

a) Accompany it with the complete corresponding machine-readable source code, which must be distributed under the terms of Sections 1 and 2 above on a medium customarily used for software interchange; or,

b) Accompany it with a written offer, valid for at least three years, to give any third party, for a charge no more than your cost of physically performing source distribution, a complete machine-readable copy of the corresponding source code, to be distributed under the terms of Sections 1 and 2 above on a medium customarily used for software interchange; or,

c) Accompany it with the information you received as to the offer to distribute corresponding source code. (This alternative is allowed only for noncommercial distribution and only if you received the program in object code or executable form with such an offer, in accord with Subsection b above.)

The source code for a work means the preferred form of the work for making modifications to it. For an executable work, complete source code means all the source code for all modules it contains, plus any associated interface definition files, plus the scripts used to control compilation and installation of the executable. However, as a special exception, the source code distributed need not include anything that is normally distributed (in either source or binary form) with the major components (compiler, kernel, and so on) of the operating system on which the executable runs, unless that component itself accompanies the executable.

If distribution of executable or object code is made by offering access to copy from a designated place, then offering equivalent access to copy the source code from the same place counts as distribution of the source code, even though third parties are not compelled to copy the source along with the object code.

4. You may not copy, modify, sublicense, or distribute the Program except as expressly provided under this License. Any attempt otherwise to copy, modify, sublicense or distribute the Program is void, and will automatically terminate your rights under this License. However, parties who have received copies, or rights, from you under this License will not have their licenses terminated so long as such parties remain in full compliance.

5. You are not required to accept this License, since you have not signed it. However, nothing else grants you permission to modify or distribute the Program or its derivative works. These actions are prohibited by law if you do not accept this License. Therefore, by modifying or distributing the Program (or any work based on the Program), you indicate your acceptance of this License to do so, and all its terms and conditions for copying, distributing or modifying the Program or works based on it.

6. Each time you redistribute the Program (or any work based on the Program), the recipient automatically receives a license from the original licensor to copy, distribute or modify the Program subject to these terms and conditions. You may not impose any further restrictions on the recipients' exercise of the rights granted herein. You are not responsible for enforcing compliance by third parties to this License.

7. If, as a consequence of a court judgment or allegation of patent infringement or for any other reason (not limited to patent issues), conditions are imposed on you (whether by court order, agreement or otherwise) that contradict the conditions of this License, they do not excuse you from the conditions of this License. If you cannot distribute so as to satisfy simultaneously your obligations under this License and any other pertinent obligations, then as a consequence you may not distribute the Program at all. For example, if a patent license would not permit royalty-free redistribution of the Program by all those who receive copies directly or indirectly through you, then the only way you could satisfy both it and this License would be to refrain entirely from distribution of the Program.

If any portion of this section is held invalid or unenforceable under any particular circumstance, the balance of the section is intended to apply and the section as a whole is intended to apply in other circumstances.

It is not the purpose of this section to induce you to infringe any patents or other property right claims or to contest validity of any such claims; this section has the sole purpose of protecting the integrity of the free software distribution system, which is implemented by public license practices. Many people have made generous contributions to the wide range of software distributed through that system in reliance on consistent application of that system; it is up to the author/donor to decide if he or she is willing to distribute software through any other system and a licensee cannot impose that choice.

This section is intended to make thoroughly clear what is believed to be a consequence of the rest of this License.

8. If the distribution and/or use of the Program is restricted in certain countries either by patents or by copyrighted interfaces, the original copyright holder who places the Program under this License may add an explicit geographical distribution limitation excluding those countries, so that distribution is permitted only in or among countries not thus excluded. In such case, this License incorporates the limitation as if written in the body of this License.

9. The Free Software Foundation may publish revised and/or new versions of the General Public License from time to time. Such new versions will be similar in spirit to the present version, but may differ in detail to address new problems or concerns.

Each version is given a distinguishing version number. If the Program specifies a version number of this License which applies to it and "any later version", you have the option of following the terms and conditions either of that version or of any later version published by the Free Software Foundation. If the Program does not specify a version number of this License, you may choose any version ever published by the Free Software Foundation.

10. If you wish to incorporate parts of the Program into other free programs whose distribution conditions are different, write to the author to ask for permission. For software which is copyrighted by the Free Software Foundation, write to the Free Software Foundation; we sometimes make exceptions for this. Our decision will be guided by the two goals of preserving the free status of all derivatives of our free software and of promoting the sharing and reuse of software generally.

No Warranty

11. BECAUSE THE PROGRAM IS LICENSED FREE OF CHARGE, THERE IS NO WARRANTY FOR THE PROGRAM, TO THE EXTENT PERMITTED BY APPLICABLE LAW. EXCEPT WHEN OTHERWISE STATED IN WRITING THE COPYRIGHT HOLDERS AND/OR OTHER PARTIES PROVIDE THE PROGRAM "AS IS" WITHOUT WARRANTY OF ANY KIND, EITHER EXPRESSED OR IMPLIED, INCLUDING, BUT NOT LIMITED TO, THE IMPLIED WARRANTIES OF MERCHANTABILITY AND FITNESS FOR A PARTICULAR PURPOSE. THE ENTIRE RISK AS TO THE QUALITY AND PERFORMANCE OF THE PROGRAM IS WITH YOU. SHOULD THE PROGRAM PROVE DEFECTIVE, YOU ASSUME THE COST OF ALL NECESSARY SERVICING, REPAIR OR CORRECTION.

12. IN NO EVENT UNLESS REQUIRED BY APPLICABLE LAW OR AGREED TO IN WRITING WILL ANY COPYRIGHT HOLDER, OR ANY OTHER PARTY WHO MAY MODIFY AND/OR REDISTRIBUTE THE PROGRAM AS PERMITTED ABOVE, BE LIABLE TO YOU FOR DAMAGES, INCLUDING ANY GENERAL, SPECIAL, INCIDENTAL OR CONSEQUENTIAL DAMAGES ARISING OUT OF THE USE OR INABILITY TO USE THE PROGRAM (INCLUDING BUT NOT LIMITED TO LOSS OF DATA OR DATA BEING RENDERED INACCURATE OR LOSSES SUSTAINED BY YOU OR THIRD PARTIES OR A FAILURE OF THE PROGRAM TO OPERATE WITH ANY OTHER PROGRAMS), EVEN IF SUCH HOLDER OR OTHER PARTY HAS BEEN ADVISED OF THE POSSIBILITY OF SUCH DAMAGES.

End Of Terms And Conditions

BSD Based License

Sudo is distributed under the following BSD-style license:
Copyright © 1994–1996,1998–1999 Todd C. Miller <Todd.Miller@courtesan.com>
All rights reserved.

Redistribution and use in source and binary forms, with or without modification, are permitted provided that the following conditions are met:

1. Redistributions of source code must retain the above copyright notice, this list of conditions and the following disclaimer.

2. Redistributions in binary form must reproduce the above copyright notice, this list of conditions and the following disclaimer in the documentation and/or other materials provided with the distribution.

3. The name of the author may not be used to endorse or promote products derived from this software without specific prior written permission from the author.

4. Products derived from this software may not be called "Sudo" nor may "Sudo" appear in their names without specific prior written permission from the author.